THE SUMMER OF DEATH

THE SUMMER OF DEATH

The Great Heat Wave of 1936 and the Making of Modern-Day America

GEOFF WILLIAMS

PEGASUS BOOKS
NEW YORK LONDON

THE SUMMER OF DEATH

Pegasus Books, Ltd.
148 West 37th Street, 12th Floor
New York, NY 10018

First Pegasus Books cloth edition June 2026

Interior design by Maria Fernandez

Library of Congress Cataloging-in-Publication Data is available.

ISBN: 979-8-89710-125-2

10 9 8 7 6 5 4 3 2 1

Printed in the United States of America
Distributed by Simon & Schuster
www.pegasusbooks.com

To my daughters, Isabelle and Lorelei, and my nieces,
Aster and Beatrice, and all their cohorts in Gen Z and Gen Alpha—who
are going to be tasked with managing a climate-change mess.

"For the sun rises with its scorching heat and withers the grass; its flower falls, and its beauty perishes."

—*James 1:11*

"All the nations will say, 'Why has the Lord done thus to this land? What caused the heat of this great anger?'"

—*Deuteronomy 29:24*

"For now, these hot days, is the mad blood stirring."

—William Shakespeare, *Romeo and Juliet*

"Too hot, too hot!"

—William Shakespeare, *The Winter's Tale*

CONTENTS

Author's Note

On November 17, 2023, during a Taylor Swift concert in Brazil, a twenty-three-year-old woman lost consciousness. She later died in the hospital of cardiorespiratory arrest. The heat index, a term coined in 1979, is what the temperature feels like when you merge the air temperature with the humidity. When the young woman fainted, the heat index was 138 degrees Fahrenheit.

She fainted, in what almost seems like a vicious prank, during the song "Cruel Summer," and while she was the only concertgoer to die that day, one thousand other Swifties passed out before the night was over.

For the last few years, the world has lived through what's become something of a heat horror show, although maybe you haven't noticed it much if you work and relax in the comfort of an air-conditioned office and home. But if you're a construction worker, a farmer, a park ranger, a botanist, or anyone who spends time outdoors, you know. It has been hotter than normal, except that isn't the right way to describe it, because the new normal is that it's always hotter than normal.

In Mexico, monkeys now routinely collapse and fall from trees. Doctors and pharmacists have warned patients that the quality of their mail-ordered prescription medicines may be diminished because temperatures inside the cargo areas of delivery trucks sometimes hit 150 degrees in the summer. When Muslims embarked on a Hajj pilgrimage in Saudi Arabia in mid-June, 2024, over 1,300 people died in the extreme high temperatures. Over ten days during the summer of 2025, approximately 2,300 people died of heat-related causes across twelve European cities; researchers determined that two-thirds of those deaths were linked to climate change.

We could spend all day scrutinizing statistics and news stories about melting polar ice caps and how climate change is shaking up the planet, but it isn't as if anyone should be surprised. We've known these summers were coming for some time. For decades, scientists have warned of climate change. But generations from long ago perhaps could have done a better job passing on their own stories of what it was like to endure a monster heat wave. Still, even if they had warned us more, would we have ignored them like many people and politicians continue to ignore today's scientists?

The summer of 1936 was a season that we should all hope is never repeated. When people think of the good old days, 1936 would not be that year. Most of 1936 was bonkers, a freak of nature. It was a year when the country appeared to be cursed.

Especially during the summer of 1936. This was a heat wave that could have been designed by Mary Shelley or Bram Stoker. Records were hit that had never been seen, many that still haven't been broken—not yet at least.

It wasn't just hot. It was scary hot. Deadly hot. Apocalyptic hot. This was a heat wave that often acted not natural, but supernatural, and it had prophetic timing.

What follows is the story of North America's worst heat wave. How many people died? Nobody can ever say for sure, but 12,000 is a conservative estimate.*

It was always a challenge to assign a cause of death. It still is. If you have a heart attack in 110-degree weather, did you die because of a bum ticker or the heat? What if you were a healthy 104-year-old who died in 104-degree weather? Did the heat finish you off, or was it your age? In more recent times during the pandemic, doctors, patients, and politicians were arguing whether an elderly person died of COVID, or if poor health or advanced age finished the person off. These things can be up for interpretation.

* A 1936 report from the U.S. Department of Commerce suggests 4,678 people died of the heat wave over the summer, which may be why 5,000 deaths is often cited whenever there's discussion of the 1936 heat wave. But on October 8, 1936, the National Safety Council, then and still a prominent safety advocacy nonprofit, estimated the heat wave was responsible for the death of at least 6,000 Americans. It also suggested that an additional 5,000 home accident deaths could be attributed to the heat. So right there, that's 11,000 deaths. The Dominion Bureau of Statistics, in 1937, suggested the heat death toll for Canada was 780. So that's at least 11,780 heat deaths. If you round that up, you've got 12,000 Americans and Canadians.

There were many heat waves before 1936 and there have been many since, but what made this heat wave so unique was its length, scope, and impact on the nation. The entire summer, most of the country resembled an overturned bowl with heat trapped inside. Only a handful of states, like Florida and Wyoming, made it through the summer of 1936 relatively unscathed.

Air-conditioning wasn't much help. It existed, but it was a rarity. Homes lacked it. The White House installed air-conditioning for the West Wing in 1930, and in 1933, President Franklin Roosevelt had it put in his residence. But most homes, even affluent ones, were without.

Most hotels lacked air-conditioning too, and almost no hospitals had it. If you were a heatstroke patient, it was probably far hotter inside the building than outside, and odds were good that you were about to become acquainted with an ice bath. You've probably heard that people cooled off in air-conditioned movie theaters during the Great Depression, but that's only 40 percent true, since 60 percent of the country's movie theaters didn't yet have it.

After the summer of 1936, nobody could credibly make the argument that air-conditioning (or keeping your food cold in a refrigerator instead of an icebox) wasn't a necessity. That said, crazy as it now sounds, there were people who thought technological marvels such as air-conditioning and refrigeration were examples of a world going soft. The critics were right to be skeptical, albeit they should have been for different reasons. Ever since air-conditioning's arrival, the world has produced AC units and refrigerators that pump out hydrofluorocarbons, chemicals now considered superpollutants because of their potential to warm the earth. They've been in a phasing-out period for some time now. And, of course, the warmer the planet gets, the more people need air-conditioning and refrigeration. Still, it's hard to argue that as a civilization, we are better off cooling ourselves and our food with blocks of ice.

The summer of 1936 changed air-conditioning, refrigeration, and how we dressed; improved public healthcare; and started conversations about climate change. Skeptics of climate change have argued that the summer of 1936 demonstrates that the planet has always run hot and cold, and the world's temperatures aren't changing appreciably. That's one way to look at it. Another is that the summer of 1936 was a warning from Mother Nature that if the planet continues to heat up, the world will continue to be one hot mess.

Before we visit the summer of 1936, several housekeeping notes are in order:

- When you see a sentence like "In Lexington (99°F), a sixty-three-year-old died," here's how to translate that: The high that day was 99. Maybe the sixty-three-year-old died when it was 94 degrees? Quite possibly.
- Regarding the daily death toll at the start of most chapters, those are estimates simply to give you a sense of the ongoing devastation.
- As for the people you are about to encounter in the book, if I know somebody's ethnicity or race, it's generally mentioned. You can make an excellent argument either way that I should or shouldn't do that (i.e., it's best to be inclusive; it's best to be color-blind if somebody's race or ethnicity isn't germane to the story of the heat wave). What I don't do is typically mention if anyone in the book, a victim or potential victim, is White. That would overpower and exhaust the reader. In 1936, the American population was mostly White; about 88 percent, according to Census records.
- Throughout the book, I stick with Fahrenheit versus Celsius, even when writing about Canada, which also got walloped by the heat wave. For our Canadian readers, I hope that doesn't annoy you.
- Back in the day, newspapers often stated exactly how hot it was. For example, they would note that it was 104.7 degrees. In the interest of accuracy and offering a 1936 ambiance, I do the same thing.
- If it helps, you can think of this book as a how-to manual on surviving a deadly heat wave. Because if the world continues to get hotter, someday this story will be the story of all of us.

Prologue

The Winter of 1936

Eight days after the American side of Niagara Falls froze over, approximately 465 miles away, at about 3 P.M. on February 8, 1936, five fishermen from Charlevoix, Michigan, found themselves in a predicament.

The ice below them broke off—and drifted into Lake Michigan.

Alarmed bystanders watching them float away contacted the coast guard. Eventually, a rescue boat came, but there was only room for three fishermen. Two would have to wait. Clayton Brown, twenty-five, and his father-in-law, Claude Beardsley, fifty-one, volunteered to stay behind.

Another boat later arrived, helmed by Earl Cunningham, a coastguardsman. By now it was dark and snowing. Brown and Beardsley gratefully scrambled into the boat and off they went. Except the snowstorm was now a blizzard. Cunningham tried to paddle them back to shore but couldn't. Not against sixty-mile gusts of wind and eight-foot waves.

It was a lousy way to spend a Saturday evening. Lakeshore thermometers indicated that it was twenty below zero. Five people in Michigan died of exposure, and a gravedigger had a heart attack provoked by the freezing temperatures. A snowplow driver fell asleep in his vehicle and died of carbon monoxide asphyxiation. In the last twenty or so days, subzero temperatures had ended the lives of two hundred people in twenty-two states.

Brown, Beardsley, and Cunningham remained in their boat, hoping not to freeze to death.

At 3 A.M., twelve hours after the ice beneath them took them into Lake Michigan, Brown, Beardsley, and Cunningham decided to start a fire, and tore up the back seat of the boat for kindling. Gusts of wind kept blowing out their matches, which was probably just as well. Maybe they could have contained the flames, but maybe not. Starting a fire when the cold has muddled your brain is risky. Around this time, Edward Grachet, a twenty-year-old farmhand in Ithaca, Michigan, also tried to warm himself. Only he did it by lighting a fire with a can of oil. He blew himself up.

The winter of 1935–1936 was one of the worst the country had ever seen. Langdon, North Dakota, became world-famous for its cold temperatures: The community experienced temperatures below 0 degrees Fahrenheit for forty-one consecutive days. Once Langdon landed on a day over zero degrees, the cold spell nonetheless continued for ninety-two more days without hitting 32 degrees. The townspeople shivered their way through sixty-seven nights with the mercury below zero.

Minneapolis achieved a record low: -34 degrees. McIntosh, South Dakota, saw temperatures plummet to -58 degrees. Parshall, North Dakota, dropped even a little bit lower: -60.

Fawns froze in the woods along with cattle on prairies. Gravediggers couldn't bury the dead; the ground was too hard. The Chicago River turned to ice for the first time in twenty-four years. On the evening of January 22, sheriff's deputies on horseback in St. Clairsville, Ohio, rescued a hundred children from school buses buried in sixteen-foot snow drifts in this hilly, sparsely settled section of the state near West Virginia. "You couldn't see the buses at all," the sheriff said. "The drifts were 15 and 16 feet deep, and snowplows that set out simply bogged down and would not budge. The temperature was about 8 below and going down all the time. It was terrible. On the way, we had to help about fifteen motorists who were stalled or blocked by the buses."

On January 24, rescuers saved thirty-five kids from having to spend a night in a Neptune, Ohio, schoolroom—and another two hundred children were rescued from a school in Geneva, Indiana, with just enough wood remaining to keep the fire going for another hour.

On the morning of February 9, Claude Beardsley, his son-in-law Clayton Brown, and coastguardsman Earl Cunningham were alive but still somewhere in the middle of Lake Michigan. They could barely tell it was morning. The blizzard hadn't stopped. The three men occasionally rowed but didn't get far. From what they could discern, they were ten miles from shore. They could see a church steeple in the fishing village of Good Hart, which they weren't from but were familiar with. The blizzard persisted. Cunningham, who was wearing his regulation coast guard uniform but not a coat, was getting weaker by the hour.

Brown, feeling intense guilt that their rescuer was not going to survive, tried keeping Cunningham alert, continually slapping him on the back with an axe handle. But nothing worked. Ice was forming on Cunningham's face and his body was stiff. Cunningham died around 9 P.M. His last words were "I wish I could see my wife and three children once more."

Claude Beardsley, who had remained as optimistic as anyone could be in such a situation, wasn't doing well either. He probably never should have been out fishing in the first place. He felt ill the night before and skipped breakfast, having no earthly notion that he would soon be stranded on an ice floe in Lake Michigan, and then a boat, without food. Nothing to drink either, other than ice-cold lake water.

At some point, Beardsley threw his tackle box into the water and swore off fishing forever. As the temperatures dropped, with Cunningham's frozen body still in the boat, Beardsley and his son-in-law watched the waves around them solidify.

Around midnight, Beardsley made a fateful and desperate decision—he was going to get help by walking to shore, across the ice.

Brown tried to dissuade his father-in-law, who he called Dad. It didn't seem safe and they weren't anywhere near shore. But Beardsley was determined and bid his son-in-law farewell. Perhaps after Cunningham's death, he felt he had nothing to lose. He made the trek for about two hundred feet—until the ice snapped underneath him. Beardsley plunged into the water, shouting for help. Brown scrambled to him and managed to get him back onto the ice and even dragged him over to the boat. But Brown was too weak to help his father-in-law climb back inside.

Claude Beardsley's last words were "I'll never go fishing again if I get out of this alive."

Brown tried to rouse his father-in-law but eventually gave up and covered his father-in-law with the tarp. He went inside the boat and jumped up and down to try to stay warm for the rest of the night.

The next morning, on February 10, Brown checked on his father-in-law, hoping for a miracle. There was none. Beardsley was frozen.

With the arrival of daylight, Brown was the last one alive, though maybe for not much longer. The blizzard was finally over, and Brown had the same epiphany as his late father-in-law: Nobody was coming. If he had any chance of survival, he was going to have to make it back home on his own. He scanned the horizon and believed he could see land about nine miles away, west of Petoskey. He tested the ice, and it seemed secure. Brown decided to chance it. Leaving the boat and two bodies behind, he began walking. He also kept falling. His feet, numb and in dire shape, kept failing.

Back at home, Brown had a wife and two daughters, a two-year-old and a four-month-old. Brown kept thinking of them. Four times, Brown saw an airplane and took off his coat to wave, attempting to attract the pilot's attention, but the aviator, searching for three men in a rowboat, didn't see him.

Brown kept walking, crossing several open cracks in the ice. In many stretches, the ice was so thin that he was scared to step on it. Hoping to disperse his weight, he crawled across. Several times mid-crawl, Brown fell asleep, but when his face hit the freezing ice, he awakened. Eventually, even when he could walk, he was too weak—he couldn't feel his legs—and was forced to crawl.

But at 4:30 P.M., on Monday, nearly three days after the ice floe broke away, Brown reached the doorstep of a shack belonging to George Andrus, a Native American living in Good Hart. "He took me in and helped me change into dry clothes. He gave me first aid and some warm soup," Brown later wrote.

Despite all he had suffered, he was one of the lucky ones.

For much of the winter of 1936, large swaths of the nation were paralyzed by cold. Why it was such a brutal winter hasn't been extensively researched, at least, not as much as one might think, according to Travis Allen O'Brien, an associate professor of earth and atmospheric sciences at Indiana University Bloomington. But what scientists believe occurred is that there was an unusual amount of precipitation in the Northeast that winter, O'Brien says, due to abnormally warm ocean temperatures in both the Atlantic and Pacific Ocean. Those same ocean temperature anomalies likely stuck around into the summer, he adds.

Whatever was responsible for the extreme temperatures, the winter was heartless. People fearful of freezing to death in snow-covered homes set fires for warmth, only to die from carbon monoxide poisoning that built up due to obstructed chimneys. Around the time Brown was out on the boat with Beardsley and Cunningham, in Cape Cod, Massachusetts, seven men around the ages of eighteen and nineteen working for a voluntary government relief program called the Civilian Conservation Corps were on an ice floe that broke apart from land. They were all rescued—twenty-two hours later. At that point, five of them were on one floe and two on another. But they were all floating in the same area when a pilot spotted them.

The day after Brown was saved, a forty-two-year-old pregnant mother of eleven children from Fulton, Michigan, was pulled on a sled for six miles to the town of Athens, where an ambulance was waiting to take her to the hospital. She gave birth on the sled. Upon reaching the ambulance, everyone discovered the baby had been smothered by the blankets covering him.

On February 12, in Marcus, South Dakota, a Presbyterian reverend and his wife were rescued after a week of being snowbound at their ranch; their fuel ran out, and for the final two days, they burned twenty-five religious books. "It was so cold that water froze in glasses near the kitchen stove. My wife and I couldn't even keep warm in bed," the reverend said. Elsewhere in Marcus, snowbound ranchers burned furniture, hay, fence posts, and parts of their homes.

February 13 was one of the worst days. Wolves were seen in great numbers around Chicago, driven south by the cold and looking for structures like chicken coops where they could seek shelter, warmth, and perhaps a hearty meal. In Austin, Minnesota, Lee Hobbe, a salesman, stopped his car to rescue a truck driver stuck in the snow. While trying to dig the truck out, two-inch-long icicles formed on both men's eyelids, freezing them shut. The two men groped their way back into the truck to thaw them out. And a fifty-five-year-old mail carrier, Lawrence Harden, was found in the Idaho wilderness. Best as people could tell, he was struck by a landslide of ice and snow. His frozen body was found in a tree.

But on February 18, something near-miraculous happened that works as a metaphor for how surreal the weather was in 1936. In Hagerstown, Maryland, a dog chased a cat up a telephone pole. The cat's owner and friends shooed away the dog and tried to convince the cat to come down, to no avail. There the cat remained until it froze and fell to the earth. The owner thawed out the cat and brought it back to life.

Across the country, people shivered under layers of clothing and quilts, wishing for warmer days ahead. They would come to regret that.

MAY

THE GREAT WARM-UP

1

MAY 2

Hotter Than Fiction

There was a reason Hollywood studio heads encouraged directors to shoot on sound stages. Your actors weren't rained on. Well-coiffed hair remained unmussed, and if you wanted it tousled, the director could create wind. It never got too cold inside a Hollywood studio, and it never got too—well, actually, it was often plenty hot. The heat radiating off the cameras and lights could be intolerable, especially from the key lights. Still, exchanging rugged and realistic terrain for a Hollywood studio was a pretty good trade-off for everybody involved. Actors focused on their craft instead of the weather, and directors controlled the environment instead of the environment controlling them.

David O. Selznick knew that. The famous Hollywood mogul had produced a slew of hits, including his blockbuster 1933 film *King Kong*, and while that story was mostly set on a jungle island or in the streets of New York City, it was largely filmed in the backlot at Culver Studios in Los Angeles. But for his latest triumph, *The Garden of Allah*, Selznick wanted the realism of the great outdoors. In fact, he shot the movie in glorious Technicolor, a rarity for the times.

The $2.2 million budget was a serious chunk of change for 1936, and while the plot involved two star-crossed lovers in the Sahara Desert, filming in North Africa would be cost-prohibitive. Buttercup Valley, twenty-three miles out from Yuma, Arizona, would have to do. Decades later, the same sands would be the setting for a scene in *Return of the Jedi*, the one in which Jabba the Hutt, with an enslaved Princess Leia at his side, makes a futile attempt to eliminate Luke Skywalker and Han Solo.

The Garden of Allah film crew built elaborate sets representing Algerian villages and an oasis near Castle Dome Peak, where rock outcroppings offered the cast and crew a little shelter from sandstorms. Thirty-four sedans, trucks, and buses brought in supplies, creating movie sets as well as a community of sorts for the cast and crew, one with barber shops, dressing rooms, lavatories, a commissary, and a schoolhouse for the children working in the picture. Most everyone slept in bunkhouses, although the stars and high-level crew members spent their nights at the Hotel San Carlos, a fancy hotel in Yuma that was built in 1928. Thanks to the luxury of air-conditioning, the prices set guests back $3.50 a night, a dollar more than the competition. Unfortunately, the actors and high-level crew members were rarely at their air-conditioned hotel long enough to enjoy it.

Years later, Maria Riva, the eleven-year-old daughter of the film's leading lady, would recall life on location. "Canvas flapped in the hot wind," Riva wrote her in her book *Marlene Dietrich: The Life*. "Like something out of Kipling, tents stretched among the sand dunes as far as my eye could see. Except for the maze of wooden walkways, the trucks, generators, reflectors, arc lamps, sound booms resting lopsided in the fine sand, I expected Gunga Din to materialize."

Riva slept in the bunkhouses. She found hotel life tedious, listening to her mother complain to her fellow actors about the quality of the script. Around the set, the weather was suffocating, but there were other kids her age and a menagerie of animal actors, including horses, donkeys, dogs, goats, sheep, rabbits, and chickens, along with their handlers.

Naturally, since the movie was set in the Sahara Desert, there were camels. Everyone fell in love with little Djemila, who was born on the set and named after a town in Algeria. Marlene Dietrich called Djemila the camp mascot. Every day, leading man Charles Boyer and director Richard Boleslawski brought snacks to feed to the infant camel.

Djemila was a pleasant distraction. While many creature comforts of home were at the film site, nothing was actually comfortable. This was no desert paradise, just a desert. With no air-conditioning for miles, Boyer showered seven or eight times a day.

Buttercup Valley was beautiful but barbaric. The production quickly became an unexpected endurance test, offering heat far worse than the

Sahara Desert. Reliable weather records for Algeria from 1936 are admittedly a little hard to come by, but the average April temperature in North Africa is 67 degrees. The April weather in Yuma had mostly been in the 90s and low 100s.

April, in general, was not a comfortable month for the country. Really, it started getting hot in some of the country on March 30. Parts of Pennsylvania saw 76-degree weather. On April 12 in Phoenix, Arizona, it was 99 degrees, a new record for the city, and Idaho was unseasonably hot: it was 83 in Boise. On April 14, the high hit 99 in Pittsburgh, Pennsylvania. On April 17, it was 86 in Spokane, Washington. On April 29, a twenty-three-year-old Black man collapsed in Washington, DC's 85-degree heat. An ambulance took him to the hospital, where he was revived.

The heat spawned extreme weather. On April 5 and 6, at least fourteen tornadoes tore through the Southeastern United States; 200 people in Georgia died, and another 254 perished in Tennessee, Mississippi, South Carolina, Arkansas, and Alabama. One house that was destroyed had two parents and eleven children in it.

Amateur weather forecasters were already predicting a harsh summer, in part because it seemed like the symmetry might be right after such a harsh winter.

Now it was May, and while the country's weather appeared to be settling into some normalcy, it was anything but at the outdoor set of *The Garden of Allah*. It was so hot that the film stock kept melting. Once Selznick was clued in, he informed his director that there would be no shooting from 11 A.M. to 3 P.M. They should wake up early to film, like in-the-middle-of-the-night early. Each day's footage would then be placed in a truck with a refrigerated compartment and driven to the studio, where it could be developed. It was the one bit of trouble encountered during filming that had a somewhat easy fix. Most problems on the set had no readily available solutions.

For starters, the actors didn't think much of Boleslawski, despite the forty-seven-year-old director having helmed critically acclaimed hits such as *Les Misérables* and *The Three Godfathers*. The language barriers didn't help the tension. Boleslawski, who everyone called "Boley," was a native of Poland. Dietrich was German. Boyer was French. Basil Rathbone was

British, though born in South Africa. Joseph Schildkraut was Austrian. Even when communication was possible, the actors didn't like what they were saying and hearing. Everybody hated the script.

But the heat made everything worse. Exhibit A: Charles Boyer's toupee. The thirty-six-year-old actor kept sweating it off. According to Riva's memoir, Dietrich took Boyer's lush black-haired hairpiece to Yuma and cleaned its hair lace with gasoline. The thirty-four-year-old actress then shampooed, styled, and returned it the next day, gluing it to Boyer's head using a half bottle of spirit gum, an adhesive often used with wigs. It worked. Boyer was delighted. So was Dietrich. The two actors filmed throughout the morning without issues. But then, while the camera filmed a close-up of an embrace, Boyer's toupee rolled off and a pool of perspiration that had collected underneath all morning doused Dietrich's face.

Dietrich had her own clammy hair issues, although she tried fixing things by having a full-length mirror placed by the camera. She also told the cinematographer how to best light her. Selznick, hearing from frustrated crew members, complained to Boleslawski that Dietrich was too concerned about her appearance. "Dear Boley," Selznick said in one of his hand-delivered memos to Boleslawski, "would you *please* speak to Marlene about the fact that her hair is getting so much attention and is being coiffed to such a degree that all reality is lost."

Still, Dietrich had reasons for her militant devotion to a mirror and brush. She was a star emerging from some recent career misfires and didn't want another one. Besides, fans paid their hard-earned Depression-era money to see her looking glamorous, and that wasn't easy to do in 100-degree weather. She knew better than to risk disappointing them.

The heat was a challenge for everyone. Boyer's sunburned face was layered with heavy makeup. Some crew members were hospitalized for heat exhaustion, and those who didn't make the trek to the hospital visited the medical staff standing by. Riva remembered the set's infirmary being especially busy: "Our specialties were sunstroke, blistered skin, diarrhea, infected eyes and lacerated shoulders."

The film crew was doing strenuous work in the worst of conditions. For starters, to get to their spot at Buttercup Valley, a mile off the highway, the crew built a plank road made of 95,000 feet of lumber and forty-five kegs of spikes. When Selznick decided the set needed an oasis, he shipped twenty-five date palm trees from Los Angeles and dispatched his crew to dig a pit for the desert lake—the size of ten swimming pools, according to Dietrich. It was no easy job; overcome by the heat, laborers kept toppling into it.

Scorpions were always underfoot. Aside from having a small uncredited role as a young girl sewing, one of Riva's jobs was to search for scorpions alongside other film crew members and, with thick gloves, remove them from the sand dunes where scenes were going to be performed. (According to Riva, the film crew kept the scorpions in a cage and had quite a little zoo by the end of the shoot.) Gadflies, also known as horse flies, thrived and swarmed the cast and crew.

The movie's cast of animals, however, were not faring as well, and on April 30, when it hit 90 degrees, two-week-old Djemila died. She was buried on a knoll near the camp while his mother, Hepzibah, and two hundred somber members of the cast and crew looked on.

Sandstorms came daily; some lasted three days, and a crew member recalled that everyone was constantly breathing sand. In fact, when crew members did an autopsy on Djemila, sand was in her stomach. Even when the wind died down, the quality of life improved little. Riva described the shoot this way: "Everyone continually searched for an unoccupied patch of man-made shade and sweated profusely."

The heat hadn't let up since April 15 when the film began shooting in 99-degree weather. On April 16, it was 101, and the next, 103. But on May 2, the heat finally caught up with the movie's biggest star, Marlene Dietrich. In the middle of a scene, Dietrich collapsed.

The high that day was 101. Press releases and breathless news reports would later say that it was 138 degrees on May 2, and PR flacks would jack that up to 148 degrees. That may have actually been true, if you factor in the additional heat from the camera lights.*

* The hottest temperature ever recorded on the planet was in 1913 at Death Valley, California, with the mercury reading 134 degrees, although there is some debate as to the accuracy of that number.

Riva wrote in her book that her mother, knowing they were about to lose the light, faked a fainting scene to get Boleslawski to wrap up for the day. Maybe that happened once—Dietrich wasn't an enthusiastic member of Team Boley—but it also seems plausible the actress, after fainting, would have told her daughter she feigned a collapse, not wanting the adolescent to worry.

But there is no doubt that on May 2, 1936, while filming in the early morning to capture the light and to avoid the worst of the day's temperatures, Dietrich fainted in the heat. Newspapers reported it, including the Associated Press, and Selznick's office sent out a press release. For those understandably skeptical about the veracity of news coming from a Hollywood set, at a time when the publicity machine thought nothing of stretching the truth, some entertainment journalists of the era were equally jaded.

On May 3, James Reid, writing for *Picturegoer Weekly*, came onto the set to write a feature and soon heard about Dietrich's fainting scare. "On every side, I heard the story. From Boleslawski, from Marlene's stand-in, from cameramen, from prop men. The story was no hoax. It had happened," wrote Reid.

Moreover, Joseph Schildkraut, a silent film star who won an Oscar the following year in *The Life of Émile Zola* and later played Otto Frank in the 1959 classic *The Diary of Anne Frank*, who had no reason to lie, wrote in his memoir that Ms. Dietrich had not one but multiple fainting spells on the sand dunes.

In Riva's book, she writes of Dietrich dismounting a horse and falling into Boyer's arms, then pretending to faint. But according to a comment Dietrich herself made to the press later, it happened after her costar Basil Rathbone came riding up to her on his horse. He dismounted and greeted Dietrich, who brushed the back of her left hand across her eyes and forehead. She must have had an odd look because Boleslawski asked: "Do you feel all right, Marlene?"

She nodded, went limp, and flopped into the sand.

Schildkraut had a weak heart, and it being the days before beta blockers and ACE inhibitors, he was carrying an ice bag with him, keeping it pressed over his heart between scenes. Schildkraut was the first at Dietrich's side and placed his ice bag on her wrists, followed by the rest of the cast and crew, which swarmed around her.

Dietrich had been up late the night before studying her lines, and there were the early wake-up calls. So Dietrich may have also been somewhat sleep-deprived, making her more susceptible to the heat. Dietrich was reportedly unconscious for five minutes. The company doctor was soon by her side, helping her to a sitting position and putting a bottle of smelling salts under her nostrils. Moments later, Schildkraut grabbed the bottle and took a whiff for himself. The doctor informed Dietrich that she had suffered a slight sunstroke and wouldn't work any more today. She protested, but Rathbone and Boleslawski carried Dietrich into a car and sped off to the hotel in Yuma.

Selznick was a brilliant producer and storyteller—maybe you're more familiar with his 1939 masterpiece *Gone With the Wind*?—but considering that *The Garden of Allah* became a box office dud, he would have been better off scrapping the script and using his footage for a weather documentary. Unbeknownst to the cast and crew, a real-life disaster worthy of a Hollywood movie was just getting started.

2

MAY 4

Heat and Weak Hearts

Today's Death Toll: 1

Most people have a body temperature of around 97 to 99 degrees, and 98.6 is considered optimal. Ninety-five degrees may not sound bad to a layperson, but if your temperature drops below it, hypothermia has probably set in. If that happens, your heart, nervous system, and other organs will start to malfunction.

You also don't want your body to go above 99 degrees. That's when you start to develop hyperthermia (not to be confused with *hypo*thermia). A small rise in body temperature is generally not a big deal, but if your body goes above 104, that's when the trouble begins. You may become confused or angry. Your pulse may quicken. You may feel faint or discover your skin is awfully dry. You may even pass out and wind up in a coma. If you have a fever of 106 or more, you may already be dead.

But depending on what is happening in your body, several outcomes can occur. As your body heats up, your blood and oxygen flow toward your skin, which means those are resources that are now not going to the stomach and intestines—and if things get really bad, toxins that were in your gastrointestinal system can start to leak into other parts of your body. That can lead to blood clots and organ failure, such as your kidneys and lungs. But maybe that won't happen. Instead, you may merely get confused, a possible sign that your brain is shutting down. Or the heat may bring on a heart attack.

When any of this happens, you've had a heatstroke, sometimes called a sunstroke.

In a heat wave, if you're healthy, your body will usually keep you cool, or cool enough. When the heat becomes unmanageable, however, your body starts to react. For instance, your blood vessels widen. But that's good, because your blood is flowing toward the skin and sending extra body heat packing. Still, the main way your body stays cool is by sweating. Your sweat carries hot water out of your body, and as it hits the surface of your skin, the water evaporates, which cools you off, even though it may not feel like that's happening.

If you remember your high school biology class, your heart pumps harder as those blood vessels widen, and it circulates two to four times more blood a minute during warmer months than cooler ones. So the hotter it gets, the harder the heart works to keep the body cool. Hearts in peak condition tend to do this just fine. Weaker hearts have trouble.

It was said that John Baden had a weak heart. Around the time that Marlene Dietrich returned to the desert set, Baden was working hard in Omaha, Nebraska. His heart was working even harder.

Baden was a sixty-nine-year-old general contractor who specialized in remodeling homes. He had been doing this for at least twenty-one years. He did it all. He could build you a cabinet, a bookcase, a stairway, a porch, and the house to go with it. In 1916, he led a team of contractors to build a bank in the city of Schuyler, about one hundred miles away. It was the talk of the town for years.

Today, Baden toiled outside, remodeling the affluent Fischer residence—the home's owner was a train engineer—and temperatures kept rising, eventually reaching 87 degrees. Baden collapsed at four P.M. Mrs. Fischer saw him fall and immediately called her family physician and then probably his wife, but there was nothing to be done.

Not surprisingly, Baden's death wasn't covered nationally, and wasn't even a topic of interest for neighboring states. But even if Baden's death had been more widely covered, it wouldn't have registered with anyone for long. Everyone was used to people dying from the heat. In fact, when Nebraska's papers reported on Baden's demise, most headlines designated Baden as "Omaha's first heat victim." In the decades before air-conditioning was mainstream, cities annually ran news stories about the community's first heat wave victim. Every summer, it was expected that sooner or later, some unlucky soul would win the heatstroke lottery.

3

MAY 7

The Sand Pit

Today's Death Toll: 3
Total Death Toll: 4

Summer showed up early in the upper Midwest. In Cleveland, Ohio, (86°F), men removed overcoats and vests. In Alpena, Michigan, it was 90, the hottest part of the country, even hotter than Yuma, Arizona, which was down to 87 degrees. Canada was hot, too. In western Ontario, farmers hustled to make good use of the warm weather, in the high 80s, only to have their horses collapse.

In Detroit, Michigan, city dwellers marveled that on February 18, it was 9 below zero, but now you could fry an egg on the sidewalk. Bemused residents observed that the local weatherman predicted today would be on the cold side: it was 86 degrees.

"What happened was this—" began an apologetic meteorologist, Clarence Root, who told the Associated Press that the problem was a stalled pressure system. Heat waves are caused by high-pressure systems that trap the warm air, which sinks to the surface of the earth. Root, who worked out of Detroit's weather bureau, said, "The pressure areas just stagnated all over the country and until they move, there won't be much change in the weather. I can't tell you why they didn't move."

Root's diagnosis was spot on. What Root didn't know and couldn't have known was that the stagnating high-pressure areas wouldn't budge for a long, long time. In 1936, weather forecasting was a mix of science, technology, and guesswork. Germany had made some strides in predicting the weather ten days out, a feat that its chancellor Adolf Hitler believed could come in handy in future battle planning. But right now, an accurate three-day forecast was about the best anyone could hope for. That people could predict the weather three days in advance was largely because of technology that allowed weather professionals and amateurs to share information and spread the word on what was coming.

"Meteorological observations are virtually useless in current service unless immediately transmitted to a wide network of stations where they can be promptly charted, analyzed, and issued in the form of bulletins and forecasts," stated a 1936 report from the United States Department of Agriculture's Weather Bureau. In fact, two to six observations were made from fifteen radio stations throughout Alaska, run by the United States Army. Weather intel from most of those stations was sent twice daily to Seattle's weather bureau, which distributed them to weather bureaus nationwide. Mexico, meanwhile, sent weather bulletins to an army station in Marsh Field, California, which distributed the information to bureaus throughout the west. The bulletins would race ahead of the actual weather, so weather forecasters generally had a sense of what was coming.

That lingering high pressure above the country would start to have serious consequences today. Several people, from Illinois to Pennsylvania, passed out in the 80-plus degree heat. And then came the deaths. A fifty-six-year-old railroad switchman in Milwaukee collapsed in 87-degree heat and never woke up.

Maybe the switchman could have avoided dying if he consumed more water or sat down more, but it's hard to imagine what Alexander Szumanski, of Detroit, Michigan, could have done differently. In fact, maybe he had no chance of survival this summer. The Polish immigrant moved to America in 1912 and ever since worked for car companies. But like many people, he lost his job during the Great Depression, and he and his wife only kept their kids fed by taking in Polish boarders. But recently he found steady employment at Chevrolet Motor Company. It must have seemed like a lucky break.

It was anything but. Szumanski had a demanding role, one that was often given to Black residents and immigrants, says John Hinshaw, a history professor at Lebanon Valley College in Annville, Pennsylvania. It was also a dangerous job during the summer, especially this summer. Because of the low-pressure area hanging over the country, Szumanski collapsed on the job, in conditions that would have been far hotter than the 87 degrees it was outside, and he was pronounced dead at Grace Hospital. Until he died, it was Szumanski's responsibility was to maintain and control Chevrolet's equipment used to melt metal. It was a sweaty, unforgiving position even in cold weather, but today, the thirty-seven-year-old didn't stand a chance. Alex Szumanski was a furnace tender.

If you were a school kid on a hot day in Michigan in 1936, you had two choices—sit in a stifling classroom and melt into your desk or engage in an American ritual as old as school itself: play hooky.

You can hardly blame Melvin Foerster and four of his pals for not showing up at Midland High School on a day when the high was 92 degrees. For high school seniors, weeks away from graduation and with the rest of their lives ahead of them, skipping school was probably an easy decision. In fact, across the country, during the summer of 1936, millions of Americans of all ages would do just what Melvin did when faced with hot, unbearable temperatures: They went swimming.

Unfortunately, there weren't many practical and safe swimming options in Midland, or in many communities in America. Public swimming pools in America only started to gain traction in the late 1800s. The modern-day Olympics, which began in 1896, popularized the sport and pastime of swimming, but pools were also inspired by public bathhouses, which were pretty much what they sound like: places to get a bath. Many homes, especially in cities, didn't have access to clean water. By 1936, public bathhouses had sort of come around full-circle; they were still being built, but people usually patronized them as a place for indoor swimming. Of course, since prehistoric times, people had been frolicking and cooling off in creeks, rivers, and the ocean, but in more land-locked places, those options were few.

By the 1920s, it was no longer unusual for a city to have a swimming pool, but many communities still lacked one during the 1930s. As the economy spiraled, building them quickly became an afterthought, with at least a quarter of the nation unemployed.

Still, after President Franklin Roosevelt debuted his New Deal and began putting people to work, more pools were constructed. In Jeff Wiltse's book *Contested Waters: A Social History of Swimming Pools in America*, he estimated that over a thousand swimming pools were built in cities across America during the 1920s and 1930s. Not many were built between 1929 and 1934, but a resurgence occurred from 1934 until the end of the decade.

Midland, Michigan, didn't yet have a city swimming pool, nor did Auburn, eight miles away, where Melvin lived. If you were a resident of the area and wanted to swim, the best and safest option was a man-made lake thirteen miles away in Francis Grove. In 1929, the lake's owners, loaded and generous, opened three acres of their land and water and allowed the public to come and swim. There was a sandy beach and shallow water—for about 150 feet until the ground began sloping deeper—and the Red Cross provided lifeguards.

But thirteen miles was a drive for five high school seniors, and roads in 1936 weren't what they are now. Instead, Melvin and his friends swam at the local swimming hole—a sand pit. Normally, this pit was used for excavating sand and gravel. But it was spring, and right on schedule, the snow melted, the rain fell, and something resembling a lake had formed. For much of the morning, Melvin and his friends swam laps.

For decades across North America, sand-pit swimming holes had been popular destinations. For instance, Larned, Kansas, had a sand-pit swimming hole that their newspaper described on August 9, 1917: "The bathing beach at the sand pit is proving the most popular place in the county these warm evenings, and crowds of bathers are there every day. The fresh, cool water and the clean sandy riverbed make it an ideal place to swim, and it is pronounced far superior to the swimming pool at Great Bend." Sounds idyllic, but many sand-pit swimming holes were not so pristine. In 1932, an editorial in Hackensack, New Jersey's *The Record* noted that most of the city's swimming choices, some of which were sand pits, contained "broken glass, wooden piles or other debris, and polluted matter, which often cause serious accident or illness."

The same editorial noted that the "sand pit at North Hackensack is usually crowded with children, some unable to swim." Part of the issue at North

Hackensack's sand pit—and most sand pits—was the unpredictability of the sand beneath everybody's feet: "In some places the drop is sheer, while in others a gradual descent forms a perfect beach except for treacherous holes where they are least expected. Filled with water, the pits are death traps for the unwary."

Indeed, that's exactly what sand-pit swimming holes were: death traps. In 1933, at the popular swimming hole in Lindsborg, Kansas, one hundred people saw either a man or a boy—nobody was sure—sink and disappear. There was an all-night search. They blew up the pit with dynamite and still couldn't find anyone. Three days later, searchers dredged up the corpse of a seventy-six-year-old man. That same year, about two miles out of Garysburg, North Carolina, a young Black woman on her honeymoon went into ten-foot water in a sand-pit swimming hole. The papers said she was seized with cramps and drowned.

Seized with cramps. That was almost always the language that the papers used when reporting about a drowning victim. While it was shorthand for "something unexplainable went wrong in the water" to the point of being ridiculous—virtually every swimmer was seized with cramps?—there was good reason for reporters suggesting it.

When the swimmer was in extremely deep water, especially if in the shade, the water could be extremely frigid, sometimes 50 degrees or colder. Swimmers would hit that chilly water and it would be a shock to the system, and their muscles would cramp.

The seized-with-cramps excuse was aided by the myth that everybody should wait a full thirty minutes to swim after a meal. It's a "rule" that has no basis in fact but is believed to have originated in 1908 when a Boy Scout manual recommended that people refrain from swimming after eating—so if people drowned within any proximity to having eaten a meal, cramps became a suspect.

Drowning happened a lot during the summer of 1936; it still happens a lot. Recent numbers from the American Red Cross suggest that eleven Americans drown every day, or a little over 4,000 people a year. Many Americans never learn how to swim even today due to a wide range of factors, many of them socioeconomic. In 1936, swimming lessons as a concept were rare. If you were a middle-aged adult in 1936, you probably remembered a time when swimming lessons essentially didn't exist. Not that there weren't swimming instructors in, say, 1890. You could find them at some bathhouses. But swimming lessons didn't really take off until the YMCA started a swimming campaign in 1909. Being the Young Men's Christian Association, it vowed to teach "every man and boy in North America to swim."* By 1936, quite a few YMCAs also provided swimming lessons to girls (even though officially girls wouldn't be allowed to become members until 1964), and some organizations, such as the Girl Scouts, stepped in and offered swimming lessons to girls and women. If you were a kid of color or of poverty, however, your odds of receiving swimming lessons in any formal capacity were fairly low—and that's still the case today.

Melvin, thirteen days past his eighteenth birthday, could swim. When he and his buddies went into the water, it was in what papers described as a sand-pit pond about seventy-five feet long and six feet deep. They spent a good chunk of the morning swimming, and as the noon hour approached, the five young men decided to dry off. And that would have been that, and this story wouldn't be in this book, except that Melvin told his friends that he wanted to take one last lap across the pond and back.

His friends waited for him. And watched. Then they could see that something was wrong. It was said later that Melvin was seized with cramps.

Clinton Callahan, one of Melvin's buddies, swam after him. He got hold of him twice, but he couldn't save him.

Panic ensued. Clinton returned to the shore and the four teenagers piled into their car, driving a mile and a half into Midland, where they notified the city fire department that they had an emergency on their hands. Firefighters scrambled toward the swimming hole. Evan Price, a Boy Scout executive, telephoned Red Cross lifesavers and drove back with Melvin's friends.

Word got around of Melvin's plight, reaching Dirk Waltz. Twenty-two years old, married, and living at his parents' home, Waltz was unemployed,

* Generally, White boys and men. In 1910, there were segregated YMCAs built for the Black community. The YMCA wouldn't officially ban racial discrimination at their facilities until 1967.

as were many people, although in the future he would become a local legend as the owner of an auto dealership and community philanthropist. Waltz swam into the lake and located Melvin, pulling the eighteen-year-old's body to shore at 12:30 P.M., forty minutes after he went under.

Everyone must have understood that this was a hopeless mission, but two Red Cross workers, the fire chief, and police officers attempted to revive Melvin anyway. They used an inhalator—a device that came with two tanks, one of which was filled with oxygen and another with carbon dioxide—a hose, and a mask. The rescue workers pumped a mixture of oxygen (93 percent) and carbon dioxide (7 percent) into Melvin's lungs. The inhalator had saved a lot of victims from drowning, but it wasn't doing anything for this teenager. Still, Melvin had two parents, two sisters, a grandfather, and numerous friends depending on the rescuers' success, so they pumped air into the eighteen-year-old's lungs for two hours. Then they had to acknowledge there was nothing more to be done.

The day before, citizens of Midland, understanding that they needed something safer than a sand-pit swimming hole, formed the Midland Swimming Pool Association and set up a meeting to discuss how to finance the creation of a city swimming pool. Melvin was the sixteenth person to drown at a swimming hole in Midland County in the last decade.

Melvin's story soon became sickeningly familiar. In fact, across the country, during the summer of 1936, thousands of Americans of all ages across North America would do just what Melvin did when faced with hot, unbearable temperatures: They went drowning.

4

MAY 9

Unseasonably Hot

Today's Death Toll: 13
Total Death Toll: 20+

Across the country, men and women traded in their fedoras and berets for cooler but also stylish straw hats.

It was a wise fashion choice, although one might have suggested that everybody simply go hatless. But generally, in 1936 if you were in public, you were going to wear a hat, hot or not.

Canadian heat waves are practically an oxymoron, but that's what Ontario was experiencing, with one heat death in the province the day before. In Toronto, it hit 89.8 degrees, an early May record that hadn't been matched for ninety-four years. New Jersey's Asbury Park and Atlantic City beaches were teeming with bathers. In California, thousands of people were flocking to the water, and a thirteen-year-old Black boy's drowning in a channel of water near the Oakland airport was blamed on the heat. In some California cities, it was in the 90s; in Imperial, it was 104 degrees. Between the coasts, people were passing out. In Hamilton, Ohio, a fifteen-year-old girl and a thirty-five-year-old man collapsed on different streets in the late afternoon, when it was 93 degrees.

The heat was affecting sidewalks. In Belleville, Ontario, the temperature rose to 84.02 degrees and the concrete exploded. This wasn't too unusual. Because concrete is porous, water can get trapped in it. When concrete gets really hot, the trapped water expands. If the temperature rises faster than the steam rises from the concrete, then it's kablooey, which may not be the actual technical term the construction industry uses. Still, it was awfully early for this type thing to be happening, especially in Canada.

Ten deaths throughout North America were attributed to the heat that day: in California, New York, Michigan, Pennsylvania, and in Ontario. Three of those deaths were in Pennsylvania.

In Phoenixville, where it was in the low 90s for the second day in a row, Frank Ingram, fifty-nine, was playing tennis when his game was interrupted by a heart attack.

In Wilkes-Barre (95°F), the heat came for Marko Vuksonovich, forty-one. His work as a miner had given him "miner's asthma," a condition also known as black lung. Half an hour before his body was found on the floor of his home by his brother, Vuksonovich appeared healthy, talking to his neighbors, who had no clue anything was amiss.

And near Hazleton, Pennsylvania (95°F), thirteen-year-old Salvadore Damato and three buddies wanted to cool off in the lake at the Sugarloaf Dam. When Salvadore reached the middle of the lake, which was eight feet deep, he was stricken with cramps. At least, that's what people said. But that isn't what the boys thought when they heard their friend groan and disappear under the water.

They believed it was a prank.

In a few seconds, Salvadore would resurface. Any second. Any minute now. Even when five minutes became ten and Salvadore didn't appear, the boys still thought it was a gag. Obviously Salvadore swam underneath the water and made his way to the shore. But thirty minutes later, Salvadore's friends started to panic. Rex Matteo, a twelve-year-old boy, went for help and found some on East Diamond Avenue. A score of men living near the dam rushed to the lake, the fire companies were notified, as was city hall. Soon, it was as if the entire town had descended upon the dam and lake to search for this boy.

There were nine state police officers present. A district attorney. The superintendent of the Wyoming Valley Water Supply Company. There were also firefighters from the 14th Ward Fire Company, shining spotlights on the dam and rushing around, trying to secure a boat. Somebody donated one to the cause, but it leaked. A second boat was found and rescuers set out to search for the boy.

A nineteen-year-old resident began diving underneath the water, looking for Salvadore Damato. Crowds formed on the edge of the lake.

Around midnight, the authorities went to Salvadore's home to alert the family while rescuers concluded they were going to have to drain the lake. To speed that up, a miner who lived nearby set off a charge of dynamite that blew away the southeast corner of the dam. That did the trick: Salvadore's body was found by a firefighter sometime after 1 A.M. Around then, Salvadore's father and sister showed up. Lifesaving equipment was used on Salvadore, just in case, but a physician soon declared the youth dead. If there was any solace for the family, maybe they hoped Salvadore was now with his mother, who died eleven years earlier.

Despite this and the other tragedies, there was still little inkling of what was to come. In Oklahoma and Texas, residents were dodging tornadoes. Farmers in Aitkin, Minnesota, were welcoming heavy rain for their crops—that is, until hundreds of acres were flooded by the Mississippi River. And road crews in Colorado were still battling the long winter, digging communities out from a fifteen-inch snowfall.

5

MAY 30
Summer Comes Early

Today's Death Toll: 20 (mostly drownings)
Total Death Toll: 50+

The May heat continued to occasionally pick people off. On May 10, in Michigan, there were two heat deaths. On May 11, *The Boston Globe* enthused, "To Mrs. Carrie M. Davis, 48, of 127 Merriam Ave., Leominster, goes the dubious honor of being New England's first heat victim for the present year. She lost consciousness in the lobby of a Leominster theatre and was held last night for observation at the Leominster Hospital."

Mrs. Davis was fine, but as May continued, more people were passing out and not waking up—and wisecracks about the heat became less amusing. Then the dogs started acting up. When temperatures shot from the 60s into the high 70s over the course of a few days, thirty Pittsburgh residents went to the hospital for dog bites.

There would be a lot of people getting treated for dog bites this summer. Heat made dogs irritable, doctors theorized, and in recent years, there has been research to give that theory more teeth. In 2023, researchers from Harvard Medical School and Spaulding Rehabilitation Hospital analyzed 69,525 dog bite cases in eight cities and found that dog bites increased 3 percent on days with high ozone pollution, 4 percent on days with higher temperatures, and 11 percent on days with elevated ultraviolet radiation (in other words, a lot of sunshine).

On May 17, in Boston (92°F), two men in their sixties became heat victims, one found in his home and the other watering his lawn. On May 18, in Pottstown, Pennsylvania (88°F), a fifty-two-year-old farmer had a heart attack while shopping.

That same day, more than one million New Yorkers, city officials estimated, mobbed the beaches. Attendance records were broken. It was 86 degrees, and on Coney Island, hundreds of men strolled along the waves without a shirt. Police held off on making arrests for public lewdness. Last year, shirtless men on the beach were dragged into court and slapped with heavy fines. But not this time. Maybe the police were more sympathetic, or just as likely, social mores had subtly shifted in twelve months' time. In fact, an NYC alderman had just announced plans to introduce a bill permitting "shirtless bathing" for men.

There was no question that cooler clothing was the smart way to dress this summer. In New York and New Jersey, several people passed out; all were revived. Drownings were harder to reverse. A father and son lost their lives in Brady Lake near Franklin, New Jersey; the boy fell out of the boat and the dad leaped into the water after him. Three more boys perished in New Jersey's rivers.

In Boston, where it was a record-breaking 91 degrees, 300,000 people headed to the beaches, and two children drowned. In Portland, Maine, it was 90. In Fresno, California, it was 100. And it was only mid-May.

The filming of *Garden of Allah* continued to slog on in 105-degree heat. Ever since Marlene Dietrich's fainting spell, most days the high temperature was over 100, sometimes well over. Boyer, Dietrich, and sometimes Rathbone sought sanctuary in the actress's deluxe tent, insulated with an inner lining of silk. On one occasion, it was so hot that Rathbone refused to come out to shoot a scene, and Boleslawski threatened to write him out of the picture.

Rathbone talked to a reporter the following year about the miserable heat the actors endured. He discussed how he fought in World War I for four years, saying it was a nightmarish experience for him, especially since his brother, also a soldier, was killed. But Rathbone said that despite the hardships he endured, "I would fight the war to the end because I believed it meant something. In Buttercup Valley, however, the whole thing seemed senseless to me. If I hadn't been bound by contract, I would have handed them back their money and left the picture."

Nobody was enjoying themselves. Boleslawski collapsed from the heat, according to news reports, though the press office said he had become ill from drinking polluted water. A week after Dietrich's fainting spell, she had another one. Thirty minutes later, she performed for the cameras, but as entertainment reporter Elizabeth Yeaman put it, Dietrich looked "deathly wan."

The sandstorms continued, the heat didn't let up, and crew members were passing out daily, all of which cost the production $20,000 a day. It surprised nobody when almost a week later, on May 30, 1936, Producer David O. Selznick finally waved the white flag and pulled everybody from Yuma, where it was 105 degrees, so the movie could finish shooting at a studio in Los Angeles, where the camera lights would still cook everybody, but at least the weather could be controlled.

JUNE

MERCURY RISING

6

JUNE 3

Hot Where You Wouldn't Expect It

Today's Death Toll: at least 8
Total Death Toll: 60+

It was hot even where you wouldn't expect it. Juneau, Alaska, hit 78 degrees; sled dogs panted and looked pained while perplexed miners shed their black woolen underwear. Kamloops, British Columbia, reached 92 degrees. In parts of Maine, it hit 95, and in the town of Norway, a horse became a casualty of the heat. Flocking to rivers and lakes for relief, half a dozen Canadians drowned. Melting snow in the mountains created the worst flooding in thirty years, washing over railways, washing away buildings and bridges, and turning telegraph and telephone lines into kindling.

It was also hot where you would expect it. In New Brunswick, New Jersey (94°F), police officers secured permission to remove coats while directing traffic—and across the country, a lot of people were waking up in the hospital covered in ice. People collapsed in Philadelphia (97°F), Washington, DC (96°F), in Newark, New Jersey (93°F), and in other scattered states like North Carolina, Virginia, and Texas. In Englewood, New Jersey (90°F), a mail carrier was discovered face down in a gravel driveway, unconscious and his eyeglasses broken. Police initially thought it was a hit-and-run.

In New York City, a fifty-year-old man died in 90-degree heat, the hottest it had been that day since 1895. And in Pottstown, Pennsylvania (93°F), Edgar Hummel's luck, such as it was, ran out.

Hummel was a sixty-five-year-old mostly unemployed painter who had a job to finish. He had painted a family's garage and other parts of the house. Only the chimney remained. In his eleven years of professional painting—before that, he was a photographer—these last few months had been the bleakest. This was only his second job in several months.

It was hot outside—a twenty-year-old Pottstown woman picking strawberries returned home, where she lived with her parents, and passed out in the doorway. Hummel's wife had implored Edgar not to go up on the ladder, but if he had to, she wanted him to do it tomorrow morning when it would be cooler. But Hummel wanted his paycheck and said he "would be all right."

He would not be. Hummel may have simply lost his grip, but everybody, including his physician, assumed the heat made him dizzy. He plunged off the ladder headfirst, falling thirty-five feet, landing on a concrete sidewalk, both his blood and the can of red paint splattered on the ground.

Summer wouldn't officially begin for another eighteen days.

7

JUNE 10

Sunburns and Skimpy Clothing

Today's Death Toll: at least 1
Total Death Toll: 60+

Scientists in 1936 didn't fully grasp how sunbathing might lead to skin cancer, but they knew there was a connection. Laymen also recognized that subjecting yourself to a sunburn wasn't the healthiest thing you could do to your body. As an op-ed that ran on July 3 in a Berwyn, Illinois, newspaper stated, "People who would shudder at the thought of burning themselves with a match or having scalding water sprinkled on them will unhesitatingly expose their entire bodies to the blazing rays of the sun. The results may be a burn which is just as severe and as deep as that made by scalding water or fiery flame, for sunburn is a true burn."

Suntans, however, were considered healthy. The same writer stated, "It is essential that human beings get into the sunlight as much as possible . . ." and wrote there was nothing wrong with getting tanned, just that one should do it gradually. That actively tanning wasn't the best idea would be more widely grasped gradually over decades.

It's too bad: While it feels wonderful to lounge outside and soak in the sunshine, the rays burn the skin, make it less elastic, and pre-age it. In fact, if a sunburn is severe enough, along with your body being dehydrated, your skin can get infected. You could even find yourself hospitalized with a high fever, chills, or nausea.

Fortunately, you could protect yourself. Sunscreen was invented in 1891 by a German scientist, and it started going mainstream in the 1920s; many people used a sponge to apply it to their skin. By 1936, there were quite a few suntan lotions on the market, many resembling the sunscreens of today.

Rexall, the drugstore chain, sold its own brand of suntan lotion, naturally called Rexall Suntan Lotion. Noxzema sold Noxzema Suntan Oil for prices between 23 cents and 79 cents. Elizabeth Arden's Ideal Suntan Oil would have set you back $1.75. Less familiar names included Gaby's Suntan Lotion, Vin-a-Balm Sun Lotion, Rubinstein Sunproof Cream, and Tussy Suntan Oil. Many suntan lotions went for $2 a bottle, or over $40 in today's dollars. It wasn't cheap.

"This year, get your tan the Norwich way," read one newspaper ad. "Slowly, evenly, without tanning your skin like leather and ruining it for the rest of the year."

There were also suntan powders, which you'd mix in with foundation cream and then rub on your face, arms, and the rest of your body.

Some people simply pooh-poohed sunbathing altogether. "This fad they have of sun-bathing is ridiculous. It is just another excuse to show the body," a Canadian reader wrote to the *Windsor Star* in mid-July.

Sunbathers had lots of opportunities to enjoy the heat so far this year. On June 6, in Spokane, Washington, it was 80 degrees, and thousands showed up at the beaches. But not everyone was enjoying the warm weather. The last several days, people around the country fainted from the heat, in states that included Kentucky, Kansas, Nebraska, Maine, Missouri, Maryland, Indiana, Oklahoma, Pennsylvania, and Kansas. On June 6, at a politician's funeral in Nashville, Tennessee (94°F), attended by President Franklin Roosevelt, six women collapsed.

Today, in El Paso, Texas, it was 102 degrees. In Phoenix, Arizona, it was 104. Across the country, the heat was becoming really hard to shrug off.

California

Today, the news broke that Jean Harlow was moving out of her palatial hilltop home in Hollywood, due to doctor's orders.

Harlow was a film actress and one of the biggest Hollywood stars of the 1930s, but she was also a twenty-five-year-old who loved to sunbathe. Harlow, who lived with her mother, owned a house with a swimming pool. Thanks to a bad case of sun poisoning in 1935 and several bad sunburns earlier in the year, her physician ordered her to stay in the shade. He certainly didn't suggest she sell her home, but Harlow quipped, "If I can't swim, what's the use of having a place with a pool to tempt me?"

Despite ridding herself of temptation, Harlow would be lured to lay in the sun's golden rays throughout the rest of the summer, and while she used many of the numerous suntan lotions on the market, they never seemed to work. There may have been reasons for that, however, which nobody would understand until much later.

Louisiana

Mike & Harry's Bar in Shreveport announced their newly installed air-conditioning, a big deal at the time. Harry Lazarous, one of the proprietors, informed the press of the change in one of those self-serving public relations comments that never seem to change no matter what decade or century: "It has always been the policy of this institution to offer the utmost in comfort as well as merchandise, and we feel that all Shreveport and Ark-La-Tex will appreciate the installation of air-conditioning."

Kentucky

A group of guys patrolled the streets, seeking teenage girls and women dressed in shorts and halter tops on the streets of Covington. These men weren't being creeps per se. A woman police offer named Elizabeth Cohran requested that her colleagues keep an eye out for any girls or women wearing any clothing that was deemed too revealing.

Miss Cohran was a product of her time, and the girls she was trying to look out for were a product of theirs. Cohran was a rarity in 1936—a female police officer, known then as a police matron. The unmarried former nurse handled situations that the city government believed needed a woman's delicate touch. For instance, if the authorities were looking for a teenage runaway girl, Cohran would get involved. If a young woman was pregnant and needed to find a home for her baby, Cohran was on the job. If a woman was the victim of abuse, you'd call Miss Cohran.

She did a lot of good in Covington, but this summer, she arguably went too far. She wanted any girl over the age of ten cited for indecent exposure if they were caught outside wearing scanty outfits, such as shorts.

"The heat of the past few days has brought them out," Cohran told a reporter. "Now, I think the shorts and halters are perfectly lovely in the right place. The streets, however, are no place for them."

She had been on a crusade against hot-weather garments since late the previous year. Not everyone in the area agreed with how Cohran saw things.

"I don't think that under the law, shorts and halters would be defined as contributing to indecent exposure. They seem to have become an accepted custom," said John Ames, acting secretary director of Cincinnati, in an interview.

Still, Cohran may have had a point, if you look at it from the viewpoint of a woman born in 1891. Maybe she encountered a lot of male deviants who couldn't handle women wearing skimpy clothing. Cohran was living in an age in which masculinity and youth were prized (she shaved four years from her age when she applied to the police force). She probably believed she was saving young women from predators by ensuring they were well clothed.

But this was 1936, not 1836, and the younger generation embraced the freedom of not being buried in layers of clothing. This was an issue that emerged repeatedly this summer, an argument made by younger folk but also by frustrated members of the older generation. When it came to loose clothing, society needed to loosen up. Some people were dying because they chose a heavy garment to wear over a lighter one.

Alaska

Temperatures hit 80 and above. Fires broke out, and glaciers melted off mountains and created floods. Cabins, some full of prospectors, trappers, and homesteaders, washed down the Stikine River. But what really confounded physicians in Juneau was a female patient suffering from a condition that no doctor could recall ever seeing in these parts. The woman had a sunburn.

Nebraska

Adolph Dahl's funeral was held today in the town of Davey. Two days earlier, in the morning, the sixty-six-year-old helped put up hay at the farm of one of his sons. But in the afternoon, nobody could find Dahl. His son, Ben, and other farmhands went looking for him.

Adolph seemed to be in good spirits, which is why it was shocking when he was found around 3:30 P.M., hanging from a low tree branch near a barn. His feet were touching the ground, but it didn't matter; the rope and gravity had done their work.

The high was 96, and everybody speculated the heat had driven the farmer mad. Of course, it was also the Great Depression, and Dahl may have been suffering from economic stress or any number of problems. These were bleak times. On July 10, in Los Angeles, Thomas Carroll, unemployed, asked for his job back at a hat factory. After being refused, he went up to the roof, sat on the edge, his feet dangling, and after ten minutes, dove off headfirst, to the horror of a thirteen-year-old girl who witnessed it from afar.

Suicide is incomprehensible to many people, and it may seem supremely simplistic that the media and healthcare professionals in 1936 would routinely suggest that a heat wave could cause somebody to kill themselves. But they did. And it is simplistic. Yet there may be something to it. In 2024, a study published by the French National Institute for Health and Medical Research analyzed the cause of deaths recorded between 1968 and 2016, of which 502,000 out of 24.4 million were suicide, and concluded that the heat *does* affect the rate of suicides. Extreme cold doesn't seem to have an impact.

Maybe Dahl was doomed to end his life before the summer ended. His family said their patriarch dreaded hot weather. Considering everything that would transpire in the weeks ahead, it is possible that Adolph Dahl never stood a chance.

8
JUNE 15
Waxing Nostalgic

Today's Death Toll: 2
Total Death Toll: 70+

The day before, Henry Helm Clayton, an esteemed seventy-five-year-old weatherman based out of Canton, Massachusetts, forecasted a brutal summer, one that would have "periods of intense heat," especially in July.

It was perhaps the country's first true warning of an impending calamity, although obviously the nation didn't mobilize for a hot summer based on one professional meteorologist's opinion. Still, the public took note. The year before, Clayton predicted the upcoming winter would have subnormal temperatures.

Scientists such as Clayton were in too short a supply, according to Edgar Calvert, head of the forecasting division of the United States. Calvert wasn't a fan of amateur weather forecasters, and in 1936, there were a lot of them. About two weeks earlier at a hurricane preparation conference in Jacksonville, Florida, Calvert urged members of the public to follow the Weather Bureau (renamed the National Weather Service in 1970) for accurate information, "instead of following inaccurate advice disseminated by so-called weather experts, of which there are thousands."

Calvert wasn't wrong, although there were some excellent amateur weather experts across the country doing yeoman's work, and many towns depended on their "unofficial" temperature readings. For instance, in Mankato, Minnesota, John Pihale was a sixty-four-year-old who had collected weather observations for the city since 1900. At first, he was a tailor who studied weather patterns as a hobby. But he was so good at what he did that in the 1920s, he was hired by the federal government to regularly furnish data to the Minneapolis weather bureau.

Then you had, just as an example, Charles Salick, a seventy-nine-year-old weatherman who collected weather data for Watertown, Wisconsin. Salick was a jewelry store owner fascinated by meteorology, and for the last fifty years kept meticulous climate data, furnishing it to the local paper and working with the United States weather bureau, all for free. On the worst day of the 1936 heat wave, July 14, Salick was found unconscious in his apartment and died in the hospital. Richard Hoge, a bank cashier and an amateur weather buff willing to work for free, replaced him.

That same day, Pihale also became ill in the 100-degree-plus heat and had to briefly shut down the city's local weather bureau and stay in bed, per doctor's orders. He rebounded.

Because weather forecasting was still in its relative infancy (the first US weather bureau opened in 1870), the amateurs outnumbered the professionals, and they relied on a variety of methods to make predictions that didn't impress Calvert. John Pos, seventy-nine, a resident of Pella, Iowa, forecast weather by observing the moon and behavior of birds. C. W. Hawk, a resident of Des Moines, Iowa, made predictions based on the movement of the planets.

Abraham Fagen was a resident of Minneapolis and had a lot of careers during his life, including one as an insurance agent and, lately, that of a trolley car operator. But he was an amateur weather forecaster and correctly predicted the summer of 1936 would be awful. He was so confident that during the worst of the summer, he produced affidavits signed on April 22, stating his prediction that the country would face "the greatest crop losses in history throughout the world through drought, with the heaviest losses in wheat." But Calvert and other weather professionals were underwhelmed by Fagen's forecast. That's because Fagen blamed the drought on atmospheric disturbances from radio broadcasting, a common belief at the time. Meteorologists understood that there was a lot about the climate they didn't know, but they knew radio waves had no effect on the weather.

But out of all the amateur weather forecasters of the era, James Forbes, a Rochester, New York barber, stood out. He raised leeches in a large glass bowl, and his forecasts depended on how they reacted. He had done this for decades, a practice he learned as a barber's apprentice. His boss was a barber from Europe, still engaged in the outdated practice of bloodletting.

Forbes told a reporter the following month, "What the leeches do is my secret. I just go into the room where I keep them in a large glass bowl, and when I come out, I can predict what the weather will be twelve hours later."

It was a technique that didn't work for him this summer. A few weeks from today, he would train an electric fan on his bowl of leeches to keep them cool. The fan didn't help. For the first summer in fifty-three years, Forbes couldn't use his leeches to forecast the weather—because they all died.

In many ways, predicting a hot summer this year was an easy call. The weather was already oppressive, with people passing out, dying, and drowning. It wasn't difficult to imagine July and August would be worse.

Weird things were also happening. In Muncie, Indiana, patrons of the newly opened Baker Hamburger Inn were settling in for lunch when the spare tire of a car parked out front exploded. Rubber harmlessly scattered into pieces, but the hubcap flew into the air, narrowly missing a passerby, crashing through the inn's front window, ricocheting off a wall, and falling harmlessly to the floor.

The tire blew up due to the heat, everybody figured. A reasonable assumption. The heat was making ordinary moments rather extraordinary.

In Frogtown, a suburb of St. Paul, Minnesota (95°F), the heat became too much for Rapinwax Paper. Nationally known for its wax paper, the conditions in the four-story factory were always hot. Paraffin wax was, after all, constantly melted before being embedded into the paper sheets. But today, the inside of the building became an inferno, fueled by the weather outside. A fire started under a loading platform at the rear of the building.

Fortunately the fire broke out at 11:40 A.M., when Rapinwax's 125 workers were outside eating lunch. Over two hours, firemen saved enough of the factory that it reopened for business two days later. Frogtown was fortunate. The fire almost reached two oil refineries and a coal company a few blocks away. While firefighters sprayed water, three workmen from Rapinwax hurriedly hooked a truck to a gasoline tank car, containing 7,000 gallons of fuel, and hauled *that* away before flames consumed it.

While frantic adults fought the fire and a plume of smoke enveloped the skies across St. Paul, Minnesota, carefree children played, creating sculptures out of paraffin wax. For years, awestruck locals talked about the flood of wax melted by the flames and the sun flowing down Frogtown's sidewalks and boulevards.

9

JUNE 16

Wally

Today's Death Toll: 3
Total Death Toll: 75+

The terms "global warming" and "climate change" were not really in the 1936 lexicon, but the concepts were discussed—and the phrase "climate change" was occasionally used. Especially this summer. A few weeks from now, in Elmira, New York, the *Star-Gazette* would run a column with the headline "Climate Changing?" The article started off with "Secretary of Agriculture Henry A. Wallace notes the possibility of a weather change in the United States that is to make drouths a frequent occurrence from year to year. He bases this suggestion upon the drouths of 1930, 1934 and 1936 and the fact that history records that climate change have turned wide areas into arid lands, forcing the migration of peoples."

In fact, this month, Brian O'Brien, a University of Rochester professor, made news for his new theory suggesting the ozone layer was keeping everyone alive. Ozone had been known to exist since the 1800s, and scientists were aware of the ozone layer since 1913. But O'Brien believed much of the reason we weren't being fried like ants under a magnifying glass was due to the ozone layer's protection. O'Brien was onto something, though the ozone hole wouldn't be discovered for almost another fifty years, and scientists would realize that the more the hole widened, the hotter the planet would become.

It was certainly hot today. People passed out in Louisiana and Pennsylvania. In Kentuck, Virginia (94°F), a thirty-year-old tobacco farmer in poor health died working in his fields. Elsewhere, there were other problems.

Alaska

The Alaskan heat wave was now "unprecedented," stated a news wire service. Firefighters in Homer battled a forest fire, where it was 72 degrees—instead of the usual 50s. Most of the state was in the 80s, although in Seward, where there was daylight twenty hours at a stretch, temperatures reached 108, causing two citizens to pass out. One year earlier, it was 55 degrees.

California

It was in the high 60s, but the morning began with 86 percent humidity. At the Herbert Fleishhacker Zoo, later renamed the San Francisco Zoological Gardens, one animal, an elephant named Wally, was particularly hot and bothered.

But, first, a little backstory: Wally was born in India in 1908 and probably came to America around the time the elephant became a teenager. He was enticed into a life of show business, mostly because Wally's "agent" was a group of animal handlers with guns and chains. Showbiz can be a rough gig.

By the summer of 1922, Wally was one of the stars of the Sells-Floto Circus based out of Chicago. Wally's name was not yet Wally—his name was Charlie Ed, named after the son of a circus executive. Wally had an interesting life as circus elephants go. He traveled around North America, was profiled in newspapers, and made headlines on August 2, 1926, when while being loaded onto a circus train, he and thirteen elephants made a break for freedom. Cranbrook, British Columbia, had never seen anything like it and probably never will again: fourteen elephants racing down Main Street, with citizens scrambling out of the way and rushing into stores' doorways. Then the elephants charged into the Canadian wilderness.

Eleven elephants were quickly recaptured, but three remained on the run: Charlie Ed, Tillie, and Myrtle. Three weeks later, Tillie was caught, convinced to return by a trail of bread that led to her captors. On September 8, Myrtle (who some people called the ringleader), hungry and weak, was cornered six miles from Cranbrook and didn't go down easily; two days later, she was dead. Some say she died of pneumonia; others claimed she was emaciated and had to be put down.

Charlie Ed was the last to be caught. He went down hard, battling men who brought him down with elephant hooks. He lost a tusk in the battle and ended up in chains.

Charlie Ed was renamed Cranbrook Ed, after the town where he escaped—but he wasn't pleased to return to circus life, at least according to his handlers. A special steel car was soon built to transport and contain the elephant.

Four years later, perhaps exhausted from caring for the restless elephant, the Sells-Floto Circus executives sold Cranbrook Ed to the Hagenbeck–Wallace Circus, which may have had no more luck with the elephant, because they soon sold Cranbrook Ed to the Al G. Barnes Circus. During that time, Cranbrook Ed was loaned out to two movies that came out in 1935—*Clive of India*, an adventure starring Ronald Colman, and *O'Shaughnessy's Boy*, a drama about a circus animal trainer starring the fifty-one-year-old actor Wallace Beery, who was a circus performer in his youth.

By now, Cranbrook Ed was called Wally due to his association with Beery, and while renting elephants to movie studios may have been profitable, perhaps the hassle of caring for a cranky pachyderm wasn't worth the money. In 1936, the Al G. Barnes Circus donated Wally to the Herbert Fleishhacker Zoo.

As far as the staff knew, Wally was a sweet, gentle animal, but some zookeepers recognized this was not a docile creature. Do not turn your back on Wally, they would say.

Ed Brown, one of the zookeepers, may have never heard the talk. Brown, forty-five years old, was no stranger to elephants. He had worked in the circus, and from 1930 to 1934, spent four years as a zookeeper at the Herbert Fleishhacker Zoo in the elephant house until deciding to quit, a bold move during the Great Depression. But he had recently been rehired. The economy was still terrible, his wife was in poor health, and he had bills to pay.

On this somewhat hot and extremely humid day, Brown decided to take Wally to get a bath. He was accompanied by an assistant keeper, Rudolph Bjork.

Bjork was preoccupied, holding off four elephants from following Brown and Wally, so he didn't see what happened. He *heard* what happened, though. Brown cursed and screamed.

Bjork spun around. Brown was down on one knee. Wally was swinging his one remaining tusk into Brown, knocking him flat onto his face. Bjork had no time to react. Wally swung his trunk again and rushed toward Brown, trampling him. After that, it was bedlam. Lions roared in their cages; tigers snarled; animals throughout the zoo were thrown into a panic. Zookeepers struggled to contain Wally so they could save Brown, or at least have something left over of him for the funeral. It took about an hour before Wally was in chains, his head, tusk, and leg splattered with blood.

Brown's body was scattered on the ground in four pieces.

Afterward, the local newspapers offered headlines blaming the heat. One newspaper headline stated, "Former Barnes Circus Animal Goes Amuck in Bay Heat Wave." "Heat-Crazed Elephant Kills Keeper," screamed a headline in Longview, Texas. One paper described Wally as "a heat and lust-maddened, one-tusked bull elephant . . ." "Maddened by the unseasonable heat," another newspaper article started. *Variety*, the Hollywood trade magazine, even weighed in, saying, "It is thought summer heat and being separated from the other elephants in the zoo brought on the rampage."

Zookeepers like Bjork and Robert Cleary couldn't help but recall why Ed Brown temporarily quit his zookeeping job two years earlier. The job, Brown said, was "too dangerous."

10

JUNE 17

The Elephant in the Room

Today's Death Toll: 20
Total Death Toll: 90+

The day after an elephant gored its zookeeper to death, the city of San Francisco was consumed with the question: What should be done about Wally?

The zoo director knew. Edmund Heller recommended that Wally's life end—immediately. He was now hearing about other disturbing incidents in Wally's past. There was a rumor that three months before he was donated to the zoo, Wally killed a circus worker, although the circus denied it. If the gossip was true, it was kept quiet; no contemporary news account of a circus worker gored to death by an elephant seems to exist. Other people recalled a moment a few years earlier when Wally reacted angrily while news camera crews took photos of him.

It really didn't matter what Wally's past was like, according to Heller. A zookeeper was dead. There would be retribution. Someone floated the idea of taking the elephant in chains onto a ship, and once it was nice and deep over the ocean, the crew would release Wally into the water. Cooler heads prevailed, however, and the zoo opted for a faster, cheaper, more humane, but still unsatisfying end. They would shoot him.

"Wally was never known to harm anyone before, but since he killed his keeper, I wouldn't want to put any others in jeopardy," Heller said.

Wally had no shortage of defenders. The Oakland mayor said his own city's zoo was discussing whether they could bring Wally into their care. Society women spoke up for Wally. Children did, too. City officials weighed in, saying Wally's life should be spared. A prominent veterinarian wondered if the San Francisco–Oakland Bay Bridge should be destroyed because twenty-two men died while building it.

Heller was having none of it. Wally would be put down today, right away. Indeed, Wally was chained to a post while two police detectives adjusted the sights of their guns, described by the press as big "moose guns," and a crowd of zoo guests gathered to watch the execution. Except . . .

An attorney, Alexander Mooslin, arrived in a taxi. He dashed up to the elephant corral of the Fleishhacker Zoo.

"Stop it, stop it," Mooslin shouted. The attorney asked which person was Heller. The zoo director identified himself. Mooslin handed Heller a writ, staying the execution until the next day. Mooslin, who just came from a courtroom, explained his law partner was suing as a "citizen," pleading that the execution would be cruel and inhumane.

A hearing was scheduled for the next day at the zoo.

"I guess that's that," Heller said.

Heller was disgusted—and resigned to the idea that Wally might live. "There are a lot of disappointed people who came out just to see the killing. As far as I'm concerned now, anybody can have Wally," Heller said. "I might ask the humane society or some nice old lady in the city to adopt him."

"Maybe," Heller wisecracked, "we can get some of the people who want the elephant protected to come out here and feed him." At one point, a frustrated Heller said, "I reckon they ought to shoot me instead of the elephant."

Heller may have felt ganged up on, but he had some allies. "If persons pleading for Wally's life could see the mangled body of his victim," said A. J. Cleary, the chief administrative officer of city hall, "I believe they would not insist upon keeping him alive."

Mabel Brown, Ed's widow, was noncommittal about Wally's fate. She acknowledged that her spouse had been a little nervous about Wally and told reporters the elephant killed her husband in what was "a touch of midsummer madness, a bit of heat and of desire," and it didn't make any difference to her what happened to the animal.

"No matter what they do, it won't bring Ed back," she said. "Now please leave me alone."

Elsewhere, the heat wave continued to spread across North America.

Oklahoma

In Tulsa, a woman's body was found partially submerged in a stream behind a house, in a neighborhood where she was a governess. Police saw no signs of murder and believed she died by suicide. After an autopsy, they concluded the 97-degree heat was the culprit. She was thirty-four.

Alaska

In Fairbanks, it was 88 degrees. Children were dressed in bathing suits and light clothing; ice cream was selling better than ever. In Seward, forest fires continued to rage.

Missouri, Kentucky, Indiana

St. Louis, Missouri, lost two citizens to the 98-degree heat. Kentucky, which saw temperatures in the low 100s today, lost two people. In Indiana, where it was in the 90s, there were two drownings.

Ohio

Twelve deaths were blamed on the heat, though in most cases, indirectly: people drowned, while others were struck by lightning in storms brought on by high temperatures, which were well into the 90s in some parts of the state.

In Troy, the heat caused a section of State Route 66 to bulge upward, and an unfortunate motorist didn't notice it. His car flipped and landed in a ditch. The driver staggered away from the wreck with a bruised shoulder.

Virginia

In Lynchburg, two boys drowned in Blackwater Creek in about eight-foot-deep water. Cornell Howard was thirteen, and Jetson Wesley York was twelve. They were swimming with two other boys when something went terribly wrong.

Lifesaving crews worked for more than two hours to save the boys, found seventy-five feet apart at the bottom of the muddy stream. York gasped a few times when he was removed from the water, and then . . . nothing. In the aftermath of their deaths, locals—at least, Black locals—floated an idea. They suggested perhaps the city could finally start building a swimming pool where there wouldn't be signs saying "Whites Only."

Lynchburg had no swimming pools for Black residents. There were, however, five swimming pools for Whites, including the YMCA and public park pools. In the past, there was talk of creating a swimming pool for Black people, but the project was shelved. This time, talk turned to action. The following summer, Jefferson Park Pool opened for Black swimmers, a welcome development that came too late for kids like Cornell Howard and Jetson York.

Pennsylvania

In Erie (90°F), two girls, eight and ten years old, wanted to cool off. The friends donned their swimming suits, and a mother drew a bath.

She then went to a nearby beauty parlor and left the kids alone. It probably didn't seem irresponsible. The girls weren't going to drown in a bathtub. But for some reason, the mom, or maybe the girls, turned on the bathtub gas heater, perhaps unaware of the many cautionary tales about bathtub heaters.

When the mother returned, what happened next must have been a blur, the kind where time stands still and you're pretty sure you've just had your soul ripped out. Because the next hours were spent in the bathroom while a fire rescue squad and physicians unsuccessfully attempted to bring the girls back to life.

The bathtub gas heater ran while the girls were playing. Water, naturally, was splashed. The water extinguished the flames in the heater. Without the fire burning, the gas that was released became carbon monoxide.

11

JUNE 18
The Trial

Today's Death Toll: 10
Total Death Toll: 100+

While the 1936 heat wave was mostly relegated to North America, other parts of the world were feeling the effect. In early June, it was 90 degrees in Siberia. On June 25, in Iceland, a heat wave melted glaciers and subsequent flooding weakened a bridge over the Öxnadalsá River. It collapsed thirty minutes before the king of Denmark and Iceland was scheduled to cross it. A few days later, Rome's humid summer sent seventy-nine-year-old Pope Pius XI to his summer retreat weeks earlier than normal.

Still, this year, Americans and Canadians—especially Americans—were primarily the ones winning the heat lottery, and other countries were taking notice. "Amazing scenes were witnessed in New York, where millionaires have chartered aeroplanes to fly to altitudes of 10,000 feet in their attempts to escape the furnace-like conditions in the city," stated an article in Liverpool, England's *Evening Express* on July 11.

"Fifty persons an hour died in the United States to-day from the heat," observed a July 15 article in *The Age*, a newspaper in Melbourne, Victoria, Australia, describing events that occurred two days earlier: "The Detroit morgue, typical of other stricken cities, presented such a scene as occurs when sudden disaster takes many lives. The dead lay in low rows, with relatives seeking to identify them. The two cities of St. Paul and Minneapolis were near panic to-day as 109 died in a temperature of 106 degrees. Detroit's experience was in the nature of a holocaust. The hospital facilities were taxed to the limit. Cases filled all the corridors and deaths occurred in such numbers that there was barely time to remove the dead to the morgue."

Today, across the country, temperatures continued to remove people from the population with scalpel-like precision, from the heartland to the coasts.

California

Wally the elephant's stay of execution the previous day was dramatic, and this morning, attorney Alexander Mooslin gave it his all, arguing the zookeepers didn't have the right to destroy the animal, that it would be inhumane. He also demanded a fair trial. That last point may have miffed the judge. They were doing a trial, weren't they? Was Mooslin suggesting the judge lacked integrity? Miffed or not, Superior Judge Frank Deasy declared the elephant's life must come to an end.

Mooslin appealed. A court turned him down again hours later, and thirty minutes after that, while a crowd watched, Wally was held down in chains, and two detectives nine feet away fired their moose guns at the elephant's head.

Mooslin cried, but not everyone was heartbroken. Walter McLain, the guy in charge of the elephants at the Al G. Barnes Circus, said, "Females and only the youngest of males are considered safe around the circus crowds. I think that the execution of Wally is a good riddance."

"If we didn't kill the elephant, there were bound to be endless accidents. He was a bad one, and there would be danger to women and children visiting the zoo, if he was allowed to live," zoo director Heller said.

Frank Buck, the famed hunter and actor who wrote the bestseller *Bring 'Em Back Alive*, said later in the day that the killing was a useless waste of life: "I knew that elephant, from the day he was on the Al G. Barnes circus." He then bragged about something perhaps not worth bragging about: "And the three females who were his companions before keepers separated them were brought to this country by me."

Wally's corpse was carved up for scientists to study, but most of his body was given to the other zoo animals as food.

Missouri

In Kansas City, hens turned up dead while grasshoppers showed up by the millions. Grasshoppers thrive in hot, dry conditions. They're cold-blooded and eat more and grow faster in high temperatures. The hot, dry weather also reduces the odds of the grasshopper's eggs being affected by a fungal infection, so more eggs hatch. Grasshoppers were now swarming in Missouri, Oklahoma, Kansas, Iowa, Nebraska, Montana, Colorado, Wisconsin, and Illinois. Farmers quickly began making bran mash, a type of food given to horses that the grasshoppers loved—and then they set it out just for the grasshoppers.

One extra special ingredient was always added: arsenic.

Alaska

For the eighth day in a row, Fairbanks's high temperature was over 80. Today, it was 87. Mosquitoes flourished, and ice cream sales soared.

Tennessee

In Nashville (99°F), city officials informed residents they could sleep outdoors at the parks if they desired. This was standard procedure in most American cities for generations. You couldn't sleep in a park—except when there was a heat wave.

If you owned a home, you could sleep in your yard, but if you lived in an apartment, it was awfully handy to have a public park where you could stretch out with dozens of your fellow neighbors.

Kansas

In Wichita, the high was 105 degrees. That night, hundreds of citizens conked out on front porches, on their lawns, and along riverbanks, as well as in the city parks. There was an unrefreshing wind, and the low that night was 78, a temperature that didn't arrive until 7 A.M.

Illinois

Ice was always an important commodity during the summer, but it was about to become especially profitable for ice manufacturers. Prices shot up in parts of the country but dropped in others. In New Orleans, wholesale price of ice would soon climb from $4 to $5 per ton, infuriating retailers. Serv-Ice, Inc. in Memphis actually lowered the price of their ice for consumers in June. They could afford to be generous with ice very much in demand.

Manufacturers had been producing and transporting ice since the 1800s. For decades, during the winter, manufacturers in the north harvested ice in lakes and rivers, and in warmer climates, ice companies were freezing water in metal cans submerged in brine (salty water). In simple science terms, the salt pulls the heat out of the water in the metal cans, allowing the water to freeze, while the brine remains liquid (salt water freezes at a much lower temperature than fresh water). If the liquid surrounding the metal containers froze, you couldn't fish them out of the water.

But just because you could purchase ice didn't mean you'd necessarily want to have that ice as cubes in your drink. It was common in the 1800s and early 1900s to learn that your local ice manufacturer was freezing sewage water. Even if the water was healthy (c'mon in, the water's fine), pond or lake grass could get into that water, so consumers had to worry about their ice being contaminated with decaying vegetation.

Keeping the ice cold was another matter. Trains experimented with refrigerated cars almost since trains were invented, and at first, refrigerated cars were cooled with (what else?) ice. By the 1920s, many refrigerated cars were cooled with chemicals like sulfur dioxide, ammonia, and methyl chloride, the latter of which wound up in a lot of the mass-produced refrigerators in the late 1920s and 1930s. Those eventually fell out of favor; the methyl chloride sometimes leaked, and some upper and middle-class families became the subjects of tragic front-page stories due to breathing in the odorless, colorless, toxic gas.

In Chicago, the *Tribune* free ice fund opened today, earlier than expected. The day before, the mercury reached 91 degrees, and everyone was bracing for another hot one. Today's high, however, was only 68.

Thanks to donations remaining from the previous year, *The Chicago Tribune* had 200,000 pounds of ice that they were giving to ten charitable agencies and ten district stations of the United Charities of Chicago, run by Miss Edna Mae Wray. These charities gave poor Chicagoans a ticket that they could redeem for free ice, which they could put in their icebox. Every summer, impoverished families needed their ice ticket, mostly to keep food and fresh milk from spoiling, but having something cold to drink on a hot, humid day didn't hurt.

Ice funds were a lifesaver to people across the country. If you lived in a big or medium-sized city, your newspaper probably had an ice fund.

"Not one penny of federal, state, county or city funds is available this summer to supply milk for undernourished Omaha children," stated a plea from *The Omaha Evening Bee-News* later in the month, urging readers to give generously to their free milk and ice fund. The paper observed that city hall was swamped "with calls from anxious mothers begging milk for their babies."

It would get far worse. As the drought and heat killed pastureland, dairy farmers were running out of product to sell and, blaming the cost of feed, they began raising the cost of milk. That put milk even further out of reach for poor families, of which there were many during the Great Depression.

Across the country, when the ice trucks arrived, the excitement was palpable, especially this summer. The commotion rivaled ice cream trucks that sold their treats for a nickel, only instead of children rushing out, desperate mothers were hurrying out onto the blistering pavement and exchanging their tickets for ice.

12

JUNE 20

The Tragedy of Martin Pee

Today's Death Toll: 10+
Total Death Toll: 110+

Taking its seasonal place in the spotlight among topics of interest to real estate, architectural and building circles, air-conditioning looms larger than ever this year, since it is being widely applied to the home for the first time," stated an article that ran in *The Cincinnati Enquirer* today, which was syndicated across the country.

Air-conditioning was invented by Willis Carrier in 1902. But it was initially a crude invention, and it took a few years before Carrier's company had clients. Textile companies were Carrier's first customers in 1906. Carrier is still in business, of course, and has been wildly successful.

While professional rainmakers were accepting money to try to improve the weather outside, an ethically questionable occupation, Willis Carrier bet on fixing the weather inside. By 1936, Carrier owned a prosperous company and was battling a slew of competitors, including General Electric and Frigidaire. In fact, there were now 15,000 air-conditioning dealers and contractors in the United States—and the industry had achieved a milestone that all new industries are excited to reach: they could make up a fake holiday to get media attention! This week was the first "National Warm Air Heating and Air-Conditioning Week." It was declared so yesterday, at a national convention of air-conditioning industry professionals in Columbus, Ohio.

But, really, the industry didn't need to promote their product. The very idea sold itself, if you had the money to buy an air-conditioning unit (and thanks to the Depression, almost nobody did). How much an air-conditioning system cost mostly depended on the size of the house, and advertisements of the time were reluctant to offer a price and scare people away. But a Camden, New Jersey, newspaper article in August 1936 stated that a small air-conditioning unit, one that could cool a room, was $400 (and weighed about 600 pounds). An air-conditioning system that cooled an entire home was generally around $600 to $1,000 in a new home and $200 a room for an already built house.

The S. R. Dresser Manufacturing Company—a few months later—announced they reduced the cost of their gas air-conditioning units from $2,000 to $800, which would be $18,000 today.

The cost was far out of reach for most Depression-era households, but most people understood an air conditioner's utility, especially on a day like today, with heat deaths in states like California, Oklahoma, and Tennessee. With air-conditioning a pipe dream for most people, the entire summer was an exercise in trying to stay cool, whether that meant sleeping outside, stripping your wardrobe down to next to nothing, sitting near an electric fan, or spending an afternoon at the ol' swimming hole.

Arkansas

Two days ago, Joe Treadway, a fifty-five-year-old farmhand, was chopping cotton in Paragould—in 106-degree heat—when he suffered a partial stroke. Treadway was likely desperate for income. He had worked as a farmhand since the spring and probably decided he wasn't going to let a little old thing like a stroke get him down.

The next day, yesterday, he returned to the fields with his boss and the boss's wife, picking cotton. The temperature went up to 109, and Treadway suffered another heatstroke. Today, at his funeral, it was 110.5 degrees.

Indiana

In Seymour (98°F), Ronald Borcherding was trimming trees when he was overcome by the heat. He slipped into the fork of a tree and lacked the strength to climb down. A fireman, probably more accustomed to rescuing cats, climbed up to get him.

Arizona

In Arizona, where much of the state suffered 117-degree weather, there were two heat victims: George Seubert, a sixty-year-old Altadena, California, resident visiting Gila Bend, who died in the evening; and a fifteen-year-old Hopi teenager, Martin Pee.

Seubuet's death shouldn't be dismissed. He was a married man, a waiter, and presumably a perfectly nice guy. But Pee's story was especially tragic, given his age and circumstances. He and a friend, Ernest Honanie, sixteen, escaped from a government-funded boarding school in Riverside, California, known as the Sherman Institute. The school opened in 1892 (at a different location and under a different name) with the goal of assimilating Native Americans into "civilized" society. Students may have graduated with useful skills, but these facilities were little more than prisons for Native American youth. It took a long time, but in October 2024, President Joe Biden issued a formal apology for the federal government's Indian boarding school system. At least 3,100 students are believed to have died at these schools.

And at least one died in the aftermath of escaping from these schools. Pee may have been a new student; student records show that his friend Ernest Honanie had been there as early as 1930, when he would have been eleven years old.

Several days before, Pee, Honanie, and three other students snuck away and rode a bus to Needles, California. Then they walked across the border into Arizona, to Topock. The three others kept going, but Pee and Honanie decided to pick up some work at a cattle ranch. It was so hot, though—unofficially, the temperature read 130 degrees—that the boys became sick. Two days later, after recuperating at the ranch, they decided to hoof it back home.

The cattle ranch owner's wife gave them some canned food. She also cautioned them to follow a road, which was really a "wash," or a dry river bottom, that would lead to the main highway. Along the gully was a lot of jungle-like brush that might provide shade. It would be better than wandering in the desert.

They headed northeast, planning to go to their Hopi reservation.

But it was scorching. The unofficial temperature was 125 degrees. Only a few miles after leaving, the boys decided they might make better time through the desert. They may have been correct, but somewhere on a steep hillside near Oatman, both Honanie and Pee blacked out. Honanie simply fell, but Pee rolled down the hill until his head struck a rock. A passerby from Oatman spotted them. Pee was dead, but Honanie was rushed to the hospital. Honanie was delirious and remained so for a while, but he slowly returned to normal. It isn't known whether he returned home or if he was taken back to the Sherman Institute.

Not everybody approved of these boarding schools. An editorial in the Redlands, California, newspaper, on June 26, referenced Pee and Honanie, and stated, "We have never professed to understand the necessity for taking young boys and girls from their reservations, meager as life may be there, and sending them to remote sections to be educated. It is little enough that they have at their hovels in the rocks and deserts—but to the boys born there it was home, and it is there that they should be entitled to educational facilities."

13

JUNE 22

Campaigning in the Heat of the Moment

Today's Death Toll: 10+
Total Death Toll: 120+

In 1936, the summer of 1934 was on everybody's minds. The summer was looking like a hot one, but would it be as bad as 1934? People were beginning to fear so. Some older adults may have been thinking of other heat waves as well, such as the one in 1901 or 1896, or if you were an old-timer, 1876.

Accurate death toll numbers are hard to come by for the heat wave of 1876, but people were still talking about it fifty years later. The heat wave of 1896 ravaged cities like New York, Boston, and Chicago, killing around 1,500 people. The 1901 heat wave was devastating; one estimate suggests as many as 9,500 people may have died. The 1934 heat death toll was probably more than 4,000, the National Safety Council suggested in 1936.

Everyone was thinking of the heat wave barely in the rearview mirror: Would 1936 be like 1934? Heat waves are essentially slow-motion disasters. On June 22, 1936, even the best meteorologists couldn't recognize that the country was going to have a heat wave that would make two years ago seem like a cool day at the beach. But the signs were there, said the aforementioned Travis O'Brien, Indiana University's weather guru.

For starters, there were the warm Atlantic and Pacific Ocean surface temperatures lingering since the previous winter. There was also an unusual amount of low springtime precipitation, which meant less moisture evaporating into the air and cooling off the country. The Dust Bowl, meanwhile, "had a double-whammy effect on extreme heat in the 1930s," O'Brien said. The dust essentially trapped the heat, making everything and everyone hotter, and also interfered with rain clouds from forming, and so there was less rain to cool people off.

California

Hot, dry air can damage the membranes in nasal cavities, causing the nose to bleed. Today, in Quincy (105°F), Marian Zimmerman, fifty-six, bled from her nose—for several hours.

There were numerous nosebleed incidents this summer, some more serious than others. In July, a Missouri woman spent several days fighting a heat-induced nosebleed. She survived, but in mid-June, Don Thompson, a twenty-nine-year-old carpenter in Juneau, Alaska, developed a nosebleed during the US territory's heat wave. Thompson's nose bled periodically and heavily for a month. Doctors gave him three blood transfusions before he died.

Washington and Oregon

Spokane, Washington, had its hottest June 22 ever: 97 degrees. Beaches and swimming pools were packed. In St. Helens, Oregon (82°F), a thirteen-year-old waded into a swimming hole at a Boy Scout camp, but got into trouble. A farmer, who knew the boy, rushed in to save him but ended up underwater himself. The boy's sister, who couldn't swim, went after them and somehow got the farmer back to the riverbank. He was revived but died days later in the hospital.

Missouri

Fighting chinch bugs is not a cinch. Native to the United States, they are pests that devour crops like wheat, oats, and corn. In Lamar, Louis Niehaus, a judge, and Otis Smith, a farmer, had a plan to attack the chinch bugs, a strategy common for the time. They brought out two barrels of creosote, a soup of chemicals often used as a pesticide. They were going to take the barrels to the trenches and pour it into their fields.

It might have worked, too, except that the hotter creosote gets, the more easily it bursts into flames. Today, it was 104 degrees—and KA-BOOM! Niehaus and Smith were severely burned on their arms and faces, and the chinch bugs continued to chomp on their farmland.

Oklahoma

Oklahoma City's Harry Wahlgren, a beloved meteorologist, joked to the local media that he was probably "the city's most unpopular man" after forecasting that the state's heat wave wouldn't be ending any time soon. "There is practically no relief in sight at present. This heat has been pretty widespread," Wahlgren said.

The day before, it was 106, and three people died. The weather was dangerous, hot, and extremely uncomfortable, which is why a man who went by the name L. C. Montgomery camped out last night at a Oklahoma City park. He set up his crude bed and removed his trousers and wrapped his pants, containing $18 in cash, around his shoes and used that for a pillow.

He woke up this morning to discover that a thief had made off with his pants-pillow. Also his dignity, since Montgomery walked home in daylight, broke, barefooted, and in his underwear.

Texas

Effie Redmond was a rarity in 1936: a forty-nine-year-old female attorney and occasional politician. She started as a stenographer at a law firm and did that, along with being a notary republic, for several years. In 1918, a year before the Texas legislature ratified the women's vote, Miss Redmond was elected county treasurer in Fort Worth. A year later, Redmond passed the bar. In 1920, Redmond ran for county tax assessor and collector—but lost.

Since then, Redmond had opened her own law firm, and while she likely struggled during the Depression—1930 census records show she was working again as an attorney's stenographer—she stayed active and employed, working for a time, for instance, as a superintendent at the humane society. But politics compelled her. Redmond ran for the state legislature and was campaigning today in Fort Worth (102°F) when she collapsed.

Redmond was admitted to Methodist Hospital on a Monday night and sent home Thursday. She was fortunate; four other Texans who lost consciousness that day were not. But Redmond lost the election the following month. Was that indirectly due to her heat hospitalization? Maybe she had little chance of winning, in a society unaccustomed to female politicians, but the time spent laid up couldn't have helped her cause. She missed, for instance, a speaking opportunity in Grapevine while she was in the hospital. Also, collapsing under the withering sun may have given some voters the impression that she was weak.

She was anything but. Less than a week after leaving the hospital, Redmond stumped for votes, speaking to a crowd of voters in Crowley in 90-plus-degree heat, explaining that she advocated for taxes on natural resources and adequate taxes for the old age pension. Of course, *that*, more than anything, may be why she lost her election—asking people to pay more taxes is rarely a winning political issue.

Redmond passed away sixteen years later, when she was sixty-five, due to injuries from a fall. While her political career never really took off, Redmond remained politically engaged, later working for the attorney general and the Texas Speaker of the House.

14

JUNE 23
Eastham Prison

Today's Death Toll: 30+
Total Death Toll: 160+

On a day when five Texans were heat victims, at the Eastham Prison farm in Houston County, where the high was 96 degrees, fifty-six prisoners decided they had enough. They informed the prison guards that they were done working in the fields.

This sort of thing was expected, according to a newspaper interview with Wirt Adams Paddock, chair of the Texas Prison board: "Every year about this time, when the weather gets hot, some of the prisoners get it into their heads that they are not going to work."

It was a daring move to go on strike in a prison, especially this prison. The infamous Clyde Barrow, of Bonnie and Clyde gangster fame, did time here. Four years earlier, Barrow visited the infirmary for a foot injury. It was said that he cut off two of his toes, or had his cellmate do it for him, so he could avoid working for the prison, if that gives you any idea of what a fun place this was.

Barrow probably regretted removing his toes; a week later, he got his parole. But Barrow's extreme work-avoidance strategy was common for the time. A month before the prisoners refused to work outside in the heat, at two other prison farms, two inmates cut off some of their toes. Another guy cut off one of his fingers.

These prisoners were desperate. They may not have been anyone's idea of a model citizen, but as inmates, they were barely considered human. Days before the strike, a forger escaped the Eastham Prison on a mule; later, he was on foot when he was sighted and shot to death.

But after the strike happened, prison officials were surprisingly reasonable (according to the prison officials). Paddock assured everyone, "The convicts are not mistreated." In fact, the general manager, Jack Ellingson, visited with the striking prisoners, and he said that they had a meeting of the minds during a pleasant two-hour discussion.

"They all agreed that they had done wrong and should be punished," Ellingson told reporters, adding, "When we parted, everybody was in a good humor."

Maybe Ellingson was overstating things. Most of the men were promptly sent into solitary confinement for several hours, but Ellingson also ordered the flogging of twelve of the prison ringleaders. The men were, depending on their involvement in the strike, to be whacked five to fifteen times. A prison physician monitored the whipping, which was done with a bat.

15

JUNE 24
Remembering the Winter

Today's Death Toll: 50+
Total Death Toll: 210+

It was hot in the south, it was hot in the north, and it was hot in between. While the heat deaths were somewhat at a minimum, a disturbing number of people, mostly kids, were drowning. But in Grand Haven, Michigan, it was cool and pleasant (59°F), and some residents were recollecting the harsh winter at a special commemoration for Earl Cunningham, the coast guard member who lost his life trying to save fishermen Clayton Brown and Claude Beardsley. Brown, as everyone remembered, crawled for miles on the Lake Michigan ice to reach the shore.

Cunningham's widow was on hand to receive a gold medal. There were also three other coast guard members receiving gold medals—the ones who saved the three other fishermen stranded on the ice flow.

Brown didn't show up to the ceremony, probably because he was still adjusting to his new situation. Doctors tried to save Brown's feet and legs, but after several weeks, his feet were amputated. Later, the lower parts of his legs were removed.

Brown got around pretty well on wooden legs. Eventually, Brown divorced and married another woman, became a father for the third time, and remained wed for thirty-seven years before he died in 1989 at the age of seventy-eight. By all accounts, Brown lived an active, happy life. Brown, who enjoyed hunting, continued to do so. He still fished and even rented out boats for a living. But he swore off the Michigan winters and its now-deadly heat, moving his family to Florida, where all he had to worry about was the occasional hurricane.

16

JUNE 28

The Sweaty Zone

Today's Death Toll: 50+
Total Death Toll: 260+

One week into the actual summer—with Memorial Day unofficially starting the season, it's easy to forget summer officially begins June 21—there was one industry thrilled by the hot weather: tourism and hospitality. If you owned a hotel with a swimming pool or any business near a well-populated body of water, you loved the heat wave.

There is a biological reason that everyone, whether you were a tourist on vacation or a hardworking individual who simply wanted to take a dip in a creek, was seeking out the water this summer. Zachary Joseph Schlader is an associate professor of physiology at Indiana University whose area of expertise is heat's impact on the human body. Schlader said water is highly thermally conductive, twenty-six times greater than air, so when you jump into a pool, for instance, it starts moving the heat from your body immediately. Because there are a lot of factors involved with removing heat from your body, like your size and how the water around you is flowing, the overall affect is that swimming pulls heat away from the body about four times faster than air.

Whether you understand the science behind it or not, everybody has learned that one of the best ways to quickly cool off on a hot day is to go into the water, which explains why beaches, swimming pools, creeks, rivers, ponds, and virtually any body of water were packed this summer. Also doing well: anywhere you could find a mountain breeze. Colorado tourism hadn't been like this since 1927. Denver was welcoming 25,000 visitors a day, flocking to places like Pikes Peak and Rocky Mountain National

Park, which boasted cooling mountain breezes. The latter spot had crowds 84 percent higher than the summer before. M. E. Rowley, secretary of the Denver Convention and Tourist Bureau, told the Associated Press that the temperatures in the nation's heat belt "undoubtedly have had a great deal to do" with the influx of tourists.

Newly air-conditioned passenger trains were now an important part of the vacation experience. Earlier in the month, an article syndicated in newspapers reminisced about how riding in a passenger train in the past meant broiling or freezing, depending on the weather. You were contending with stuffy and dirty cars, and—because the train windows would be open in the summer—breathing in the locomotive's billowing smoke and cinders. "Yesterday's vacationist usually needed a 'rest cure' upon his return home," the writer stated, explaining, ". . . today Mr. and Mrs. America's vacation begins the moment they step on the train . . . No more dread of heat waves and stuffy atmosphere."

Missouri

St. Louis lost three people today, including Alson Smith, a Black widowed mechanic, only forty-four years old. Smith came down with pneumonia that was blamed on the heat. Studies have shown that extreme temperatures often set the table for pneumonia, making people more at risk for the lung infection. Today, it was 100 degrees. Smith was visiting a rooming house on a Sunday afternoon when he collapsed. He was taken to the hospital but had already fallen into a life-ending coma.

Nebraska

In Lincoln (103°F), Elmer Schmidt, twenty-two, was involved in two back-to-back automobile accidents. He hit a car but kept driving for another block until he hit another car. He stopped this time and was taken to the police station. Schmidt said he remembered the first accident but not the second. Doctors said his mental fog was caused by the heat and possibly due to a lack of sleep. Of course—who could sleep in this heat?

Tennessee

In Chattanooga, tourism was flourishing, although its customers were wilting. Swimming pools and mountain resorts were full. Today, with a high of 101.4 degrees (110 if you believed the unofficial readings), visitors overwhelmed Chattanooga's popular Warner Park: There was a 10,000 square foot beach and a large modern swimming pool with concrete and filters. People were sunbathing in the sand, swimming in the pool, and playing cards at tables. People crowded every inch of shade from the trees and buildings. You could also go to the skating rink and create a breeze. It was the type of large crowd normally seen during the Fourth of July.

As hot as the day was—still 100 when 6 P.M. rolled around—the city avoided direct deaths from the heat. *The Chattanooga News* reported that nobody was admitted to the hospital due to the temperatures and observed wryly, "The group that is perhaps the hardest hit by a heat wave—hospital patients—took it lying down yesterday." A hospital superintendent said that the visitors complained more about the hot weather than the patients.

But the heat was unsafe, and Judge Martin Fleming probably saved lives when he did something that nobody remembered ever being done before. At 8 P.M., he released prisoners, the lighter offenders, most of whom were behind bars for public drunkenness, allowing them to sleep at home, provided they came back the next day. "Thirty sweat-drenched men walked out of the city jail to spend the night in their homes," *The Chattanooga News* reported.

The next morning, half the offenders returned, mostly Black men, who probably figured it wasn't worth taking a chance with the law given the racial climate of the 1930s. But anyone in trouble with the law, provided they weren't violent, had a friend in Fleming.

The judge was known around the city as a champion of the underdog, and during the early 1930s, when unemployment was at its worst, he ran what everyone called the Fleming Flop House, until somebody else came up with a more inviting name: The Good Samaritan Inn. It was a homeless shelter for anyone who needed it, of any race. Merchant friends of the judge contributed food and clothing, and doctors volunteered their services.

As for releasing the prisoners for the night, Fleming said, "I did it because it would have been heartlessly cruel to let these men suffer from our inferior jail facilities."

The prisoners who went home probably slept outside with their families in the yard or on open and screened-in porches. Soon, virtually the entire country would sleep outside.

Illinois

In central Illinois, a seventeen-year-old boy stepped into a big hole in the Wabash River and drowned, while a seventeen-year-old girl at a public pool in Roodhouse, Illinois (100°F), ended up being no safer. This, however, was a "pool" that was nothing like Chattanooga's Warner Park or what we would find in a city today. It was a reservoir with a sandy bottom. In the early afternoon, Virginia Eileen Turner, a junior at Roosevelt High School in St. Louis, who was planning on becoming a nurse, came to the Roodhouse Reservoir Park with a group of friends. For a time, she got some sun, lying on a floating raft. Eventually, Turner slid off and waded from the raft to the shore, twenty feet away.

But she lost her balance on an incline and sank into water only four feet deep. Whether it was watery quicksand that did her in, her inexperience as a swimmer, or a combination of both, she disappeared before she could scream or shout for help. A fourteen-year-old boy saw her go down and alerted the park manager, who organized a search posse. About fifteen minutes later, at 1:10 P.M., two men found her.

Physicians worked on Turner, at first doing mouth-to-mouth resuscitation, then they used an inhalator and adrenaline. They detected a strong pulse several times early on, but as the afternoon dragged on, six oxygen tanks later, hope diminished. At 4:30 P.M., they called the time of death, and another life full of so much promise was stilled.

Indiana

There were five drownings in the state, and in Evansville (101.6°F), there were two heat victims. Thousands of Evansville residents crowded the beaches along the Ohio River, and hundreds left the city, looking for cooler places to go, but there was nowhere to be found. It was hot enough that a pile of coal at the Deep Vein Coal Company burst into flames. Firemen spent an hour extinguishing the blaze.

Arkansas

What happened to George Allen Stephens almost sounds like a grim episode of the future TV series *The Twilight Zone*. Stephens, a nineteen-year-old from Pine Bluff, was hot and sweaty, and wanted relief from the 100-degree heat. He dove into the Saline River—and was pulled out, with two broken vertebrae in his neck. But Stephens no longer had to worry about being sweaty. Due to the damage to a nerve that controls perspiration, Stephens could no longer sweat.

The national media treated the story as one that was kind of eerie, surreal, and the type of incident that *The Twilight Zone* would be famous for playing up in twenty-three years.

Still, it wasn't as though Stephens couldn't get hot; his body simply couldn't use perspiration to help him stay cool. Of course, Stephens' story was too tragic and terrible to have made for an entertaining episode of *The Twilight Zone*. The accident also paralyzed Stephens below the waist, and although he was transported from an Arkansas hospital to one in Memphis, where doctors hoped to make sense of the young man's condition, his paralysis never improved. Stephens died in 1955 at the age of thirty-seven.

But for those familiar with the famous TV series, it's worth recalling that there was a memorable 1961 *Twilight Zone* episode called "The Midnight Sun," and the way that story plays out feels oddly reminiscent of the summer of 1936. The episode focused on two women trying to stay cool, an increasingly impossible proposition since the earth had left its normal orbit and was moving closer to the sun.

"The place is New York City, and this is the eve of the end because even at midnight, it's high noon, the hottest day in history, and you're about to spend it in *The Twilight Zone*," executive producer and host Rod Serling intones at the beginning of the episode.

During the episode, a radio announcer says that the temperature is 110, adding, "At 11 this morning, humidity, 91 percent. Forecast for tomorrow: Hot. More of the same, only hotter." Later, a male stranger barges into the women's apartment to take some of her water and shares how his family died from the heat.

"She was so fragile, just . . . just a little thing," the stranger says of his wife. "She couldn't take this heat. I tried to keep her cool. But she couldn't take the heat." Nor could their newborn, he adds.

If Rod Serling was influenced by the heat wave enough to write "The Midnight Sun," Anne Serling, his daughter, said in an email that she wasn't aware of it. But it seems probable that the heat wave may have had some effect, even if subconsciously, on Serling. He was eleven years old during the summer of 1936 and living in Binghamton, New York, a city that suffered through some very unpleasant days. In mid-July, the temperature was often in the 90s—and over 100 for three days. The hottest day in Binghamton was 105 degrees: three residents passed out on the city sidewalks, a plumber collapsed in a restaurant, and a woman working in a perfume factory fainted and was taken to the hospital.

While there appear to have been no direct heat deaths Serling's hometown, a sixty-six-year-old Binghamton family doctor died from the heat at his summer home in Pennsylvania. And "in the Binghamton area," the heat ended the lives of three people, according to *The Binghamton Press*. The local paper described the temperatures and weather as "breath-taking" and "sweltering" and "unrelenting heat." Throughout New York state, people were dropping dead, and on a day when the high was 103 degrees in Binghamton, ten-year-old Rudolph Slecak lost his life by trying to cool off in the Chenango River. It was front-page news, and the Slecak family lived approximately a mile away from the Serlings.

It seems impossible that the 1936 heat wave wouldn't have had *some* impact on Rod Serling. But was it actually on his mind when he penned the episode "The Midnight Sun"? That's a mystery that may forever exist . . . in *The Twilight Zone.*

17

JUNE 29

Water Is Swell

Today's Death Toll: 60+
Total Death Toll: 320+

Drinking fountains had been part of the landscape for a couple decades, but this summer, cities across the nation couldn't install them fast enough, adding them to a variety of public places, especially parks.

During the early 1900s, drinking fountains were essentially water pumps: If you wanted a sip of cool water, you pumped water into a metal cup attached to the fountain with a chain. But eventually health experts started saying that, gosh, maybe it isn't the best idea to drink from a metal cup that countless strangers are using. By the time 1936 rolled around, it was more common to find drinking fountains, or bubblers, like you'll see now, where you press a button and cold water comes out, and you lean in and quench your thirst and try to avoid having your lips touch the actual fountain. Of course, almost a century later, during the COVID-19 pandemic, health experts would question the safety of drinking fountains altogether.

Electric pumps were now utilized instead of hand pumps, but many new drinking fountains were still supplied by well water. In fact, the word "swell" was popularized in the 1930s, and there's some evidence to suggest that satisfied kids at the playground would drink from fountains and determine its well water was "swell." True or not, it's interesting how vocabulary changes over the years. In 1936, some old-timers didn't think "swell" was an appropriate word—and still cringed when they heard the word "sweat," which a generation or two earlier had been considered a word you wouldn't use in polite company.

The nation was dehydrated. In Sioux City, Iowa, it was 104 degrees. In Peoria, Illinois, it reached 105 and was still over 100 by nightfall. In Kansas City, Missouri, the high was 106. Across the country, people were drowning and dying from the heat, and firefighters were believed to be battling 121 forest fires throughout Southern California.

Tennessee

People were dying, partly because they weren't respecting the heat wave. When temperatures are insanely high, it's best to stay in the shade. Take it easy. Drink a lot of water.

Two people who died today didn't take the advice: a twenty-three-year-old playing a baseball game in Trenton (103°F), and a fifty-three-year-old engaging in farmwork in Cleveland (102°F). The Lehews, a family in Nashville (102°F), did their best to stay hydrated but their well was dry. They had no drinking fountain on the farm. Their icebox wasn't stocked with bottled water.

Somebody decided it would be a good idea to try a common tactic to produce more water: They would ignite a stick of dynamite and toss it into the well.

The first fuse didn't go off. So Marcus Lehew, fifty-three, and his twenty-two-year-old son, Howell, lit a second stick and dropped it in. Then a third. Again, nothing happened. They were in the process of lighting a fourth stick when the first three exploded, creating a gruesome scene. The two men were essentially blown to smithereens, but they were still alive.

Twelve-year-old Riley, Howell's younger brother, saw the whole thing, and the only reason he wasn't among the living dead was because his father told him to keep his distance. Riley sprinted for his mother, Ida Lee Lehew. She stayed on the scene while Riley ran to the neighbors, who were, according to one account, two miles away. Foster Marrs, a farmer, and his son, Cawley, returned with Riley, and they all waited for the ambulance.

Until it arrived, Ida Lee, forty-nine, held her son's severed arm in place to staunch the bleeding. Her son was conscious but barely; his eyes were disfigured and his body mangled. Her husband was still alive but not talking. They did not survive the night.

Illinois

Charles Morgan, a sixty-five-year-old carpenter, husband, and father of four, kept a diary since 1896, and described virtually every day of his life up until his eyesight got the better of him and he had to quit writing, on New Year's Day, 1948. He had a lot of time to write during the Great Depression, employed on and off but mostly off. As he observed in a diary entry, "People expect one to work now for nearly nothing."

His hot take on the weather in his hometown of Bloomington for June 29, 1936? "A very sultry warm day," he wrote. "Like blasts from a furnace. The thermometer went up to as high as 110 degrees in some localities. I put in the day trying to find a place to keep cool. Tonight is suffocating."

It didn't get much better this evening. Morgan and his wife, Alverta, tried sleeping but they didn't get any deep sleep until around daybreak. Morgan, having no concept of the summer that was about to descend upon him, wrote, "Inside the house is like a baker's oven."

Missouri

Work hard, play hard—either way, you were putting your life at risk. In Springfield (109°F), Roxey Ellis Sypolt, a thirty-two-year-old laborer, collapsed while working on a bridge and was shuttled to the hospital. This was a trauma layered on top of more trauma for the Sypolt family. Roxey's wife, Dellia, was dangerously ill due to asthma. Their nine-year-old son was in a nursing home, recovering from kerosene explosion burns suffered during the harsh winter. There were five young kids in the family, including a newborn, now without a parent to care for them.

Dellia eventually overcame her asthma, but Roxey could not overcome what the heat did to him, possibly because he also had syphilis. He hung on for several days and died July 3.

Webster Maupin had more fun today, but still came to the same end. In Versailles, where records suggest it was possibly 110 degrees, twenty-seven-year-old Maupin was the third baseman for the Moniteau County Negro baseball team, the Tipton Colored Giants, who were playing against the Versailles Midgets. (These were definitely different times.)

Maupin went up to bat during the second inning. From there, accounts differ. Most reports suggest that before his bat met the ball, he passed out at the plate. Some said that he hit what would have been a home run, something he was known for doing, then collapsed before reaching home plate. Either way, for Maupin, it was the end of the game.

Minnesota and Iowa

Minnesota has never been known for high temperatures, which may be why 82 degrees was too much for a few people—plus, the humidity was 75 percent. A forty-eight-year-old Minneapolis housepainter got woozy and fell off scaffolding. He recovered, but less fortunate was Emil Nelson, fifty-six, who died shopping at a drugstore.

It was in the 100s throughout Iowa. Secretary of Agriculture Henry A. Wallace announced plans to visit twelve drought-suffering states, which included Iowa, and in discussing this trip, weatherman Charles Reed told a reporter that the farmers in Iowa were doing all right, as far as water went. Said Reed, presciently: "In Iowa, our main trouble is heat."

Georgia

Lewis Bross, a fourteen-year-old boy, was admitted to an Augusta hospital as a heat victim. He didn't have much time left, and one can imagine the conversations between his terrified parents and the doctors. One moment, around noon, Bross was chopping cotton on his family's farm in Thomson (105°F), and the next he was on the ground, suffering convulsions.

Indiana

In Greenfield, it was 98 degrees. In Vincennes, 106. Muncie's high was 93, but it felt far worse because of a strong wind: Customers leaving stores were so startled by the heat that some became sick, especially asthma sufferers. It was so hot that it was hard to breathe. Confused motorists stopped their cars, believing their vehicles were overheating.

In Franklin (100°F), the heat triggered a forty-eight-year-old man's epilepsy. He was bathing in Hurricane Creek and fell face down, drowning in water that was one foot deep.

The heat caused Michael Bauer's left rear tire to blow out, which turned out to be a serious problem since he was driving fast (about fifty-five miles an hour) around a curve. Bauer, an employee at Roy Burns Groceries in Bloomington, and his two passengers were near Seymour (102°F) heading to a Reds and Cubs baseball game in Cincinnati.

The blowout happened somewhere between Schneider's Filling Station and Emil Schneider's residence, and the car swerved to the left of the road. That, too, was a problem: Bauer was about to drive into an oncoming truck. He swerved to the right side of the road, missing the truck, but his blown-out tire hit loose gravel. Bauer's vehicle turned over and over, eight times in all, before landing upside down in the middle of the road. Bauer and his passengers, his brother and a friend, were no longer in the car; they were thrown clear before it stopped.

Bauer survived. His brother died at the hospital soon after. His friend's chest was crushed; he wouldn't last through the night.

The year 1936 started off with one of the country's worst blizzards. Babies were depending on milk, which is how the Huntley Milk Transfer truck found itself struggling to get through snow-blocked roads in Huntley, Illinois. At least, it looks like there's probably a road down there, somewhere. *Huntley Area Public Library: Huntley Area History; Illinois Digital Archives.*

The man's identity has apparently been lost to the mists of time, but in February 1936, he was serving a noble purpose, harvesting ice on the Ottauquechee River in Coos County, New Hampshire. There were commercial ice manufacturing plants in the 1930s, but when it could be done naturally, ice makers took advantage of it. *Farm Security Administration, Office of War Information Photograph Collection, Library of Congress.*

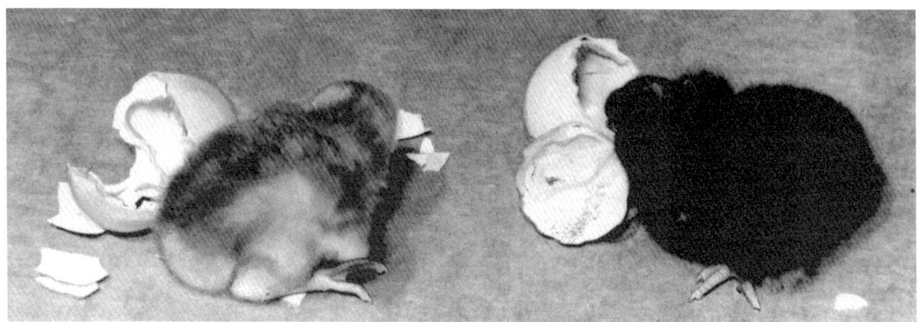

ABOVE: These two chicks hatched on August 19, 1936, in Oklahoma City, when the high was 102 degrees. A photographer from *The Daily Oklahoman* (now, *The Oklahoman*) set two eggs on the sidewalk and waited to see what would happen. In about 15 minutes, the eggs started cracking. It would have taken three times longer in an egg incubator. *Published with permission from the Oklahoma Historical Society.* BELOW: Unidentified women swimming in pool filled with ice on July 13, 1936, in Oklahoma City, when the high was 103 degrees. The photograph was published in *The Oklahoma Times.* As the caption noted, "It is fun to play around with ice in a swimming pool while the temperature soars above the 100 mark—fun for a while, but it has little psychological effect on making the bathers any cooler." *Published with permission from the Oklahoma Historical Society.*

ABOVE: A group of sweaty Oklahoma City veterans on June 17, 1936, waiting at Central High School, to pick up their "bonus bonds," money owed to them from the Great War (World War I). Originally, they were going to receive the funds in 1945, but due to the Great Depression, a law had just been passed allowing them to receive their funds early. The high was 97 degrees, and as *The Daily Oklahoman* noted in their caption, "The day was sweltering hot." *Published with permission from the Oklahoma Historical Society.* BELOW: Jack Buhia, a seventeen-year-old in Bloomington, Illinois, on July 8, 1936, stuck a flag in the road to alert people that they shouldn't be driving here. The 108-degree heat mangled the road, as the high temperatures tended to do. *Published with permission from the McLean County Museum of History.*

ABOVE (LEFT AND RIGHT): Chloe Keefe, a local model, came to Lake Bloomington in Illinois, to cool off on July 13, 1936. It was 109 degrees. *Published with permission from the McLean County Museum of History.* BELOW: Jean Harlow, in a photo taken by *The San Francisco Examiner*, three years before she was mauled by the sun. *Published with permission from The Bancroft Library, University of California, Berkeley.*

ABOVE: Poor Wally the elephant, in a photo taken by *The San Francisco Examiner* on June 18, 1936, two days after he mauled a zookeeper and on the day he was put down. The heat was blamed for him losing his temper. *Published with permission from The Bancroft Library, University of California, Berkeley.* BELOW: Taken in Gregory County, South Dakota, in 1936, believed to be shortly after the July 19 dust storm that blew through the middle of the country. That car you barely see, covered in dust and sand, belonged to the county commissioner. *Courtesy of the South Dakota State Historical Society.*

In July 1936, in Terry, Montana, as you can see, aside from the withering heat and grasshoppers, this was otherwise a pretty successful corn crop. *Farm Security Administration, Office of War Information Photograph Collection, Library of Congress.*

In Grassy Butte, North Dakota, a farmer went into church, said to be there to pray for rain. This was taken in July 1936. Grassy Butte and surrounding areas were seeing temperatures over 100 many days, the highest temperature that month was 110 degrees on July 5. *Library of Congress Prints and Photographs Division.*

Marlene Dietrich, in a 1936 photo, apparently taken in cool weather, given the fur she is wearing.

Robert Wadlow, in 1937. At 8'5" tall, and weighing 425 pounds, he had a particularly rough time dealing with the 1936 summer heat. *Courtesy of the McLean County Historical Society.*

A mugshot of Rattlesnake James, also known as Robert S. James in the press (his actual name was Major Raymond Lisenba). Lisenba was a sideshow during the heat wave of 1936. Was he relevant to the history of the heat wave? No. Was he a distraction for people looking to get their minds off the heat? Absolutely.

ABOVE: Corn, dried up and lying in the field, after being subjected to weeks of temperatures over 100 degrees. Yum. The photo was taken somewhere between Dallas and Waco, Texas. *Courtesy of the New York Public Library Digital Collections.* BELOW: A migrant farmer taking a water break, part of a mass exodus of farmers leaving South Dakota due to the drought. (It was real life scenes such as this, playing out in states throughout the Dust Bowl, that would inspire John Steinbeck's 1939 classic novel, *The Grapes of Wrath.*) This is a photo taken by Arthur Rothstein, one of a slew of photographers hired by the federal government to document the rural poor in the United States. Whatever day this was isn't known, but South Dakota was broiling. The state was experiencing temperatures over 110 degrees in July and August. *The Miriam and Ira D. Wallach Division of Art, Prints and Photographs: Photography Collection, The New York Public Library.*

18

JUNE 30

The Umbrella

Today's Death Toll: 20+
Total Death Toll: 350+

In Fort Worth, Texas, the city health director observed that more people died in the city this week—sixty deaths—than any other in the year so far. He concluded the extreme heat was a contributing factor. There were heat deaths in scattered states, including Ohio, Missouri, and Virginia, and a forest fire was consuming eastern Kentucky, engulfing an estimated three million acres and spanning fourteen counties.

Actually, it was a lot of fires and not just one; 1,500 firefighters and volunteers fought the inferno. Michigan was also suffering forest fires. Tennessee was battling six big ones. Wyoming had a brief fire that started and ended today, but had lots more before the summer was over. In San Bernardino, California, 1,200 men battled a fire that had swept over 1,000 acres of timber and brush in San Bernardino National Forest.

According to a 1938 issue of *Forestry News Digest*, there were 226,285 forest fires in the United States in 1936. Usually, you could expect about 101,000 forest fires a year. In recent decades, that number has dropped. In 2024, there were 64,897 wildfires reported, according to the National Interagency Coordination Center.

Soon, the entire country would feel as if it was on fire. But today was bad enough.

Illinois

In Marissa, Mary Ida Wylie, a seventy-four-year-old widow, was on a mission. With one hand, Wylie carried a basket full of Sunday school literature intended for children who weren't able to attend church the previous weekend. With her other hand, she gripped an umbrella. She wielded it to block her from the scorching sun and heat, already 90 degrees at 8:05 A.M. Unfortunately, as she crossed railroad tracks, the umbrella also blocked her view of an oncoming train.

Georgia

In Montezuma (100°F), a husband, wife, and their children, an eleven-year-old and seven-year-old, swam at the Lewis millpond. They should have gone somewhere else. A millpond is what it sounds like: A pond created by a dam, and it has a water mill. There was an undercurrent. And Luther Parks, a dairy manager, got caught up in it. Parks was not a skilled swimmer, and when the undertow caught him, he shouted for help.

A couple of things happened that should make people feel good about humanity. Parks's wife, Ila, couldn't swim. She bravely rushed into the pond to help him anyway. In this racially charged climate, a Black man—whose name the local news never bothered to get—happened to be passing by and heard the cries. He dove into the water and heroically saved Mr. Parks.

It would be a far better feel-good story if Ila hadn't drowned.

Tennessee

Willie Mae Jones, one day from her tenth birthday, lived in a tenement building, structures that were notoriously hot.

It was 100 degrees outside, and worse indoors. So Willie and her friend, Will Stigall, who was seven, went to the railroads, hoping to find scraps of ice that might fall their way. As they probably had done many times, the two Black children stood underneath a car-icing platform—a structure where blocks of ice, weighing as much as fifty to a hundred pounds, went down a chute into a refrigerated railroad car. Somehow, several blocks of ice fell off the chute, crushing the children. Will survived and led a long life; Willie did not.

The summer was nine days old. But as tragic as June was, it was nothing compared to what was coming.

JULY

HELLSCAPE

19
JULY 4
Fireworks

Today's Death Toll: 80+
Total Death Toll: 500+

Despite the surge in fatalities the previous two months across the country, the average adult was not concerned about dying of heatstroke. You were worried about putting food on the table. The unemployment rate was 17 percent. You might have been frantic about polio; small outbreaks were happening across the country. You might have fretted about any number of things—but probably not the heat.

The hot summer wasn't yet front-page news. The Associated Press would soon regularly publish a tally of heat fatalities, starting on July 3. But the general public hadn't yet noticed any great swell of deaths. In these days before air-conditioning, there were always a handful of heat-related deaths and drownings every summer.

But the heat was becoming impossible to avoid. Appliances with motors, like a refrigerator or a supply pump in a boiler room, were overheating and catching on fire. Twenty-five-year-old aviator Ruth Barron Nason ended a promising life and vocation by landing at the Omaha airport with her plane engulfed in flames, nose-diving into the earth.

In Norfolk, Nebraska (111°F), a pile of manure caught fire. In Ponca City, Oklahoma (102°F), a woman detected an odd smell—before realizing the celluloid on her sunglasses was burning. And the heat was selectively removing some people from the population: a sixty-three-year-old woman in Council Bluffs, Iowa (110°F), a fifty-year-old railroad switchman in Des Moines (106°F), and in Omaha (110°F), a fifty-five-year-old grain executive in excellent health who collapsed and never woke up.

According to a report from the United Press, nationwide, seventy-seven people went to watery graves, most of them swimming at Fourth of July picnics.

Two additional men either drowned or burned to death—nobody was sure which happened first. They were trapped aboard a burning fireworks barge on the shores of Lake Huron, near Lexington, Michigan. As two other men escaped by diving into the water, their legs burned, a hundred rockets, fifty Roman candles, and other fireworks exploded. A thousand spectators helplessly watched their Independence Day celebration transform from something joyous into utter carnage.

20

JULY 5

"... A Terrible, Hot Time"

Today's Death Toll: 100+
Total Death Toll: 600+

There were heat deaths today throughout the country—three citizens died in St. Louis (109°F)—but people were still mostly focused on what the weather was doing to the crops, which made a lot of sense. A few people dying here and there in the heat was to be expected, but when a crop went down, that threatened everyone's livelihood. According to a May 26, 1936 issue of *Oklahoma Live Stock News*, farm families made up 22 percent of the population, and 44 percent of Americans lived in the countryside and often were working for a farmer. But the heat wave was really beginning to ramp up, and soon, so would the human death toll.

Oregon

In Silverton, an incensed crowd gathered around a car with a Washington license plate. A baby was inside, wailing. The high was 79 degrees. Smashing a window was on the agenda, and someone called the cops. Right before the police came, a woman rushed to the car, unlocked it, and spirited the baby away—going into a restaurant where she and others had been eating.

Inexplicably, the police didn't have a chat with the mother.

Illinois

Buddy Branson, seven years old, also had a near-death experience. The high in Mattoon was 104 degrees, and Buddy was parched. Buddy removed the cover of the family's well—and fell into it.

It's something of a miracle Buddy didn't drown or hit his head on the well's walls, the bucket, or the iron pipe below. In fact, the iron pipe saved him from drowning. Buddy grabbed it, and he climbed up it enough that once he started shouting, his mother and a neighbor were able to hear him and pull him to safety.

Other than a few bruises, Buddy was feeling well (perhaps a poor choice of words), but the rest of the state was not. In Bloomington (109°F), Charles Morgan, the carpenter, wrote in his diary, "Clear and hot, a very sultry day . . . Today and tonight was a terrible hot time." Mostly, death by heat stayed away from Illinois today, though a Springfield policeman seeking relief drowned in a lake. In Tuscola, a married couple went on a social call and left a trough full of water on their farm for their fifty hogs. They underestimated evaporation in the 104-degree heat, however, and how thirsty several dozen hogs might be, perhaps unaware that pigs don't have functional sweat glands. By evening, when they returned, they had a dry trough—and forty dead hogs.

Ohio

On a day when the high was 87 degrees, Hans Meuser, a bassoonist with the Cincinnati Symphony Orchestra, passed out during a rousing performance of *Carmen* at the Cincinnati Zoo. Despite that, musicians would continue wearing their jackets, the head of the opera said, arguing that artists are conditioned to undergo discomfort. Meuser possibly had a different point of view. He spent the next several days in his bed, unable to sit up.

Alabama

A Selma prison announced that they had been allowing twenty model inmates to go home to sleep at night. Since June 1, the high had been at least 90 every day, and hitting or surpassing 100 occasionally.

Not all Alabama prisons were so accommodating. Later in the month, the newspaper in Dothan described their prison as having twenty "sweaty, unbathed" human beings confined to a 16×18-foot jail block, with conditions that "would prove distasteful to the average farm hog." The editors reported that Black prisoners were "using their neighbors' bodies for pillows because of crowded conditions" and going unbathed due to obsolete plumbing.

Iowa

Dr. George Mogridge was eighty years old, semi-retired as an honorary superintendent at the Asylum for Feeble-Minded Children, a state institution in Glenwood that had been around since 1867. (The asylum's unfortunate name was common for the time.) Mogridge started a diary earlier in the year, and he had written a lot the previous day, his July 4 entry, most of it in a stereotypical physician's illegible scrawl, but he noted that a large crowd had celebrated the Fourth—despite it being 110 degrees in the afternoon.

But for July 5? All Dr. Mogridge could muster to say was that it was over 100, he was "home all day," and that he didn't even go to chapel.

There were at least three drownings in the state, and in Council Bluffs (104°F), there were two heat deaths. In Des Moines (105°F), a twenty-two-year-old minor league baseball player decided to withdraw from the game, then passed out when leaving the mound. He recovered, but the game never should have been played. The county fair in Algona (106°F) should have also been canceled. The sun beat down on the fairground stage, and when performers wearing thin-soled shoes stepped onto the wooden floorboards, the audience could see they were in agony. Two bears performed in an act later on the same stage, and from their jerky, agonized movements, spectators could see that they, too, were being scorched.

That evening, in Ames, two college men visited a girls' dorm at Iowa State College, planning to serenade two women. They showed up at the dormitory's porch, surprised to see the ladies they wanted to sing to—and a bunch of other young women, since it was too hot for anyone to sleep inside. Only in Davenport (105°F) did anyone seem to be having fun. Fifty youths were swimming in the Mississippi River, upsetting residents and boat traffic. Police officers extracted them but not before being taunted with playful chants of "Come in, and get us out."

21

JULY 6

Beware the Electric Fan

Today's Death Toll: 100+
Total Death Toll: 700+

The first electric fan was invented fifty years earlier, in 1886. For years, they were only accessible for the wealthy. Not only were fans expensive, but your home had to be set up for electricity. By 1936, lots of people still didn't have electric fans, especially those in the countryside.

But if you were one of the first people to own an electric fan, you might be safe from the heat, but you were not *safe*. For starters, the first electric fans had no protective cage. In 1899, a twenty-year-old Milwaukee waitress washed her hair at the hotel where she worked and dried her hair near an electric fan. Her very long locks got caught in the blades, and her head was dragged toward the fan—you can unfortunately imagine the rest. In 1901, in El Paso, a widow's dress got caught in a fan. She was pulled to the floor and broke her hip, which led to her death a couple weeks later. In 1925, a Louisville, Kentucky, painter had his hand mangled by an electric fan; the loss of blood, the shock to his body, or both led to his demise. During the 1934 heat wave, a lumber mill employee in Scotia, California, was believed to have fainted—and then fell into an electric fan. That was a guess since nobody saw what happened; they just found his bloodied corpse.

Industrial fans also had their risks. In 1913, an electrician at the Philadelphia Electric Company got too close to one of the utility's giant fans and was sucked into it.

Of course, we haven't even mentioned the accidents in the annals of electric fan history that were due to faulty wiring. There were several such incidents this summer. In May, the third floor of a Pittsburgh library was set ablaze after an electric fan shorted out. In July, a fan motor overheated in a Michigan home, and curtains caught fire. That same month, in Bethany, Illinois, Michael Sconce, seventy, was resting on a cot in his basement. He reached for his electric fan and received an electric shock so bad that he fell out of the cot and onto the concrete floor, breaking his hip. But he recovered and stuck around for another six years.

Sometimes fans were not built well. Blades occasionally flew off and struck the person cooling off. Protective cages were on electric fans in the 1930s, but they were often decorative and almost an afterthought, barely doing the job of keeping hands away from the spinning metal blades. By 1936, electric fans with rubber blades were just arriving on the market, but most consumers still owned fans with spinning metal blades.

This summer, there were many electric fan injuries, probably due to the odds: so many fans were being used that bad stuff was bound to happen. For instance, in May, a Columbus, Georgia, policeman caught his hand in a fan (the most common injury when it comes to fans) and was treated at a hospital for lacerations. In June, in Atlantic City, a twenty-two-year-old dishwasher accidentally stuck his left hand into spinning blades, and doctors were forced to amputate.

In July, in Seneca, Kansas, a guy played a practical joke on his sleeping cousin, splashing water on him. The startled cousin awakened and his foot jutted out, kicking a fan at the end of his bed, and he lost his big toe. D. M. Hutton, editor at the *Harrodsburg Herald* in Kentucky, on August 22, severed an artery on his right hand when it inadvertently encountered an electric fan. On August 30, an employee was on his boss's yacht in Long Island Sound and, not yet having his sea legs, lost his footing. When he tried to save himself from falling, his left outstretched hand went into the whirring blades of an electric fan. He lost his fourth finger.

Still, it was more dangerous to be without an electric fan. The heat was getting worse, and people were dying in Indiana, Minnesota, Wisconsin, South Carolina, and Kentucky, among other states. In Wishek, North Dakota, it was 120 degrees. That nobody died in Wishek was probably due to a relatively low population of about a thousand people—and low humidity of around 8 percent.

Iowa

Beed's Lake, near Hampton, was recently restored as a Civilian Conservation Corps (CCC) project. Similar to the Works Progress Administration (WPA), the CCC was a Depression-era program that put young, unmarried, and unemployed men to work in national forests. For six months at a time, enlistees received three square meals a day and worked on public land projects. Beed's Lake was still under construction, however, and everyone was told not to swim here. But some swam anyway, and it was 103 degrees. The Koch family may have been unaware of the warnings, or figured that wading in the water couldn't hurt anyone.

At about 2:30 P.M., the eleven-year-old boy and two girls, eleven and fourteen, were trying to rescue a toy boat from a stream that fed into the lake. One of them may have stepped into a deep hole, and things went downhill from there. The mom, Lucretia Koch, thirty-two, waded in after them.

Two young children in the family were on the beach and shouted for their father, who had left but was in earshot. Alfred, a farmer three days from his fifty-first birthday, rushed into the water but couldn't find Lucretia or the kids, so he hurried to his vehicle and sped back to his house, less than a mile away, to find their oldest son, Albert.

The father and his twenty-year-old son returned, and Albert brought his stepmother and siblings from the water. A medical team spent an hour trying to bring the three children and mother back to life, but everyone recognized the futility of it all. Before Albert found them, they had been six feet underwater for thirty-five minutes.

Nebraska

At 3 A.M., it was 78 degrees. That's why Jerry Jantas, a restaurant owner in Omaha, slept outside. He found a comfortable spot at a grass knoll in the countryside and brought with him an army cot and a honeydew melon, thinking ahead to breakfast. Jantas woke up at dawn this morning and reached for his melon, which was now just a husk covered with grasshoppers. The grasshoppers also consumed most of his socks, and there was a large hole in the seat in his trousers.

The heat had a way of bringing out the grasshoppers. Three days earlier in Grand Island, one observer claimed the insects were everywhere you looked for a twenty-mile stretch.

Omaha's high today was 98, hot but cooler than the hamlet of Fort Yates, where a federal meteorologist determined that it was 119. There was no official temperature, but it was said the city of Steele hit 121 degrees.

Missouri

In Kansas City, a man who is only known as M. H. Winner found himself freezing to death on a day when the high was 99 degrees.

Winner was the manager of an ice station, which is what it sounds like: you'd drop by, pay for a block of ice, and take it home. Shortly after opening at 4 A.M., he supervised the unloading of the contents of an ice truck. After the truck left, a car pulled up, and two armed men in their twenties got out. They forced Winner to take $188 from a safe, then ushered him into the icehouse, padlocking him inside.

Winner yelled for help, but the room was well-insulated to keep inventory cold and thus practically soundproof. Winner felt his toes getting numb. His nose was starting to turn blue. The day before, it was 103 degrees. Today's high would be 99, and Winner was anticipating freezing to death.

But Winner noticed that when he rattled the door handle, it made a loud noise, and so he kept shaking it, hoping somebody might hear or notice the door handle moving. Eventually, the noise woke Dudley Knepp, a twenty-eight-year-old dozing in Slope Park about half a block away. Fortunately, Knepp got up to investigate. When he was at the locked door, he could hear Winner pleading, "Get the key from the safe and let me out."

"I will," Knepp reportedly said, "if you'll let me finish my nap in the ice house."

"Done," Winner said.

As for the thieves, they robbed at least one other icehouse, and the local press bestowed upon them the moniker "the ice house bandits." About a week later, they were caught stripping a car for parts.

Illinois

"Clear and very sultry today. Thermometer rose to 112 degrees today," wrote Charles Morgan, carpenter and expert diary writer. He was describing life in Bloomington, although he could have been speaking for most of the country. "This hot, dry weather is becoming very serious. No rain anywhere now. Farmers in the Dakotas and the northwest have given up. Everything is burnt up."

About forty miles away, in Peoria (106°F), at about 5:30 P.M., as Alvin Rocke, twenty-nine, a factory welder, collapsed, his sweaty right arm bumped against the electric current of his welding torch. He died instantly.

That night, Morgan and his wife, along with other family members, dozed at their daughter Lucille's house. "None of us slept much," wrote Morgan the next day. "Out under the trees, on the grass, we tried to find relief from the awful heat."

22

JULY 7
Heat Wave Skepticism

Today's Death Toll: 200+
Total Death Toll: 900+

In Bismarck, North Dakota, where it was 106 degrees, ducks fainted. For months now, pretty much as soon as the winter ended, the ongoing drought started drying up streams and making mother ducks and ducklings vulnerable to temperatures and predators. In the last week, state fish and game department officials moved approximately 1,500 ducks to available water. It was estimated that the drought had already killed 300,000 ducks this year—half of the state's duck population.

The human population across the country was struggling, too. The heat was blamed for two suicides today, one in New Windsor, Illinois (105°F), where a twenty-year-old shot himself, and in Gary, Indiana (95°F), where a married woman hanged herself from a tree. In Grand Rapids, Michigan (98°F), William Turnbull, a train crossing watchman, died on the job. This was before the era of flashing lights and lowering gates; it was Turnbull's job to stand on the road with a STOP sign to warn pedestrians and motorists that a locomotive was coming. It was a job that required being outside under the pounding sun. The heat, doctors concluded, was too much for him.

Some cynics were skeptical about blaming so many deaths on the heat. An op-ed that ran in today's *Beatrice Daily Sun* featured an anonymous Nebraska writer griping that the media was hyping up the heat wave. The writer referred to an eighty-eight-year-old citizen of Iowa who was dubbed a heat victim.

"If the old gentleman had passed away while a blizzard was raging, he probably would have been advertised as a blizzard victim," the writer charged. "If his last day of life had been in a balmy day in May or October, his taking off would have been accounted for as due to the natural causes incident to age. The 88 birthdays probably had more to do with ending his career than the heat of one of his many days. But the heat wave is the news of the day, and heat victims must be found." The complaining scribe didn't name the guy, but it was clearly Bartney Cox, an eighty-eight-year-old retired Council Bluffs farmer who died July 5.

It might have been a valid point any other year. But the coroner who examined Cox wrote on his death certificate that "heat exhaustion" was a contributing factor to the retired farmer's demise, and before the day was up, twenty-eight deaths nationwide were attributed directly to the heat, seven in Peoria (106°F). Twenty-five people throughout the country were known to have drowned. In Mobile, Alabama, where you'd expect it to be hot, it was 100. In Racine, Wisconsin, where you would not expect it to be, it was 98 degrees, and the heat took out a fifty-six-year-old fire captain. All national and local media play up natural disasters in their news coverage—always have, always will—but you couldn't hype this weather event enough.

Indiana

A fire ignited on a farm—how and why, nobody knew—in Winchester (109°F). The farmhouse and milk house were saved, but a barn was destroyed, along with five horses, two cows, several hogs, fifty chickens, farming equipment, two hundred bushels of corn, twenty tons of hay, and other feed.

Two thousand cars with lookie-loos showed up. One man drove twenty miles, explaining to a reporter that he thought the fire was much closer to his home than it turned out to be. Townsfolk said that Everett Shultz and his widowed mother had some insurance on the farm, and others said they had none. Either way, it was financial devastation.

Indianapolis had a different challenge: no raging fires, but a raging bull, said to be crazed by the 107-degree heat and foaming at the mouth. The bull escaped from the stockyards and made its way to Indianola Park. It was a family friendly park, except on days when there was a wild bull on the loose. Once the police arrived, the bull took off. The animal charged a workman on West Sixteenth Street, but the man hurled his thermos bottle and lunch bucket at it, and the bull ran away. The police, hot and tired, eventually gave up chasing the bull, who knocked over a man but didn't hurt him much then raced off to who knows where. With any luck, the bull made a happy life for himself somewhere in Indiana's farmland.

Massachusetts

In the town of Lynn (89°F), Nicholas Nicoletta returned home from work early in the afternoon. Next to nothing can be found about his life history, other than *The Boston Globe*'s mention of him. But along with over a hundred thousand residents, Nicoletta decided to go swimming. Only he couldn't find his bathing suit. Nicoletta searched a closet and decided it was too dark to his liking, and so he lit some matches. Unfortunately, some of his clothing caught fire and about $500 in damage was done by the time the blaze was extinguished.

But maybe it was for the best. That night, a twenty-three-year-old male in Quincy (89°F) found his bathing suit just fine. He went to a quarry's swimming hole to cool off and promptly became a drowning statistic.

Minnesota

Nelson Edstrom, a seventy-one-year-old Minneapolis resident, was found floating in the Mississippi River. The coroner suspected that Edstrom, who went missing on Sunday when it was 104 degrees, became overcome by the heat and toppled in. It was a reasonable assumption, with the state suffering a dozen heat victims and drownings today. In the evening, an eighty-year-old went to a baseball game and keeled over from a heat-induced heart attack as the ninth inning concluded, though on the plus side, everyone noted, he got to see his team win.

Ohio

Robert Cass, twenty, was driving in Marion when the road exploded underneath his car, throwing his vehicle into the air while bricks crashed against his shock absorbers. Cass wasn't injured, but where his car had been, now there was an eight-foot-long hole in the road. Across the county, seven additional roads were damaged by heat explosions.

Cass didn't have a good year as a driver. In November, there would be snow on the road, and he would skid, his car turning over on its left side, injuring his wrist, and costing about $200 in repairs. The heat explosion only cost him $18.50 in damages. In these early days of car insurance and twenty-two years before it would be mandatory to have it in Ohio, Cass tried multiple times to get the city to reimburse him for the heat explosion damages, but the Marion councilmen always voted against him.

Michigan

Albert Lemkau was Midwest born and bred. He came to the world in Iowa, grew up in Illinois, went to college in Indiana, and was currently a geology graduate student in Wisconsin. But now, after doing surveying for a gold mining company, the twenty-three-year-old was lost in the Michigan woods, near Ishpeming. After Lemkau didn't show up at camp, a search party formed, although nearby forest fires limited where they could look. The next day, an airplane spotted no sign of a young hiker. Three of the sheriff's bloodhounds were enlisted, but the 100-degree heat destroyed any scent Lemkau might have left behind.

His geology professor, Stanley Tyler, was likely shaken. He had been hiking back to the camp with Lemkau when his student insisted on taking a shortcut. They still had another two miles to trek, and Professor Tyler thought it was best to stay on the trail. Lemkau disagreed.

Lemkau was found almost a week later, with no happy ending. His body was so badly decomposed that the coroner could only assume the heat did him in.

23

JULY 8
America Goes to Hell

Today's Death Toll: 300+
Total Death Toll: 1200+

In the morning, in Des Moines, Iowa, wealthy families woke up at their country clubs on blankets in the grass, under the trees.

They were trying to beat the heat, but there was no escaping it. Across the country, drivers pulled off the sides of roads to let their overheated vehicles cool off.

New York City and New Jersey hospitals were overcrowded with heat-exhaustion patients. In Montana, Wyoming, and Ontario, Canada, forest fires were raging, and the death toll went up in numerous states, including California, Missouri, Iowa, Ohio, Tennessee, Rhode Island, and Massachusetts. There weren't many states not feeling the heat wave. There was even a drowning today in Lewiston, Maine (98°F). That may beg the question: What was the government doing during this time?

Depending on your point of view, a lot or not much. Today President Roosevelt announced a vast drought relief program:

- Twenty thousand farmers would be employed on Works Progress Administration projects in the drought districts in several Southern states.
- Some 55,000 distressed soil tillers were going to be hired for similar undertakings in the Northwest.
- A reduction on freight rates for moving Montana cattle to grazing ground was approved.

- Tens of thousands of families in "drought emergency counties," mostly in the Dakotas, Wyoming, and Montana, paying rural rehabilitation loans for a time would no longer have to.

But what the government could do to help people stay cooler and comfortable was limited. If there were actually internal government discussions about shipping millions of Americans free electric fans or millions of pounds of free ice to impoverished families, those ideas would likely have been dismissed as too expensive or impractical. Government officials also probably figured that soon temperatures would drop and go back to something relatively normal. They always did.

Only not this summer.

There was another reason why the government likely didn't get more involved with helping the public find ways to cool off: the demand wasn't there. People were asking for help with their crops, and throughout the 1930s, soup kitchens did a brisk business, but it wasn't really in the public's nature to insist on too much, observed the aforementioned John Hinshaw, a history professor at Lebanon Valley College: "Americans were just a lot poorer in the past, and their expectations were likely lower."

Kentucky

In Louisville, a woman called the *Courier-Journal* city desk at 8:45 A.M. and asked, "Hello, what's the temperature?"

"You mean the highest for the day?"

"No, I mean right now! Right this minute! It feels like somebody has just taken the lid off of hell!"

Hell was an apt description. At 11 A.M., it reached a high of 102. Before the day was over, a Louisville army sergeant, a World War veteran, ended his life; the coroner speculated that the heat was a motivating factor. Three more people in Kentucky took their last breaths, including a one-year-old boy who died in his mother's arms as she carried him to the hospital.

Ontario

Canadians couldn't remember anything like this. In Toronto (105°F), a married woman found two black squirrels in her backyard, one passed out and the other struggling to crawl—and brought them water. A local radio station stopped allowing audiences in their studio to watch the orchestra because the musicians agreed to perform only if they could strip down to their underwear.

That evening, a Toronto policeman on a bicycle was informed that somebody collapsed in the grass along University Avenue. The officer cycled over to find hundreds of people sleeping. Perplexed, he wondered, how do you determine who is asleep and who is unconscious? So he walked through the crowd, waking hundreds of people, as a *Toronto Star* reporter followed along. "You all right? I hear somebody's passed out around here," the officer kept repeating, getting responses like, "Sure, I'm alive." He traveled several blocks before saying, "Everything OK here. Somebody must 'a been crazy with the heat." The officer pedaled away, never finding who he was looking for.

Michigan

In the unincorporated community of Hell, it was 100 degrees. So naturally, in any town that had a higher temperature, people were quick to say that their community was hotter than Hell. The previous winter, when it was super cold in Hell, newspaper editors fell over themselves to point out that Hell had frozen over.

In Hell and out, it *was* hot. Three people died from the heat in Grand Rapids, two died in Saginaw, and one in Muskegon, Escanaba, and Flint. Cherries ripened so fast in Traverse City that orchardists feared they would run short of pickers, even though WPA labor was helping them out.

In Detroit police stations, officers stood sweltering at attention, wondering one thing: Who was the moron who decided that today would be a good day to do the annual winter uniform inspection? The uniforms weighed ten pounds.

In Battle Creek, street department workers spread sand across Michigan Avenue's crosswalks because melted asphalt stuck to pedestrians' shoes in the 102-degree heat. One woman lost her shoes to the street, and people tracked tar into stores as well as on rugs at home, and cars collected tar as they drove.* The brick roads in Battle Creek didn't fare any better; those blew up.

Minnesota

In the 1920s, tourism boards began promoting Minnesota as the "Land of 10,000 Lakes." But the state known for its water and cool temperatures was now knocking out tourists and residents, and sometimes killing them. In Minneapolis (101°F), the body of a one-legged dead man was fished out of the Mississippi River. In Fremont (99°F), a three-year-old boy died. Children in St. Paul (101°F) were cooling themselves off with a garden hose and playing, the way kids do, when a six-year-old boy darted off the grass and onto the road in front of a fast-moving truck.

In Moorhead, Pipestone, and Campbell, it was 104 degrees. Duluth was 98, but there was a rumor of a fifteen-mile-per-hour breeze coming across Lake Superior. Thousands of hopeful people showed up. At night, they camped along the lakeshore and at parks. Instead of covering themselves with blankets, most just used a blanket of stars.

Illinois

In Oak Park, where temperatures reached 100, street superintendent William Barry learned that some of his streets were oozing into the gutters—the heat was melting the asphalt. Cars skidded, as if on icy roads. Mr. Barry sent out a squad of workers to spread sand on the streets, just as he had six months earlier, when he was trying to keep cars from sliding on ice.

* The only people happy: shoeshiners and car wash owners.

In Evanston, a suburb of Chicago, officers on motorcycles were called off the streets when heat-loving sandflies flew in clouds so dense that they blinded drivers. Theaters turned off lights to avoid attracting bugs, and street sweepers were ordered out during the night to clear the pavement of dead insects.

In Chicago, park officials estimated that half a million people were sleeping at beaches and forest reserves.

Funeral homes in Decatur were overwhelmed. It was the worst tragedy since the influenza epidemic in 1918, funeral officials said. Charles Morgan, carpenter–diarist, continued to observe Bloomington's weather: "The excessive heat spell and the absence of rain makes things take on a critical mood."

Of course, there were drownings; there were always drownings. In the towns of Chester, Earlville, and Wilmington, there were four victims. Thirty minutes before midnight, Eleanor Bowersock, twenty-one, was on her way to becoming a fifth.

Eleanor was swimming toward the shore from a raft in the middle of the lake at the South Side Country Club. That's when the trouble started. Something went wrong—later, it was suggested to be a heat-induced heart attack—and Eleanor disappeared under the water. Fortunately, her twice-widowed mother, Margaret Lou, who went by Lou, was watching closely. The fifty-one-year-old was a private nurse for a family that had a membership at the club—and after Eleanor failed to resurface, Lou dove into the lake, submerged, found her daughter, and brought her back to shore.

For more than an hour, medics administered oxygen—two tanks—before they could get Eleanor breathing so they could take her to the hospital. One can imagine how distraught Lou felt. She lost her husband in 1906, several months after they married, though how he died isn't clear. In 1916, she lost her son James Robert. The papers didn't list a cause, but a polio epidemic was running rampant. She lost her second husband and Eleanor's dad, Clark Bowersock, to influenza in 1919.

The next day, fearing the worst for her daughter, who was still in the hospital, Lou fainted due to a combination of anxiety, the heat, and whatever cruel circumstances caused her employer to have her working instead of being at Eleanor's side. But it turned out that Lou needn't have worried. Several hours later, Eleanor and Lou were both discharged from the hospital, alive and well.

In fact, from what one can piece together of their paper trail, mother and daughter both led happy lives after what was probably the worst night of their lives. Lou, who lived to be eighty-five, moved to California with Eleanor in the 1940s. Eleanor went into show business. She started landing work in 1945 and didn't exactly become a big star, but she led a full life during her eighty-seven years. She changed her name to the more Hollywood-friendly Elle Bowers, married at least once, lived in Beverly Hills, and for several decades found steady work in theater, the movies, and TV, doing everything from working as June Allyson's body double to appearing in some *Perry Mason* episodes.

Indiana

Hogs were dying in farm fields. The streets of South Bend were cracking in the heat. Highways in and around Lafayette, Indiana, blew up. Fortunately, someone at the Greenfield Packing Company in Greenfield (108°F) had the sense to call off their bean pickers, many of them children, from working in the fields.

A twenty-six-year-old married woman was found dead on the floor of her home in Gaston (105°F) after working outside on the family farm. In Brazil (109°F), a ninety-eight-year-old Civil War widow, in good health, was rubbed out by the heat. So was a seventy-one-year-old, who the local paper described as developing "an attack of paralysis." A forty-eight-year-old from Kendallville died in 108-degree heat; he was on his honeymoon at Lake Wawasee.

There were six drownings, including a man and a boy who had been wading in the water searching for clams. One bystander said later that in the evening, "We looked and saw them floundering in the water and shouting quite a distance upstream. We thought they were swimming, so we didn't pay any attention to them."

And one day after the heat was blamed for an ill woman hanging herself in Gary, newspapers reported that in the same city, a witness saw an unidentified man, "believed to have been temporarily deranged from the intense heat of the afternoon," throw himself in front of a fast freight train.

New York

Scores of people headed to the parks in New York City tonight to sleep, and sixty-three men were arrested for vagrancy. Their sentences were suspended, but everybody was warned not to sleep in public again.

Colorado

Willie Aragon was a seventeen-year-old Latina girl who became another heat fatality statistic. She was the third daughter of nine children. Her parents were farm laborers, and Willie was following in their footsteps, putting in long hours in the fields. In the evening, at a farm in Delta, she was picking beets when her body decided the 98-degree heat was too much for her.

Washington, DC

The heat wave finally caught up with the nation's capital, reaching 93 degrees. Ira Gabrielson, head of the Bureau of Biological Survey, kept a diary from 1936 to 1939, and while most of his journal was about his job, peppered with occasional mentions of his wife or life, he couldn't not comment about the heat. "Hotter than hot in the first real heat of the season," Gabrielson wrote. "Worked like a trojan in the office all day with the sweat pouring off me, and the evening was no better."

Pennsylvania

The heat eliminated three people, including a forty-nine-year-old woman near Pittsburgh (96.5°F) engaged in housework until she wasn't. It must have been unsettling for people to realize that you could just be living your regular life, and if the heat wanted you, the heat was going to get you.

Sometimes, in the cruelest way possible. Claude Mattice, a fifty-six-year-old driver from Geneva, New York, stopped at 5:30 P.M. at a Canton, Pennsylvania, service station to change a tire. His truck had four rear tires, with two dual tires on the left side and two dual tires on the right. One of the inside tires had gone flat, and so before he could change it, Mattice needed to first remove the outside good tire.

Changing tires even on a pleasant day could be dangerous, since you could easily overtax your body and send it spiraling. The high was 97 degrees. Regrettably, Mattice didn't have a heart attack. That would have been a far more enjoyable experience.

Mattice wasn't aware that his other tires were barely in better shape than the flat one. While Mattice was removing the outside "good" tire, it exploded. A piece of the metal rim, or possibly a lug nut, struck his forehead and lodged itself in his brain. Mattice was rushed to the hospital. He died eleven days later.

People as far as a quarter mile away heard the tire explosion.

Missouri

In Kansas City (100°F), a courtroom was filled with nineteen people hoping to talk their way out of paying a speeding ticket fine. At least one defendant—the guy who was charged the most—blamed the heat for his infraction. Samuel Levitch explained that when he drove forty miles over the twenty-mile-per-hour speed limit, he was only trying to cool off. The judge, probably melting under his robe in the courtroom, wasn't sympathetic and fined him $25.

Courtrooms were infamous for their heat. During the summer, in Madison, Wisconsin, a jury foreman passed out while the verdict was read. In Birmingham, Alabama, a juror became ill but recovered after drinking copious amounts of ice water and getting fanned off by his fellow jurors. In Cincinnati, Ohio, a member of the jury collapsed, leading to a mistrial. In Bowling Green, Kentucky, a sixty-five-year-old man became ill in a courthouse after testifying and died outside the building.

In Mishawaka, Indiana, a city judge declared that the jail cells in the basement of the courthouse were far more comfortable than the actual courthouse and arranged it so trials would be held downstairs. Call it equal justice, if you will: across sweaty courtrooms in America, judges, attorneys, defendants, plaintiffs, and jurors were all suffering.

Kansas

In the town of Seneca (100°F), a plumber and a farmer picked up a long water pipe that had been lying in the sun. They both burned their hands.

They were in good company. Motorists nationwide shrieked when reaching for their car's metal door handles. In Mitchell, Indiana, workers constructing a water filtration plant fried their hands picking up tools; there was zero shade, so they stuck the tools in water when they weren't using them. Workmen in Marion, Ohio, buried tools in the dirt to keep them cool. In McCook, Nebraska, the post office's brass-handled doorknobs, heated by the sun, caused blisters on hands until they were covered with cloths.

And then there was Orval Millard, an iceman who lived in Arapahoe, Nebraska. He picked up a garden hose nozzle and scorched his hand—so he grabbed the rubber part of the hose, but water dripped out, burning his *other* hand.

Wisconsin

After enduring a 102-degree day yesterday, students from the University of Wisconsin, in Madison, slept on the roof of the university YMCA—until the sun came up and beat down on them so hard that everybody had to make a hasty retreat.

There were about a dozen heat fatalities in the state and three drownings. There was slightly less water to drown in, however; Beaver Dam Lake and Fox Lake were each losing one inch of water per day.

For the three million people in Wisconsin, it was unbearably hot (108°F in Janesville), but most people went about the business of the day, unless suddenly, everything changed. As evening fell, Francis Jorgensen, eleven, was accompanying his father, Carl, fifty-one, on a trip to Green Bay (102°F). Carl was a butcher–turned–truck farmer, growing crops and hauling his bounty in his truck to suppliers around the area.

Before setting off for home, Carl had an argument with a client. Carl wanted too much for his radishes, the client said. Carl vehemently disagreed. Shortly afterward, the father and son stopped at a filling station in De Pere. After his truck was serviced, Carl, still fuming, started driving to their farm in Glenmore.

During a spate of heavy traffic, Carl slumped over the wheel, his foot pressing down on the gas. Francis grabbed the wheel and tried shoving his dad's foot off the pedal. When that didn't work, the boy had the presence of mind to turn off the ignition and guide the car to the curb, all while not crashing into anyone. Francis had driven the vehicle for a quarter of a mile.

Carl wasn't looking good. The physician who examined him remarked that Francis's dad probably died before the car pulled to a stop. Carl had a heart issue that acted up several weeks earlier, but the doctor concluded that the heat killed him. Also, the doc said, squabbling over the price of radishes didn't help.

Illinois

For the foreseeable future, funeral directors knew there would be no trouble making payroll. In Decatur (106°F), one funeral home had sixteen bodies come in between the morning and early afternoon.

In Bloomington, Charles Morgan lamented in his diary, "We had a rain north of us early this morning, but none here. Turned off awful hot and another sultry day." In Macon, ten portions of highway exploded under the withering sun; before the month ended, there would be approximately 440 heat-caused road explosions throughout Illinois.

In Prophetstown, Mayor George Brydia, who also owned the town's grocery store, opened an envelope that immediately commanded his attention. It was a letter, written in pencil on ruled tablet paper, from an extortionist. The writer demanded $1,000 in exchange for not setting a bomb off in the town.

Brydia started considering how hot and dry it had been and wondered if a bomb, along with destruction and death, might set the entire city on fire.

Here is the letter in full, with a few interruptions for explanation:

> *We have selected you to obtain from each manager of a store twenty dollars to be delivered to us including yours in the deal. We believe there are fifty stores that will—mean you get together one thousand dollars. We know all the store managers and intended to get the rest of them in a short time if the [ristun?] simply refuses to pay his tribute to us, the Camorra.*

That is how the letter was written, according to the local media, which could not figure what a ristun was and why it was in brackets with a question mark. The Camorra was a reference to an Italian secret social organization of criminals similar to the Mafia. They've been around since the fifteenth century and are still operational.

> *If you want to live in peace and not be bothered the rest of your life you had better do as instructed. The same goes for the store men, we mean business—or else.*

We mean business—or else? The extortionist apparently enjoyed the gangster movies that were popular during the 1930s.

> *There is more than one hundred of us and you can not get more than one or two; then the rest will give their lives to get yours. If you are willing to obey our demands—place the following ad in the personal ad Sterling Gazette dated July 9.*

Did the writer provide a clue of where he lived?* The *Sterling Gazette* was a weekly newspaper in Sterling, about eighteen miles from Prophetstown. On the other hand, the return address said Walnut, Iowa. But maybe that was just a dodge to throw everyone off the scent, since the letter was post-marked in nearby Wyoming, Illinois. Hmmm.

At the end of the page was a note: "turn over." On the other side the letter continued:

> *This is the ad:*
>
> *"Meet me at the Rockford public library in the reference room at 7 P.M. Sat.—July 11, G.S.B."*

The public library in Rockford was about sixty miles away. But what the extortionist means by G.S.B. seems less clear. General Services Building? A note to himself to get some bread? Oh, wait, there's more.

> *And you had better make up your mind by July 11, and deal with us straight or it will never be safe for you or anyone in Prophetstown, Ill. We know the art of setting fire and the art of using dynamite. Now get busy and get $500 in ten dollar bills and $500 in twenty dollar bills, one thousand dollars in all—all of these must be used bills and none of the numbers must run in rotation. Put the money in a shoe box and tie with red cord. You had better not pull any of the dummy package stuff.*

Mayor Brydia decided to comply with the demands, which would make for several interesting days. The letter writer may have been a kook, but in this dry and hot climate, the mayor didn't want to risk the community going up in flames.

---

* Do we know for sure the extortionist was a "he"? No, but Brydia assumed it was a man. Plus, not to sell my gender down the river, but we all know it was a guy.

24

JULY 9

Stay Cool, America

Today's Death Toll: 400+
Total Death Toll: 1,600+

In the war against the heat, newspapers were filled with stories of citizens who were workshopping the best ways to stay cool. For instance, a resident in Port Huron, Michigan, filled flat glass bottles with cold water and put them between her bedsheets. Then she'd remove them before getting into bed, an hour later. It was important, she added, to have the water in a container that wouldn't "sweat" and get the sheets wet.

But in Cushing, Oklahoma, residents wrapped themselves in wet sheets before sleeping. Some people soaked their bedsheets in cold water, hung them over the clotheslines, and slept under the wet sheets. This was mostly attempted outdoors, but some tried it with the clothesline strung up indoors. One woman in Sedalia, Missouri, filled her iron with ice cubes and ironed the sheets before going to bed.

An Iowa family made it a practice to water their lawn and sit in the wet grass.

People filled hot water bottles with ice water and took them to bed. Folks suggested resting a cold water bottle on a wrist or sticking it near your chin. A Ponca City, Oklahoma, woman asked her husband to fill the bathtub with ice water. She did housework in a bathing suit, and every thirty minutes had a dip in the tub.

Some people wore wet headbands under their hats. Of course, not wearing any hat at all might have been even better.

In Ann Arbor, University of Michigan students and townspeople organized midnight swimming parties in the Huron River. A Lansing woman suggested people take the bag off their vacuum cleaner; the blowing apparatus made a decent fan.

In Cincinnati, Ohio, a fourteen-year-old boy tied a sheet to the top of his bedposts and aimed an electric fan at it. He said it created an air-conditioning effect in his room.

Newspapers suggested the best parks to sleep in—and offered tips for a productive slumber. "Avoid the low places, where the mosquitoes are bad," suggested the Murphysboro, Illinois, newspaper, steering readers to Riverside Park. "Pick out a nice hillside, take a long a pillow and a sheet, and choose six feet of sod free from rocks." The paper advised against sleeping in the nude, even if it was pitch black: "Some automobile headlights might pick you out."

A guy in Moberly, Missouri, suggested trying what he did to cool off: sit alongside a busy road and enjoy the breeze stirred up. There was a downside: the highway wasn't paved, and the cars sent a cloud of dust over him.

Some families in Detroit turned their kitchen into an icebox. At night, they put their mattresses and pillows on the floor and sealed the windows and doors with paper, opened their refrigerator or icebox, and put an electric fan inside. Then they'd go to bed and hope for the best.

Another simple cooling trick that had been around for a while—set down your electric fan and put a pan of ice in front of it. Hospitals did that, though it could be a safety issue. Several years earlier, a Chicago homeowner wound up with a skull fracture and lacerations. In the dark, he stepped on the pan of ice, slipped, fell over a banister, and crashed on a first-floor landing.

Nationwide, homeowners with cellars and basements basically moved down there with furniture and bedding and pets.

Businesses experimented with strategies to keep employees and customers cool. Wood Davis, a plumber, was hired by an Anadarko, Oklahoma, company to install a sprinkling system on the concrete roof of a bank building: five hundred gallons of water were sprayed per hour. With a three-inch thick sheet of water falling off the roof, Davis cooled off the second-story floor by 17 degrees.

The sprinkler system was effective—until the temperature reached 110. Then, the evaporation was so heavy that the sprinkler became useless: the water stopped pouring off the roof.

In Carlinville, Illinois, a business owner with a large electric fan in the basement wanted to cool his store. Next to the fan, he created a chute of cardboard boxes up the stairs so that the air was directed to the first floor.

Some motorists put a cake of dry ice in their cars under the cowl ventilator or in front of the fan in the car heater. It was expensive (a ten-pound chunk of dry ice, generally costing a buck, would typically cool off your car for five hours) and a little risky. Dry ice has a temperature of 110 below zero, so you'd only want to touch it wearing gloves, lest you destroy your hands. It's also a solid form of carbon dioxide. As dry ice melts, it turns into carbon dioxide gas, and if enough carbon dioxide fills the space that you're in, similar to carbon monoxide, you can pass out and die. Even without the dying part, it was dangerous. In late June, a fourteen-year-old boy in Olive Chapel, Ohio, put dry ice in a glass jar for some reason. When the gas expanded, the jar blew up, shards of glass flying everywhere, and he lost an eye.

Drivers cooling off cars with dry ice kept at least one window cracked open. As one doctor of the time noted, if you hadn't already opened your windows, once you started choking, you sure would.

Some motorists put hundred-pound blocks of actual ice in their cars, in a tub to collect melting water, much of which evaporated. Then they'd close the windows and drive in comfort.

One Texas driver displayed colossally poor judgment, however; instead of having his foot near the brake, his feet rested on a chunk of ice. When he needed to brake in a hurry, he couldn't find the pedal in time, crashed into another car, and suffered a broken collarbone.

Still, people had to do *something* to try to stay cool. There were heat deaths today in states like New Jersey, Vermont, Connecticut, Kentucky, Missouri, Minnesota, and California. The Associated Press pointed out that in the last six months, the country experienced a 175-degree variation from six months earlier. "Mercury columns then shrank as low as 55 below zero," the anonymous AP writer wrote. "Now they are up to 120 above.

The difference is summed up in the three words: The wind shifted. In the chill of winter, the weatherman blamed it all on a steady flow of air from the Arctic. Now the flow is just as steady—from the tropics."

Ohio

Shortly before 3 A.M., in Trenton, coming off a 105-degree day, two parents were awakened by their worst nightmare. The heat caused blood vessels in their ten-day-old son's nose to rupture. He was dead within the hour.

The day didn't improve. At least eighteen cities throughout the state reported temperatures of over 100. In Columbus (105°F), seventy circus workers fell ill. In Cincinnati (103°F), workers at a manufacturing plant initially thought there was a fire when the automatic sprinkler system was set off—by hot, dry air. In Lancaster (103°F), motorists abandoned unair-conditioned cars on the side of the road, finding it more preferable to hoof it. In Bettsville (100°F), the high school almost burned down; firefighters saved it, but not the chemistry lab where the fire likely started. Firefighters suspected the heat caused lab chemicals to explode.

At least one reporter in Cleveland asked whether these high temperatures were unprecedented. "Don't worry about records now," said an unidentified and prescient assistant to the weatherman Ralph Mize. "This thing is just beginning."

Indiana

There was a heat death each in the towns of Bluffton, Kendallville, Laporte, and Brazil. There were three drownings. In Evansville (104°F), one of the zoo's monkeys died. In Richmond (98°F), a pigeon flopped about on Main Street, struggling to survive—until a car ran over it.

In Indianapolis (103.4°F), at 4 P.M., a three-foot long strip of road blew up; a woman inside her house said she felt it shake.

A milk shortage was announced. Cows struggled to find pasture to eat due to the drought, so farmers slaughtered them to sell their meat, which meant less milk for everyone. Which may have been just as well. The milk in delivery trucks usually spoiled before it could reach Indianapolis.

Celstino Gonzalez may have been the first person this summer to go crazy from the heat, but he wasn't the last.

Most people affected by the heat didn't turn into a homicidal maniac, and as wretched as the temperatures were, it seems unfair to blame the weather for murder, especially this one, when the man had a clear motive. But the media of the time certainly made the connection, and studies have shown that there is a correlation between rising heat and murder and assault. We could talk about these studies all day, but to pull one out at random: a 2021 study from the National Bureau of Economic Research concluded that violence between inmates increases by 18 percent on extremely hot days.

Gonzalez was a thirty-six-year-old blacksmith, a resident of East Chicago, Indiana, and an employee at a steel plant at Indiana Harbor. He discovered proof that his wife, Maria, was having an affair with their boarder, Jose Haro, who promptly moved out. Still, while Gonzalez committed his murders in the heat, it was not in the heat of the moment. For two days, he mulled things over and took the time to write an apologetic note to one of his daughters, explaining his actions, although it was not the note of somebody who sounded rational.

The evening of July 8, before he did what he did, he went to visit Jose Haro. What was said, nobody knows. He then took his family to a lakeside park with a beach. He was possibly considering not doing anything drastic. In the note he left under his pillow, written in Spanish, to his oldest daughter, Juana, he said, among other things, "Right now my head is so confused that I don't know what road to take."

Really, it's impossible to say what went through Gonzalez's mind in the wee hours of July 9, coming off a day when it was 97 degrees—and whether the 80-plus-degree heat at night pushed him over the edge, or if he would have also lashed out in 55-degree weather. But whatever was firing his neurons, it wasn't good, and he took the wrong road, the worst that can be taken by a human being.

In the evening of July 8 and the early hours of July 9, Gonzalez slept—or perhaps pretended to sleep—in a front room of the house, with his two daughters, a sixteen-year-old and fourteen-year-old, and his seven-year-old son. At the rear of the home, three more sons—eight, eleven, and thirteen years of age—slept in the kitchen. The back door was open so the kids might catch a breeze. Gonzalez's estranged wife seems to have been in a side room near the boys.

Around 2 A.M., having abandoned the idea of sparing his daughters, Gonzalez started his killing spree. Gonzalez, who was described by local media as "brawny," tied up his daughters and stuffed handkerchiefs down their mouths. After doing the unthinkable, he left the room with a bloody axe and went toward the kitchen. His seven-year-old son ran ahead of him, shouting for help. His three brothers were asleep and didn't hear him, but Maria did. She left her room, but by the time she saw her husband, it was too late. After Gonzalez killed her, he went for his seven-year-old, then his three other sons, who were still asleep, police believed.

As all of this went on, a neighbor thought she heard a boy scream, but when she heard nothing else, she went back to sleep.

After slaughtering his family, Gonzalez waited in the home for several hours and washed the blood off him. That may be when he wrote another note in Spanish, which was translated into English and later run in newspapers. It was long and rambling; he said that he didn't plan on killing everyone in his family. He tried to defend himself, saying, "The deception that I have received is very great. I couldn't tolerate it." He also wrote, "I want all my intimate friends to forgive me for the great dishonor which I have brought them, but I can't hold myself." He ended the letter, saying, "It is Jose Haro who is the one responsible for this tragedy and who, I believe, will not escape from me."

At 7 A.M., Gonzalez armed himself with a gun and made his daily commute to his employer, the Inland Steel Company plant, where Haro also worked as a blacksmith's helper. Haro had finished the night shift and was changing into his street clothes when a wordless Gonzalez entered the locker room, according to the one witness in the room. Gonzalez shot

Haro four times in the head. Then Gonzalez put the gun to his own head and pulled the trigger. He never woke up, but it took him an hour to die.

Police, after getting the addresses of the two dead men, knocked on the door of the Gonzalez home to inform Maria of her husband's death. Upon finding the doors locked, the police left after hearing from a neighbor who thought Maria and the kids had gone to the beach. Later in the afternoon, they returned. The doors were still locked. This time, the police bashed in the door, discovering a gruesome crime scene. Near some of the bodies was the axe.

Why did the newspaper reporters and police blame the murders on the heat? Partly, the heat was so pervasive that everybody was blaming it for anything bad that happened that summer. Still, the temperatures were barbaric. During the day, Gonzalez was toiling as a blacksmith in a steel plant, subject to inhumane temperatures. *Nothing* can excuse what he did, but given that he was described as a sober hardworking husband and father who took pride in his family, one could imagine that a combination of anger, jealousy, and embarrassment, along with days and nights of heat and sleep deprivation, caused him to crack and lose his mind. There was, in any case, evidence that the weather was a toxic influence on the family. Heat rises, and so a lot of families were making improvised mattresses on the floor, sometimes next to their bed frames, hoping that sleeping a few feet lower to the ground might make a difference in getting a little more rest. That's where several mutilated bodies were discovered—on the floor, lying on straw mattresses.

Kentucky

A reporter from the *Lexington Herald-Leader* reporter sat in at the weather bureau, listening to someone managing the phones: "Yes, this is the weather bureau . . . It's 106 right now . . . No, I'm sorry, but there is no relief in sight . . . It certainly is mighty hot . . . Uh, huh . . . Well, I hope it cools off soon, too . . . You're entirely welcome."

Albin Baxter Kinkead, wife of a deputy sheriff, hung up the phone. She was one of the country's few woman forecasters and known around Lexington as the "weather lady." She began working at the weather bureau in 1915 as an assistant and was running it from her home by 1945, when the office was moved, and she thus lost her job. Kinkead's interview with the *Herald-Leader* was constantly derailed by phone calls from residents wanting to know the temperature and forecast.

But she was able to tell the reporter that she wouldn't worry about the heat unless it got hotter than 125 degrees, which was as high as her backyard thermometer went. "But if it gets that high, probably none of us will be able to do much worrying," she said, implying that a lot of Kentuckians wouldn't survive that.

Ontario, Canada

Lillian Kyte, twenty-three, complained of a headache and told her mother that she was going to lie down. Two hours later, Kyte was semiconscious, with a fever of 110. She spent her final moments at Toronto East General Hospital. Her grief-stricken mother, Amy, said of her and her husband's only child, "She hadn't been doing any work around the house, for it was altogether too warm. She had been sitting around all day trying to keep cool. It was at supper time that she started to complain of a headache and not being well. She went upstairs and tried to sleep. Shortly afterward she went unconscious, and we had to take her to the hospital. It was too much heat all right."

There was no way to tell who the heat wave would kill and who it wouldn't. A retired storeowner, James Robinson, ninety-six, collapsed in Toronto, but he lived to see his one hundredth birthday. Betty Langford, seventeen months old, lost consciousness and was rushed to the Hospital for Sick Children. She, too, survived, but another seventeen-month-old boy who lapsed into unconsciousness didn't.

The heat disaster was unfolding at the speed of a sundial, although when something went wrong, it often went wrong quickly. In Hamilton (105.5°F), the motorman of a streetcar fainted. His streetcar hit another streetcar, throwing that car's motorman, Basil Prokos, off the vehicle. While Prokos struggled to his feet, now fighting extreme back pain, his streetcar caught on fire. Everybody survived.

That night, more than ten thousand people slept at Toronto's Exhibition Park. At Lake Ontario, pajama-clad families showed up with alarm clocks and mattresses, while other families came to watch the spectacle of pajama-clad families taking alarm clocks and mattresses to the lake. In Trinity Park, people wrapped their shoes in newspaper and used them as pillows.

The police announced that laws about sleeping in public places weren't being enforced. For now, sleep where you want. One woman left her heat-baked apartment for a nearby cemetery, where she scrambled over a fence and laid out some blankets. Sleeping among tombstones may have been a thing across North America that summer. The next evening, five boys in Palmerton, Pennsylvania, slept in their local cemetery.

Factories throughout the province closed for the day prematurely or didn't open. One plant in Stratford shut down after an employee took a temperature reading inside the factory: 120 degrees. Another factory couldn't have workers do anything until after midnight; the heat expanded the metal machinery so it couldn't be operated properly.

At St. Joseph's Hospital in London, a surgeon finished an operation and asked a student nurse for some ginger ale. Noreen Coughlin, a twenty-year-old, obliged and grabbed a glass bottle of ginger ale out of an electric refrigerator. When she brought it out into the hot room, it exploded: a razor-like fragment of glass shot into her face, creating a gash across her lips and chin.

If this was going to happen, a hospital was the best place Coughlin could have been. She was stitched right up.

Pop bottles exploded throughout the summer. A few hours after Coughlin's experience, in Chicago, before bedtime, thirteen-year-old Kermit Krantz went to the kitchen to get a bottle of cold root beer from the icebox, or maybe the family also had one of those new Westinghouse electric refrigerators. But once the bottle met the hot air and Krantz's hot hand, it exploded, glass slicing him in the abdomen and wrist. But Krantz would also be okay and go on to have a successful career as a respected physician and the inventor of an expandable woman's tampon.

In Central City, Nebraska, when it was 111 degrees, a man put a bottle of soda pop in ice water to keep it cold, and it, too, exploded, sending six shards of glass into his face, barely missing his eyeball. Not that this was a phenomenon synonymous only with the summer of 1936. In 2024, there were reports of cans of soda becoming too hot before being loaded onto Southwest Airlines flights, then exploding and injuring attendants.

Missouri

August Beilmann, an arboriculturist at the Missouri Botanical Gardens, said in an interview that the average tree had an internal temperature of 74 degrees—and that trees begin to lose their leaves when their internal temperature reaches 85 degrees.

About a week later, in mid-July, fall came early. States such as Missouri, Oklahoma, Indiana, and New York, and in Canadian provinces such as Ontario, communities reported leaves falling from the trees as if it were already autumn. On July 18, in Indianapolis, the assistant state entomologist H. K. Rippey told a reporter: "The leaves are cooking on the trees, and there isn't enough moisture in the ground to supply them with nourishment to withstand the heat attack. Maple trees have been hardest hit, elms are second, and even sturdy oaks are dropping their leaves."

In Michigan, trees weren't merely shedding leaves; they were dying. In 1949, the US Department of Agriculture mentioned in a bulletin that 28 percent of the trees in the Huron National Forest were killed by heat and drought during the summer of 1936—and an additional 20 percent of the trees were wiped out solely due to the high temperatures.

Wisconsin

In Milwaukee, a twenty-six-year-old iceman, carrying a hundred-pound block of ice, passed out. He lived, but newspaper editors appreciated the irony, and his little story was circulated around the country. Man carries ice, collapses in the heat; ha-ha. But it wasn't amusing or even odd. Years later, Milton Miller, an Evansville, Indiana doctor, recalled in a 1983 newspaper interview that it was common for icemen to wind up at the hospital. "They'd have heat exhaustion and would have convulsions from the salt they lost [through perspiration] while carrying the ice," Miller said.

Even if carrying around the ice didn't deplete your energy, there was always the chance you might drop a three-hundred-pound block of ice on your right foot, which happened today to Matt Calkins in Chippewa, who was quickly taken to the hospital.

There was another odd cold-hot story today in Wisconsin. In the town of Two Rivers, where it was 100 degrees in the shade, WPA workers on a city park project dug through a foot of snow. Let's back up a bit: Dirt was piled on a snowdrift back in March, keeping it cool. Today, the workers dug through the dirt and discovered the snow. City officials tried to make the most of it the following summer when they marketed themselves as a tourist destination, branding themselves "The Coolest Spot in Wisconsin."

But mostly, the ground throughout Wisconsin was dangerous, as a two-year-old boy discovered the hard way today: in Green Bay (100°F), a toddler burned his feet on sidewalks badly enough that his parents kept him in a wheelchair for several days.

It was a bad time in the country to be without shoes. Yesterday, in Glen Falls, New York, an eight-year-old girl seeking relief from the heat walked around in her bare feet—only to step on a broken bottle. Today, in Dayton, Kentucky, a thirty-eight-year-old male and three children were treated at a hospital for first and second-degree burns after walking on a beach along the Ohio River. Also today, in Fair Oaks, Indiana (108°F), a two-year-old boy was at his grandfather's house, walking in sand—he suffered second-degree burns on his toes and feet.

On and on these stories went. Dogs weren't safe either. Several days from now, in Alton, Illinois, a dog would run on a paved road after his boy and the boy's friends, who were all on bicycles. The dog spent the next few days resting at home due to burned paws.

New Jersey

A factory fire in Newark (104°F) sent fourteen people to the hospital after a pile of celluloid film, destined to be thrown away, burned under the glare of the sun, setting off an explosion that sent scraps of fiery celluloid film fluttering a quarter-mile away, catching a steel forging plant on fire. Soon, seven other buildings were in flames.

Bridgeton (100°F) had a different problem—residents who lived too close to the State Fish and Bone Fertilizer Plant were struggling. The company was allowed to store fertilizer but not manufacture it, but it was obvious that they were making it and breaking the law. The smell from the plant was overpowering, and on miserable hot nights, residents chose between closing their windows and being cooked inside their homes—or opening windows and gagging on the smell of fertilizer.

New York

Today, in New York City, the weather department for *The Daily News* received more than three thousand phone calls, a record for the paper. The largest previous number had been two thousand calls on January 23, the coldest day of the year. It was 2 below zero then; now, in parts of the city, it was 109 degrees.

In Troy (104°F), at a convention for the Women's Auxiliary, State Veterans of Foreign Wars, twenty-nine women fainted. In Hornell (104°F), there were two forest fires, and a fifty-six-year-old retired policeman was found dead on his porch after a long day of working on his farm. In Watkins Glen (107°F), three people died. In New York City, the heat killed a dozen people, including a three-year-old boy who, seeking relief from the broiling heat inside his family's apartment, went onto the fire escape alone, four stories high, and fell off.

In Mount Vernon, streets and sidewalks buckled in the heat, and while repairing Gramatan Avenue, six men collapsed, causing the commissioner to call employees off the job. Later that evening, the heat came for a sixty-year-old man just sitting on his porch.

It was so hot that the ticket window to the Thomas Jefferson Pool was mobbed with swimmers, and three police cars came to manage the crowd. At a payroll office, nine thousand WPA employees waited in line to get their checks; forty young men and women collapsed. Heat-irritable people started shoving and fighting with each other to keep their position in line, and the police were called here, too, to restore calm and take heat victims to the hospital.

The nation's First Lady, Eleanor Roosevelt, was visiting New York City and braving the heat. Several days later, she wrote a newspaper column about July 9 and her time speaking at the Teachers College at Columbia University.

"I must record my admiration for the devotion of these summer school students," Mrs. Roosevelt wrote. "The hall was packed for the opening of this course, and as the day was very warm, I could not help sympathizing with everybody present." She wrote that the drive to the university "cooled us off, but when we arrived, we had to go indoors to eat our supper, and it was almost like stepping into a furnace."

Eleanor also wrote that she spoke to her husband that night and asked how everybody was surviving in Washington, DC. The president responded cheerfully, "The heat is fearful, and I am so busy all I hope is to live until I get on the train and start off on my trip."

Washington, DC

While President Roosevelt anticipated his air-conditioned presidential train, the rest of the city muddled along. The White House press room was unusually packed; political reporters were drawn to the air-conditioning, which kept the room at 70 degrees.

Ira Gabrielson, head of the Bureau of Biological Survey, in his diary, recorded, "Hot again. Up to 104°. Worked all day & did not suffer much. In evening tried to work at home but not much success as the kids made too much noise."

Gabrielson fared far better than some fellow citizens. A retired postal auditor and a dishwasher died. A horse collapsed on K Street. Residents and tourists soldiered on, although Roosevelt spread the word that government offices should close if it was needed. Many government buildings were being outfitted with air-conditioning, and so fewer offices closed than had in the past.

People were asleep under virtually every shade tree in every park. Typically, the capital consumed 107 million gallons of water in twenty-four hours; today, it consumed 137 million. Vacationing continued: 86 tourists climbed up 365 steps to the Capitol dome (which was then open to the public; now, it is only accessible for members of Congress). At the Washington Monument, 168 tourists were crazy enough to walk up the stairs instead of riding the elevator.

Kansas

An agriculture-themed press conference in Topeka (102°F) was held in the office of Governor Alf Landon, who was running for president against Roosevelt. Frank Lowden, a former governor of Illinois, removed his coat, saying, "I'm not used to such hot weather." Landon, trying to look presidential and not offend voters, kept his coat on.

Massachusetts

In Quincy (83°F), the Pawsey Dump caught fire after the sun reflected through discarded glass bottles. The postmaster in Lawrence (86°F) canceled afternoon mail delivery, fearing today might be like yesterday, when twelve carriers became sick in the 97-degree heat.

Seven citizens died from the heat or drowning, and pets were hurting, too. "This heat is tough on dogs," said John Sullivan, Boston's chief of police. With it being in the 90s, Sullivan urged residents to keep their dogs in the shade and do whatever they could to keep them comfortable. Local journalists found that interesting. Sullivan had been on the record previously as saying "The only good dog is a dead dog." Maybe, one reporter speculated, the heat melted Sullivan's heart.

Tennessee

In the dark of night, near the town of Limestone, twenty-three-year-old John Baldwin went outside to his front yard to sit down and cool off. His wife explained this after she found his mangled corpse. Baldwin was a laborer, and all day, he toiled in 97-degree heat. Exhausted, he wasn't thinking properly—because no rational person would have done what he did.

After Baldwin sat down, he fell asleep. On railroad tracks.

Pennsylvania

The state was having a rough day:

- Farmers threw buckets of water on hen houses' floors, trying to lower the temperature through evaporation. Other farmers carried stricken hens into their cellars and doused water on them. One chicken farmer lost 150 hens.
- In Berwick (104°F), hoping to cool off, motorcyclists jumped on their bikes, only to report feeling like the air from a hot oven was blowing on them. The golf course was deserted; the few who attempted to play abandoned their games midway.
- In Wilkes-Barre, a twenty-five-year-old mental institution escapee drowned in the Susquehanna River. The coroner suggested the heat may have pushed him to flee, especially since he went straight to water.

Pittsburgh (103°F) had three heat deaths and a drowning. In Philadelphia (107°F), six people died, and four transformers exploded and cut off electricity for the southwest part of the city. Firemen rushed to put the fires out, several of them collapsing in the heat.

Philadelphia's police were busy, too. They were called to check out the top floor room of a bandbox, also known as a rowhouse. When two officers entered the room, they were appalled by what they found: a two-year-old boy, Charles, in a crib, and a four-year-old boy, John, with a collar around his neck and a rope leading from the collar to the floor, fastened there by a staple. Only one window was open a few inches—and covered with chicken wire.

"It was so hot, you could barely breathe," said patrolman Herbert Walker. He and sergeant Frank Harkin forced their way in because neighbors alerted them to the screams and sobs that had been coming from the house. When he saw the two officers, John was said to have cried, "Water, water, gimme a drink!"

The father was long gone or dead, and the mother wasn't around. The police rescued the dehydrated boys, who had siblings: Richard, a six-year-old being raised by another family, and Margaret, eight, who lived with her maternal grandmother. The cops, certain the mother would return, waited around, as did a growing crowd that swelled to five hundred people. When Marion Shanks, the twenty-nine-year-old woman vying for worst mother of the year, arrived with her boyfriend, William Davis, thirty-nine, the police greeted them and had to restrain a crowd of irate women from attacking them. The officers steered both Shanks and Davis to the patrol car. "Kill her, kill her," the crowd yelled.

Michigan

The night before, in Detroit, Earl Brown slept outside in a vacant lot next to his house. Two of his kids, Lloyd, four years old, and Robert, two, accompanied him. We can assume the fifty-year-old factory worker, along with hoping for a better night's sleep, thought the outdoors might provide some peace and quiet. He and his wife had nine children. It was a crowded house. So very crowded.

Earl forgot that not everyone was home.

His son George returned in the family car early in the morning, driving into the vacant lot and straight for the garage. He ran over his father.

Earl survived, suffering three fractured ribs and a fractured skull. Earl would (eventually) be okay and even become a dad for the tenth time. But it's a safe bet that he never slept outside again.

Twelve people in Detroit died, and it didn't pay to be overcome by the heat in the wrong place. Walter Flemming Jr., twenty years old, of the Detroit suburb Grosse Pointe Shores, was in a canoe when he had a heart attack and fell into the water. Another Michigander, forty-six years old, was on the top of a lumber pile when he fainted and was seriously injured. But when Garfield A. Nichols, an assistant prosecutor conducting a case in a hot Detroit courtroom, passed out, he fell onto the floor. Instead of riding in an ambulance or hearse, he was taken home in a police car.

There were numerous drownings, too many to mention. Scores of heat-stroke victims were shuttled to the hospital, and the Detroit weather bureau office, staffed with only three men, received so many calls from citizens inquiring about the temperature that the guys rotated who answered. Each clerk would pick up the phone, shout "102 degrees" into the mouthpiece, and hang up.

Illinois

In Alton, a seventy-nine-year-old Black man, Henry Hunter, a widower and a flour mill engineer, died at home this afternoon—from the heat, according to his physician. He had been spiraling since yesterday. It was a loss for the town. Hunter had lived there since he was six and seems to have thrived. His parents had been enslaved, but it isn't clear if they still were when he was born in 1857, in Washington, Missouri. Hunter married, fathered three kids, and was politically active, starting a chapter of the Alton Republican Club and a charter member of a lodge. Hunter started off at the mill as a coal-passer (he shoveled coal). But he rose up the ranks until he was an engineer, running the whole thing. Of course, the heat wave destroyed all of that for Henry Hunter.

The heat wave was merciless in that way, targeting people who were practically living history museums. On the same day, in Chicago (95°F), Matilda Steiger, a 108-year-old woman born in 1828 in Belgrade, Serbia, had been getting along just fine until the heat wave; she was found dead in bed by her seventy-year-old daughter. Later in the summer, the heat took out hundred-year-old Gaius Paddock, a retired St. Louis merchant who enjoyed recounting how he used to clerk at a Springfield, Illinois, store where lawyers used the shop as a meeting place and spun yarns and talked politics. Paddock particularly enjoyed sharing stories about a regular visitor, a young, six-foot and four-inch attorney named Abraham Lincoln.

At the Northwestern Barb Wire Company, in the city of Sterling (101°F), 550 employees went on strike. They demanded a raise in wages—and electric fans.

Executives quickly agreed, promising fans and higher wages: four additional cents an hour. Workers were not impressed. They continued a strike that lasted three weeks and became violent at times, but when it was all said and done, the perspiring workers got a ten-cent-an-hour raise and electric fans.

If the Sterling factory workers read the paper today, they might have spotted a message assuring an extortionist that he would receive his money in the coming days.

The day after being instructed to place a newspaper ad alerting an extortionist that the money would be forthcoming, Mayor Brydia of Prophetstown did just that. He also contacted Sim Mee, a United States district attorney from Sterling, for advice, and made the rounds with the local businessmen, collecting money for the mad bomber.

If the politician asked everybody to keep quiet about it, somebody didn't listen. Hardly a surprise; Prophetstown was a community of 1,400 residents. All you'd need is a local news editor or reporter to get wind of what was happening.

That may explain why word spread and newspapers around the country reported today on the letter Brydia received. Now, Brydia was no shrinking violet. He was only too happy to talk about the extortionist and, like any good politician, used the threat to his political advantage. For starters, Brydia issued a blanket statement about the extortionist to the media: "I am not disturbed in any way, but I will meet their demand. Business will continue in Prophetstown without any deflection in any way. We'll protect the city at all costs."

Brydia also conducted local interviews. "I have no personal fear in connection with this threat," he told a reporter, "but I expect to protect

Prophetstown and its businessmen just as far as possible. With buildings as dry as they are after many weeks without rain, attempted arson might have serious consequences."

"I don't think this is the work of a crank," Brydia added. "The letter is too well written, and the plan has been worked out too carefully."

"Continues very hot and sultry," wrote carpenter–diarist Charles Morgan from his perch in Bloomington. "With record breaking temperatures, people seek cool places for retreat. But cool places cannot be found." He said that people were living in their basements and sleeping on porches and backyards.

"Pastures are dried up. Crops are about gone unless rain comes soon. Work has been eliminated," although Morgan spelled it as "illiminated." Still, for a man with an eighth-grade education, Morgan was doing just fine. He would have made an excellent journalist. He described a city where "nothing is done, only as emergency demands it. Death tolls are running higher and higher. . . . creeks and streams are diminishing, and at present the situation looks very grave."

Edna Mae Wray, director of the *Chicago Tribune*'s free ice fund, was working overtime, trying to get ice (and milk) to the city's poorest families on a day when it was 106 degrees. She outlined the problems to a *Tribune* reporter, in a story that would run in a couple days: "One woman with eight babies came in here today. The oldest child was nine. The baby is six months old. They all have to have milk. She said she tried to cool it with running water, but you know how little good that does."

Wray said that she gave the mom tickets she could redeem for free ice. "I haven't turned anyone down yet," she said. "You just can't do anything else in this heat but give them ice—as long as you have it."

That evening, Charles Morgan and his wife dined on vegetable stew with one of their sons and a daughter-in-law for dinner, then went to visit friends or family. "Came home near midnight and found our rooms very warm and stuffy," Morgan wrote. "Each evening is very calm, and no breeze makes it very stifling and hard to breathe good."

As uncomfortable as the nights were, they were easier to maneuver in than the day. Which is why in Tallula, and other places around the country, wheat farmers were waking up around midnight and harvesting their crops in the moonlight. Typically, it would be impossible to harvest wheat after midnight because it would be too damp—but not any more.

Stifling nights also explain why some people slept on their roofs, people like Carl Dohrman, sixty, who went to his Chicago apartment's roof shortly after midnight. It was hot and dry everywhere, but maybe up here, there would be a breeze. Dohrman's plan worked: he fell asleep. But his plan didn't work as he hoped, because somewhere in the middle of the night, he rolled off the roof and plummeted to his death.

25

JULY 10

Attack of the Heat-Crazed Squirrels!

Today's Death Toll: 400+
Total Death Toll: 2,000+

For years, movie theater owners hated heat waves. Audiences stayed away and ticket sales took a nosedive. But as air-conditioning caught on among theaters in the last half of the 1920s and throughout the 1930s, movie theater owners started to eagerly anticipate summers—the hotter, the better. Heat waves were excellent for business.

Movie theaters were far from the only business to use the heat wave as leverage to draw crowds. All summer, advertisers used the heat wave to promote their products and services. "Weather too hot to write a letter?" asked a newspaper ad. "Send a Gibson Greeting Card instead." "These summer days are too hot to spend in the kitchen. Bring the family down for one of our fine fish suppers," enthused a newspaper ad for a restaurant in Manchac, Louisiana. An ad in a Cincinnati, Ohio, paper suggested people try a popular local beer: "When the going gets too hot, cool off with Felsenbrau!" "It's too hot these August days to lick stamps and envelope flaps. Let Sengbusch Sanitary Moisteners work for you," read another ad in Jackson, Tennessee. Kellogg's, in late August, promoted a "hot-weather special" for its cereal in newspapers across the country. "Buy now!" the ad urged.

But unlike a lot of companies trying to get consumers' attention and make a few bucks, air-conditioned movie theaters were providing a true service to the community. Cinemas throughout the country started advertising lodging for the night. In Chicago, twenty-four theaters opened for night sleeping. You could pay for the last show and stick around until dawn. Just bring a pillow and maybe a blanket. Some theaters allowed you to bring in your own food, and at least one theater—the Iowa Theatre in Des Moines—opened doors for the sleeping public at 11 P.M., promising to keep their cooling system operating all night. You didn't even have to pay for a movie ticket.

"Bring your own pillows," the theater owner advised. He said the idea came to him after a young woman the evening before asked permission to sleep in the theater. So he opened it up to her and anyone; three hundred people showed up.

At the Capitol Theater in Madison, Wisconsin, they separated genders: women slept in the downstairs lounges; men were upstairs in the aisles and on the stage. No minors allowed. Policemen stood watch, probably enjoying the assignment, since the temperature was 70 degrees. One person really got some serious shuteye, sleepwalking through the theater.

The LeClaire theater in Moline, Illinois, also welcomed people. The manager, William Pras, invited his friends to stay. Word got out, and he soon had to tell frustrated members of the public that there wasn't enough room for everyone. Most Moline residents were stuck sleeping in parks, lawns, and as low to the ground as you could get, sprawled in ditches and ravines.

Massachusetts

Alphonse Albano and his fellow welders repaired trolley tracks in Springfield, in 101-degree heat and 95 percent humidity. Albano, thirty-eight, was found lying at the corner of Mill and Locust Streets. The medical examiner and superintendent concluded that Albano passed out and fell over his welding equipment, which was hooked up to the high-tension trolley line; his chin touched an exposed wire.

Washington, DC

Late in the evening, after a day of 105-degree heat that took out a middle-aged woman walking on the street, President Franklin Roosevelt boarded a train which would take him to the Maine coast for a summer vacation. Frederick Storm, a United Press newspaper correspondent, observed to readers, "The President has been a victim of blistering heat with all other residents."

True enough. But between the air-conditioned train and ocean breezes over the next two weeks, it's safe to say that the president had some advantages to keeping himself cool and comfortable that most Americans didn't have.

Maryland

In Federalsburg (108°F), Claude Howard, a chicken farmer, tried saving his flock of nine hundred by spraying them with cold water. He even tore down one side of the chicken house to allow more air to get inside. The chickens still all died. Factories shut down early. The mayor of Baltimore (107.4°F) shortened hours for city workers, especially those who toiled outside, a decision that likely saved some lives.

South Dakota

In Mitchell (104°F), eleven thousand residents participated in a day of prayer, asking the heavens for rain. Churches remained open all day so people could come in and plead their case.

Grasshoppers, out of control as usual, battered themselves to death against a downtown store window in Aberdeen (114°F) as they made a futile pursuit for the only green grass in sight—an artificial window display. Photographers for the city paper couldn't get a photo of that or much else; when they tried developing their negatives, the 83-degree water melted them.

Near Aberdeen, Roy Schaunaman, twenty-six years old, wanted to cool off in a lake behind a dam in Richmond. Schaunaman became yet another example of the country's desperate need for more swimming pools and lessons. Schaunaman couldn't swim, but the lakebed on one side of the dam was known for not being deep. So Schaunaman waded there, oblivious to the crevice he was about to fall into.

Illinois

In Chicago (102°F), 107 people reported being bitten by dogs. It was a new record, the board of health declared. A few days later, they would reach 120 dog bites.

About 130 miles away from Chicago, George Brydia, mayor of Prophetstown, continued raising money for his extortionist (or at least pretended to). "The whole town's talking about this, and everybody's behind me 100 percent," Brydia told reporters. "We haven't had any rain in twenty days, and we're afraid the whole town would be burned up if somebody started playing with matches." In an abundance of caution, Brydia deputized people and doubled the police force. Prophetstown now had four police officers.

Brydia planned to leave the money with the extortioner the next day, although like all good politicians, he kept his options open, saying, "I am not afraid personally, but I want to protect Prophetstown property, and I probably will comply with the demand." But townspeople were afraid, and so Brydia told the press, "The residents of Prophetstown are becoming convinced that the extortionist plans to carry out his threat. On requests from them, I have organized a vigilante committee, armed with sawed-off shotguns. We're ready to meet any trouble, if there is any."

Pierce Kyles, said to be 109 years old, was named a heat victim and probably the oldest person taken out by the heat wave. If he was as old as he believed, Kyles was born into slavery in 1827, in Columbus, Georgia, and remained enslaved until the Civil War. He moved to Chicago with his family almost a hundred years later in 1924.

Important surviving-a-heat-wave tip: Lighting anything on fire is not a good idea. Edward Nolan, a forty-five-year-old farmer in Harvard, Illinois (106°F), burned Canada thistle, an invasive plant from Europe (not Canada) that has plagued American farmers since the 1600s. Nolan was trying to rid the thistle from the family farm. One of his brothers found him later, and when it was all pieced together, everyone concluded that while watching the thistle burn, Nolan passed out. His body was charred almost beyond recognition.

Minnesota

Seventeen baby chicks scurried around in the city in Ada (100°F). The chick hatchery had discarded what they believed were bad eggs. Two boys, who were good eggs, were searching for old brass and rescued the chicks, bringing them home in their hats. This sort of thing occurred probably hundreds of times this summer, with the heat acting as an incubator and causing eggs to hatch. Farmers, homeowners, and truck drivers delivering eggs to the market often heard cracking, only to look and see a chick pecking its way out to freedom.

Iowa

It was 100 degrees throughout the state. At least eight people died, including a woman in Storm Lake. Her husband was driving when she fainted and fell against the car door, which sprung open, and she went tumbling out onto the gravel highway.

It was getting hard to cope. In Des Moines, Edward and Florence Rayhorn, sixty-four and sixty-two years old respectively, admitted to Judge Frank Shankland that high temperatures were a factor in deciding to end their marriage. "It's the heat, it's got us down," they reportedly said. Shankland declined to grant the divorce, suggesting they first see an attorney. Shankland told a reporter, "By the time the petition is filed, and the weather is cooler, they probably will change their minds." The judge may have been onto something; the couple had been married for thirty-nine years.

The news broke today that when Des Moines households were bringing in their laundry to laundromats, pajamas and nightgowns weren't among them. The laundry officials were too polite to come out and say it, but the heat was driving people to sleep in their birthday suits.

And if you didn't have enough to worry about, you might be attacked by a heat-crazed squirrel. John Brawford, seventy-five, was trekking through a residential district in Estherville in the 104-degree heat when a squirrel landed on his sweaty head. The squirrel knocked his hat right off and started biting him. Brawford shook off the attacking animal. The squirrel fell to the ground, ran for one of Brawford's legs, and bit him again.

Brawford escaped and limped to a hospital. Word got out that a psycho squirrel was on the loose, and Police Chief J. C. Lilley went out to see for himself. The squirrel wasn't hard to find—it charged Lilley. After the police chief shot the squirrel with a rifle, it was packed in ice and sent to the University of Iowa in Iowa City for a rabies analysis. In fact, there were several tests done. The conclusion? The squirrel did not have rabies, and Brawford lived another twenty-one years.

Indiana

Plenty of people who left pants, with their wallets inside pockets, in their car while they went swimming this summer had them stolen. But in East Chicago, at Indiana Harbor, while a resident cooled off at the beach, a thief made off with his new $800 sedan. The crook had a good day; nobody else did. A six-month-old baby girl in Michigan City, Indiana, died from acidosis (too much acid in her fluids), which was triggered by the heat. In Hammond (100°F), there were two deaths: a landscaper, and a businessman who complained about the heat, walked into another room with a 32-caliber revolver, and blew his brains out.

Another heat-crazed squirrel was on the loose. In Indianapolis (109°F), a squirrel bit Betty Kracke, a reverend's eight-year-old daughter. The squirrel also bit Betty's mother and three men, and chased three more people before racing off to who knows where.

Indiana's animals were not doing well at all. The Muncie Tanking Company, a rendering company that picked up dead animals for free then turned them into usable materials, such as ingredients for glue and fertilizer, had thirty-two requests today to pick up carcasses. In the last week, they picked up over 150 animals. Hogs, sheep, cows, and horses were all dying off at farms. "The situation has just been terrible, that's all," one official told Muncie's newspaper, *The Star Press*. "We've been running all our trucks. We just can't catch up with orders." It was a similar situation across the country; some farmers were burying their dead livestock when the rendering firms couldn't come for them.

Not every animal was off their game. In Dunkirk (104°F), Jack Rhodes, a twenty-eight-year-old salesman, was at his office when he received a phone call from concerned neighbors. They didn't have a phone but made a call from a local store. We have to connect the dots as to how the conversation went, but the neighbors probably couldn't open the door to Rhodes's apartment and were worried because their dog was at the open window, barking furiously. Jack's wife, Nina, was doing nothing to calm him down. Perhaps because she couldn't?

Jack hurried home. The dog, who probably was treated like royalty for the rest of his life, led Jack to an immense wardrobe. Locked inside was his twenty-three-year-old wife, Nina, semiconscious. A rare breeze had come at just the wrong time and blown the door shut.

Kentucky

In Louisville, an intoxicated (at 10:30 A.M.) truck driver overturned his vehicle. The truck was carrying 2,400 pounds of ice, and regrettably, the temperature was racing toward 104 degrees. By the time another ice truck arrived, only 600 pounds of ice remained.

In Newport (105°F), citizens descended upon the Ohio River. Or they would have, if the city hadn't banned them from swimming due to fears of catching typhoid. It isn't a disease you want; it can dole out a massive headache, diarrhea, loss of appetite, and, in rare cases, internal bleeding. Police officers patrolled the river and warned that anybody caught trying to take a dip would be thrown in jail, which was likely to be far hotter than anywhere else. Indeed, prisoners were being allowed to walk around in their cells naked, and one thirty-eight-year-old in the slammer for receiving stolen goods went a little crazy, ramming his head against the bars repeatedly until five officers wrestled him into a straitjacket and hauled him to the hospital.

On the other side of the river, in Cincinnati, Ohio, there was no typhoid ban—not for another day—and satisfied residents frolicked in the sewage-polluted waters.

Ohio

In the last three days, eight Cincinnati residents died from the heat, so maybe it was no surprise that people were desperate enough to wade into the Ohio River and risk catching a little typhoid.

Meanwhile, to help the animals in distress, a Cincinnati entrepreneur who owned a chain of gas stations announced that his filling stations would offer fresh water for dogs and horses. The businessman may have started a trend. Later in the month, in Wisconsin, Michigan, and Illinois, gas stations started doing something similar for horses.

The Ringling Brothers and Barnum Bailey Circus announced that Cincinnatians who showed up would be greeted by a new air-cooling system. It was sorely needed. Last summer, when there wasn't a massive heat wave, aerialists went to the peak of the big top with thermometers and found that it was 130 degrees.

The circus surely helped maintain attendance and probably saved a few people's and circus animals' lives, but their cooling system wasn't *that* sophisticated—it was essentially a bunch of electric fans. In fact, one of the Wallendas, the famous high-wire family circus act, reported that even with the cooling system in place, the temperature was still miserable at the top of the tent—at least 135 degrees.

C. C. Lanley, a sixty-year-old laborer in Sandusky, snapped and shot his forty-eight-year-old wife, then ended his own life. "Mentally deranged because of the heat," one newspaper said. One of Lanley's sons agreed the heat was to blame. He said his father had been irritable for days and seemed paranoid, especially toward his wife.

The son had worried about his father's temper. He told police he had said to Lanley, "Don't do anything you'll be sorry for."

Children are sometimes incredibly hard to wake when they are asleep, which in this case was a blessing: The Lanley's six-year-old granddaughter, sleeping next to Mrs. Lanley, didn't hear the gunshots. Nor did several other children in the house or an elderly boarder. Neighbors heard the noise, however, and called police; after the authorities arrived, the children and boarder awakened to a real-life blood-splattered nightmare.

Michigan

For the first time since the weather bureau opened in 1871, Detroit experienced three consecutive days of temperatures over 100 degrees. There were seven drownings around the state, including one in Kalamazoo involving a thirty-nine-year-old man who lost his life after his boat flipped over, while his four children and father watched helplessly from the shore.

Nineteen people died in Detroit. There were three heat deaths in Mt. Clemens. Another in Lansing. Another in Monroe. There was a death in Stony Point. A fifty-seven-year-old factory worker in Flint bit the dust. A death in Grand Rapids. South Lyons. Bay City. Three heat deaths in Owosso. A man died in Alma. In Fairfax. In Saginaw. As evening fell in a Wayland neighborhood, children playing hide-and-seek found a seventy-eight-year-old heat victim dead on her porch.

Wisconsin

It wasn't easy being a kid in 1936. Children were expected to be seen, not heard. If they got into trouble, an old-fashioned whipping was a respectable form of punishment in many families, though some child experts cautioned against it. And there were shady characters lurking about. A San Francisco shopkeeper was recently arrested because he believed neighborhood kids were stealing from him; hoping to catch them in the act, he put play money that resembled dimes in his backyard. If any children had picked them up, their hands would have been caught in a wolf trap.

Today, in Jamestown (102°F), Melvin Vanderah, twenty-two years old, and his two younger brothers, seventeen and eight years old, refreshed themselves in a creek that ran through somebody's farm. They hadn't been splashing for long, however, when Frank Freyberger, the farmer, appeared with a shotgun and said, "Get and get fast!"

Melvin and his brothers scrambled up the riverbank, and despite making his point, Freyberger shot his rifle anyway, missing. Freyberger gave a little chase, and as the boys ran across a field, he fired, missing. He fired again, and this time, fifteen lead pellets struck the oldest brother in the back and his legs.

Melvin recovered, although doctors couldn't remove the slugs in his back, and Freyberger was arrested. It was bizarre behavior. Freyberger was a father himself with adult kids helping to run his farm. He also wasn't exactly a doddering old man who had lost his grip on reality. He was forty-eight. It seems doubtful the heat addled his mind and caused him to fire his gun, because he didn't come to his senses and apologize. If anything, he dug in, and for the next several months had the threat of jail hovering over him before his case was dismissed.

"He doesn't seem to understand that one just can't do such things nowadays," said Sheriff Joe Green. Indeed, Freyberger was flabbergasted, saying, "It's a funny thing if a fellow can't shoot a man who trespasses on his property."

In Janesville (104°F), factories, including Chevrolet Motors, closed their plants. Milwaukee (101°F) should have followed their lead: Sixteen women employed on a WPA sewing project fainted. Thirty others, too weak to continue, were sent home. Along Milwaukee's Lake Shore Park, motorists stopped to rescue pigeons whose feet were stuck in the melting asphalt.

And in Oshkosh (99°F), Joseph Jarvis, sixty-two, sat at his window, watching the world go by. Everyone knew Jarvis. He once owned a tavern but in recent years, with diabetes slowing him down, he sold his place and tended bar as an employee. Now, he was trying to catch some fresh, cool air. That, at least, is what everybody assumed when he sat there on a Thursday evening, on a day that reached 102 degrees. But now it was Friday morning, and passersby noticed, well, hey, wait a minute, Jarvis has been sitting there for a long time.

Somebody checked on Jarvis and discovered that he had checked out. Until he could be removed later in the afternoon, his body remained in his chair, appearing as if he was still looking out the window.

Nebraska

In Omaha (101°F), there were six heat victims, including a forty-seven-year-old man who slept tonight on his roof and either rolled off or inadvertently stepped off it in the darkness. Charles Harvey, forty-six years old, meanwhile, seemed poised to die not from the heat, but perhaps an errant shoelace. Harvey was a car checker for a railroad, where a train stopped to switch some cars. At some point, Harvey stepped off the engine's footboard and started walking in front of the locomotive. Unfortunately, he tripped and fell on his face, in the middle of the track. That's when the engine started moving.

Harvey's feet were pointed toward the engine, which was fast approaching. There was nothing he could do except to edge over near one rail and lay still, on his stomach, with his hands stretched out ahead of him, and pray for divine intervention. He got it, because the engine safely passed over him—*and so did sixty-one cars.*

He wasn't hurt beyond bruises and cuts, but his clothes were shredded by the brake riggings of the cars that passed over him. By the end, he was only wearing shoes and socks.

"I might have been able to jump out of the way if I hadn't fallen so hard," he told a reporter for the *Omaha World-Herald* later. "But by the time I had collected myself, it was too late."

Harvey said his life was spared because he was dressed for the hot weather. If he had worn thicker clothing, the cars might have caught some of his layers and dragged him into a bloody oblivion.

Tennessee

Even without the heat, prison life was a tough existence, no matter what your skin color, but the summer of 1936 may have been the absolute worst time to be Black prisoner. It was particularly terrible at a rock quarry in Avondale, a neighborhood in Chattanooga. Black prisoners from a workhouse were regularly sent here.

Next to nothing is known about the life of George Davidson, except for the color of his skin and that he looked to be in his late forties. It's not even certain that George Davidson was George Davidson, because later, authorities suggested his last name was Erskine, and that he also had an alias last name—Taylor—and that he might have hailed from either Alabama or Georgia. He also may have robbed a post office once, and may have been a coal miner. What we do know was that while he was in the quarry, he was essentially cooked to death.

Davidson became a prisoner in Chattanooga on Independence Day. He was arrested for loitering and committed to the workhouse for vagrancy. The cure for that in these parts, or for any infraction that got you into a workhouse, was the quarry. Rather, that was the punishment you received if you were Black, charged Charles Hutchings, a Black ex-prisoner who spoke out after news broke of Davidson's death, in an interview with *The Chattanooga Times*. Hutchings wanted to get the word out that Black prisoners were being mistreated. Not that the White prisoners were feted like royalty, but they worked on road crews, where the weather was a little cooler, and they were probably less likely to be beaten out in public.

Hutchings, a former schoolteacher turned insurance agent, was allegedly drunk and disorderly earlier in the year, and for those infractions was fined $20 and sentenced to seventy days at the workhouse. He was freed on June 1, about a month before Davidson was arrested—but stayed in touch with some of the prisoners and became something of an advocate for them. Hutchings told *The Chattanooga Times* that one of the prisoner employees, Lowell McAfee, who was Black, beat the inmates if they weren't working enough.

According to Hutchings, in the hours before dying of heat exhaustion, Davidson was beaten twice with a stick. McAfee, questioned by reporters, denied that he beat prisoners, especially not with a stick. McAfee also said that during a break, Davidson went swimming in a pond of still water near the quarry, ate some beans, and returned to the pond for another swim. It's not entirely clear what McAfee was suggesting. That Davidson had a lovely final afternoon consisting of a swim and a hearty lunch and another dip in the water? That the quarry was practically a vacation resort? Or that Davidson overexerted himself by swimming?

Hutchings said that McAfee's story was doubtful. For starters, prisoners weren't allowed near the pool of water, and typically, if they slacked off, they were thumped. With sticks.

"When McAfee took over the job, the prisoners were excavating about 50 cubic yards of rock a day," Hutchings said. "He beat them and worked them so hard, the production increased to more than 100 cubic yards, daily." Hutchings said that McAfee always told his superiors that beatings happened because the prisoners were out of line. That, Hutchings said, was ridiculous—the prisoners knew it was hopeless and foolish to do anything other than what they were told.

Referring to the foreman above McAfee, Bill Akins, Hutchings asked, "Does he think that one of those prisoners, shacked and guarded with guns, would attempt to strike him when he is armed with a stick and a knife?"

Hutchings also volunteered this information: "McAfee and the others armed with sticks inflicted most of their beatings on Negro prisoners who did not live in Chattanooga. They knew those men would leave town when released, and there would be no complaint."

It wasn't only McAfee administering the thrashings either, Hutchings said: "We were not allowed to rest until a dynamite blast was set. While working, we were continually ordered to speed up and if a prisoner fell behind in his work, he was beaten by McAfee or his two henchmen."

One of those henchmen was very large. Hutchings and the other prisoners referred to him as King Kong.

King Kong roughed up Hutchings a few times. On March 23, McAfee hit Hutchings on the head with a stick, leaving a scar, and on April 2, struck him with his fist. Hutchings described a miserable existence where the prisoners worked from 7 or 7:30 in the morning to 11:30 in the morning.

There was a thirty-minute lunch break, and at 4 P.M., they were shuttled back to the workhouse.

"When I was there in March, we had to sleep in the same dirty, sweaty clothes we worked in," Hutchings said. "We wore leg irons all the time." Hutchings said he had his leg irons on for seventy days. "When we got back to the workhouse and were locked in cells, the leg irons went with us. They were not removed until the fine was worked out," he said.

Hutchings said that one Black man on crutches, who is only known as J. F. Conley, was forced to work on a rock crusher at the quarry. During Hutchings' time there, Conley had been there for almost eight months, working off two $50 fines.

"I will probably be the victim of an attempt at bodily harm for making these statements, but it is time the inhumane treatment given those Negroes in the quarry is stopped," Hutchings said.

It wasn't halted soon enough for Davidson, however. Three days into his time at the rock quarry and three days before his death, he possibly became sick. At least, the workhouse superintendent Frank Brown said, "He was ill several days before his death, and we found out he was stricken with epilepsy. He was treated and kept away from the quarry work for several days and did not return until he told foreman Bill Akins he felt able to work."

Maybe, or perhaps that was a cover story designed to suggest that Davidson's poor health sealed his fate. In an interview, Brown said the prisoner didn't complain about the heat until the day he died. Brown said Davidson mentioned the heat was too much, took an hour's break, and said he was well enough to return to breaking rocks. In other words, nothing to see here, folks.

Another workhouse superintendent, E. G. Murrell, put out a statement to the press that the prisoners were supposed to be on the job ten hours a day but that it often was less. He also suggested that none of the prisoners even spent time in a quarry. "All of our work is done on the roads, where the men have plenty of fresh air," Murrell said, adding, "We don't take a man straight off the streets and put him to work building roads. When they first come to the workhouse, we give them light work to do, and as they become hardened to the work, we place them out on the roads."

Sure. The facts seem pretty obvious. Murrell was lying, and around 4:15 P.M., a little past the usual quitting time, Davidson was breaking rocks when he collapsed. He was taken to Erlanger Hospital, which had already treated three men with heat exhaustion that day alone. Davidson, however, was dead on arrival.

Missouri

There was a heat victim in Kirksville. Another in Poplar Bluff. And Kansas City. And St. Louis, where at least ten people went to the White hospital to be treated for heat prostration, and six went to the hospital for Black patients.

Ontario

In Brantford (104.5°F), the metal components that secure trolleys to the overhead tracks, called "trolley ears," were melting. Several streetcars became immobile until crews could make repairs.

Dead robins and sparrows were turning up throughout Toronto (104.8°F), and the city's humane society practically begged the public to pay more attention to their pets. Hundreds of cats and dogs were ill, part of an epidemic of summer influenza that was intensified by the heat. Anyone with a vomiting cat was urged to take their pet to a vet. Humane society officials also encouraged business owners to leave out water for heat-tormented horses and said they could pick up cards at the society reading "Drivers May Water Their Horses Here."

People weren't faring any better: today, thirty-five men, women, and children in Toronto died. Over one hundred heat patients were admitted into hospitals.

A. W. Miles, an undertaker, told the *Toronto Star*: "Our deaths have just about doubled in the past day or so. Of course, I believe heat always does that. Last May, when we had a heat wave, the death rate jumped immediately. It doesn't appear on the certificates as death due to the heat, but there is no doubt in my mind that heat is what aggravates the diseases or weaknesses which carry them off."

That evening, in a cottage at the summer resort of Sandy Beach, off Lake Simcoe, the heat wave, just as it saved a railroad worker's life through lighter clothes, prevented the deaths of two children, according to a widely circulated newspaper report. A mother told her kids to go to bed, and the father said, "Let them stay up. It's too hot to sleep." The mother agreed. Minutes later, a windstorm knocked over a large tree that flattened the kids' bedroom.

Pennsylvania

There were twenty heat victims today. A forty-five-year-old in Tyrone (102°F) was practically destined to see a grim end. He died cleaning the bottom of a steel car in a stone quarry.

In Harrisburg, postmen collapsed on their rounds, and dead dogs and cats were in the streets. The working theory was that if the heat wasn't killing them outright, it was slowing them down and making them more vulnerable to being hit by cars.

Thirty-seven Philadelphia residents were hospitalized for heat sickness. Meanwhile, Marion Shanks, Philadelphia's worst mom, showed up in court to answer charges that she left her two little boys alone in a crib, in a hot room, without food or water. Magistrate Edward J. Holland demanded an explanation, and inexplicably, Shanks smiled. Her boyfriend said he had no idea what was going on. The judge declared they would each be held on $800 bail.

Lillian Peachy, an agent for the Society to Protect Children from Cruelty, told the judge the Shanks family had been under their observation for several years. They kept moving about and were hard to trace, Peachy said. A year earlier, Peachy visited the house and they were living amid "indescribable squalor and so strong a stench that I had to talk to the woman outside."

"This is the most pathetic case I have ever seen in all my experience as a magistrate," the judge declared, before giving Peachy temporary custody of the children.

In the evening, around 7:30 P.M., at Lake Carey in Hughestown (103°F), eighteen-year-old Doris Schmaltz heard a boy screaming. A fifteen-year-old was about to become another drowning victim.

From her back porch, Schmaltz charged through her home, ran out to the front yard, and, upon reaching the shore, kicked off her shoes and flung off her belt before diving into the water. She swam underwater for several seconds, traveling about forty feet, and found Willard Craig, who had been screaming and searching for his friend, Andrew Weiskerger, also fifteen.

Schmaltz tried to get Craig to show her where Weiskerger went down, but he couldn't figure it out, and he was losing his strength. Schmaltz ordered him to go to the shore, and she swam underwater. She found Weiskerger at the lake bottom, covered in weeds, eight-feet deep, and unconscious.

Schmaltz freed the boy and brought him to the shore. A doctor who lived nearby showed up and gave Weiskerger mouth-to-mouth resuscitation and brought him back to life. Andrew had a sore back the next day, but otherwise, thanks to Schmaltz, he got to have a future, serving in World War II and becoming a grandfather. He died in 1994. Schmaltz was around long enough to become a great-great-grandmother. She passed away in 2016, at the age of ninety-eight.

New York

Harold Harger, a homeowner in Dansville (100°F), learned why tin roofs, popular in the 1800s, were going out of fashion. The tin roof became so hot that it caught fire, and his entire house burned down.

At least Harger wasn't injured. There was a lot of dying going on today. A fourteen-year-old Black girl from Buffalo drowned in Lake Erie. In the same city, a sixty-four-year-old man visiting his daughter with his wife decided to drive around for some fresh air. His wife found him in the car, still at the front of the house, slumped over in the driver's seat.

Three people in Rochester died, including Aquilino Donato, a WPA workman, who was trying to get fresh air standing at his third-floor window. Whether he passed out and fell or lost his balance was up for dispute.

In Brooklyn, the heat was blamed for a suicide. In Dobbs Ferry, Jennie Eustace was also dubbed a heat victim. She was a stage actress for over forty years, acting in once-popular plays such as *Jim the Penman*, *Sunlight and Shadow*, and *Alabama*. She also played the Queen in *Hamlet*. Eustace was sixty-nine years old and living in a nursing home, but until the heat wave, had been getting along okay.

Across New York City, thirty-eight city dwellers were erased from existence, and 115 people were taken to hospitals. There were ten drownings. New York City's official temperature was 100, but thermometers were taken to the streets, where temperatures ranged from 105 to 111 degrees. At 2 P.M. Mayor Fiorello H. La Guardia said that city employees, except for police officers and firefighters, should go home for the rest of the day. He ordered the swimming pools to be open until midnight and finally decided people could sleep in the parks without fear of arrest. Policemen sent to turn off fire hydrants, it was said, traveled to their destinations slowly. It was so hot that a judge in New York City ordered male jurors to take off their coats and open the necks of their shirts.

Two thousand women were employed on a sewing project run by the WPA, and when workers stood in line to get their employment checks, forty women passed out. Later, after the sewing machines began operating and the machines made the rooms even hotter, more women collapsed. Doctors, police, and ambulance drivers descended on the building; six women were taken to St. Vincent's Hospital; everybody else was ordered to go home.

It was also for a lot of New Yorkers, simply a strange and surreal day:

- Antonio Noa, twenty-six years old, was dragged into court for opening a hydrant near Lexington Avenue at 12:30 A.M. He had help but was the only one caught. He was charged with disorderly conduct and told if he couldn't raise $250 (he could not), he would have to stay in a jail cell for the next few days until he was sentenced. Noa couldn't convincingly claim the authorities had the wrong man: he was still wearing his bathing suit.

- Two bridges over the Harlem River were opened to let ships go through. But the metal expanded four feet in the heat and couldn't be closed, jamming traffic. The same thing happened to the Lincoln Highway bridge over the Hackensack River in Jersey City and bridges across the country.
- In Brooklyn, a horse fainted at Washington and Atlantic Avenues. Police officers formed what *The New York Times* referred to as a bucket brigade, passing containers of water to each other, until the final officer doused and eventually revived the horse.

New Jersey

In Demarest, New Jersey, a 102-year-old woman, Louisa Marie Hale, sat at her son and daughter-in-law's house with an electric fan blowing on her instead of celebrating her birthday. The year before, they had a lawn party. But with the heat, and Hale's health in decline, they weren't about to chance a celebration.

Just about everything on the social calendar was canceled. Nationwide, colleges nixed summer classes or held classes outside under shady trees. Summer camps were delayed until slightly cooler weather. Parties, parades, picnics, dances, family reunions, class reunions, and virtually every social event imaginable were being scrubbed. Couples put off getting their marriage licenses—and requests for divorces went up. Lodge meetings were rescheduled, golf outings were postponed, and church attendance dropped. If you didn't *have* to do something, you often didn't.

An editor at the *Grant County Herald*, the Lancaster, Wisconsin, newspaper, wrote a society column in a few days that said it all: "Because of the hot weather the past week, the social column must necessarily be brief." She also noted that, especially with June being over, there were no weddings to write about and asked readers to "be patient, and in a short time, the old column will look as hale and hearty as ever."

The one social function not being put off was the funeral. Those sad and sweaty affairs were happening at great frequency. One elderly woman from southern Indiana was said to have been a regular presence whenever there was a chance to attend a funeral. In mid-July, a neighbor asked her about it, and the elderly woman said, "Yes, I went, but the weather was just too hot for me to enjoy it."

In a Camden, New Jersey, courthouse, a judge weighed in on the case of two teenage boys fighting over a dime. One dropped it, the other picked it up, and fists started flying. In the courthouse, one of the boys said that he wouldn't have hit his friend, but he needed the dime.

An Associated Press reporter captured the ensuing dialogue.

"What was the dime for?" the judge asked.

"So I could go swimming," one of the boys said.

"Well, here's a dime for you," said the prosecutor.

"How about me?" the other teenager asked.

"Sure," said the prosecutor, fishing another dime from his pockets.

"You are sentenced to go swimming together," said the judge.

"Hey, about us?" said some of the spectators.

"Next case," said the judge, wiping his brow.

Charles Kimble went for a walk, and his daughter called the police. It was 102 degrees, and Kimble had been gone for three hours. Plus, Mr. Kimble was ninety-nine years old.

But no need to worry. Safe and sound, Kimble, a Civil War veteran, returned from his two-mile stroll into downtown Fort Lee. He went there, he said, "to see how things looked." And he snapped to a reporter, "No need to kick up a fuss. I'm not ten years old. I'm old enough to take care of myself."

Indeed, Kimble stuck around for another three years. But his daughter wasn't wrong to be concerned. Three members of New Jersey's National Guard fainted in a parade today, and twenty-one people died from the heat, including a nine-month-old and a very famous sixty-three-year-old: Joe Humphreys.

Humphreys may barely be remembered today, but he was one of the country's most popular prize fight announcers, even turning up in a handful of silent films during the 1920s. For forty-six years, ever since his big break at a boxing tournament in 1890, Humphreys gave audiences blow-by-blow accounts between the sport's winners and losers. He had, by some accounts, a voice like a foghorn. When Madison Square Garden introduced the revolutionary technology called a microphone, Humphreys wasn't interested. He didn't need one.

The last several years, Humphreys had battled health issues, and was already ill when the temperature in Fairhaven climbed to 106 degrees. But he was planning his return to announcing fights. The heat, doctors said, sped up the inevitable. This afternoon, Joe Humphreys finally went down for the count.

26

JULY 11

Monkeys and a Mad Bomber

Today's Death Toll: 400+
Total Death Toll: 2,400+

A political cartoon that ran in papers today featured a baby and mother bird in a nest watching a man in a suit and a straw hat, shuffling along under a hot sun. The birds offered some commentary.

Baby bird: "What is a man, momma?"

Momma bird: "Man is a very remarkable animal, which invents automobiles and cooling systems and all kinds of complicated gadgets to make life more comfortable."

Baby bird: "Oh—is that what makes the man look so weary, Momma?"

Momma bird: "Oh, no. That man looks weary on account of he is too dumb to take off his hat and coat and collar, which are very uncomfortable."

The cartoonist wasn't wrong. American society was having an impromptu national discussion about what was appropriate to wear in a heat wave. In not quite a week, there would be a headline in the *Des Moines Tribune* on the front page blaring, "Wear Little Clothing If You Like—It's Legal," and right underneath, the reassuring banner "There's No Law Against Bathing Suits or Shorts Downtown."

Nobody had a byline for the article, which was common for the era, but the writer explained that the law in Des Moines was open-minded when it came to wardrobe choices. "There is, of course, the law forbidding indecent exposure," the article stated, "but that still leaves the way wide open for more comfortable fashions in clothing if anyone wishes to start setting them. It appears to be legal, for instance, if your stenographer wants to come to work in a bathing suit, even one of the skimpiest kind. If she wears shorts, too, it's quite all right with the police. Or if a man desires to wear shorts, that's all right. In fact, the attorneys see no legal reason that a man could not go about his daily work, clad only in bathing trunks if he wishes to. In other words, just about anything permissible on an Iowa beach or at an Iowa swimming pool is permissible anywhere, so just make it easy on yourself. But watch out for sunburn."

But what flew in Iowa might not fly in New York. Yesterday, a city judge in Yonkers, New York, found a man and woman, both in their mid-twenties and reporters for the *New York Daily News*, guilty of wearing shorts in public a month earlier. He fined them each $10, which would be around $220 today. But the judge was sympathetic to their cause and suspended the fines.

Rose O'Gorman and William Matthias appealed that decision. They thought it was a dumb law begging to be overturned. That's why in June, O'Gorman and Matthias went hiking in shorts and then ambled into the streets of Yonkers, knowing they'd likely be arrested for challenging the city's anti-shorts ban. It took until 1937 for the legal process to play out, but New York's Court of Appeals sided with O'Gorman and Matthias. So if you live in Yonkers and have always enjoyed wearing shorts, you know who to thank.

On the other hand, New York City, at least in some areas, had no issues with shorts. A Hope, Arkansas, newspaper columnist marveled in July 24 column about recently being in New York City and seeing "three brave men sauntering 42nd street in shorts, sleeveless shirts and moccasins. There were no complaints." Times Square has always been ahead of the times.

A Cleveland, Ohio, safety director was asked what he thought about women wearing shorts, given the commotion in New York. "They can wear all the shorts they want," said Eliot Ness, who was world-famous for having helped to bring down Al Capone, now spending his days in Alcatraz.

There were other law enforcement officials who were supportive of the idea of people wearing less clothing, or cooler clothing. C. W. Wood, a policeman interviewed by the *Charlotte News* in a July 2, 1936, article, snapped, "I wish the guy who designed these woolen uniforms had to wear them."

But generally, if you dressed casually in public in 1936, you were nervous about the consequences. In Ann Arbor, Michigan, Robert Elbel Jr., who owned Elbel & Co., a family business that had sold pianos since 1852 and also offered radios and other appliances, told his four male clerks that they could wear short pants in his store until the heat subsided. Smart decision; trousers during this time were generally made of wool.

"I was fearful of the reaction of the public," Elbel admitted to the *Detroit Free Press*. "But it has been received as a grand idea. If the hot weather continues, I predict other stores in Ann Arbor and other places will fall in line."

In Kingston, Ontario, a perspiring young man came to a Queen's University dance with his coat off, wearing a shirt and suspenders, which was considered rather uncouth. Other young men approved, however, and removed their coats; soon after, the university instituted a ban on suspenders being visible. The coats were required to go back on.

In New Jersey, the law and social mores were also rigid. In early July, a Jersey City officer on patrol, Edward Higgins, spotted a resident, Walter Konicski, fifty-one, trudging through Van Vorst Park at 5:30 A.M. with pant legs rolled up. He was also in bare feet.

According to one account, their exchange went like this:

> **Higgins:** "Hey, you can't do that."
> **Konicski:** "Why not?"
> **Higgins:** "Well, it don't look right."
> **Konicski:** "But there's nobody to see it."

With Konicski at his side, Higgins telephoned the desk sergeant to ask what should be done about this pant-leg and bare-feet situation. The sergeant recommended not arresting Konicski but suggested inquiring with the police captain for guidance. The captain recommended that William McGovern, the commissioner of the Jersey City's Department of Parks and Public Properties, be roped in. That led to a conversation with Konicski and McGovern. Konicski explained that he sometimes got anxious, and he remembered as a little boy, in his native Poland, padding around barefoot after cows through the cool, dewy grass. He was trying to recreate that feeling in the park, two blocks from his house, and it kind of worked. He felt less anxious, and he figured that nobody was around at 5 A.M. to see him.

McGovern agreed that Konicski should be allowed to go barefoot in the park. He issued a special permit stating that he was allowed to do so between 5 A.M. to 5:30 A.M.

People who lived in the countryside thought the whole episode was a little kooky. "The ways of the metropolitan area are strange," a writer for *The Marion Star* concluded. "In Ohio, of course, everyone walks in the dew almost at will—well, nearly everyone would like to walk bare foot in the dew, wouldn't you?"

On July 20, Dave Smith, a sixty-five-year-old gardener, strolled through East Orange, New Jersey, in the early morning hours, wearing an athletic undershirt and bright blue underwear shorts. He was also swigging a bottle of soda pop. After weeks of being in the 100s, 90s, and 80s, he was dressing for the weather.

But a cop saw him. Smith was dragged to police headquarters and charged with public intoxication, even though he was drinking soda. Smith was displeased, telling Gerald Duncan, reporter with the *New York Daily News*: "If these young people can wear shorts, why the hell can't I or any older person who wants a little relief from the heat?"

Smith continued, "The kids of East Orange have been going around for a couple years in shorts, and nobody interferes. I don't mind telling you, I've been a little envious, especially on some of the hot days we've had. Is there an age limit on shorts? I'll take this case to the highest court in the land to get an answer to that."

That may have been mere talk. There does not appear to be a court case called *Smith v. United States* that revolved around wearing underwear and calling them shorts during a heat wave.

The debate over whether to shed some clothing was silly, considering that this had turned into a life-and-death issue. But for generations, people imprisoned themselves under layers of clothing, no matter what the weather. Women wore corsets; men wore suits and sometimes also a trench coat. From the neck to the toes, people were bundled up, but this summer, that was subtly changing. Fashion experts suggested men wear belts instead of suspenders, since belts did the job while suspenders added another partial layer of clothing. Sandals for men and women were selling well, but they were still frowned upon if you wore them to the wrong place, like a store. Stick to the beach.

Women still wore gloves in the heat, and men and women wore hats. But some influencers of the era were encouraging the public to give genders a break with all the social mores, at least on hot days. Today, the Associated Press reported that American fashion designer Herman Patrick Tappé said men should be using paper fans. Women wielded them, but it was considered unmasculine for a man to in most situations. "Only at a ball game when a man is in shirt sleeves is it considered proper for a man to use a fan. We are cursed with such nonsense," Tappé said. "Why not twirl a fan whether the weather is hot?" Tappé, who was sixty but far ahead of the times for a man his age, also pointed out that he was one of the first men in America to wear a wristwatch. He wore one when the rest of society called it "sissified."

Fearing what society would think was possibly why backless shirts for men were not the rage after they debuted, reportedly for the first time, on July 5, 1936, at a hotel in West End, New Jersey. The thinking was that policemen, clerks, laborers, or even bank executives might wear them, especially in hot weather. A thin band from the collar to the small of the back connected with a band around the waist.

It did not catch on. Still hasn't. But society was thinking long and hard about easing up some of the fashion rules that kept men and women passing out in the heat.

Ohio

If you were to worry about the strange and awful ways you could die, you would probably not have on your bingo card "Be overcome by heat, topple into a vat of sewage, and drown." But that happened to a thirty-five-year-old sewage disposal plant employee in Akron (100°F).

Cleveland (99°F) came through most of the heat wave in decent shape, thanks to those Lake Erie winds, but this was not a good day. Nine people met their end under the sun, one of them forty-eight-year-old John Stacy, who collapsed playing golf at the Ridgewood Country Club. "Stacy was an outstanding Ridgewood golfer," the *Cleveland Plain Dealer* helpfully noted when reporting his death, as if that kind of made everything all right.

Toledo (101°F) suffered twelve heat deaths. In Fremont (100°F), police officer Fred Strohl smelled smoke. His pants were on fire. More than three dozen matches that he had stuffed in one of his pockets had burst into flames. That he wasn't badly burned was probably because his pants were soaked with sweat.

This type of thing had happened before and continued. In a few days, in Pittsburgh, a celluloid fountain pen, a celluloid card case, and a comb rubbed together, creating friction and fire in a man's hot coat pocket; later in the month, a Hot Springs, South Dakota, resident stamped out his problem in the nick of time: the sun ignited eyeglasses in the pocket of his shirt.

Indiana

While many social engagements were canceled, some people held them anyway, perhaps to their everlasting dismay. In La Porte (102°F), Adelbert Frantz, a sixty-one-year-old grocer from Mishawaka, Indiana, showed up as a guest to a wedding reception alive—and left dead. Frantz wasn't the only one.

There was at least one heat death today each in the cities of Terre Haute, Washington, Vincennes, Kokomo, Columbia City, Jonesboro, Connersville, Logansport, and Elkhart. Two babies, already ill with pneumonia, died at an orphanage in Mishawaka. In Indianapolis, three adults died. That was also where two policemen were making rounds on their motorcycles when they heard a report on their radio that a squirrel had gone mad, biting a man and a boy. This was, it was believed, the same squirrel that terrorized the same neighborhood the night before. There was even a report that the squirrel attacked a cat. It may have not been a battle for the ages, but the officers eventually hunted the squirrel down.

The heat was also blamed by some newspapers for a pet monkey in Evansville going berserk. Granted, maybe he would have escaped regardless, but the heat may have made the animal more desperate to flee. Yesterday, it was 99 degrees. Today, the temperature hit 105, and somehow, Mike, a fifteen-year-old rhesus monkey, got out of his cage.

Of all people, Clem Kevekordes should have known better than to have a pet monkey. For starters, two years ago, Mike escaped and severely bit and clawed a grocer named Arthur Sanders. Sanders was now in the midst of suing Evansville for $3,000 in damages. Second, Mr. Kevekordes was the superintendent of the local zoo.

Still, while today it would be unthinkable for a zoo superintendent to have a monkey as a pet, this was an era in which it wasn't considered all that unusual or irresponsible. In fact, pet stores sold them, amusement parks and circuses often had them, and numerous universities and hospitals kept them for experimentation. Because of that, monkeys escaping owners was a common occurrence. If you were a police officer in 1936, pursuing a monkey was practically part of the job description. Harvard had two monkeys escape a few months earlier. Later in the summer, two monkey escapees from a carnival in Warren, Ohio, tied up downtown traffic for two hours because motorists were watching the police try to get the animals out of a tree.

Pet monkeys, most frequently rhesus monkeys or sometimes chimpanzees, were always on the lam. Monkeys would flee the steamer ships bringing them into the country, and so they'd race around the vessel or port. St. Paul, Minnesota, was just twenty-four hours away from having a monkey—also named Mike—break out of their zoo. That Mike roamed around St. Paul for at least a week, stealing lunches from WPA workers in the park.

This particular Mike, the one in Evansville, Indiana, like any normal monkey, ran for his newfound freedom, or more accurately, swung for it. Bounding from tree to tree, Mike was in his element while neighborhood dogs barked, alerting interested and excited children, who gathered to watch. It was Mike's first chance to be a regular monkey in some time. Eight years earlier, he was part of a vaudeville act, where he was known as the world's only high-diving monkey. If his act was like all the other world's only high-diving monkey acts, Mike ascended a tall ladder and jumped into a net.

Soon, four police officers gave chase, with scores of neighborhood children on bicycles following behind. The police had orders to capture the primate alive, but that was easier said than done. Block after block, under the punishing sun, the officers quickly became weary of the pursuit.

Kevekordes circled back to the zoo and brought with him a female monkey named Josie, who Mike was fond of. With her help, Kevekordes lured Mike from the trees into his car. But once Mike was back in the vehicle, he attacked Josie, slightly wounding her, and fled again through an open car window. (Kevekordes evidently wasn't about to drive home with two monkeys with the windows closed in an unair-conditioned car.)

The officers continued lumbering after the monkey, but it began to dawn on Kevekordes that they were never going to catch his pet, and even if they did, who was to say this wouldn't happen again, and maybe a neighborhood child would get hurt? That was the rationale he gave after telling the police they should shoot to kill, but it also may be that the zookeeper's patience for continuing the chase in the heat was wearing thin.

But to shoot Mike, they had to get a good shot. One of the officers cornered Mike in an alley, or so he thought. Mike, teeth bared, rushed for him. The officer, either unarmed or with no time to shoot, ran for his squad car's front door, which was locked. Racing around to the passenger side, it was unlocked, and he scrambled into the vehicle just before Mike attacked. Then a police dog chased Mike back into the alley. Another officer took his shot.

After Mike went down, Kevekordes wept over the body. "Mike wasn't bad. He was just scared," Kevekordes said.

Kevekordes purportedly loved animals, but his track record for taking good care of them was shaky. Earlier in the year, a lion cub at the zoo was mysteriously poisoned, and the year before, three bears walked over a frozen moat and climbed out of their enclosure. Years later, there would be at least one more escape into Evansville by one of Kevekordes's monkeys. By then, he owned both a dog kennel and a pet store (which sold monkeys). He was hastily terminated from the zoo in 1942, but not for mistreating animals. Details are scant, but Kevekordes pled guilty to assaulting an eight-year-old girl.

In another, poorer part of Evansville, Herschel Reeves, an eleven-year-old Black boy, went swimming. Unfortunately, the Booker T. Washington pool—the one place Black families were allowed to swim—was closed when Herschel decided to take a dip. Herschel, the son of a mill worker, scaled the fence and went into the water, about to become another cautionary tale.

Somebody saw Herschel climb over the fence and started to fret. Garland Johnson was asked to fetch the lad. Johnson, an eighteen-year-old who was also Black, was the perfect person for this assignment. He worked for the CCC and was a certified lifeguard. He went to the pool and spotted Reeves under the water. The boy wasn't moving.

Johnson hauled him out of the water and started artificial respiration. The police were called and showed up within ten minutes. An inhalator that the city had just purchased was brought out, and everybody went to work. After about five minutes, Herschel was breathing again. He was weeks away from his twelfth birthday. Thanks to Johnson, Herschel Reeves would someday see his seventy-sixth.

Michigan

In northern Michigan, where it was over 100 degrees, thousands of firefighters, CCC workers, lumber camp employees, and residents of nearby towns battled 2,500 acres that were on fire in Hiawatha Forest. In Mio, a town located in the northern part of the bottom half of Michigan, thirty separate fires were reported.

Another senseless murder was blamed for the heat in Bancroft, which had been in the high 90s. Victor Yanson killed his wife, Elizabeth. It likely occurred at 4 A.M.; a neighbor heard three shots but thought somebody was shooting at a noisy owl. After Victor murdered his sleeping spouse, he walked to the other side of the bed, lay down beside her, and shot himself. In his twisted mind, maybe he thought that it was a romantic gesture.

Friends discussing the murder-suicide suggested that Victor might have been driven mad by the heat, but he also had money and health issues. Lloyd Yanson, their adult son, was distraught. "Dad couldn't have killed my mother," he insisted. Still, he wasn't entirely surprised, since he admitted, "But he had treated her like a dog."

North Dakota

Thorvald and Stella Dihle, residents of Columbus (101°F), had a swim with two of their youngest children.

The family went to a dam on the edge of a creek. While the parents walked, their boys, Allan and Donald, eight and six, ran for the creek but slipped on clay and fell into deep water. Stella jumped in after them but was soon drowning with her sons. When she woke on dry land, an unsettling moment must have turned into abject horror as she realized she was all alone—no kids, no Thorvald—and had to piece together what happened after she lost consciousness.

California

Lambert Schnaible was on vacation. The twelve-year-old's parents had brought him to Lodi, to stay with a relative and escape the heat in South Dakota, where the high temperature had been over 100 degrees for days. They would have been better off staying put. That night, Lambert rode his bicycle near the town of Victor without a bicycle lamp.

After a car hit Lambert, the aghast driver took the boy to the hospital, but there was nothing anyone could do. It was one of many sad stories in which, no, the heat wasn't responsible for a death, and yet, yes, it was.

Wisconsin

The Genrich family—George, Marguerite, and their twenty-year-old son, George Jr.—began milking their six cows on their farm in Rosendale at the crack of dawn, since it was cooler. Unfortunately, a storm came in, and at 6:15 A.M., lightning struck the barn's silo, shaking the building, killing the five cows, and knocking the family unconscious. But once they woke up, they were all in good spirits, although Marguerite had the unpleasant experience of realizing a dead cow was on her leg.

Missouri

Eight citizens in St. Louis (102.8°F) took their final bow today and stepped off the stage of life. St. Louis's City Hospital, from sunrise to sunset, had lines of patients on rolling stretchers, waiting for an ice bath. A saloon owner set out buckets and pots and pans on the floor; his tar roof was dripping through the ceiling. St. Louis's night was miserable, too: at 11 P.M., it was 94 degrees.

In Joplin (90°F), Lloyd Campbell, a band director, led a drum and bugle corps at a state competition at a Veterans of Foreign Wars (VFW) stadium. They already had a rough go of things; at a parade yesterday, a drummer fainted. But now, everything was smooth sailing. Until Campbell collapsed.

Campbell was attired in full marching band uniform, including a wool flannel coat and a blue trench helmet.

Another musician took Campbell's place. After the performance, two drummers, standing in the shade, blacked out. An ambulance was called, but all three men decided to recover in their hotel. At the same competition, a women's auxiliary drill team finished their performance, and soon after, in the hotel lobby, most of the nine members fainted. They, too, were all revived. Marching band musicians are a hardy breed.

Iowa

It was over 100 degrees in Des Moines, but the low humidity helped reduce deaths. Still, one person died in Decorah, and a Canadian bishop's wife, on a road trip with her husband, suffered a fatal sunstroke in Cedar Falls. In Maquoketa, the heat took out George Wolfe, a resident of the Jackson County Poor Farm. Wolfe had no known relatives. He outlived them all, since he was 140 years old.

Actually, Wolfe only *said* he was 140 years old. The head of the Poor Farm later clarified that Wolfe was ninety and, alas, not a marvel of nature.

In Waterloo (106°F), there was a drowning and three deaths, and there was almost a fourth: James Caley, a fifty-year-old plumber, who finished work and started walking home or perhaps to the streetcar. Actually, nobody was sure where Caley was going, including Caley. In a daze, he staggered onto the road in front of an approaching car. Bystanders waiting for the streetcar yanked Caley out of the vehicle's path and took him to a hospital. Caley had an internal temperature of 107 degrees. He was swiftly ushered to a lifesaving ice bath.

Nebraska

"The situation is more critical than I can describe," declared Gov. Walter Welford of North Dakota as he appealed to President Roosevelt to hasten aid on a day when there were at least three heat deaths, including a two-month-old boy. Welford forwarded to Roosevelt a suggestion for Deputy WPA Administrator Aubrey Williams that half a million dollars be allocated to his state at once. Economically, ranchers and farmers were being crushed. Corn crops, oats, barley, potatoes—just about anything you could grow—were being wiped out, due to the heat and lack of rain.

And on this day, according to the Associated Press, a woman—nobody ever learned her name—was severely addled by the heat. She got off a bus in Nebraska City (105°F) but insisted that she was in Omaha. She proceeded to a hotel, where she took keys without permission and entered an empty room. A little later, she left via the fire escape, naked, and walked to a nearby apartment, knocking on doors and asking for "a drink, even water." Later, she was, presumably fully clothed, put on a bus for Omaha.

Wyoming

If only Medicine Bow Peak in the Medicine Bow National Forest had been more accessible to the rest of the country. At noon it was 32 degrees and an inch of snow was on the ground. Wyoming (and its southern neighbor, Colorado) was one of the few states to endure the summer of 1936 without much of a death toll. Most days, there were no heat deaths, while surrounding states were filling their graveyards with new tenants. It was likely due to the two states' geography, surmised Travis Allen O'Brien, *The Summer of Death*'s on-call weather expert. "The Rockies often produce a 'lee-side low,' a low pressure that develops right along the eastern edge of the Rockies," O'Brien said. "It's possible that these lee-side lows occasionally interrupted the heat dome, which would help abate heatwave conditions."

O'Brien said that according to surface maps from the summer of 1936, lee-side lows appeared multiple times. He says that the occasional downslope flow of air from the mountains may have also helped cool off Wyoming and Colorado.

Virginia

An Abilene railroad employee was zapped in 97-degree heat, another case of a sweaty man working too close to power lines. In the evening, after a long, humid day, a squirrel was spotted in Danville (107°F), appearing as if it was going to pass out, bobbing and weaving on a sidewalk.

New Jersey

Today was a Saturday, and by the end of the weekend, poultry farmers around the state estimated that the heat had taken the lives of ten thousand chickens. Some birds, it was said, were so ravaged by the sun that, aside from the feathers, they almost looked like fully cooked, roasted chickens.

For any chickens still alive, it was recommended that farmers stick their heads into cold water.

The humans weren't faring much better. A fifty-eight-year-old wiredrawer (he made wire) died at a factory in Trenton (100°F), and the heat took down Emma Zimmermann, a resident of East Rutherford.

Zimmermann was a century old, celebrating her birthday last February 21. Upon her death, *The New York Times* reported: "Pronounced in splendid physical condition when she was 100, doctors said Mrs. Zimmermann probably had ten more years of life before her."

Pennsylvania

Cities saw temperatures hit 100-plus degrees, and predictably, there were deaths. In Central City. In Altoona. In Allentown. Three in Harrisburg. And John Brown, twenty years old, a Sunnyside resident and the father of a three-month-old, became a cautionary tale. Brown visited his uncle, who had a cottage near the water. It was in the mid-90s, and Brown couldn't swim. So he floated in the middle of Conestoga Creek on an inflated inner tube. It was a fine plan—until the tube started to lose air.

North Carolina

In Raleigh (93°F), two timber wolves died at North Carolina State College (now North Carolina State University). They were the mascots of the football team, the Wolfpack. The wolves, captured in West Virginia and given to the student body in the spring, were doing well until the heat wave. Minnesota government officials volunteered to give the college two of their wolves, and North Carolina State accepted, but it was decided they would stay put until the heat wave concluded.

Minnesota

It wasn't as if Minnesota was a comfortable paradise. There were nineteen heat victims today, including Alice Masheter, a sixty-nine-year-old Minneapolis nun who died serving dinner to residents at a nursing home.

There were also seven drownings, including four family members from the Sybrandt family in Rush City (106°F). Duane Sybrandt, a five-year-old, was in the St. Croix River when the current started to carry him away. His twenty-one-year-old sister, Blythe, rushed into the water to save him, but her layers of clothing weighed her down and she began screaming. Her older brothers, Jerry, sixteen, and Dallas, twenty-seven, charged after her, but they couldn't swim.

New York

New York City was a hellscape, according to Clifford Langford-Baker. The forty-four-year-old newspaper scribe had lived here for the last thirteen years. His day job was reporting and writing a column for *The Montreal Star* called "New York in Review." Langford-Baker was not a fan of the hot weather, which was unfortunate for him but fortunate for his readers.

"The subway is something Dante forgot to include in the Inferno," Langford-Baker complained in a column that ran today. "The fans are on in the cars, but they do not make much difference. They only circulate hot air and blow it into your face. Men and women are in various stages of greasiness. Many of the former, those of the lower but more sensible order, are coatless. The fat ones mop their brows constantly."

According to Langford-Baker, being a New Yorker was currently a miserable existence: "You know that there will probably be no let-up for at least forty-eight hours, no comfort in sleep, no joy in living. In company with six million other New Yorkers, you wonder why you are there at all when there are so many other places in the world. There isn't any answer."

Later in the day, in a syndicated article that ran in the *Evening Express*, a British paper, Langford-Baker wrote, "In the great tenement districts conditions defy description. More than 100,000 people spent the night on mattresses thrown on the iron fire escapes of these huge dwellings. Another 100,000 slept on the beaches and in the parks of New York."

Langford-Baker went onto to say that "the damage throughout the country from drought, heat fires and associated causes is mounting up at the rate of 1,000,000 dollars an hour." But mostly he described the public's daily life: "Grocery stores and restaurants are doing very little business. On the other hand, soda fountains and ice cream parlors are doing a roaring business in cooling drinks and ices. The minimum of clothing is being worn. Coats have not been seen for days. In offices and even the law courts, shirt sleeves are the garb of the day. A water shortage threatens in New York. Householders have been warned to curtail the use of water, but little attention is paid to this."

Speaking of water, Langford-Baker suggested children were the only residents having a decent time: "In many parts of New York, children, wearing swimming suits, unscrewed fire hydrants released a powerful rush of water, and danced gleefully under these impromptu showers while their sweltering elders looked on with envy."

Another well-known columnist of the day also wrote about the heat wave in New York City, although Ed Sullivan, the future TV variety host, tackled it in a comically exaggerated manner. Sullivan described waking up and having "staggered" to a cold shower and then of walking "out of the house and into the street, where people were falling like tenpins." He added, "Unfortunately, I did not recognize any people I disliked, so carried on, walking in and out between the bodies littering the sidewalks."

He was kidding and not kidding. Today, throughout the state, there were at least another thirty-eight heat victims.

Sullivan also wrote that the Paramount Theater manager scolded him and other "refugees from the heat" to move away from the front doors, where air-conditioning could be felt. "Get out of here," the manager said to one aristocratic-looking gentleman. "You've been standing here for two days. Give somebody else a chance."

Georgia

The entire state was unbearable. In Blakely, the high hit 106. Still, there were few, if any, heat deaths today. Georgians were just extremely uncomfortable. "The heat wave here will continue in full force, there being no immediate relief in sight," said George Mindling, head of the Atlanta Weather Bureau.

Mindling was quite a character, one of several weather forecasters of the time who were creating a template for future offbeat, comic TV meteorologists to follow, like Willard Scott and Al Roker. The day before, when it was 100 degrees in Atlanta, reporters located Mindling in his front lawn, attired in a bathing suit, sitting down in a pool of water he created from his garden hose. "No relief in sight, boys," he said. "But why not try this?"

The fifty-four-year-old, who lived to be ninety-five, had an interest in writing poetry, often about the weather. In late July, Mindling wrote:

The Weather molds the life of man;
Has done so since the world began.
It sends the water down the rivers;
Makes Springtime floods and wintry shivers
White torrid heat upsets the livers.

Probably no surprise that he was better known for his weather forecasts.

Ontario

In Sarnia, neighbors feared the worst when they heard five loud gunshots from a liquor store. But the noise was alcohol bottles exploding from the heat. It was as high as 108 in some parts of Ontario, but the obituary pages in the *Toronto Star* really told the story of the heat wave in Canada. On July 9, a Thursday, there were thirty-two obituaries in the paper. Friday, there were eighty-four. Today, there were 156.

Six Native Canadians perished on reservations. A forty-five-year-old road crew worker died in Niagara Falls, digging a ditch in 110-degree weather. In Toronto, Percy Wray, a fifty-five-year-old dishwasher, left his shift at a café on Queen Street, disoriented. He went to his neighbors, believing he was at his boarding house. They directed him to where he lived. Wray staggered to his bed and never woke up.

In one Toronto house, Susan Wilson, sixty-seven, took care of her eighty-three-year-old brother-in-law, William Harding, bedridden and ill from the heat. But caring for Harding wore Wilson out. She died this afternoon, and he died the next morning.

Reginald Sparkes, a wealthy Toronto dog breeder and kennel owner, spent the day trying to save his dog. This was no ordinary dog. This was Bunjie, a bulldog who won Best in Show last March. The fifty-four-pound canine beat 772 other thoroughbreds, going against competitors from Canada, England, and the United States, and was now valued at $10,000. Despite having a kennel equipped with electric fans, he became ill the night before, and Sparkes, who traveled everywhere with Bunjie, leaped into action, probably more invested in his dog's health than his worth. He hired veterinarians to take care of Bunjie, who was soon packed in ice. They also administered oxygen. Sparkes did everything he could think of to save Bunjie, but it wasn't enough. His bark was stilled today.

Another dog, a six-year-old beagle named Friday and known as "Toronto's fattest dog," had better luck. For weeks, Friday, weighing just under a hundred pounds, lay in some shade of the house and remained there throughout much of the heat wave, according to his owner, Maude Grigg. She may sound like Toronto's worst pet owner due to his weight, but Friday was dognapped from her four years earlier, experimented on by a lab, and given glycerin injections. The Toronto Humane Society got involved and was able to return Friday to Mrs. Grigg.

"When the heat wave was here, I thought he would die for certain," Grigg told a reporter. "We believed it would overtax his heart, and he would pass out, but as soon as it began to get really warm, he seemed to realize it and went outside and crawled away under the veranda where it is cool. He never did this before."

Friday emerged from his shady spot once there was some rain. "Then he went outside and just stood there getting wet all over," Grigg said.

Manitoba

Robert Richmond, a night watchman at the Crescent Creamery, a dairy plant in Winnipeg, dodged the heat by going into the cooling room, where the temperature was seven degrees below zero. Richmond overcompensated and stayed in the room for far too long. When he left and returned to the land of the sweltering, his ears were frozen.

National media, knowing a good story when they read it, quickly picked up the short, quirky news item and, for the rest of the summer, editors would run the story, never following up on how the poor guy was doing. Even into October, papers were reporting on Robert Richmond, night watchman who hilariously froze his ears during a heat wave.

Of course, weird incongruities were bound to happen. Months earlier, on February 8, in Davenport, Iowa, where it was -11 degrees, Elmer Rhodes, a janitor, collapsed from the heat. He was indoors, repairing a boiler.

Washington, DC

After two days of over 100-degree heat and with today's high hitting 99 degrees, the US Weather Bureau on M Street decided the temperatures were too dangerous for the entire staff to work. Most people were sent home—leaving just a few people to answer the hundreds of calls from people wanting to know how hot it was.

Illinois

Charles Morgan, Bloomington's diarist-carpenter, wrote about living with 109-degree heat: "Clear and hot again this morning. And indications of another torrid day. A blazing sun makes existing a torture. I make my way uptown these days, very cautiously, avoiding as much as possible the blistering heat of the sun's scorching rays."

Morgan had reason to be careful. "Three fatal heat prostrations occurred yesterday in this vicinity," he wrote.

It was miserable everywhere.

- In Chicago (97°F), pools were so crowded that children were required to swim in half-hour shifts to give everyone a chance to cool off. In North Chicago, a parade went on despite the heat; four marines and three sailors collapsed.
- An eighteen-year-old woman in Chicago, frolicking in a fire hydrant's water, slipped and fell, fracturing her skull.
- In Kewanee (111°F), Kenneth Downs, twenty-nine years old, tried to cool off with an ice cream cone. He died before finishing it.

Prophetstown's mayor spent most of the day preparing to meet his extortionist and talking to the press about it, though it must have been clear to him that his demented pen pal was never going to appear. Mayor George Brydia was increasingly showing his cards to the press, which meant that if the extortionist was following current events, he knew there was no point in trying to collect his money.

"I slept like a bull moose last night in spite of the heat. All I've done has been to answer phones and hold conferences," the mayor said. "Businessmen have swamped me with requests to take their money and send it to Rockford but not to go myself. Even some of the city officials have demanded that no chance be taken."

But Brydia said he would meet the extortionist. "I want to meet the man who wrote that letter. There has been so much publicity that I doubt he will show up. On the other hand, if he does, we will let circumstances govern our procedure," Brydia said.

In another interview, Brydia said, "What I wish more than anything else is that if this threat writer is fooling, he'd drop a postal card and say that the whole thing is off. This strain is getting me down. Now, understand, I'm not afraid, but the idea of the whole thing, and the heat wave, are beginning to tell."

Brydia now claimed that he never really intended to collect money for the blackmailer, that it was all a ruse to put the extortioner's mind at ease. "When I get to Rockford, the extortionist is going to be a very much disappointed gentleman. He's going to be presented with a very nicely tied package—with nothing in it," Brydia said, who later vowed, "What we're really going to do is give him a box of bricks in it—provided he shows up."

By the end of the day, Brydia was no longer suggesting the mad bomber was a mad genius. Instead, Brydia theorized, he was "probably some lunk who wanted to get a barrel of easy money in a hurry" and suggested the extortioner was likely "'tetched in the head."

Brydia added, "If he doesn't show up, I'm going home. I'm not afraid of him. As a matter of fact, I wish he would show up. I'd like to take one crack at him."

Easy to say, of course, when your plan is to head to the meeting spot with a few of your law enforcement friends. That night, Mayor Brydia drove to Rockford with the sheriff of Whiteside County and a shoebox stuffed full of newspapers tied with easy-to-spot red string, just like the blackmailer asked. The two men joined the sheriff of Winnebago County and dined at a restaurant half a mile from the Rockford public library. Brydia, with two sheriffs in the car, drove past the library several times. They actually ran a little late, arriving a little after 7 P.M. Not surprisingly, the extortionist was nowhere in sight. Even if he did show and then left before Brydia showed up, which seems very doubtful (reporters would have surely noticed), the villain and hero mayor wouldn't have been able to meet. Not inside, anyway.

The library was closed. It shut down three hours earlier than usual, according to a sign explaining that the building emptied at 6 P.M. due to the intense heat.

27

JULY 12

In the Heat of Competition

Today's Death Toll: 400+
Total Death Toll: 2,800+

After what seems to have been a night of deep sleep, Blair Miller, Indianapolis newsstand proprietor, woke on the courthouse lawn. He soon discovered that somebody had cut off the chain of his old-fashioned stem-winder watch, attached to his waistcoat. It was a family heirloom, and now probably being sold on the black market.

Throughout this heat wave, crooks were taking advantage of other people's misery. For instance, throughout the United States and Canada, some families who went outside to sleep returned to their homes to find that they had been burglarized. It's much safer to sneak into a home in the dark of night, after all, if you know that all the tenants are sleeping in the front yard.

In Hammond, Indiana, Joe Haback, a manager of an ice station, was visited by two couples. One of the four customers kept fingering a $5 bill. Haback kept lugging ice into their car, sweating profusely. Once he was finished, somebody asked the exhausted Haback for change for their $5. Haback gave it to them.

After they drove away with their ice, Haback realized he made change for a five-dollar bill that he never received.

And naturally some thievery involved merchandise that would sell well during a summer like this. Yesterday, in Kansas City, Missouri, six electric fans were stolen from St. Francis Xavier Church. In a couple days, in

Fremont, Ohio, three children's bathing suits would be stolen from Stanley Nikonluzikis's clothesline.

It was turning out to be a hell of a summer, though not every state was suffering. *The Palm Beach Post* offered an op-ed on this day, starting off with "While most of the other sections of the United States have suffered from heat waves, drought and other discomforts of the present summer, West Palm Beach and South Florida have enjoyed comfortable weather. True, it has been hot to residents, but not that dry enervating heat. No nights have been too warm to sleep."

Florida's lucky talisman was probably its sea breezes, theorized our weather authority Travis Allen O'Brien: "The air temperatures over Florida are often tied very closely to the temperatures of the surrounding water, and those water temperatures were not as extremely warm as the temperatures in the middle of the continent."

Illinois

In Cook County, where Chicago is located, the morgue was overcrowded for the first time in the staff's memory, worse than even the 1918 influenza pandemic. The morgue had 150 crypts and 200 bodies. It was 97 degrees outside, and surely well over 100 inside the crowded tenement buildings, in the stores, in the restaurant kitchens and at the drycleaners. At a Walgreen drugstore in Chicago—the store wasn't known yet as Walgreens—the heat melted lead connections on pipes of the store's refrigerating plant in the basement. A fire broke out. Sixteen firemen passed out while fighting the blaze.

"Clear and very sultry as usual, all morning," Charles Morgan penned in his diary, writing from Bloomington, adding that the afternoon was a little cloudy, "and maybe slightly cooler, with a southwesterly wind." Still, it wasn't a day for moving around. "We stayed around the rooms all day," he wrote. "Entirely too warm and sultry to venture out anywhere. We all swelter in the terrific heat all day."

You get the idea that Morgan was writing his diary with the idea that somebody, maybe his children, might be interested in pages such as these. He seemed to understand that his community was going through something newsworthy and unprecedented.

"Each day there is some breeze," Morgan wrote. "But very stifling and calm . . . scarcely a breath of air stirs at nighttime. People lay around everywhere in backyards, on porches, in the parks, anywhere to keep cool. Anywhere people are allowed to sleep without molestation. The temperature ran up to 109 degrees today. Lawns and gardens and pastures, all burnt up. For the last two weeks, it has daily run up from 105 to 112 degrees. Several fatalities from the heat now. And increasingly daily. Farmers do their work at night. In order to save what is left."

About 130 miles away, Mayor Brydia was talking tough about the extortioner. "I promised to meet him, and I kept my appointment," he told reporters. "The next move is up to him, but we'll be ready for him if he tries to carry out his plans."

Jane Hubbell, the sixty-six-year-old librarian who shut down the library early, was pestered by journalists who wanted to know if the closing was really influenced by the heat or the extortionist. She admitted nothing, but those close to her said that she didn't like the idea of reporters and townspeople huddling in the reference room, hoping to see Brydia meeting an extortionist.

Brydia said he planned to continue running his grocery business and conducting his mayor's duties as usual. Still, for a few days, Prophetstown was on edge. At some point, Brydia told the press they needed to stop asking him questions about the extortion. "Forget it, boys—it was fun while it lasted," he said.

The extortionist never turned up, but if pressed, Brydia and shopkeepers probably would have admitted that he had been great for business. Just in case the extortioner did strike, retailers hired security guards, and residents armed themselves with newly purchased guns. Insurance agents scattered around the town, selling property insurance and writing out life insurance policies. Tourism was up, too, as thousands of people came to visit Prophetstown, hoping to get a glimpse of a mad bomber intent on turning the city into kindling.

Indiana

In South Bend (105°F), younger male churchgoers attended services without their sportscoats; older churchgoers highly disapproved. But even religious leaders get hot, and that afternoon in Decker (110°F), Reverend Benjamin Eisman, a good swimmer, went to the White River, which was low, and the forty-eight-year-old was wading across it when something went wrong.

Nobody knew what happened, but Eisman shouted for his twenty-year-old son, David, and told him, "Call help quick." Then Eisman sank like a stone. David couldn't find him. Nobody could. A crowd gathered and a search party started. David, distraught, tried to drown himself. Family and friends pulled him out of the water, and he was taken home.

By evening, four hundred people were gathered along the riverbank as a search party of five boats attempted to recover the reverend's body with grappling hooks. The next day, with about a hundred people remaining on the riverbank and after about forty sticks of dynamite, the body floated to the surface.

Seventeen people throughout Indiana drowned or were taken down by the heat today. Late at night in Muncie, when it was still in the 80s, one woman gave up trying to sleep and discovered she had a condition known as blepharitis. Her perspiration formed a temporary glue; she couldn't open her eyelids.

Around the same time, at 10:30 P.M., in the same city, Hubert Gaston, a professional glasscutter and future World War II machine gunner, was at home handling a pistol when a freak accident occurred. The intense heat ignited the pistol's gunpowder, Gaston explained later. That seems logical. At the time of the explosion, it was 89 degrees outside, and earlier it was far hotter. Which is why one moment, Gaston was handling his gun, and the next, he was reeling from powder-burn injuries on his hand and a bullet ripping through his thigh.

Kentucky

Mrs. Eddie Berry, a resident of Covington, couldn't sleep in the heat and took some sleeping powder. It had been 106 earlier in the day and would be 104 degrees the next day, and desperate times call for desperate measures, but this was a terrible decision. Many sleeping powders on the market were highly addictive, and some were extremely dangerous.

After Eddie went to bed, her husband, George, could tell something was horribly wrong—she may have gone into a seizure—and she was spirited to the hospital. Mrs. Berry's doctors guessed that she may have taken more of the sleeping powder than usual, hoping that it would knock her out. It did. She never woke up.

Wisconsin

In Madison (104°F), residents who lived near the Vilas Park Zoo spotted a refugee from Monkey Island in their trees. The police pursued the primate in the afternoon heat but soon gave up. They would try again, they decided, in the early morning the next day.

Minnesota

The high in Minneapolis was 106.2. Hospitals were overrun with heat patients. University Hospital nurses, after their shifts, volunteered at General Hospital and Parkview Sanitorium. Retired nurses were enlisted to take care of patients as well.

In Duluth (102.2°F), a seventy-year-old man died, and his cocker spaniel was found dead in the home the next day. One newspaper said that the dog died of a broken heart. Awww, but unlikely: it was now 106 degrees outside, and inside the home wasn't fit for man or pet. Two other dogs were wearily lying on their deceased master's bed, and the man's family members got them outside.

In the evening, a fifty-three-year-old man decided to sleep on the roof of his house in Minneapolis, and he was lucky enough to only suffer a broken ankle after falling sixteen feet. It was safer to sleep at a park or the beach. A Minneapolis park official estimated that 230,000 residents had been to the state's lake beaches in the last week. A lot of families went there. Housewives on two streets reported forming a "round robin" method of taking care of their kids, where one or two parents would take the kids for a drive in the morning, to cool off. In the afternoon, they'd visit an air-conditioned theater. In the evening, some moms would take the kids to the beach to swim and then sleep on the sand.

Missouri

In the morning, in Seneca (99°F), Christine Wallace, fifty-six years old, was walking to her Baptist church when she collapsed. One can imagine the reverend playing up her devotion to the church when presiding over her funeral several days later. A death like that is eulogy gold.

In St. Louis (104°F), yet another guy decided to sleep on his roof, and after falling forty feet, lived to regret it. Francis O'Brien fell onto brick pavement, fracturing his right hip.

Iowa

Extreme heat—111 degrees in some towns—was blamed for sixteen deaths. There were also close calls—people saved because they were lucky enough to be around others who could swing into action. For instance, one guy collapsed frying fish at an American Legion picnic, and a nine-year-old boy fainted in a wading pool.

Everybody wanted to be near the water. The municipal swimming pool in Traer had seven hundred visitors, which was almost a record, and people came from thirty miles away, which may not sound like a big deal, but these were cars without air-conditioning, and during the pre-interstate days when travel took longer.

Pennsylvania

Another senseless drowning occurred in front of friends and family at the Lehigh River near Bethlehem (97°F). A fourteen-year-old girl lost her life when she spotted a water snake. Frightened, she hurried away into deeper water than she could handle. She wasn't the only one to seek relief in the water and encounter animals. On July 25, a teenager from Boston (80°F) went into the ocean, only to be killed by a shark. Numerous adults and children in states like the Carolinas and Florida cooled themselves off in swimming holes and rivers only to flee when they spotted an alligator (in one terrifying moment, a pet dog was snatched, but at least the boys scampered out of the water), and on August 7, in Pomona, Illinois (92°F), George Beasley, a twenty-year-old, swam at Cedar Lake and was bitten by a copperhead snake. Beasley spent the next couple weeks with his hand and arm swollen to almost twice its size and clinging to life before he recovered.

Michigan

Sixty people in Detroit died today. They expired at home, work, at the hospital, and any old place: a thirty-four-year-old was found in his car, in front of his home, badly sunburned, having died from an internal hemorrhage.

In Detroit, in the evening, the heat took out Jack Sanders, the second centenarian and ex-slave to die within about two days. Sanders was said to be 107 and active until the last moments of his life. Sanders had memories of being sold as a twelve-year-old. Before that happened, Jack and his mother escaped and hid in a swamp for three days until bloodhounds found them. His mother's fate isn't known, but Sanders was sold to a family in Aiken, South Carolina. After the Civil War, Sanders became a farmer. He retired at eighty and lived in a cabin, and when he was ninety-five, he moved to Detroit with his thirty-four-year-old daughter.

The heat also (indirectly) ended the life of Bernard Price, thirty years old, in the most surreal way. The high was 99—and Price and two buddies found a fun way to keep cool on a Sunday afternoon. They were at Pleasant Lake, which had what folks called a "speeding water merry-go-round." It was a merry-go-round, the kind that used to be popular in playgrounds, that you propelled yourself and kept spinning around. It was surrounded by water. At some point, Price's two buddies, invigorated by the wind, jumped off and were again refreshed by the water.

Then Price made his leap, flying into the air and disappearing under the water. He did not reappear. Neither Price nor his pals considered that it might be problematic to fling yourself into shallow water with a rocky bottom.

New Jersey

In Hackettstown, thunderstorms dropped hail, and that's how Margaret Swackhamer, in above 100-degree weather, found her car sliding on ice, sideswiping two vehicles, overturning, and catching on fire. She (somehow) survived.

Along the Jersey shore, about 400,000 beachgoers cavorted in the sand and surf. One of those beachgoers was Ira Funston, who left his dog in his locked car in Ocean City (92°F). Even worse, a painfully short rope was around the dog's neck and the other end was tied to a footrest.

Fortunately, a woman noticed the dog gasping for air and alerted the authorities. A police officer and a resident who lived nearby broke into the car. By this time, the dog was unconscious. The men applied ice packs and massaged the dog for half an hour until he came to. The officer gave the dog water and received a grateful lick.

Three hours later, Funston returned. He was arrested. Funston would see the judge in about a week—who would say that what he did was "an act of gross thoughtlessness." Funston was fined $25 (over $560 in today's dollars), while the woman who alerted the authorities received praise from people writing into her local paper, and the officer who rescued the dog received thank-you letters from people around the country and a $5 bill.

If his punishment doesn't seem that severe, you'll be happy to know that Funston waited in a hot jail cell until the $10 in bail money was raised and saw his name sullied in newspapers as far away as England. His lousy behavior was even mentioned in a book almost a century later.

Ohio

David Caldwell, a sixty-two-year-old pastor, struggled to deliver his sermon. The service at St. Paul's Evangelical Church started in Findlay at 9 A.M., and it was already 88 degrees outside, heading to a high of 101. In a church filled with people and no air-conditioning, there's no telling how hot it was inside. Parishioners called the heat "oppressive."

Indeed, Caldwell couldn't finish the service, and so he enlisted an active church member, Elliot George, to take charge. As the services concluded, George asked a sixty-nine-year-old parishioner, Charles Wheeler, to lead the church in prayer. Wheeler, owner of a secondhand furniture store, stepped into the pulpit and, as everyone was finishing the prayer, collapsed.

Wheeler was moved to the basement, where services probably should have been held (around the country, some churches moved their proceedings to their cooler basements). He was then taken to the hospital, where Wheeler suffered a cerebral hemorrhage, and doctors declared him dead at 2:30 P.M. Several days later, Pastor Caldwell oversaw Wheeler's funeral.

Henry Hart, sixty-eight-year-old Sandusky mayor and a Democrat running for Senate, planned to give a speech at a country fairground. He was going to speak to members of the National Union of Social Justice, a group that had endorsed him for Congress and was run by the well-known and controversial Father Charles E. Coughlin. But the heat was too much for Hart, who collapsed and was taken home.

For the next several days, Mayor Hart seemed to improve, even today, when it hit 105 degrees, but in the evening, his health deteriorated. A doctor was called at 6:30 P.M., and forty-five minutes later, the last breaths were taken by Henry Hart, who might have in another alternative timeline one day been a Democratic senator and even president of the United States (hey, you never know).

Hours after Hart passed out at the fairgrounds, Harry Harris, a thirty-nine-year-old newspaper pressman, enjoyed the waters of an abandoned gravel pit, a swimming hole a little northeast of Dayton, Ohio, that everybody called Garbage Lake.

Garbage Lake was actually pleasant. A decade or more earlier, a passing train's refrigerator car doors came open, and fruit and vegetables tumbled into the pit of water. For weeks, a faint odor of rotting refuse emitted from the lake. The smell disappeared, but the name stuck.

On this day, Harris—probably with his wife and four kids—was among several hundred swimmers trying to cheat the heat on a day when the high was 107 degrees. He had every reason to assume he was not going to drown. But at 7:15 P.M., something happened. Maybe cramps, people said. Or Harris may have been walking through the water and just got out of his depth, unable to swim and finding himself stumbling among the loose gravel. It was a mystery.

Many people recognized gravel-pit and sand-pit swimming holes were places to steer clear of. "There have been two drownings in gravel pits near Muncie already this year, and there will be more before summer ends unless something is done to close these deep and dangerous holes to the public," declared an op-ed in Muncie, Indiana's *The Star Press* on June 26.

The *Winston-Salem Journal* ran an op-ed titled "Dangerous Business" on July 18, inspired after a fourteen-year-old girl was bathing at a boathouse at Lake Lure in North Carolina. She stepped off a rock ledge into water twenty feet deep. She drowned while her aunt, who also couldn't swim, helplessly watched. "It is best to take the children where the waters are much frequented by other bathers and swimmers, perhaps, or where lifeguards are at elbow. But at any rate they should not be without adult company, which, ideally, should include someone who is a good swimmer," the op-ed stated.

Gravel pits, even more than sand pits, were especially treacherous. When you had a rocky floor and walls surrounding you, it provided lots of shade—and so you were swimming in warm currents mixed in with extremely cold currents of water, which was exactly what was needed for a swimmer to be seized with muscle cramps. Also, if you were wading in shallow water, even more so than the sand pits, the ground beneath you could disappear at any moment, with a deep hole or a steep drop off into a watery abyss. Since the walls of the gravel pits often were rocky hills, some unlucky swimmers discovered that if you had bad timing, you might suddenly find yourself buried in a landslide of rocks and boulders.

When everything went right, gravel pits were fun, idyllic places to swim. But too often, something was going wrong.

Ontario

In London (100°F), Joseph Crapps, a janitor, went to the St. George's Anglican Church, assuming he was going to do what he always did. He would unlock the door, clean, and prepare the building for Sunday school. That was the plan.

He did not know what was waiting for him on the other side.

For an entire week, a heat-mad black squirrel was trapped in the church. As people were discovering, squirrels do not enjoy extreme temperatures. The squirrel suffered through approximately 168 hours without food or water, though one would think it must have subsisted on some liquid somewhere in the last week; perhaps it found some holy water. But one thing was for sure. The squirrel was livid, and while it may not have understood the concept of revenge, the animal's instincts told it to give whoever let him out a piece of his mind.

Crapps unlocked the church door.

The squirrel went, as one paper described it, "berserk." There are few details about the fight, but the squirrel did not run for its freedom in the great outdoors. It attacked Crapps, repeatedly, and the battle ended with a dead squirrel. Crapps then entered the church, horrified by what he saw. Each window frame had been gnawed on, with wood shavings covering the floor. The window blinds were in shreds. It was all a futile attempt to escape a sanctuary that had become anything but.

At Hamilton Beach, along Lake Ontario, the first aid station had their busiest day ever as far as anyone could recall. At least sixty people came for help, either half-conscious or severely sunburned.

Sunday trading laws were lifted so ice could be transported to households. A week earlier, a driver was arrested for making Sunday deliveries, but the judge refused to jail him. One ice company reported delivering six thousand tons of ice today, more than six times the normal rate.

The ice was desperately needed. Four out of five patients visiting the emergency room at Toronto Western Hospital were heat cases. That night, Toronto nursing home resident Margaret O'Donnell knelt in prayer at her bedside. The seventy-four-year-old was closer to God than she possibly could have realized; she died mid-prayer.

New York

James Romeo, a sales manager, returned to his Seneca Falls home after an all night drive to help his four-year-old son sleep during a hot night. Claire, the mom and wife, evidently decided she wasn't up for a road trip. Romeo drove 157 miles, an arduous journey on country roads in pre-interstate days. An exhausted Romeo said, "It was worth it, for it put the kid to sleep."

In Buffalo, it was 96 degrees, leading to two deaths and a drowning. And in Rochester (90°F), Leon Cole, fifty-nine, turned up—alive, to everybody's surprise. Some people are terrible at communicating, thoughtless, or both, and some were perhaps inept at living before the era of cell phones. About a week earlier, when the temperature was in the 100s, Cole was nowhere to be found, and his sister—also his roommate—feared her brother was a heat victim. For days, the police searched the woods for Cole's body. And then Cole showed up, explaining that, oh, he was simply visiting some friends about twenty miles away.

In New York City, George Varoff was functioning on little sleep—and preparing to compete and qualify for the Olympic track team. Yesterday, Olympic hopefuls descended on the first of a two-day competition at Randall's Island Stadium,* which was now, for the first time ever, open for business—along with Randalls Island Park and the Triborough Bridge.

This was a very big deal for New York City, attracting to the dedication the mayor and President Franklin Delano Roosevelt, en route to Maine in his air-conditioned train. Twenty-five thousand fans were expected to appear to see the Olympic hopefuls, but far shorter numbers showed, with estimates ranging between 10,000 and 15,000 spectators.

The high was 96, but the stadium, people said, was far worse, and one unofficial temperature reading declared it was 108 degrees. One newspaper called the stadium, "boiling." Still, despite the heat, somehow some athletes wowed the world. Today, Jesse Owens won the 100-meter race in 10.4 seconds and the broad jump (jumping 25 feet 10 ¾ inches). Tomorrow, he would win the 200-meter in twenty-one seconds.

Owens was less than a month away from becoming an Olympic legend and winning four gold medals in Berlin. Louis Zamperini was also at the trials; he would tie in the 5,000-meter race and later become a World War II hero and the subject of Laura Hillenbrand's best-selling book *Unbroken*. Zamperini recalled in Hillenbrand's book that the heat at the Olympic trials "made a wreck of me." Zamperini remembered athletes being carted off to hospitals.

There were six heat victims around the city, on the first day the Olympic trials; the second day, today, the day George Varoff competed for the Olympics, only one New Yorker is known to have died: a thirty-two-year woman sitting on her apartment's front steps. That the humidity was at least 70 percent wasn't helping matters. In fact, the humidity was climbing at night, just when temperatures were lowering. That may explain why Varoff recalled the nights in New York City being worse than the days.

---

* Now known as Icahn Stadium.

A student at the University of Oregon, twenty-two-year-old Varoff had, earlier in the month, set a new world's record in pole-vaulting, soaring 14 feet 6½ inches at the Amateur Athletic Union. Next stop: the Olympics. But first, he needed to make the team. Varoff came to New York City for the trials about a week before his July 12 competition, but the Oregon college student, who grew up in San Francisco, found himself thinking about little else but the heat. Nobody was thriving in this weather, but it was always worse for people used to a cooler climate.

Varoff could tell that he wasn't performing well at practice. Several days before his Sunday competition, he predicted his doom. "I knew I was going to fail," he later said in an interview. The day of his finals, "my legs were dead." The problem was that Varoff's body was attempting to rest and recuperate during the hot, humid nights in a hotel that lacked air-conditioning and was situated in a concrete jungle.

"It was so hot, sleep was impossible," Varoff said.

Varoff evidently didn't run into Ken Griffin, who might have given him some good advice. Griffin competed as a gymnast at the Olympics in 1936. As Griffin recalled in a 1988 oral interview with the LA84 Foundation, he stayed at the YMCA, and there was no air-conditioning: "My only relief was to go an all-night theater where it was air-conditioned and get a little sleep, which I did several nights a week. At least I could sleep. Don't ask me what the performance was, the motion picture, because I didn't even look at it."

In his suffocating hotel room, Varoff slept in the nude on the top of the blankets, but it didn't help. By the time he competed to make the Olympic pole-vaulting team, he hadn't had true sleep for at least forty-eight hours. "On the day of the finals, when I should have been at my best, I was tired and loggy," said Varoff, who didn't make the Olympic team.

Varoff wasn't the only one having trouble sleeping. "Neither could the other kids from out this way—Eastman especially," Varoff said.

Ben Eastman earned a silver medal in the 400-meter race at the 1932 Olympics, and everyone expected Blazin' Ben to go to the 1936 Olympics. It didn't happen. "Gosh—he was even lower than me," Varoff said of Ben. "He didn't say anything, and I guess that was because he was afraid if he opened his lips, he might burst out crying. I sure felt sorry for Ben."

Later, Eastman broke down, sobbing in the showers, according to a LA84 Foundation oral history in 1980 with the track and field Olympic athlete Malcolm Metcalf. "He had just set a new world's record a few weeks earlier but had an off day apparently," said Metcalf, who recalled how the 1936 heat wave sapped athletes strength: "We all lost a great deal of weight."

Metcalf, in fact, lost almost fifteen pounds and estimated that most athletes dropped ten pounds. The women athletes also struggled, said Dee Boeckman in an interview with the Associated Press. Boeckman was a middle-distance Olympic runner who was now coaching the women's national track and field team—and America's first female Olympics coach. The women qualified for the Olympics on July 4, but they were stuck in New York City for the time being. The Olympic fund would pay for their expenses once they left for Germany on July 15, but until then, the female athletes were on their own.

"They are eating so very little, they cannot train in this severe heat," Boeckman said. "The money some of them saved for buying souvenirs in Germany has been used for food and hotel expenses, and they are now living on sandwiches."

Ben Eastman soon hung up his cleats and went into business, and eventually became a part-time track coach at a university. The heat, and being born at the wrong time, destroyed Varoff's athletic career. Varoff planned to shake off the 1936 disappointment and go into the 1940 Olympics, but that was canceled due to World War II, and so he was going to compete in the 1944 Olympics, but that, too, was scrubbed due to the same war. Varoff competed in more contests, but for all practical purposes, on July 12, 1936, his pole-vaulting career effectively ended. Later, after serving in World War II and working at Stanford University, he was employed as a track and field coach at his alma mater, Fresno State.

While the Randall's Island Stadium Olympic trials will always have a place in history for helping Jesse Owens achieve greatness, the actual competition wasn't much to brag about. *The Washington Herald* said at the time, "It was one of the worst conducted meets in American or any other country's history." Nobody knew when track and field events were being held. Sports reporters couldn't get timely information, often receiving news on athletes' performances an hour after a competition. Officials blamed the heat wave, saying the public address system had been "fried in the sun."

Many athletes were struggling. Still, generally, professional athletes seem to have all made it through the summer alive, possibly because common sense sometimes prevailed before some sporting events occurred. For instance, in Omaha, on July 9, the Midwestern tennis championship went on as scheduled, but the game was paused several times between sets so players could cool off.

On July 10, John Wood Platt, better known as J. Wood Platt, a prominent golfer in Philadelphia, decided to not defend his state amateur golf title. Platt, thirty-seven, suffered a sunstroke several years earlier and didn't want to risk another episode. With temperatures topping out at 102 degrees and three people in the area dropping dead that day, it was a prudent decision.

On July 15, a sportswriter wrote, "for the first time in the memory of the oldest fan, hot weather caused postponement today of a schedule major league baseball game—that between the Cincinnati Reds and the Brooklyn Dodgers tomorrow." (As it turned out, the high on July 15 was 104, the eighth day in a row of plus-100 degree heat; if the game had been played the next day, it would have been 91.) The game was postponed until August 28, to be played as part of a doubleheader. That seems to have been the only major league baseball game during the summer to be called off due to the heat, but numerous minor league games were delayed days or weeks. In Windsor, Ontario, horse races were scrubbed for several days in mid-July due to the heat wave, probably saving a lot of horses' and jockeys' lives.

Still, even with games and races being called off, and buckets of ice water placed in locker rooms and sponges and towels for players to use, there were a lot of close shaves. In St. Louis, on July 11, the legendary Jerome Herman "Dizzy" Dean, star pitcher of the St. Louis Cardinals, was knocked out in the sixth inning—from a line drive, not the heat—but shortly afterward, the Giants' catcher Gus Mancuso was removed from the game because he was struggling to play in the 102.8-degree weather. In the stands, several fans collapsed, and one spectator, a forty-nine-year-old railroad clerk, was taken to the hospital where he died. His death certificate read "excessive heat." (If you're wondering, the Cardinals won the game, 9–3.)

On July 14, in St. Louis, Terry Moore, the Cardinals' center fielder, collapsed on the field in the fifth inning of the game with the Brooklyn Dodgers, when the temperature was 108. Teammates rushed to his aid, and he was revived.

On August 23, Cliff Melton, Max Bishop, and Fred Blake, Baltimore Orioles players, couldn't finish a game due to the heat. Blake was bedridden for the next several days.

In late August, Luke Sewell, a Chicago White Sox catcher, finished a game in 100-degree heat against the Detroit Tigers only because he kept whiffing smelling salts.

Rabid sports fans also had to be careful. On June 19, Joe Louis, the legendary boxer, was famously knocked out by Germany's Max Schmeling (Louis got his revenge in the ring two years later). For a while, there was an unfounded rumor that Louis, after being slugged, died from the heat, a rumor that didn't make much sense since the high that day in New York City was 75 degrees. But the country itself was starting to swelter, and twelve people listening to the game got agitated and excited listening to the fight on the radio and died while listening to the match—and many of their physicians blamed a combination of excitement and the heat.

North Carolina

A Durham, North Carolina, columnist for *The Herald Sun*, whose byline was simply "the Bishop," felt something was amiss with the weather and said so in a column that appeared in today's paper. The Bishop mused, "With a blistering sun spreading his July fury over most of the United States, we wonder again whether the world is getting warmer."

The Bishop admitted that assuming that the world was getting hotter "may because considerable eye lifting" with skeptics, before stating, "but facts are facts, and some of them can't be hurdled with mere gestures."

28

JULY 13
Heat Vacations

Today's death toll: 500+
Total Death Toll: 3,300+

Heat vacations" wasn't a phrase people used, but it describes what everyone was doing this summer: traveling somewhere cooler. Although they didn't furnish numbers, newspapers of the time reported that the Department of Commerce stated that during the week of July 5 through July 11 records were set for the number of people traveling to escape the scorching heat and drought.

Later in the summer, on August 16, a headline in a Springfield, Massachusetts, newspaper said it all: "Vacation Exodus Spurred by Heat With Shore and Lake Resorts Beckoning."

In 2010, a former resident of Kansas City, Missouri, Gloria Schusterman recalled, in an oral history for the Harry S. Truman Library, what was basically a heat vacation. "My grandfather died in July, and we decided to get out of Kansas City for a while. It was terribly hot," Schusterman said. She was six years old at the time. "We left in three cars—family, mostly family—and one car full of friends, and we made a caravan and drove north to Minnesota. We rented a great big family house. It was like a farm, but it was on a lake."

Granted, Minnesota was really no cooler than Kansas City, Missouri, but it did cool down deeper into July, and, plus, it had 10,000 lakes, making Minnesota a hotbed for tourism this summer. In mid-July, Frisco Lines, a Midwestern railroad, ran ads in newspapers, saying, "Take a vacation from the heat wave . . . step aboard a Frisco air-conditioned train. There are many short trips which can be made between sunset and sunset—and this brief change of climate will refresh and invigorate you. The cost is very low."

Crops were dying; food prices were climbing. Henry A. Wallace, secretary of agriculture, lashed out at "alarmists and propagandists" trying to scare consumers about "food scarcity." But even without propagandists, people *were* scared. Some states hadn't seen rain for over a month. Twenty-two states were in a serious drought. Cornfields were curling up. Pastureland was brown. Livestock were dying. Wheat and oat fields were burned and inedible. The whole country needed a vacation.

Missouri

Weldon Willis didn't feel right. Suspecting he was going to have a heatstroke while driving from Springfield to Ash Grove, Willis, a grocery store owner, parked his car by the road, five minutes from his destination. It was 2 P.M., and Willis lay down in the shade of a nearby tree.

That decision, and a well-meaning woman, may have saved his life. Soon after lying down, a local funeral home received a call from a lady screaming, "There's a murdered man beside the road out here!" Police officers located Weldon, alive but ill. They took him home, and family members later returned for his car.

That wasn't the only mistaken dead body incident during the summer. A few weeks later, in Toledo, Ohio, the medics were called to revive Herbert Heintz, a dentist. The rescue squad immediately began admitting artificial respiration. A flabbergasted Heintz insisted that he was just taking a nap.

Across Missouri, hospitals and ambulance drivers were overworked, but no city was suffering like St. Louis. The hospitals were crammed with patients who needed an immediate ice bath but had to wait in a line until a tub was freed.

From sunrise to sunset, sixty-four residents died in St. Louis. Years later in a local newspaper interview, Thomas Cook, an ambulance driver for City Hospital, recalled his career and said this week stood out. Cook began driving a horse-drawn wagon ambulance to the hospital in 1906. He took patients to the hospital in 1909 after two streetcars collided and ninety-one people were injured. He transported about five hundred smallpox victims a year, early in his job, without getting sick himself, and he delivered several hundred babies on the way to the hospital, including four sets of twins. But nothing compared to the summer of 1936, Cook said, when he constantly took heat victims to the hospital—or to the city morgue. Thirty-five of his passengers died before he reached the hospital.

Iowa

There were eighty heat victims in Iowa today.

According to an enormous thermometer on the roof of the Maybohm garage in Preston, the temperature hit 108 degrees. Around that time, the heat beating on the glass tube below the mercury set fire to the building. Fortunately, the garage owner, Nick Maybohm, was also the fire chief.

Thermometers were exploding all summer. On July 14, at the University of Wisconsin's medical school, $25 worth of thermometers exploded from the 107-degree heat. A village doctor in Goldsmith, Indiana (110°F), reported that his trusty thermometer exploded in his pocket. Perhaps Maybohm should have attempted what an insurance company did in London, Ontario. They, too, had an immense thermometer, but it only went to 100 degrees or, rather, 37.7 Celsius. On extremely hot days, the insurance executives packed the thermometer in ice.

Connecticut

Joseph Geraci, a bespectacled sixty-two-year-old chauffeur with a mustache, was enjoying some down time on a late Monday afternoon and fishing, trying to catch "shiners," a type of fish, for eel bait. Geraci had been fishing with no luck for almost an hour, and at 4:50 P.M., and he threw his double-hooked line further out, about thirty feet. That's when he saw the face of a woman and her body, half submerged, floating by.

He froze—but not for long. Geraci made a snap decision, one that resulted in probably the best example of fishing that didn't involve fish in the history of fishing. Geraci brought his line back in and cast it out again.

One hook snagged the woman's stocking; the other, her dress. Geraci reeled her toward him and shouted for help in Italian, all the while fearing the hooks might cut her skin. A little boy heard Geraci and found some policemen. Two officers pulled her out of the water and started mouth-to-mouth on the thirty-three-year-old woman while Geraci watched, stunned and speechless. A small crowd formed. She stirred. People shouted, "She's alive!"

Indeed, she was. The woman was revived before the inhalators were needed and taken to the hospital. At first, she couldn't remember her name or how she got in the water. Did she faint in the heat? Or was her fall into the river just a matter of bad luck? Later, she remembered her name—Mary Maloney—and as far as she recalled, she missed her footing and fell into the water. Maybe that's all it was, though it seems plausible that the heat did get her, given that her memory was foggy and considering how common it was to collapse in the summer heat. The heat wasn't brutal today, but it wasn't cool either. It was 85 degrees, with no heat victims' deaths in Hartford today, except for a twenty-seven-year-old male who had been admitted to the hospital when it was 100 degrees.

Geraci was naturally excited by his big catch and saving a life. When a reporter asked what he thought when he saw Maloney floating by, he said through an interpreter, "I was very nervous. But I determined to pull her to shore if I could."

Maloney, for her part, had just finished a vacation and was supposed to have returned to her job at a department store. But for reasons she didn't seem to know, before her fateful fall, she didn't. Instead, she spent the afternoon wandering around Riverside Park.

New York

Elisabeth Luther Cary had seen her share of heat waves after living in New York City for sixty-nine years. Forty years earlier, when Cary was twenty-nine and becoming known for her translations of French literature into English, the summer of 1896 had been agonizing. From August 4 to August 14, the city was in the 90s, and the heat torched the lives of 564 people. Barges took away piles of dead horses from the city.

When Cary was thirty-four, the 1901 heat wave was exceptionally lethal: an estimated 750 New Yorkers died.

When Cary was forty-four and three years into her job as art critic for *The New York Times*, the first person to hold such a position at the paper, the summer of 1911 killed 158 New Yorkers.

On August 7, 1918, when Cary was fifty-one and ten years into her job as art critic for *The New York Times*, the mercury reached 104 degrees. Approximately 200,000 people, mostly kids, flocked to the beach at Coney Island. People died, drowned, and slept in parks.

In 1934, when Cary was sixty-seven and still the art critic for *The New York Times* with legions of admirers, on June 29, the temperature reached 101 degrees. At least five New Yorkers died that day, and many people passed out on the sidewalk.

All of which is to say that Cary was no stranger to the city's unbearable heat. In fact, on June 14, 1936, she began a review or an appreciation of the Whitney Museum in *The New York Times* that led off with the observation "Nothing is much pleasanter now that Summer heat approaches than to find yourself in a gallery furnished for coolness, surrounded by paintings, prints and drawings that are neither puzzling nor commonplace, but gently stimulating."

If only Cary had spent more of the summer in cooler museums. On July 9, Cary got through the 106-degree heat okay, but on July 10, when it was 102, Cary collapsed. She was revived, however, and didn't go to the hospital. That was a mistake. According to a friend who saw Cary shortly before she became ill, she seemed healthy and alert during their encounter. Maybe after she awakened, she felt she would quickly get past this. Or perhaps Cary was reluctant to join the mob of patients at the hospitals. There were so many heat patients being admitted on the day that Cary became sick that the police who normally counted such numbers gave up.

Cary also may have lacked the support group of intimates who might have rushed her to the hospital. Cary had no children. She was only married to her work, although for the last ten years, she scaled back some of her duties, so she was writing what she wanted and not covering every art exhibit in the city. In any event, Cary remained at home, but the air was asphyxiating. "Heat in New York City does not feel like heat on an Iowa or Dakota farm. Heat has weight in New York," wrote one anonymous reporter for in a newspaper column syndicated by United Press. "It presses on the chest and fills up the lungs. Perspiration does not evaporate. And every brick, stone, concrete slab and piece of steel throws waves that bleat the eye."

Two days after her collapse, a cousin took Cary to Brooklyn Hospital. That day, Sunday, July 12, her last story was published in *The New York Times*, a look at modern lithography. She would die Monday morning, July 13. Three days later, at the funeral, Cary was surrounded by members of the art community and fellow coworkers, including Arthur Hays Sulzberger, president and publisher of *The New York Times*. There was no music or eulogy, simply a hymn that was read: "Jerusalem, My Happy Home." The next day, Cary was buried, one week after falling ill. The heat wave was nothing if not an efficient killing machine.

Michigan

A man driving from Lansing to Detroit reported an eerie sight: On his route, hundreds of people sleeping on the grass "islands" between streets, as late as 6:30 A.M., with the bright sun streaming down upon them. Men, women, and children, wearing pajamas, nightgowns, and underwear, were all lying there, he said, as if they were dead.

It would have been a reasonable assumption. There were problems throughout the state.

St. Joseph (94°F) At 8 A.M., when it was in the 80s, a young married woman named Catherine Tiffany swam in Lake Michigan, emerged, and took a nap on some sand dunes. Big mistake. Tiffany awakened three and a half hours later with her legs and arms fiery red.

Saginaw (111°F) Over a dozen people were spirited to hospitals for ice baths. Meanwhile, the heat was killing off the dreaded cutworm, but the high temperatures were bringing out grasshoppers, chinch bugs, red spiders, and flea beetles.

Lansing (99°F) Factory workers—too many to count—passed out on assembly lines, and women in downtown offices collapsed. General Motors reduced its hours for their workers, from nine and a half hours in a day to . . . seven (way to go, guys). At the North Side pharmacy, a customer ordered a generous helping of ice cream and sat at a table with a glass top. An aluminum pitcher filled with ice and water was set down. Two minutes later, the table split in two with a loud boom. Nobody was hurt, but the glass table was useless, and the customer was only able to save some of his ice cream.

Port Huron (97°F) Gabrielle Margaret Dielman, thirteen, was asked to bring in a mare on the family farm. But the horse, witnesses said, was "heat-crazed." The horse knocked Gabrielle down to the ground and trampled on her. She was taken to the hospital with injuries to her face, chest, and legs. She was dying. Except somehow, the girl rallied and ten days later left the hospital. Before leaving, Gabrielle told a reporter, "Everybody—even papa—thought I was going to die, but here I am."

Traverse City (100°F) Eli Kallio, twenty-four, was believed to have suffered a heart attack before drowning in Long Lake, near Traverse City. His body was quickly pulled out of the water, and Eli's distraught sister, Lillian, twenty-eight, and a friend sped off to get a doctor, but the car skidded off a road at an intersection, and they were both severely injured. The Kallio family simply couldn't catch a break: two months later, with Eli long dead and Lillian still in the hospital, Lillian's and Eli's thirty-year-old brother, Toiva, was unloading logs at a railroad when the racker broke and a log got loose and crushed him to death.

Detroit (99°F) In the morning, in federal court, the judges showed up in their customary black robes, and bailiffs warned attorneys and visitors to keep their coats on in court, no matter how hot it got.

At 2 P.M., Suzie Mendi, an eight-year-old chimpanzee, died at the Detroit Zoo. (Suzie was the sister of several chimpanzees at the zoo, all with the last name Mendi.) The previous day, at the zoo's theater, Suzie, wearing a blouse and checkered skirt, roller-skated, pedaled a bicycle, pushed a scooter, and walked a tightrope, among other tricks. It was 98 degrees, however, and during the day's last show, Suzie passed out. So did her sister Mary Lou. "It was this Detroit heat that got her," said the city's zoo director. "Although Suzie came from West Africa, where it gets plenty warm, she just couldn't stand this."

A store in Highland Park, a Detroit suburb, had a shipment of one hundred fans come in at 4 P.M. By 5:30 P.M., ten remained.

There were 108 heat victims in Detroit today, many of them auto factory workers, and in a fourteen-hour period, the Associated Press reported, people died every ten minutes. It was estimated that nationwide, seventy-five people an hour were dying.

Dr. William Ryan, the county's medical examiner in Detroit, told reporters, "I have been chief medical examiner for 16 years, and I have never seen anything like it. Perhaps we have been busier for a few hours at a time, but there has been nothing like this over a protracted period." In the last three days, he and three assistants performed 150 autopsies. For the last two days, four telephones in the morgue had been ringing nonstop.

Dr. Thomas Gruber, superintendent of the Wayne County Hospital at Eloise, in Detroit, told a reporter the heat wave had caused "the most ghastly death wave I have ever witnessed. I have been in hospitals since 1912, and I have never seen anything to equal the heat plague at Eloise. We are doing all we can to combat the heat—yet the patients die by the dozens."

Gruber said that usually during a heat wave there would be some relief to break up high temperatures, "but now we have had no breathing spell for five days. Ordinarily in an institution, the largest of its kind in the world, we have about two deaths a day. During the past five days, 63 persons have died."

Eloise, originally a poor house, was a psychiatric hospital that now had a poor record of keeping their patients alive. Still, that more patients weren't dead was likely due to Dr. Gruber, whose first decision when he was hired in 1929 was to get rid of the triple bunk beds that the male patients were sleeping in, recognizing that diseases tended to spread when you crammed in as many people as possible to a room. Gruber once said, "Michigan takes better care of its prize herds and swine than it does of mental patients."

But doctors fought the good fight. G. R. Harris, the superintendent of Receiving Hospital, told the press that they were working on getting two portable air-conditioning units to their building, one that could be put in the admitting room and the other in the ward where the heat-affected patients would be cared for. Of the eighty-two heat patients who arrived at the hospital in the last thirty hours or so, Harris said that twenty-one had died.

But caring for children was the hardest task. Infants, too weak to raise their arms, lay in cribs while nurses drew shades and kept rooms as cool as possible; if the babies weren't listless, they were shrieking. In Albion, at 4:30 P.M., frantic parents tried to cool off their eighteen-month-old, John Philip Oeschger, in a bath at home when he suffered heatstroke. A physician worked on the boy for over an hour, fruitlessly trying to pump air back into his lungs.

Ontario

In Toronto (100°F), twenty-eight people met their maker today. In fact, four out of every five people who came to Toronto Western Hospital's emergency room were heat patients, officials estimated. The city's cemeteries recruited extra gravediggers. One cemetery reported triple the number of burials as usual, and casket makers throughout the region added hours to shifts.

The high temperature in Windsor was 104 degrees, and by the day's end, twelve more funerals were being planned. Two police officers fainted; the chief a couple days ago started allowing officers to work in short sleeves, or perhaps the entire police force might have gone down.

The heat just wouldn't let up. In Essex County, five people died. In Hamilton, five as well. Four people died in St. Thomas. In Brantford, a nine-month-old baby died; in Sarnia, a farmer; in Goderich, an insurance agent. In Peterborough, the heat took out two nonagenarians in a nursing home. In Timmins (103°F), only the good died young: a thirty-one-year-old woman, a three-month-old boy, and a newborn, just a few hours old.

Thousands of dead fish were on the shores of shallow lakes.

A farmer left Milton in his truck with eighty hens to sell. When he reached Toronto, only ten were alive.

At the Peel Memorial Hospital in Brampton, doctors were so desperate to cool off their patients that they asked the fire department to spray the walls with water, which lowered the temperature a dozen degrees.

In the evening, in Dorchester, two horses, bothered by the heat, reared when their owner, Edgar Lea, led them to the barn. Lea, weak from the heat and probably scared out of his mind, fainted. If he was unlucky enough to wake up, it was only long enough to feel horse hooves crushing his chest. Somebody carried Lea, barely alive, into the house, causing his ninety-three-year-old mother, Annie, to faint. Any parent would have been gutted, but in Annie's case, it was doubly traumatic: five years earlier, another son had perished in a barn fire. Annie and Edgar both died that night.

Manitoba, Saskatchewan, and Alberta

In Emerson, Manitoba, it was 112 degrees. In Medicine Hat, Alberta, 91 degrees. Saskatchewan was in the 80s or less. But across all three provinces, there were twenty-six heat deaths and drownings today.

Tennessee

Evening fell in Memphis (97°F), and John Thomas died at home. Thomas, forty-five, was probably doomed to a relatively short life, no matter what the weather. He was an asbestos worker.

North Dakota

In the last ten days, it was often over 100 degrees, and the train tracks between St. John and Devils Lake had enough of the heat: they split apart. Soon after, a passenger train derailed into an eight-foot ditch, and several people were injured. This sort of thing occurs enough that there is a word to describe the heat warping railroad tracks, a term that's been around since at least as early as the early 1880s. It's called a "sun-kink," and there were many during the summer of 1936.

South Dakota

One year earlier, the Waubay Bluehill Migratory Bird Refuge opened; it was a scenic paradise for migratory birds and other wildlife to feel safe and welcome. They didn't feel safe or welcome today: more than three hundred acres were on fire.

Minnesota

5 A.M. In Minneapolis, it was 86 degrees. As daylight broke, near the old post office building, police woke up men sleeping on the sidewalks. The one man who didn't wake up was taken to the morgue.

10 A.M. In Minneapolis, it was 100 degrees. Frank Giebenhain, a former alderman, went to a dentist to replace a gold filling that melted. His dentist blamed the heat. That doesn't seem possible since gold melts at 1,947 degrees. But who are we to argue with a dentist?

Throughout the day. As the high hit 105 degrees, Dr. Charles Remy, superintendent of city hospitals in Minneapolis, appealed to his community for electric fans. He said that General Hospital needed a hundred fans and Parkview, fifty. Remy said residents could attach notes with their names and addresses so the fans could be returned once the heat wave was over.

Minneapolis hospitals were now only performing emergency operations; inside the operating rooms, thermometers read between 120 and 130 degrees. (In Hamilton, Ontario, the same decision was made, following a man's death after a minor surgery.) But there were other problems in Minneapolis—so many people were collapsing, ambulances were having trouble keeping up with calls. Two drivers on the job for twenty years said they had never been so busy.

7 P.M. Having cared for 135 heat victims in one day, with an ambulance full of heat victims arriving, on average, once every eight minutes, General Hospital refused to allow anyone else to come in. Instead, they diverted patients to other hospitals. F. O. Hanson, superintendent at the Minneapolis Swedish Hospital, said, "Ice is now the most important medicine in our cabinet. I have never seen this situation equaled."

One newswriter described the morgue looking like the scene of a major shipwreck, as crying relatives pushed their way through sweltering autopsy rooms to claim their dead. Today, St. Paul's coroner gave up trying to keep a complete record of the deaths, which, when listed in newspapers, filled two columns.

The bodies kept piling up. Near the town of Red Wing (112°F), two people died—and in Red Wing itself, Katie Grosse, sixty-four, discovered her brother-in-law passed out in their home, moments from death. The next morning, Katie checked on her eighty-nine-year-old mother, who was dead in bed.

Pennsylvania

Murray Fries emerged from the rubble of his Ford coach car, assisted by police and medics. Fries's chest was crushed, and his face and arms were bruised, but the thirty-five-year-old was alive. His four other passengers were banged up, including his twelve-year-old nephew, who had a broken nose and arm. Fries remembered nothing of the wreck.

The guy Fries plowed into remembered everything. Mcclellan Mains, a laborer, was taking his family to Conneaut Lake to cool off from the 100-degree heat, and he slowed down at a curve, but Fries's car didn't. In fact, Fries plowed into the Mainses' new 1936 Pontiac sedan. It was incredible that nobody died; the cars went airborne, and between both vehicles, there were a lot of broken bones and internal injuries.

Fries blacked out while driving, said police, pointing to two clues. For starters, Fries's passengers said that he complained about the heat. Second, before Fries was pulled from the wreckage, the police found a cloth on his forehead—still cold and wet.

New Jersey

At least one tragedy averted: Cape May lifeguards saved the life of a nine-year-old boy caught in an undertow. In Trenton, the heat struck down two men and a five-month-old, and in Wyckoff, the body of Mary Otte, fifty-five, was recovered from Sam Braen's Sons Sand Pit, a popular swimming hole. She was found around 7:30 P.M., about two hours after her family reported her missing. The weather hadn't been too bad—in the 80s, although earlier in the morning the humidity was 85 percent. It was the perfect day to go swimming, if you knew how to swim. Mrs. Otte did not.

Family members noticed Mrs. Otte wasn't around, but they figured she was somewhere, never dreaming that somewhere might be at the bottom of the pit. Everyone later speculated whether she went into the water willingly or perhaps fainted and toppled in. She was last seen sitting on a rock, about eighteen feet above the water.

Ohio

Cincinnati hospitals were hopping. Howard Raver, a longtime reporter for *The Cincinnati Post*, went into General Hospital to watch the arrival of heat victims; his story ran the next day. Ambulances or police officers would bring in a victim, usually on a stretcher, and Raver referred to one heat victim as about sixty years old and a "ghastly purplish color."

"His eyes rolled; mouth was open, and his under lip quivered convulsively as he sucked in sobbing breaths of air," Raver wrote. "The officers rolled the victim through the ward into a small room containing a bathtub partially filled with ice water."

Raver described interns undressing the man and putting him in a bathtub. "Nurses carried in large pans filled with chunks of ice and placed them around the victim," Raver wrote, explaining that several interns "rubbed his chest vigorously with the ice water and tried to cool off his head. The victim never moved except for his laborious breathing. In the background stood a priest, ready to administer the last rites of the church."

Raver never said if the man made it, writing, "Each successive day of abnormal temperatures brings with it an increasing toll of heat victims. Each day, they come in more rapidly, physicians said. The hospital has several ice tubs ready." Sometimes, Raver noted, heat victims were in ice baths for as long as seven hours.

In Urbana (104°F), pedestrians walked by a dying kitten. One bystander commented, "It certainly is hot when it even kills the cats." But Bob LaRue, a waterworks superintendent, took the animal into the city building's basement, where it was cool and dark. He fed the kitten milk, bathed it, and nursed it back to life.

In nearby Piqua, there were grassfires and a factory fire from an overheated motor. Highways were still blowing up. The next day, Ohio's state highway director listed 682 roads damaged by the heat.

Death was everywhere, and the streets of Oak Harbor were a little sadder. A prominent Sandusky engineer in Oak Harbor (97°F) was felled by the heat at 4:30 P.M. and everyone was talking about the heat death of Otto Domrose, the superintendent of the Ottawa County Infirmary, also known as the "poor home," where people who couldn't afford to live on their own were housed. There were nine victims in Cleveland (94°F), five in Toledo (100°F), seven in Akron (99°F), and sixteen in Cincinnati (102°F). And, of course, there were drownings. There were always drownings.

Laura Snyder, eighteen, and her friend Gertrude Spitler, seventeen, swam at an old lime kiln, north of the village of Portage (104°F). It was a popular spot ever since it opened in 1921, with members of the Portage Athletic club often acting as lifeguards. The local paper described the lime kiln as "two quarries connected by a channel," and noted that "the quarries are fed by water from springs in their bottom, supplying fresh water constantly." There was also a diving board and bath houses. For 1936, and considering it wasn't an actual swimming pool, this was about as good as you got.

It wasn't good enough. Snyder was in the water, unable to swim and apparently unaware of a ledge in the kiln. Snyder was probably not thinking much about water safety, blissfully unaware that there had been several drownings over the weekend already.

In fact, the day before, when it was 99 degrees in Millbury, Vernal Lutman, a seven-year-old girl, playing with friends, lost her life in what was known as the Diefenthaler Mud Pit. Probably enough said, though this mud pit was often described as a pond. Local accounts suggest that it wasn't very deep, but it was deep enough.

On the same day Vernal died, Harry Komisarek, twenty-six, was in a boat that capsized on the Maumee River. He couldn't swim but his two cousins could, and they held him up in the water at first, but fighting the river currents and exhaustion, they eventually had to let him go. Rufus Pinkey, a twenty-seven-year-old Black man from Rossford, was also in the Maumee River, floating down it in an inner tube from an auto tire. Like others before him who tried something similar, his gambit didn't work. He fell out of the inner tube.

Today, near New Philadelphia (100°F), a husband and wife, Bert and Mary Board, from nearby Canton, came to the Sandy River to cool off. Signs had been posted warning people that it was dangerous to swim here—but they were torn down. Mary, just twenty-one, found herself caught up in some sort of whirlpool, according to about a dozen Ohio newspapers, and Bert, a thirty-four-year-old furniture store manager, tried to rescue her. On the riverbanks, townspeople and family members—including Mary's and Bert's mothers—watched in horror as they were sucked underneath the water.

And so now, 150 or so miles away, Laura Snyder found herself stepping off the shallow part of the kiln into the deep end and instantly panicking. Snyder frantically grabbed for her friend, pulling Spitler's bathing cap over her eyes. Spitler couldn't swim either but blindly grabbed the side of the kiln. She pulled herself out of the water—and screamed for someone to save Laura.

Laura was fighting for her life, trying to get back to the safety of the ledge, already having disappeared underwater twice. She was submerging a third time when a bystander dove into the water after her.

Halford Whitacre, a thirty-six-year-old navy veteran who swam here every day, grabbed her hair and pulled her to safety.

But if things had worked out just a little differently, Whitacre would have still met Laura. He had already crossed paths with the Lutman girl and Komisarek, two of the community's weekend drowning victims. Whitacre was the county coroner.

Indiana

After a day of eight deaths, the Erie Band were playing an evening concert at Memorial Park in Huntington (109°F) when the instruments stopped working. The lack of moisture in the air caused the valves to stick. Ice water was poured over the instruments to "thaw" the valves and the concert continued.

In Hope (109°F), Hattie Dorrell, a seventy-three-year-old, collapsed. She was taken to a neighbor's home and then to an Indianapolis hospital. While doctors and nurses revived her, the hospital staff contacted some of her children. They learned that Hattie's daughter, Ruth Talbert, couldn't visit her mother. Ruth was also hospitalized, recovering from heatstroke.

One of Ruth's sons, Harris, hopped into his truck and headed for Indianapolis to see his mom, but he was delayed. There's no record of whether this was a heat-related accident or not, but a car crashed into Harris's truck, which then went up into flames. Harris escaped, and fortunately, his mother and sister all lived to maybe laugh about it later, much later.

Illinois

The weather bureau employees in Chicago had a thankless day. The city experienced slightly cooler temperatures (91°F) than most of the state, but their building's elevator was broken. They had to hoof it up six flights.

"Another terrible hot day. With no relief in sight. 112 degrees," wrote Charles Morgan from Bloomington. Morgan spent part of his day at the new township relief office, filling out an application for financial assistance from the government.

"I am compelled to use great caution when venturing out," wrote the sixty-five-year-old. "One can soon become overcome from the heat." Morgan spent most of the day at Tom's Bargain Store, not because he wanted a discount on a suit, handbag, wristwatch, or any of the other merchandise. The owner, Tom Noonan, was a friend. Plus, the store was in a basement, where the air was cooler.

"One cannot retire before midnight. Even then, it is much too warm. No breeze at night to carry the heat out of the bedrooms," Morgan wrote, adding that he and his wife spent the night outside in downtown Bloomington. "Mom and I went up to Franklin Park tonight. Many came out with covers and spread out in the grass. And toss all night."

While Morgan bedded down in Franklin Park, in another part of the city, Abby Jolly, a thirty-two-year-old secretary, slept on a crude bed on the roof of her boarding house with several other tenants. The roof was flat, and so nobody was worried about rolling off. But Jolly was a sleepwalker. She tied one end of a rope around her ankle and the other end to a post embedded in the building.

It was a long night for a lot of people. In Rock Island, Samuel Ralph Wright, fifty-six, had been living in a camp trailer for two weeks with a guy named Charles "Chip" Evans. Almost another century later, it's hard to say if they were in a relationship, but it seems plausible. Wright, who worked at a laundry, was single, and newspapers referred to Evans as a "companion." Everybody called Wright "Peg" due to his artificial peg leg. Wright lost part of his leg as a teenager, when he injured himself playfully wrestling another teenager, it was said. He persevered, however, and became one of the best swimmers in the area, saving a number of lives.

That night, Evans went to bed outside the trailer. Wright slept inside. About 4 A.M., when it was 82 degrees, Evans went back into the stifling trailer, where he found Wright—dead.

In Paris (108°F), Emmett Wilson, a laborer, was also struggling to sleep. On July 5, it was 102, and every single day from then until now, July 13, it had been over 100 degrees. The low never dropped below 71. Desperate,

Wilson decided to use a sleep aid to help him get some shuteye. On his front porch, he mixed five ounces of chloroform with a glass of water.

Somebody suggested after the autopsy that perhaps Wilson had simply intended to breathe in the fumes to knock himself out, not actually drink it. Perhaps he forgot what he put into the water and later took a swig? Nobody believed he really intended to kill himself with his lethal bedtime cocktail. But tomorrow morning, he would be found sitting on his porch, finally getting the rest he craved.

Kentucky

At least thirteen heat victims today. In Lincoln and Casey counties, kids started school, beginning the year in midsummer and ending in midwinter, in order to help with planting on the farm. If you remember not being excited to start school in mid-to-late August or early September, imagine how thrilled children must have been to return inside a classroom in mid-July, in an unair-conditioned building in the middle of the country's worst heat wave.

Before the week was over, three adults in Lincoln County passed out. That kids didn't drop at their desks seems like a minor miracle.

Wisconsin

At 3 A.M., in Madison, it was 81 degrees. By 10:30 A.M., it was 100. By 3:30 P.M., it was 106.3, and the city's sanitation crew were really having a tough go of it. Three men stopped working because of the heat, and so those remaining were outside longer—working more slowly with fewer people on the job. Plus, they were continually giving their horses water and sponging them off.

Frederick Nieman Jr., twenty-two, a candymaker and a student pilot who built his own plane, traveled in his one-seater monoplane from Milwaukee to the village of Rubicon. He went to visit his fiancé's uncle and show off his aircraft. Weather records for Rubicon are hard to come by, but the high seems to have been 95 and possibly into the 100s. Nieman made it there just fine and likely created a lot of bittersweet memories for his fiancé's uncle.

Because soon, Nieman left for home. It's possible that Nieman's homemade aircraft wasn't up to code because it was, well, homemade, but other pilots warned the young man not to fly today. They argued that he wasn't familiar with the area around Rubicon, but more importantly, they said it was too hot. Because of the heat, the air lacked sufficient buoyancy and lift, they said. Nieman waved those concerns off. At an altitude of four hundred feet after literally crossing the Rubicon, as his aircraft suddenly pitched straight downward, Nieman had only a few seconds to contemplate that perhaps his fellow pilots were right.

Nobody would recommend that a seven-year-old boy get into a rowboat and paddle out into the middle of something called Devil's Lake, but that's what happened in Baraboo (107°F).

The Fishers, who lived in Cincinnati, Ohio, were visiting family members and camping at Devil's Lake State Park, and Herman, who everybody called Tuppy, was looking for something to do. He found it—the rowboat was just there on the shore, as if it were meant for him. And so, paddling by hand, Tuppy took his find into the beautiful, calm waters of Devil's Lake. He was having fun in the 10,000-acre body of water until he realized that he was much farther out than he intended. Panicking, Tuppy jumped out of the rowboat. Not a great idea. Tuppy couldn't swim.

That would have been the end of Tuppy, except that his aunt saw him fall in and started screaming.

Fortunately, the aunt's thirteen-year-old daughter heard the screaming and immediately spotted her cousin. Marjorie Anne Stekl, a Girl Scout, was an excellent swimmer. Marjorie Anne swam after Tuppy, and, despite him flailing about and threatening to pull her under, she dragged the boy to shore, alive and well.

In the autumn months of 1936, Marjorie Anne received a medal of bravery from the Girl Scouts. It was a moment that she was justifiably proud of her entire life. In fact, Marjorie Anne became a lifeguard and swam into her eighties. She lived to be ninety-four.

It was a rare feel-good story in a state sorely lacking them. People by the scores were dying and drowning today—in Madison, Milwaukee, and Green Bay. There were five deaths in Waukesha, four in Stoughton, and heat deaths in numerous cities including Wausau, Chippewa Falls, Two Rivers, New Denmark, Racine, Baraboo, Waterloo, Stevens Point, and Oshkosh. Hundreds of people went as high as they could on Rib Mountain (elevation: 1,924 feet), Wisconsin's highest point, hoping to catch a breeze.

At the Morpheus Theatre in Madison, 176 people took up an offer to spend the night in a room cooled off to 70 degrees. People brought pillows and blankets and lay down wherever it looked somewhat comfortable—on the stage, in the balcony, and in aisles. Men and women were segregated, and there were no minors. Police watched over everyone but decided not to disturb a sleepwalker strolling through the theater.

Less amusing was what happened in Goodrich (107°F). William Stillman, a seventy-four-year-old farmer, wasn't around for much of the day, and his children weren't initially concerned. Their widowed father liked his space and sometimes disappeared for a while. But by nightfall, his worried offspring started a search that ended inside their chicken house. Somehow, after Stillman went inside to check on his flock, the door locked on the outside. Stillman was trapped, and there he remained, slowly broiling to death.

29

JULY 14

The Worst Day

Today's Death Toll: 1,000+
Total Death Toll: 4,300+

If there was a worst day of the summer of 1936, it was today, when over one thousand people were known to be slaughtered by the sun, though the actual number was probably considerably higher. The Great North American Heat Wave came for almost everyone today, in virtually every state and many Canadian provinces. If a state or province you live in isn't mentioned, it doesn't necessarily mean there wasn't a heat death or drowning, but it does mean the region came through mostly unscathed.

Alabama

A polio outbreak was distressing everybody, even more than the heat, which was in the high 80s and 90s. Polio is deadly and highly contagious, and everyone was advised to stay far away from others and remain inside their hot, hot homes.

Arkansas

From June 19 to July 14, the heat took out at least a dozen Arkansans. Today, 103 degrees throughout much of Arkansas, there were four heat deaths and one drowning. Thunderstorms also showed up, which would have been a welcome relief, except that a lightning bolt struck a farmhouse in Van Buren, frying the porch, roof, and the thirty-three-year-old owner inside.

California

Outside of the heat dome, on Catalina Island, where actress Jean Harlow was spotted once again not listening to her physician's advice about not sunbathing, it was in the usual pleasant 70s, but in other parts of the state, the temperatures were intolerable. Sacramento was 103 degrees. Needles, 112. In Brawley—121 (but only 14 percent humidity). There were some drownings, and no known heat victims, but those were coming. Some Californians thrived because of the heat: Ventura County citrus farmers. Because of the hot summer, demand was outstripping supply, and boxes of lemons and oranges that were fetching $3 a box were now selling for $7.

Colorado

It was 91 in Greeley, and the cool waters of Neff Lake beckoned to a sixteen-year-old boy who couldn't resist but should have.

Georgia

Drought-savaged cotton crops were four to six weeks behind schedule. The peach crop was undersized. Cantaloupe, watermelon, peanuts, and sugar cane crops were struggling. Still, for non-farming public, today wasn't too miserable. The highest temperature in the state was 85, the coolest day since July 4.

Idaho

Boise's high temperature was 94 degrees. As if to signal what was coming for the state, a twenty-eight-year-old man from North Carolina drowned near Shoshone, looking for relief from the heat in Little Wood River. His body would be found in two days, two miles away, in some brush by two young boys looking for a place to swim.

Illinois

"Clear, hot and suffocating again this morning," Charles Morgan wrote in his diary from the town of Bloomington (111°F). "We are now going on our fourth week of record breaking heat. And no relief in sight yet. I managed to get uptown and back. Was awful hot. People are [beginning] to grow weaker and weaker, day by day."

There were four heat deaths in Decatur and at least one each in the communities of Spring Valley, Cicero, Tower Hill, Shelby, and Fayette. In Chicago (96°F), Arne Reitan, a forty-three-year-old Norwegian American janitor, told his wife, Margaret, "I can't stand the heat any longer." Then he walked into their bathroom, grabbed his razor, and slashed his throat and wrists. Margaret quickly got her husband to the hospital. Incredibly, he survived and lived another thirty-four years.

That night, Morgan and his wife, Alverta, went to Franklin Park once again. "Very warm as usual tonight, calm and still," he wrote.

As night fell, in Rock Island, at 11 P.M., at the end of 24th Street near Black Hawk Road, there were approximately seven hundred parked cars; families were sleeping in fields and woods. There was talk of the city establishing official sleeping camps here where families could come for relief at night, but the plan didn't come to fruition.

Elsewhere in Rock Island, Reverend Frederick Rolf, pastor of the Evangelical Church of Peace, slept on his porch with an electric fan cooling him off, and his family slept on the lawn.

But on a night when the heat would claim four lives in Rock Island, at least one fellow citizen decided that, hey, this is a good time to rob people. A burglar snuck into the Rolf residence through the front door and took $23 in cash and $200 worth of jewelry, including a watch given to the reverend by the congregation on the twentieth anniversary of his ordination. Rolf surmised that the noise of the electric fan muffled any sounds the thieves might have made.

About two blocks over, at the widow Mary Selby's home, perhaps the same crook helped himself to $3 in cash lying about the house and a cheap watch. The Selbys—Mary and her two grandsons—slept inside their home that night but practically invited thieves in. To help ventilate their home, they left the front door wide open.

Indiana

Adolph Breight, eighty-four, left his home in Fort Wayne to take the saddest walk of his life. Breight was going to view the body of his fifty-three-year-old son, Charles, a heat victim. But Breight never made it there, passing out and dying in the 106-degree heat.

The sun also set its death rays onto Robert Bunn, a sixty-five-year-old farmer, who died in Adams township at his home, at five in the evening. His sickly wife, Louise, couldn't walk and had no access to a telephone, and so when Bunn passed out from the heat, she was helpless to help him—or herself. Some accounts suggest Robert went into distress the day before, and Louise watched him suffer for twenty-four hours before he died. At the very least, she was with his dead body for three hours until a nephew, James White, arrived, intending to help with evening farm work.

Frank Ujj, a sixty-seven-year-old farmer, complained to his family all day about the 100-degree weather. Around 4:30 P.M., when he didn't return from rounding up his cattle, his family went looking for him. With any luck, Ujj died when he collapsed and not afterward. He fell against a barbed wire fence.

Approximately sixty Indiana citizens died from today's heat. Dr. Charles Myers, superintendent of City Hospital in Indianapolis, described to *The Indianapolis Star* a process that was going on throughout hospitals across the country: "When a person affected by the heat is brought in, his clothing is removed immediately, and he is put under a sheet on a table and then his legs and body are put under ice packs. There have been so many cases lately that sometimes we have to use the ice without any covering for it. We also have just poured ice water over them. Then the patients are given an intravenous salt solution and a heart stimulant."

Assuming the patient responded favorably, they were taken to their rooms for the same treatment in modified form, Myers said. He added,

"Last night, I ordered some 100-pound cakes of ice which were placed in the patients' rooms before fans, which blow the cold air on them. Patients are kept in the hospital until they return to normal."

Timothy Donlon's evening started promisingly. The fifty-five-year-old Indianapolis plumber visited his niece, Dorothy Marshall. But she left to do some grocery shopping, perhaps to make them dinner, and while she was out, Donlon walked onto the apartment's fire escape, three stories high, two floors above a liquor store. The newspapers said that he was out there to cool off.

Understandable. It hit 106.1 degrees at 2:10 P.M., and the temperatures came down, but not fast; by 9 P.M., it was still 94 degrees. Maybe Donlon became dizzy, or perhaps he wasn't familiar with the fire escape's quirks. Whatever happened, he lost his balance and pitched over the fire escape.

But, like out of a scene from a movie, Donlon grabbed the iron railing and stopped his fall. But now he was dangling at least sixty feet above the sidewalk.

Donlon's palms were probably leathery tough from years of working with his hands. He may have also been quite strong; he wasn't sitting behind a desk all day. But the heat surely sapped Donlon's energy, and the iron bar may have been hot, even in the shade of the building. And his hands may have been sweaty.

Donlon shouted for help, and a passerby, Roy Lawrence, spotted him. Lawrence told Donlon to hang on while he telephoned for help. But as Lawrence turned to sprint for a phone, Donlon lost his grip.

An hour later, Donlon died in the hospital due to a broken back. One can only imagine what his niece thought upon returning with her groceries. If only he had gone with her to the store.

Iowa

The good folks of Clinton were having trouble with squirrels desperate for relief from the heat. A squirrel got into a store on North Third street, and there was trouble ejecting it. There were also reports of squirrels making their way into homes.

At the State Institution for Feeble-Minded Children in Glenwood, a young patient died. Dr. George Mogridge referenced it in his diary the following day: "Only one child so far has succumbed to this heat," he wrote and then, in his illegible penmanship, mentioned a couple other adults who died. It may be that Mogridge simply couldn't keep his hand steady in the high temperatures. Today, he simply wrote, "No relief from heat in sight."

There was a death in Independence. In Davenport. In New Hampton. In Nashua, two "bachelor farmers," as the paper put it, died from the heat while working.

In the town of Ryan, Caroline Steinkopf, a sixty-eight-year-old, was found unconscious on her bed by her husband. Time of death: 8:30 P.M. At 9 P.M., fifteen miles away, in Manchester, William Mangold, a fifty-four-year-old farmer, died. Caroline's and William's families were devastated; they were brother and sister.

Kansas

It looked like James Hanson discovered a new danger attached to the heat wave: exploding ketchup bottles (or if you prefer: exploding catsup bottles). The Wichita resident told police and medics that he put a ketchup bottle on ice in his refrigerator and it blew up, sending glass flying everywhere, including his face. In fact, Hanson's nose was almost cut off, which is why he called the authorities. But one of the police officers, George London, was quite the detective because he didn't think the story sounded quite right, despite glass clearly having shattered and the high being 107 degrees.

"Let me see that catsup bottle," London said to Hanson, who had already been administered first aid. Moments later, London found several more bottles containing not ketchup, but a very illegal homemade alcohol. The police officers destroyed the bottles of "ketchup," except for two that they took to headquarters for evidence. His face bandaged up, Hanson was taken to jail.

Kentucky

In Newport, Sam Roberts was found unconscious on the corner of Third and York streets by two police officers, John Dance and Kenneth Collins. Roberts, a fifty-seven-year-old Black man, was a junk dealer who had a permit to push a cart in the city, collecting whatever he believed he could sell. It was a job in which he got far too much exercise on a day like this.

And now, Roberts was close to death, on a day when there were twenty-one other known Kentucky heat victims, including four from Newport. The lawmen lifted Roberts into the back of their patrol car and headed toward Speers Memorial Hospital in Dayton, Kentucky. Collins was driving—until he lost consciousness.

Dance somehow stopped the vehicle. Then the forty-five-year-old officer moved his thirty-eight-year-old partner to the passenger seat, and Dance sped to the hospital. Once at Speers Memorial, Dance got both men into the building with the help of medical staff. Then, Dance headed back to the police car—until he, too, passed out right in front of the hospital.

Dance was revived, and a patrol car was sent to pick him up and take him home. Dance refused to go off duty, however. In fact, the next day, Dance was back on the streets, investigating the assault of a fifty-year-old who had been attacked the night before. His partner remained in the hospital, although he was back on the job before too long. Sam Roberts wasn't so fortunate. He didn't make it through the night.

Louisiana

It was in the 90s throughout the state, but people were accustomed to that. The following day, after so much death throughout North America, the *Shreveport Times* produced an editorial with a pat on the back for the city and good advice for everyone—slow down: "So many residents of northern states do not know how to change their pace. They live at a certain tempo in cool weather. When prolonged heat comes, they either attempt to maintain the same tempo, or undergo nervous exhaustion wondering why mere temperature should cause them serious discomfort."

The Shreveport Times blamed modern culture for some of the Northerners' struggle to take it easy: "This inability to relax is an American failing. It has made inroads in the South in the past fifteen years, with automobiles, the radio, movies and other influences bringing more speed and restlessness. The South is beginning to have its full share of those nervous ailments caused by plain, downright lack of calm."

Maryland

In Cumberland, it was 104 degrees. People flocked to the water, and in exchange, the heat gods demanded a sacrifice: a twenty-two-year-old swimmer on a Baltimore wharf slipped and fell in shallow water, breaking his back.

Massachusetts

Two tourists temporarily passed out in Marblehead, a beach town known for cool temperatures but currently in the 90s. Elsewhere in the state, there were two heat deaths and four drownings. The 80 percent humidity didn't help, and in Boston, five heat patients were admitted to the hospital. One guy who collapsed was extremely fortunate he was discovered before too much time went by. He was lying on railroad tracks.

Michigan

In downtown Owosso, concerned bystanders alerted a police officer.

Babies were inside a car crying, blistered, and gasping for air. An officer freed the infants and was about to take them to a hospital when two mothers showed up. When they demanded their children back, the officer complied. The ladies explained that one of the women's husbands had deserted her and they were consulting an attorney.

If this had happened in modern times, or with a different officer in another city like Philadelphia (just ask Marion Shanks), they would have needed an attorney. They would have been cuffed and hauled in front of a judge. But the mothers were allowed to go home with their children. The infants were five weeks old and seven weeks old. It was 110 degrees outside.

About fifty miles away, in Bay City, Michigan, a similar situation occurred at a state park: a police officer discovered a two-and-a-half-year-old locked in a car with most of the windows rolled up (one window was rolled down a few inches). The child was suffocating and severely sunburned. The parents returned, refreshed from swimming in Saginaw Bay, explaining that when they left the toddler was asleep and the vehicle was (but no longer) in shade. Prosecutors started looking into whether they could charge the parents with anything, which gives one an idea of how weak laws were back then when it came to child abuse, neglect, and parental stupidity.

In Lansing, it hit 100 degrees at 1 P.M., but by 2:30 P.M., as the skies became overcast, it dropped to 90. By 3 P.M., it was pouring. People across the city cheered. Rain came rushing into open windows in homes, buildings, and cars, but nobody cared. Two sweaty and weary gas station attendants stood in the rain. Then they spotted one of their colleagues trying not to get wet. They ran and grabbed him and carried him into the rain and laid him down on the concrete. He didn't resist. They were all happy.

The rest of the state couldn't say the same. Edna Nevins, a fifty-nine-year-old divorced woman who was now a housemother for a sorority at Michigan State College in East Lansing, had just come to Detroit with her brother, Clarence, to visit family or friends. But the heat was too much, she decided, and she boarded a bus to return home. Clarence could drive back himself. But as usual, smart thinking collided with the reality of the relentless heat wave: forty miles into the trip, the road was slippery from melting tar, and the bus skidded into a tractor. Seventeen people were banged up and bruised, including Nevins.

In Detroit (104°F), Dr. W. T. Ryan, chief medical examiner at the Wayne County morgue, told reporters, "I have never seen anything like it in sixteen years of experience here." With three assistants helping, Dr. Ryan performed 150 autopsies within thirty-six hours.

All day at Receiving Hospital, dozens of patients arrived in ambulances, taxis, and private cars, with forty physicians and 250 nurses working around the clock. "One thing saves us," said Dr. Austin Howard, Receiving Hospital's superintendent. "Heat patients, even the most serious, recover rapidly, if at all, and few are in the hospital more than 24 hours."

At the Eloise Infirmary in Detroit, many of the eight thousand patients were milling about the grounds, trying to find a cool breeze. At least five Eloise patients died today, ranging from ages six to eighty-three.

The Detroit newspapers were filled with the names of people who died and where they were found. Harry Renz, a sixty-one-year-old, "died in Ford Emergency Hospital." Mrs. Rose Pagley, thirty-eight, "died in Receiving Hospital." Grattan Dwyer, forty-five, "died in Highland Park General Hospital." Many people were listed as "died at home," interspersed with references such as "died while attempting to reach a doctor's office in Pittston." "Died on his farm near Escanaba." "Died in front of an Escanaba hotel." "Found dead near one of his farm buildings." Henri Brassel, ninety-two, "last surviving Civil War veteran in Manistique. Died after a three-day illness." "Died of heart attack while swimming." "Died in a Mt. Clemens hotel." "Found dead in his kitchen." "Found dead in a field near his home." Sometimes there were no names or descriptions. The *Detroit Free Press*, among their dead, listed "Eight unidentified men."

There were nine drownings in Detroit. Another in Cedar Springs. In Ontonagon, three children drowned when a log they were playing on was caught in an undertow. In Oakland County, the bodies of a young engaged couple were pulled out of a lake. They were the seventh and eighth drowning victims to be found in the county's lakes since the week began. It was only Tuesday.

After dark, the rush eased at Receiving Hospital, and the staff received what Detroit doctors were calling a "breathing spell." At 11 P.M., Dr. Howard, the superintendent, announced that no heat victim had been admitted since 9 o'clock. "We are able for the time being to get back to regular hospital routine," Howard said. "And our overworked staff has a well-earned chance to recover from the worst experience we have ever been through."

The Wayne County morgue was still overloaded with phone calls and visitors.

Minnesota

Like Michiganders, Minnesotans were novices to this weather. In Fergus Falls, five people from ages forty to ninety were annihilated by 99.5-degree heat. In Minneapolis, the St. Paul coroner told the press, "We are absolutely unable to keep track of the mounting toll of deaths."

The business of life continued, however, and notorious gangster Alvin Karpis showed up at a Minneapolis courtroom. For most of the summer, he had been held in a jail cell on a kidnapping charge, but approaching his trial date and understanding that the jig was up, Karpis told his attorney that he would plead guilty.

Karpis was most known for his bank robberies and was only one of four men to be dubbed "Public Enemy #1" by the FBI, and the only of those four to be taken alive. Karpis was only twenty-six, almost twenty-seven, but his own gang was so afraid of him that they started calling him "Old Creepy," and the name stuck.

Not surprisingly, the courtroom was swarmed with photographers, reporters, court staff, and police.

Outside, the high was 107 degrees. Inside the courtroom, the thermometer read 110. The judge opened his collar and allowed everybody to remove their coats. Old Creepy kept his on. He wore a fashionable gray suit and white suede shoes, and was carrying a white sailor hat. He also held a linen handkerchief and kept mopping his brow. Sweat was visibly showing on the back of his suit.

Karpis pled guilty to conspiracy in a ransom kidnapping of William Hamm Jr., a St. Paul brewer. Three years earlier, then-thirty-nine-year-old Hamm was walking home from his family's brewery when he was jumped by the notorious Barker-Karpis gang. Hamm was shoved into the back of Karpis's car, a pillowcase thrown over his head, and taken to the gang's Chicago hideout. Ransom notes were delivered, and the Barker-Karpis gang collected $100,000 and freed Hamm, unharmed. Then the gang did another kidnapping the following year and scored $200,000. But they left their fingerprints everywhere, and the FBI started catching up with the gang members. Karpis was nabbed in early May.

"This 100-degree temperature. It would be awful to have to spend three or four weeks at trial in this stuffy courtroom," Karpis said to the judge. "I'd rather plead guilty and have it over with."

Karpis, who would spend some time in the infamous Alcatraz, was hardly the only incarcerated criminal struggling with the heat. The same day, two young men in Caldwell, Idaho, were in a county jail awaiting a trial for stabbing a guy with a knife, and they found the prison unbearably hot and wanted to speed the legal process up. They told officers, "It's too warm here. We plead guilty. We waive everything but our shirts."*

Several days earlier, Ernest Desmond De Hagen, whose nickname was Lord Desmond, was taken in for questioning in New York City. He was accused of being the leader of a blackmail ring that tried to extort money from Alfred E. Smith Jr., a politician and the son of the former New York governor. At the district attorney's office, during questioning, De Hagen fainted from the heat. A doctor helped revive him, and after that, De Hagen told them everything they wanted to know.

Mississippi

The Deep South has never been thought of as a place to cool off, but it was in the low 90s in the state. Mississippians found that refreshing when comparing it to the alternative. The next day, the *Biloxi Daily Herald* commented that two of their business owners had just returned (probably today) from Chicago, where the sidewalks were cracking in the high temperatures:

* That quote sounds like some clever wordplay from a United Press reporter and perhaps not an actual quote, but we'll let it stand.

"They made purchases for the Mississippi Coast stores and were pleased to be back in Biloxi to get relief from the heat."

Missouri

The temperature shot up to 100 degrees at 10 A.M., in St. Louis, and remained at 100 until 9:40 P.M. Offices shortened shifts; at one firm, five stenographers fainted. In City Hospital's nursery, the body temperature of some of the thirty-plus newborns climbed as high as 105; the staff set blocks of ice in front of seven large fans. In the rest of the hospital, doctors and nurses cared for 120 bedridden heat-tortured patients. Another 108 patients were treated and sent home.

Throughout St. Louis County, eighty-two citizens were scrubbed out of existence. There were 601 calls to police cars and ambulances, mostly about the heat; sirens were heard throughout the city all day. In one of the ambulances was Louise Darrigs, an eighty-year-old who tried to climb over the railing of Eads Bridge and plunge to her death in the Mississippi River. Good Samaritans prevented that. The following month, they were not, unfortunately, able to stop a woman in her mid-thirties from leaping to her death from the same bridge on another hot day.

On the way to the hospital where she would be diagnosed with a sunstroke, the ambulance driver asked Mrs. Darrigs why she wanted to jump in. "That water looks awfully cool, and plenty of other people are doing it," she said, adding, "Besides, it is just too hot to live."

Nebraska

In Omaha (109°F), a fifty-four-year-old physician dropped dead on the sidewalk, and people were flopping down on city streets, drugstores, and in their homes. Loyce Montgomery, six years old, returned from school and found her forty-five-year-old mother on the floor, unconscious. Loyce ran to the neighbors, who called the ambulance and administered first aid.

Then they waited. And waited. The ambulance arrived two hours after being called because the city and county bickered over who should pick up the mom in Pershing, a suburb of Omaha.

In spite of that, Loyce's mom recovered after a night in the hospital.

Nevada

In Las Vegas, the high was 103. It's always hot in Nevada, but because everyone was used to the heat, and particularly because the desert nights were cool (the low on the 14th was 67 degrees), heat deaths were at a minimum. A few days later, Letson Balliet, a mining engineer writing for *Nevada State Journal*, started a column with a familiar refrain: "After three months in the sun-baked East and Middle West, I am about the happiest man in the state merely because I am back home in Nevada." He added that when he left Des Moines, Iowa, it was 108. For comparison's sake, the high in his home city of Reno today was 93.

New Hampshire

New Hampshire had at least one day this summer in which the heat hit 100 degrees, but otherwise, if you lived here, you had decent weather. Just don't do anything foolish like cross the border. Today, a seventy-seven-year-old Newmarket man went to Lowell, Massachusetts (92°F), and collapsed and died in a bank.

New Jersey

In the city of Cape May, an ordinance went into effect: Men could no longer remove their shirts on the beach. Any shirtless male beachgoer would be fined $50 or spend ten days in the county jail. Cape May instituted a few other new rules. No bathing suits or shorts on the boardwalk or public streets. You also couldn't disrobe in cars or on beaches—or eat food on the beaches. (But, hey, have fun!)

Throughout New Jersey, it was mostly in the 80s and 90s, but four days earlier, it hit 110 degrees in Runyon, an all-time record for the state. This new law had pretty stupid timing.

Three days later, by coincidence, *of course*, some city council wiseacres in Stone Harbor, practically a stone's throw from Cape May, decided they would table a rule forbidding topless bathing suits for men that they considered the previous month. Any would-be shirtless guys displeased with Cape May's decision could instead visit and improve the local economy of Stone Harbor.

New Mexico

The state was in the low 90s, but nobody was complaining. The rain was only 25 percent lower than usual, so New Mexico largely avoided a drought. Tourism was also up. People were actually coming to New Mexico to cool off.

New York

Floyd Heitman was a watchman on a road construction job near the town of Burt. He had been sleeping nightly in his car, parked alongside the road. Tonight, Heitman found somewhere cooler to sleep—a nearby orchard. The next morning, he returned to his car, now a heap of scrap metal. In the night, another vehicle hit it, and Heitman became one of a handful of people who could credit the 1936 heat wave for *saving* his life.

North Carolina

In Charlotte, the high was 89. Generally, the state was never affected by the heat wave as badly as the rest of the country, though a North Carolina resident drowned in Idaho today. Still, there was a heat wave ripple effect affecting the state: a milk shortage. The drought meant a heavier demand for milk, and North Carolinians were having trouble getting their usual share.

North Dakota

Today, in 100-plus heat, there were deaths in Grand Folks and Inkster, among other communities, and a seventy-eight-year-old merchant drowned in Cannonball River; he was standing on the dam, cooling off, when he slipped and struck his head, and down he went. A twelve-year-old boy from Raleigh (93°F) who couldn't swim waded in a shallow area of a water-filled coal mine—and stepped into a ten-foot hole. His fourteen-year-old brother galloped on a horse to seek help, which would never arrive in time.

Ohio

Such a variety of incidents happened here that it's hard to know where to start.

- In the morning, in Cincinnati (105.6°F), Margaret Conners, a heat victim, was laid to rest. For the first time, as far as anyone recalled, St. Xavier Church allowed mourners to wear white to the funeral instead of traditional black. That's because, for those who missed this information in science class, the color black absorbs light and white reflects it, and so you're always going to be cooler wearing white. Mourners, the church suggested, could bring black handkerchiefs.
- In Cincinnati, brewery workers were emptying a vat of scalding water when one of them passed out and fell into it. The forty-year-old died at the hospital.
- The Cincinnati Public Library set a new, temporary, schedule. The library was a four-story building. Heat rises, and with an iron roof, the top floor was dangerously toasty.

The librarians were concerned because on the fourth floor, only a small railing prevented employees from falling into an open space and pancaking on the first floor of the reading room. Nobody needed much imagination to visualize a librarian securing a book for a patron, becoming dizzy, and pitching over the railing. For the foreseeable future, the library would close at 1 P.M.

- Mary Smith, a sixty-nine-year-old Cleveland resident, was at the Thistledown racetrack with her family. During the fourth race between eight horses, with names like Dame Grundy and Yankee Waters, Black Miss won a neck-and-neck race with All Devil. An exhilarated Smith, with winning ticket in hand, collapsed in front of the grandstand. The track physician who examined her was skeptical that the heat had done her in, feeling that the excitement of winning was the overriding factor. Still, considering that 94 was the high, and there were nineteen other heat victims in Cleveland today, it's hard to dismiss the weather's contribution to her demise. (If Smith's family cashed in her $2 ticket, they received $8.40.)
- In Dayton (104°F), a married couple were holed up in their basement, staying out of the heat. But maybe the close quarters hurt the husband's psyche. He was stressed over a speeding ticket and had been ill for weeks; today, he shot and killed his wife and himself.
- In Lancaster, the heat brought down Jack Greenhowe, a Black laborer on a construction crew. They were building the Calvary Orthodox Lutheran Church. Greenhowe was bused in from Ohio's capital, Columbus. He was a few hours into his first day on the job, carrying bricks, when he suddenly felt unwell. Greenhowe sat in the shade but a moment later fell over—dead. It's a beautiful church, but nobody should have been working on it today. It was 116 degrees.
- In Oak Harbor, there were rumors of a ghost walking the streets. Otto Domrose, superintendent of Ottawa County's

poorhouse, had not been killed the night before by the heat, as everybody heard. In fact, Domrose said that he wasn't even sick. The fifty-six-year-old wasn't sure how the talk of his death started but wondered on a morning walk why townspeople were looking at him strangely. Then he came home, and it all made sense when a newspaper reporter in Port Clinton called, requesting details on Domrose's life for the obituary. Domrose remarked that he was relieved that the truth got out before there was a funeral.

- James Blake was a Zanesville city employee who arrived to his car and saw an extremely flat tire. The high was 107, and one can imagine the heavy sigh or swearing that followed, but Blake brought out some tools, either from his office or from the trunk of his vehicle, pulled out his spare tire, and went to work. It took a long time to get everything right, and he was sweaty and miserable the entire time, but he did what had to be done and put away his tools. Then he realized . . . he changed the wrong tire.

Oklahoma

Few people have had worse first days on the job. Mrs. Marie Mansker was thirty-five years old, a divorced woman who told everybody she was a widow (it was easier that way). She was also the mother of a nine-year-old boy and was a longtime housekeeper, ever since she needed to find employment once her husband, Earnest, skipped town. Mansker had just moved out of a friend's home, which may be where her son still was. Thanks to the help of the YWCA Employment Bureau, she started working yesterday as a live-in maid for a prominent architect in Tulsa.

She started work early. Throughout the day, she complained about the heat. It was 107 degrees, and even though the family was wealthy, there wasn't air-conditioning. Mansker retired early to her room.

Her body was found in bed at 7 A.M. by the architect's wife. Mansker died around 3 A.M., the coroner concluded. The heat wouldn't be better today with Tulsa seeing 108 degrees and parts of the state hitting 117. A hearing for her son's guardianship was set for early August.

Ontario

Pastures and crops were suffering due to the drought, and in Woodstock (93°F) farmer Tom Dent became concerned about his champion Holstein cow, Springbank Snow Countess. She gave birth the day before to a calf, which died in the heat. Dent took no chances today. He led his cow into a room in his barn filled with ice and electric fans. Springbank Snow Countess hung on a few more weeks but died in August. She was buried on the farm, with a marker and a fence surrounding her grave.

Pennsylvania

There were heat deaths in Fredonia, Pittsburgh, Latrobe, Ambridge, Homewood-Brushton, and Sheraden. A depressing repetition played out with many victims. In Fredonia, everybody was shocked to learn about the death of an eighteen-year-old who collapsed while on a ladder painting a house. Near the town of Henrietta (99°F), around 9 P.M., a sixteen-year-old boy decided to cool off in a swimming hole, an abandoned quarry where minerals had once been dug. Soon, his friends couldn't find him. At midnight, using searchlights and headlamps, rescuers were still searching for his body.

Quebec

In Montreal, the high was 84 degrees. But most days this summer, if you lived in Quebec, you were not sweating the heat wave.

Rhode Island

Rhode Island was in the low 80s. No heat deaths today—but violent thunderstorms throttled the state, with one bolt of lightning hitting a house and briefly knocking out the twenty-one-year-old housewife inside.

South Carolina

Much of the state today was in the 90s. The heat and sunshine were taking a toll on crops, said G. C. Merchant, the meteorologist at the Columbia weather bureau.

South Dakota

South Dakota's open tennis tournament in Sioux Falls was held after delaying it for ten days. But today's high was 103, similar to the last ten days. The tournament went on, carefully; over the next few days, players suffered, but nobody passed out or died mid-serve.

Tennessee

Much of the state was in the mid-90s. People were hospitalized due to the heat, including a police officer who collapsed in his car in Memphis (93°F) and a water meter reader in Nashville (97°F).

Texas

The high in Pampa was 101 degrees. In Wichita Falls, it was 105. Clarendon was 110. Most Texans were accustomed to the heat, but there were heat deaths, including one in Pampa yesterday, and more were coming.

Utah

No official heat deaths were reported today, but there was probably one: James George, an eighty-year-old Los Angeles resident visiting Provo. He became ill walking down a street and entered a billiards hall to get out of the sun. Minutes later, he had a heart attack and fell off his stool. The last several days of George's visit, temperatures were in the 70s and 80s. Today, the high was 95.

Virginia

In Fries (92°F), a twenty-year-old woman drowned in New River. In Danville (93°F), the city engineer assigned workers to monitor the steel drawbridges. The bridges were expanding in the heat, making it difficult to lower and raise them, and workers were instructed to make sure the expansion joints were operating properly.

Wisconsin

Fred Winkelman, the director of the Vilas Park Zoo, wasn't concerned that a fugitive monkey was roaming around Madison.

"This is no kind of weather to be chasing monkeys," he told the city's newspaper. "The kids are having a lot of fun with him, but they can't catch him. If you climb the tree he's in, he'll jump to the roof of a house, and if you climb up on the house, he'll jump back into another tree. Sooner or later, he'll get into a garage or some other building for shelter. They always do. And then we catch them."

As evening fell, Stanley Feeney, a thirty-five-year-old police officer in Madison, spotted a pile of men's and women's clothing on the beach of Brittingham Park, at Lake Monona, a popular swimming spot (and the place where, in thirty-one years, singer Otis Redding's plane would crash during a storm).

The pile of clothes made Officer Feeney suspicious, and sure enough, upon getting closer, he saw a naked couple in their twenties dashing out of the water. Feeney ran and caught up with Dolores Westly, who had circled back to the clothes and was grabbing some to cover herself.

Feeney then cornered Fred Kleinert in the bathhouse. He arrested the young adults—who both gave false names at first, which wouldn't help them in the coming days when they mounted a defense. Feeney dropped Westly off at her house with the promise that she would get properly dressed and come to the police station to be booked. He then drove Kleinert to the police station. It was the start of a three-day legal headache for the couple.

Feeney was following the letter of the law. Still, one hopes that he was a little empathetic to the couple. He wasn't a model citizen either. Earlier in the year, he was caught drinking on the job and lost forty-five days of pay.

But from sunset to sundown and in between, this was simply not a good day for Wisconsin. It was estimated that at least 130 people lost their lives to the heat in the state today. There were heat deaths in numerous cities, including Madison, Milwaukee, Green Bay, Beloit, Menasha, Racine, Eleva, Darlington, Oshkosh, Ridgeway, and Eau Claire. It might be easier to name the communities that didn't have a heat death.

One of those deaths was somebody whose name will probably never be known and whose bones are probably now part of the soil in some potter's field somewhere. Two miles south of Stetsonville, an unidentified transient in his late forties rode a freight train, as many people did throughout the Great Depression. The hobo was in a gondola car—low walls and no roof—on top of a carload of wooden railroad ties, and he was receiving a constant rush of welcome, cool air.

But at 2:12 P.M., the tracks underneath the train buckled in the heat, the result of a sun-kink. Five train cars flew off the tracks. The man catapulted into the air. He crashed into the earth. Then the wooden railroad ties landed, covering his body.

30

JULY 15

The Rainmakers

Today's Death Toll: 800+
Total Death Toll: 5,100+

Ever since agriculture became an industry, people have tried to make it rain. The parched public has prayed for water to come from the heavens. Native Americans have engaged in rain dances, also a form of prayer. And in 1936, the profession of rainmakers was still hanging on, albeit barely.

But once upon a time, particularly in the 1800s and early 1900s, you could make a decent living as a rainmaker. Robert George Dyrenforth was one of the first well-known rainmakers. He was a "concussionist," a term for a professional who makes it rain (in theory, anyway) by blasting water from the sky with explosives.

In the late 1800s and early 1900s, the government dabbled with hiring professional rainmakers. In 1871, a civil engineer, Edward Powers, wrote a book called *War and the Weather*. Powers noticed—as had others, including Napoleon—that it often seemed to rain after a battle. Maybe, Powers theorized, it had something to do with the explosives?

Or maybe generals were monitoring the weather and trying to time it so they didn't conduct a battle in the rain? Maybe it was simply a coincidence?

Twenty years later, a congressman read Powers's book and convinced his fellow lawmakers to invest thousands of dollars to conduct rain-explosive experiments, and the aforementioned Dyrenforth, a patent attorney, was selected to run them. Dyrenforth had no background in explosives or weather. But as a patent attorney, he worked with many clients who had rainmaking contraptions, and he was intrigued to try his hand at making weather.

Dyrenforth conducted numerous experiments, mostly in 1891 and 1892, blowing up lots of stuff, but nothing really came of it. But Dyrenforth had a lot of unearned confidence and appeared fully convinced in his ability to make it rain. He went by R. G. Dyrenforth, professionally, and joked that the R. G. stood for Rain-Getter.

Clayton Jewell was another prominent rainmaker. In 1893, Jewell, from Goodland, Kansas, was a thirty-year-old railroad dispatcher who traveled in a train with a large water tank on one of the railroad cars, which he claimed could generate rain. Part of Jewell's secret was releasing 5,000 cubic feet of gases per hour into the atmosphere, but what the gases were, he wouldn't say. If he couldn't produce rain within a certain amount of time, often around five days, he usually found an excuse, such as he had never worked at this particular altitude.

From 1911 to 1914, Charles W. Post, the cereal magnate who created Kellogg's, also experimented with rainmaking via dynamite explosions. When you become rich beyond belief, you can do these things.

Post should have invested his money with Willis Carrier, the inventor of the air conditioner who was, around this time, getting somewhere with his new creation. You could also argue that Carrier shared some DNA with the professional rainmakers. Carrier sometimes referred to his invention as "weather making" machinery.

And today, Frank Clark, a forty-six-year-old barber and part-time rainmaker from Brantford, Ontario, was turned away at the Canadian border. He was on a Chicago-bound bus with a fellow rainmaker, Edward Twardus, thirty-nine, who lived in New York City and had been a professional rainmaker for the last eight years. Clark's visa wasn't up to date, and despite vowing that he could end the drought in the United States, the border patrol refused to allow him, and his four suitcases of rainmaking equipment, into America.

Twardus also tried reasoning with the border patrol, to no avail. He told the Associated Press that he and Clark were going to the west, and for free, they would make it rain, "just as a demonstration." Clark's machinery, according to Twardus, consisted of batteries, magnets, and coils, creating static that would be broadcast "to attract rain clouds."

"There is always rain somewhere, and Clark's machine gets it where it is needed," Twardus said. "Last September, he caused six rainfalls of about one inch between Chatham and Brantford, and ended a two months' drought. I have invented a machine that operates much like Clark's apparatus, but he can cause rain over an area of 55 to 60 square miles while mine has a more limited effective area."

Sadly, Clark never got to go to America and change history by ending the drought and the Dust Bowl.

Of all the professional rainmakers, the most successful was Charles Mallory Hatfield.

Hatfield got his start in April 1902, on his father's ranch, when his first experiment with rainmaking netted 0.03 inches of rain (or so he said). Since then, he had worked on dozens of commercial contracts, and Hatfield either knew what he was doing or he was quite lucky, because he did make money over the years—and his contracts stated that he wouldn't be paid unless there was rain.

That said, Hatfield's contracts almost guaranteed success. In 1904, he went before the Los Angeles's city council and promised to make eighteen inches of rain within five months, by May 1—for $1,000. The city agreed, and Hatfield went to work, and the rain came (18.96 inches in March) and Hatfield got his money. But within five months, and in the spring? Even in Southern California, those weren't terrible odds.

As for his work, Hatfield erected thirty five foot towers and on top of each, he placed a shallow galvanized tray, four inches deep and four feet wide. Inside the trays, he placed a secret chemical solution, only known to him and his younger brother, Paul, who was his assistant almost from the beginning. Over the years, the towers got shorter, going down to twenty-five feet, and by 1936, twelve feet.

Hatfield always sounded reasonable, which was helpful in attracting skeptical members of the public who might be receptive to his message. "I do not claim full credit for the downpour, but I do say that I was responsible for holding the storm in southern California as long as it stayed," Hatfield told reporters in 1904, shortly after the deluge. Years later, he would say,

"My system consists of chemical combinations working in harmony with the law which makes rain in a natural way."

The following year, Hatfield explained the secret of his success: "When it comes to my knowledge that there is a moisture-laden atmosphere hovering, say, over the Pacific, I immediately begin to attract that atmosphere with the assistance of my chemicals, basing my efforts on the scientific principles of cohesion."

That sounds as if Hatfield was essentially saying: If I hear of a rain forecast, I pull out my chemicals and take credit for however long the rain sticks around.

Hatfield told a reporter, "I do not fight nature, as Dyrenforth, Jewell and several others have done, by means of dynamite, bombs and other explosives. I woo her by means of this subtle attraction."

His strategy wasn't entirely gobbledygook. Hatfield seems to have been on the same track researchers were when they began seeding clouds in the 1940s. Seeding clouds is still an ongoing practice, in which particulars like silver iodide are added to a cloud so water molecules can freeze around them and produce more rain than there otherwise would be. Whether this works, however, is still up for debate.

Most of Hatfield's income was as a full-time sewing machine salesman, but as a side hustle, rainmaking was profitable. For instance, in the summer of 1921, the United Agricultural Association paid him $4,000 per inch of rain for every additional inch beyond three inches (they assumed it would rain at least three inches) up to six inches, then they would stop payment (Hatfield netted $8,000). Professional rainmaking essentially came to an end in late 1929, however, when the depression hit, and nobody had extra funds to gamble that maybe a guy could rig the weather. By 1931, Hatfield was in the throes of an ugly divorce and obliged to pay child support—$7 a week—to his wife, who was raising their thirteen-year-old son.

Now, Hatfield was sixty-one years old and described as a tall, stooped figure with a long thin face, a professional manner, and a profound faith in his profession. He hadn't been employed to make rain since the Wall Street crash, so it was a little more than surprising when he turned down an offer to make rain in early June. A bigwig Hollywood producer, Jesse Lasky, whose film *Wings* was the first to win an Oscar, asked Hatfield if he could create a storm for him to promote an upcoming movie, possibly *The Gay Desperado*, a 1936 film, but one in which rain doesn't figure prominently into the plot. Hatfield remarkably declined.

"I could bring the rain all right," Hatfield said. "Yes, sir. But it'd cause more damage to the crops than I care to do." That had never been a fear of his before, skeptical critics noted. Perhaps Hatfield sensed that there was going to be little rain in the forecast? But today, on July 15, either he felt more confident about the possibility of rain, or he really needed the money. Hatfield declared that he was offering his services to any American city that wanted him. For no charge, sort of.

"I could make it rain anywhere you name and will do it gratis free and will do it for the bare expenses," Hatfield told a United Press reporter. "It is because it makes me sad to think of crops drying up and cattle dying, when it's all so unnecessary." Yes, so unnecessary, when Hatfield could easily make all of the dry weather go away, if somebody would just pay him: "All rainfall, whether natural or artificial, is produced from ionization," Hatfield explained.

Hatfield had no takers. The country would continue to bake to death.

Missouri

"It's bad news, but I can't help it. Fair and continued warm," said Andrew Hamrick, who was based out of Kansas City and being interviewed by the press. Calling the weather "warm" was a ridiculous understatement, with today's high of 107 degrees, but Hamrick was using the government meteorology vernacular of the time. "There is not a sign of relief in sight," Hamrick added.

Hamrick explained how "these cool waves come in on high pressure areas from the Pacific Ocean and down from Alaska." He said that the waves from Alaska were always "strong, sturdy fellows," but the ones from the Pacific tended to collapse when they arrived in Kansas.

"They don't have any stamina. Kansas can stop one of them without even trying," Hamrick said. "We had a good one headed this way, but after sticking its head into Kansas a few miles, it gave up. It's too Pacific; it won't do battle." Hamrick said that he had concluded it was useless to hope for a Pacific cool wave.

"From now on, a Pacific high is just a pain in the neck to me. If it isn't from Canada, it isn't genuine," Hamrick said, dispirited. "It's going to be warm again today, again tomorrow, and so far as we can see now, right on up to Christmas. There isn't a thing in sight to indicate relief."

Relief wasn't in sight, and the death toll was mounting. Overnight, and into the morning, the heat eradicated another seventy-seven lives in St. Louis. There were six more deaths in Kansas City, six in Hannibal, three in Kirksville, where a grass fire was out of control, and there were deaths in other cities like Joplin, Maryville, and Piedmont. Warrensburg (114°F) was the hottest town in the state. Rolla (102°F) was the coolest. In Cape Girardeau (108°F), a seventy-six-year-old told his relatives that he "couldn't stand the heat" and took a razor to his throat.

In Kansas City (107°F), forty construction workers who were walking on steel beams, working on the new city hall building that was going to be thirty floors high, left their jobs, telling their boss that it was too dangerous. The air, they said, was "absolutely still," and everyone feared passing out and falling 410 feet to the ground.

Michigan

The worst of the heat wave was over in Detroit (86°F), but twenty people still died there. Around the state, there were another seventeen deaths, and bodies of heat victims were still turning up. One woman who died several days earlier was discovered in a ditch. Witnesses said the forty-six-year-old was on a bus and, feeling beat up from the heat, got off. After the bus left, she must have collapsed. Her body had blood covering her hands and clothing. Doctors examined her and concluded that there had been no foul play, just internal bleeding.

California

In Los Angeles (90°F), the trial of Rattlesnake James was in full swing. For weeks now, the country had been learning about Robert S. James, dubbed Rattlesnake James by reporters, and his efforts to murder his seventh wife, Mary Busch James, who was twenty-eight and pregnant. It was a sordid, ongoing legal drama, one that likely allowed people to almost forget about the heat for a few minutes as they read about it in the paper or listened to the news on the radio. James initially confessed—but a day later said the police should be talking to his pal, Charles Hope. Hope said he had nothing to do with the murder and helpfully explained that Mr. James tortured his wife with rattlesnakes.

No, not true, James argued, adding that, by the way, Hope suggested he use black widow spiders to kill her.

The prosecution asserted that James attempted to kill Mary with rattlesnakes in order to collect on her life insurance policy. When that didn't work, he drowned her in the bathtub. He then dumped her body in their backyard's koi fishpond, trying to make it look like she had had an accident. The prosecution also charged that this wasn't the first time James had bumped off a spouse. His third wife, Winona Wallace James, he knocked out in 1932, put her body into a car, and rolled it off an embankment. But Winona survived, so he took her to a cabin and murdered her in the bathtub. At the time, he explained to authorities that his wife had fallen into the tub and died. That excuse was accepted.

But James was out of luck this time since law enforcement couldn't buy that a guy could have seven wives and two of them would end up drowning. That just seemed . . . suspicious.

Today, the prosecutors brought into the courtroom the two rattlesnakes they said James used to kill his wife. One of the rattlesnakes, named Lethal, escaped his box, creating a mild panic. Women and children screamed. People climbed onto their chairs. Bailiffs yelled for order. The snake expert searched for Lethal, who was nowhere to be seen. About five minutes later, he fished it out from behind a bookcase with a wire fork attached to a pole and got it back into its box, where Lightning, the other rattlesnake, was still coiled.

In Riverside (105°F), Ben White, a public administrator and the county coroner, strolled down Main Street in a fur coat and fur cap and, draped over his arm, a fur robe. White explained to a reporter, "I was appraising these furs with the tax appraiser when he bet me a $10 hat I wouldn't wear 'em down to the courthouse." White mopped his brow and said, "I guess I win."

White, however, was far from the only adult making silly bets about the heat. There were several heat challenges this week across North America:

- In response to a friend ribbing him about the heat, on July 9, Gavin Hamilton, eighty-six, of Galt, Ontario (98.96°F), successfully walked down the city's main street in a fur coat and woolen mittens.
- On July 13, In Royal Oak, Michigan (104°F), Caspar Schroff, thirty-nine, bet his Elks Temple lodge brothers that he could stand as much heat as anyone could dish out. Which is how he came to sit for twenty-three minutes before a roaring bonfire wearing a fur-collared leather jacket, a blanket wrapped around his knees and a towel around his head. To win the bet, Schroff had to sit for twenty minutes, but to account for any variation in everybody's watches, he did it for twenty-three. No word on how much the bet was, but Schroff claimed that his weight dropped from 203 to 187 pounds.
- A milkman in Goderich, Ontario, on July 14, was discussing the best ways to stay cool, which led to him boasting that his milk truck could make sixty miles an hour. Nobody believed him, and he challenged them to a bet. At midnight, the milkman's truck took off down the road, but after a quarter mile, he didn't make a turn, and his vehicle went flying into a frog pond, landing upside down. The milkman crawled out, smelling of frog, some said, and he got to a telephone and called for a tow truck. He didn't win the bet, but as a cooling-off strategy, trying to reach sixty miles an hour in the dead of night and landing upside down in a frog pond worked beautifully.

Kansas

Grasshoppers were one of the few animals still thriving. There were so many in Hutchinson that fishermen put away their poles. Enough grasshoppers fell into lakes and creeks that fish gobbled them up and were no longer tempted by bait. In Wichita (107°F), pavement on West Douglas buckled, sending bricks flying into the air as residents and tourists watched in awe.

The heat wave continued its killing spree:

- In Manhattan (111°F), a forty-four-year-old woman getting a tumor removed died on the operating table; she had been suffering from the heat and doctors said the high temperatures hurt any chance of a recovery.
- Near Muscotah (108°F), the Freeman family—a man, woman and their nineteen-year-old daughter—decided to move a suffering calf to a shady part of the farm. But the calf's heat-crazed mother wasn't pleased and attacked all three family members. Mrs. Freeman was gored to death.
- A sixty-seven-year-old farmer passed out in the town of Columbus (110°F) and fell off a load of hay in a field. But the heat technically didn't kill him. The iron wagon wheel that his head hit did.

Virginia

In Danville (104°F), soda fountains at pharmacies were crowded—at 9 A.M. Customers clamored for cold drinks, and extra workers were added to keep up with the demand. Free water was given out more frequently than anyone could remember. Staying hydrated was crucial: a Danville carpenter working on a building in Forest Hills, laboring in 104-degree weather and perhaps not drinking enough, became ill and was taken home, where he died.

That evening, Danville homeowners slept in their yards; apartment dwellers swarmed the parks. The streets at night were busier than anyone remembered. People drove around, trying to cool off with the breeze they were creating. The temperature eventually dropped that night, but it never got cooler than 79 degrees.

Illinois

The mercury hit 114 in Peoria, a new record. The three city hospitals (Procter, Methodist, and St. Francis) were swamped with heat patients. Procter had so many, they put adults in the nursery; St. Francis's patients lay in beds in the hallways; Methodist was at a 95 percent capacity. There were ninety-three deaths in the Peoria area so far, thirty-six in about the last thirty hours.

People died in Cicero, Shelbyville, Ohio, Cowden, Vorhees, Irving Township, and Sullivan. In Bloomington, Charles Morgan, the carpenter, wrote, "Seems hotter than ever today. I can hardly stand it. People are beginning to wither. Several prostrations. Many people die now from the terrible heat." One of those deceased people was Morgan's friend, Tom Noonan, who owned a store and was a local musician who was in a marching band boasting thirty members. Despite his shop being in a cool basement, the heat was too much for Noonan.

That evening, Morgan and his wife went to participate in the annual Railroad Week, a train festival. Ten thousand people descended upon the town to watch a parade and hand car races. The local marching band also performed, now featuring twenty-nine members.

About the time the Morgans were celebrating trains, the body of William Huffman, seventy-eight, was found in Sycamore, and everybody started piecing together what happened. Two days earlier, on Monday, Huffman told a neighbor that he was going to change his storm windows. A widower for a year with no children, nobody noticed his absence on Tuesday. By Wednesday evening, his neighbor realized she hadn't seen Huffman lately. She walked to the back of his house, where she saw a startling sight.

There was the ladder, resting against the back porch roof. Huffman had collapsed on the roof. His body would have tumbled off and dropped to the ground except that his hammer was in his back pocket. The tool's claw had stuck into the roof, preventing him from falling.

Indiana

On page four of *The Indianapolis Star*, an advertisement from the Colonial Furniture Company spoke volumes:

> *Hooray! We have FANS Again!*
>
> *We thought we had a stock large enough for all season. We guessed wrong! Rather we didn't count on the worst heat wave of all time. Anyhow, we ran out of fans—and disappointed hundreds of customers. Finally we located a new supply—plenty, we believe.*

Everyone wanted an electric fan. It was common to see streetcar passengers heading to work carrying electric fans with them to their offices.

In Evansville, the humidity hit 81 percent at 7 A.M., and the high was 105.7 degrees. That morning, Elizabeth Jones, seventy-four, left her husband at their house and went on a somber errand. Their roommate, Mrs. Jones's seventy-seven-year-old sister, died the previous day from the heat. So Mrs. Jones arranged the burial, picking out a casket and making her sister's funeral arrangements for the next day.

After returning home, Jones became a heat victim herself, dying at 5:30 P.M., the tenth heat fatality in Evansville in about twenty-four hours. Tomorrow afternoon, there was a double funeral, and working out the details for it was easy. The family added a second casket. Elizabeth Jones hadn't realized it but she planned her own funeral.

Tennessee

It was morning and the temperature was approaching a high of 96. Leon McCanless, thirty-eight, and a Tennessee Electric Power Company employee, was on a telephone pole in Nashville (96°F) working with a high-voltage line. At 9:30 A.M., his clothing was soaked in sweat, and he brushed up against a wire. A safety strap kept his body from falling. Once he was removed from the pole, two of his colleagues and medical staff spent hours trying to bring the electrocuted McCanless back to life.

The heat wave wasn't finished with Nashville, talking aim at three citizens:

- At 11:30 A.M., Louise Madison, a Black maid, was walking downtown on Fifth Avenue and passing a ten-cent store when she conked out. Fortunately, Madison awakened, although it must have been disconcerting to find a crowd of people looking down at her—and even more so to realize that about $200 worth of belongings were gone: her ring, wristwatch, and fountain pen, and $3.35 in cash.
- Nobody knew Buford Jackson's age. The coroner made a guess—suggesting that he was "about 80" on the death certificate. Papers described Jackson as an "aging farmhand." The farmer he worked for said Jackson had been working for him for twenty years and was probably between seventy and eighty. Jackson may have been born into slavery, which would explain why he has such a scant paper trail. He was found dead in a field.
- Herbert Burch was a twenty-eight-year-old criminal attorney and in poor health ever since he contracted pneumonia last winter. He was in a hotel when the heat attacked, and Mother Nature finally took him out.

Wisconsin

At the Madison police station, Dolores Westly and Fred Kleinert were informed they would go on trial tomorrow for swimming unclothed.

They protested that they had been swimming apart. No hanky-panky, just swimming.

Police Chief William McCormick was having none of it. After dismissing them, McCormick told reporters, "If this couple can get by with swimming in the nude, then others can, and I'm not in favor of making Madison a nudist colony."

It was a valid concern from his perspective. Nudism, as a trend, first caught on big in 1927 in France, and while it was something of a scandal, in 1929, a French reporter, sans clothes, infiltrated a nudist colony and wrote about how flabby and unattractive everyone looked, and the controversy died down. By 1931, however, nudist colonies started popping up in states like New York, California, and Florida. In 1935, the president of the International Nudist conference stated that there were eighty-three nudist colonies throughout the United States.

This summer, the Lorain, Ohio, police force campaigned against nude bathing after getting wind of naked swimmers cavorting on Lake Erie's shore—and promised jail time in a hot cell for anyone who tried it.

About a week earlier, on a Friday night about 11 o'clock, in Waupun, Wisconsin, nine men from two softball teams swam in the nude at a county park pool, in the darkness. A crowd gathered to watch. When law enforcement showed up, the nude bathers unsuccessfully scattered, many going into the brush, getting stuck with nettles; on Monday, the men faced a judge who probably thought it was all kind of inane because he only fined them $1 each, a little over $20 in today's dollars.

Two days earlier, in Daly City, California, where you might think the law would have been far more permissive than in the Midwest, two male nudists pushing forty years of age pled guilty for indecent exposure after being caught on a public beach sunbathing au naturel. There had been other nude bathers, but they got away, it was said at the hearing.

The two men were asked if they were in a cult. (It was a common belief that if you liked parading around without clothes, you must be brainwashed.) They denied being cult members, and the men were each handed the maximum sentence of six months of jail time, with no chance to pay a fine instead.

Minnesota

In Minneapolis, the high was 98 degrees, and nineteen people died. Gilbert Seashore, the Minneapolis coroner, said fatalities in the city had been second in volume only to the deaths recorded during the influenza epidemic of 1918, a time when he had been just a year into his career.

John Mondorf, a thirty-six-year-old from Idaho, disembarked a bus and went to the Minneapolis sheriff to share that a gangster was trying to kill him. The sheriff didn't see Mondorf as credible, just confused. Mondorf was taken to a hospital, where he barricaded himself in his room, leaped out a window, and fled. He was returned to the sheriff, who along with the deputies tried to cool the man off until he came to his senses.

What Mondorf and the entire country needed was a good air-conditioning system. Today, *The Minneapolis Star* ran an article that included an interview with an air-cooling equipment distributor executive, who said he "could have sold 10 times as many units" if they could have been secured. "Right now, we are a month behind on our orders," he said. "We have had heavy demands from hospitals and business offices as well as from householders."

Air-conditioning couldn't come to the country soon enough. This evening, Minneapolis resident Rose Minder, fifty-eight, took bedding to her backyard and became at least the second person in the country to be hit by a vehicle. Her neighbor backed his car out of the alley the next morning, unaware she was there. Minder wasn't injured too badly; she took her blanket and pillow and finished sleeping in the house.

New York

Jack Carter was a well-known—at least in theater circles—dramatic actor. Born in 1902, John Richard Carter was a light-skinned Black man who could have passed for White but didn't try to, a guy who had as colorful a life as they come. It's said that he had mob ties and ran a brothel in Washington, DC, before he started to get serious about acting. And when he did get serious, he seized everybody's attention. In 1927, he was a smash as Crown in the original *Porgy*, a stage play that led to the famous opera *Porgy and Bess*.

By 1936, Carter was in New York City and working with future film director and legend Orson Welles. But Welles, currently an occasional radio performer and stage actor, was establishing himself as a theater director. This summer, Welles directed William Shakespeare's *Macbeth*, with an all-Black cast, as part of the Federal Theatre Project, a program that was part of Franklin Roosevelt's New Deal. The WPA was fronting the money for the play, as part of a way to give employment to actors and juice the economy.

For several months, Carter starred in *Macbeth* to rave reviews, and today, he delivered another spellbinding performance. Then he went to his dressing room, showered, got into his street clothes, and left the Adelphi Theatre, all of which would have been swell except that it was the intermission. There were still two acts to go.

An announcer, needing to explain Carter's absence somehow, told the audience that the intense heat had gotten to their star, and an understudy took over the rest of the role.

The cast and crew were skeptical that the heat got to Carter. Today's high was 87, hot but cooler than it had been, and there was low humidity. In fact, by the evening, the heat wave in Gotham was starting to break.

Still, it's difficult not to give Carter some benefit of the doubt. While the only person known to have died in New York City directly from the heat today was a seventy-six-year-old who passed out days earlier from the heat, residents fainted and were treated by doctors, and one million people descended upon Coney Island to enjoy the surf. Also: Shakespearean costumes are heavy.

But some said that Carter's heavy drinking led to his mercurial behavior. Others felt his early departure had something to do with his romance with Blanche Williams, an office employee at the theater; they married almost two weeks later. Whatever prompted Carter to leave the show midway, apparently without conferring with the director or cast, whether it was heat, drinking, or just having an off day, Carter did himself no favors by ending his workday early.

After hearing how well the understudy performed in the last two acts, Jack Carter said to the theater manager, "I suppose I cut my throat." "You said it, kid," the manager responded.

Carter and the manager were not wrong. Carter landed sporadic work on the stage and screen well into the 1940s, but whether he was justified or not for abandoning the play, the actor sabotaged his career by leaving mid-performance. In more ways than one, he was no longer hot.

Ohio

Carl Tremaine fought many of the greats like Johnny Buff, Cannonball Eddie Martin, and Bad News Eber, with Joe Humphreys announcing to the audience the details of some of those fights. But Tremaine was never really a boxing champion in his own right. Still, Tremaine knew what to do with a fist. One sportswriter recalled a fight in Pittsburgh in 1923, where Tremaine clocked Pete Zivic in the seventh round. "Down he went," wrote Regis M. Welsh. "Fans thought he had been killed. Not a muscle moved. He was counted out, carried out, and it was a long time before he or the fans realized what happened."

But that was when Tremaine was twenty-four. Two years later, after a violent fight that Tremaine lost after twelve rounds, his nickname was "the uncrowned champion." He was starting to be seen as someone with a lot of unfulfilled promise. Last year, in 1935, a drunk, moaning Tremaine was picked up by police in a Cleveland, Ohio, alley. The judge, a boxing fan, regarded the bloated Tremaine with stunned curiosity. But fame wasn't much of a currency for the judge, who ordered the ex-boxer to a workhouse for "the cure."

The cure did not cure Tremaine, who developed pneumonia and was taken to the hospital. He survived that round, but this summer, the thirty-seven-year-old was again sentenced to sixty days in a workhouse for intoxication. During his stay, the heat picked a fight and landed a final knockout punch.

Kentucky

In Ross (104°F), a coroner, an assistant fire chief, and a life squad tried to save a six-year-old boy found in the shallow end of a swimming pool but nothing, including emergency surgery, worked. They concluded that the boy died from the heat; no water was found in his lungs.

Late in the day, in Louisville (111°F), there were two rainstorms. Excited residents raced outside, pulling up trousers and skirts and racing through the puddles.

Pennsylvania

About thirty drivers who delivered ice selected today to walk off the job and go on strike in the city of Sharon. It was 100 degrees.

The icemen demanded higher wages and wanted union recognition like the factory workers cranking out the ice. Their cause was just, but the strike may have imperiled lives. At least one hospital didn't get an ice delivery and one farmer fifteen miles away from Sharon died from the heat. The strike ended the next day, with drivers not getting what they wanted.

About fifty miles away, in Ambridge, iceman Louis Mercedant made his delivery and found the overheated dead body of a sixty-seven-year-old woman inside her home.

It was a day where it was hard to find much to be optimistic about. In Pittsburgh, Joseph D'Ambrosia, a thirty-two-year-old married man, rigged a device to spray water on the sweltering neighborhood kids to cool them off. It was a thoughtful gesture, and the kids probably created memories they cherished for a lifetime. Not D'Ambrosia, however. He was arrested. His device was hooked up to the city's fire hydrant.

In another almost-feel-good story since it doesn't involve death but a broken shoulder, Charles Jones, twenty-one, slept at his family's home in Derry with his bed next to a large open window. Jones fitfully tossed and turned before he fell asleep. His sisters on the front porch awakened after they heard the thud of their brother's body smashing into the ground.

Nebraska

In Omaha, Joe Rosen was struggling, not just with the heat but life. Rosen was forty-six years old and probably still suffering the effects of living through World War I as a soldier, where he fought for eleven months in France and was exposed to poison gas. He seemed to be in a good place lately, working in the CCC. But yesterday, after receiving a nice fat paycheck, he quit the CCC and bought some whiskey.

After getting drunk, Rosen got paranoid, grabbed a knife, and threatened a clerk at the hotel where he was staying. Rosen believed the clerk was trying to attack him. The police were called and took Rosen to jail.

He was released this morning, and Rosen bought another round of whiskey. Soon, drunk on a day when the high was 105, Rosen passed out the street. At a hospital, he was diagnosed with heatstroke and released in the afternoon, perhaps prematurely: Rosen decided to hurl his body in front of a moving car.

The car stopped and tried moving around Rosen, who wasn't finished with his impromptu suicide mission. He ran in front of the vehicle again, and this time the front tire went over his body, and Rosen's head hit the bumper. He was taken back to the hospital. That evening, Rosen managed to get hold of a knife and slashed his throat. The hospital staff swarmed him, treated him, and saved his life. This time, saving his life worked.

Rosen lived another twenty-one years without, it appears, getting into too much trouble. Right after getting out of the hospital, he assured his hometown paper that he no longer had a death wish. "It was a case of too much liquor and heat," he said.

Iowa

Four of Iowa's state psychiatric hospitals lost eighty-four people in the last week. H. C. White, a state board member, told the press, "Most of the victims are aged, feeble and sick patients unable to stand the intense heat.

We are taking all possible steps to protect them. Many are bed patients who cannot be moved out in yards or to cool places elsewhere. They are getting every attention possible from our doctors and nurses."

White described extra doctors and nurses being called in to give patients baths and special diets. Dr. R. H. Stewart, at Independence Hospital in Iowa, told reporters that the problem was mostly with their patients over the age of seventy. "They don't sleep well, and they quarrel and are noisy and active," Stewart said. "That is what starts their trouble. The only real remedy would be cool air, and we are powerless to give that."

Even houseflies were hot and bothered: In Newton (108°F), there were reports of the insects swarming the shade of residents' front porches.

The heat picked off people in Davenport, Northwood, and Harlan. Near Polk City, a forty-year-old man from Missouri was found lying next to Highway 60 and taken to the hospital; he could understand questions being asked of him, but he couldn't answer them.

And in Lineville, a tiny farming community that got its name for being on the border of Iowa and Missouri, several residents would embark today on an ambitious project: saving John Keeton from himself.

When John Keeton, a twenty-five-year-old farmhand, started his job at 7 A.M., it was a day like all others. Except that temperatures were heading toward 115 degrees. But there was something else different about the day. Keeton noticed that despite working hard, he wasn't sweating. He also felt like he was burning up inside.

Keeton had been outside for most of the week. He and his wife and children, a two-year-old girl and a five-year-old son, were sleeping on cots and old beds outside. Keeton, his wife, and kids lived with his wife's dad, and seven sisters and brothers. This was the Great Depression, after all, and nobody had much money. But at least Keeton had a job. It helped.

Keeton went to a neighbor's home and asked for some water. He mentioned to the woman, Emma Bright, a thirty-year-old housewife, that he wasn't sweating. Exactly what happened next isn't clear, but ninety minutes after starting work, at 8:30 A.M., Keeton's employer, Rulf Wilder, found him. Keeton did not look well.

Wilder had brought a gallon pail of water to the hay field that Keeton was mowing with horses and a tractor. Only Keeton wasn't mowing the way he typically would have.

Wilder was witnessing something that in his fifty years on the planet he didn't realize was possible: You really can go crazy from the heat. But this wasn't the type of crazy where you pull out a gun or knife and start killing people. Keeton was bananas.

"I found the boy singing wildly," Wilder said later. "You could hear him for a quarter of a mile. He was laughing at times and was driving the team and mower in all sorts of circles and figure 8's on this slope."

Wilder ran to Keeton and poured the gallon pail of cold water over his head. Then Wilder pulled Keeton by the arm, half dragging him into the shade at the side of the field. Wilder spotted Emma Bright about a quarter of a mile away and shouted, but she couldn't hear him, so he left Keeton where he was. He ran to the Bright home and used the phone to call Dr. Charles Lovett, a fifty-two-year-old country doctor who had been practicing in the area for at least thirty years.

Wilder then made his way back to Keeton, who was now throwing heavy tree limbs and logs into a creek.

"I was afraid he might feel like fighting, and I took his knife out of his pocket," Wilder said.

Wilder then monitored Keeton, who was now sitting on the bank of the creek. Keeton had removed his overalls and was tearing them into strips—and pulling out his own hair.

"He would mumble something and then give one of those fiendish, blood-curdling laughs like you get in the movies," Wilder said. "It was a hysterical laugh. He didn't recognize me. He didn't recognize anybody. Once he yelled, 'I'm the greatest sweater in the world, and I can't sweat a drop!' And then he gave that awful, hysterical laugh. He paid no attention to me."

Lovett arrived thirty minutes later. Lovett had seen a lot over the years. Lovett had set broken bones and delivered babies, including twins and triplets, and once tried to help a man who was shot in a restaurant three times by the owner, although there was nothing to be done for him. Lovett dressed wounds, nursed car accident victims back to life, removed appendixes, and fixed up a man who was kicked in the face by a horse. He also treated a man whose eyeball was almost torn out, hanging out by a socket, after a fight; surgeons later removed it.

But Lovett had never seen anything like this. As he described it, "Boy, he was crazy. He beat his breast. He tore his hair out in bunches. He ripped his overalls to shreds with his hands and tore his felt hat to bits. Only a week ago, I saw an item in the paper about a man in Detroit, crazed by the heat, and it took four men to hold him. I told my wife, 'That's all hooey.' But now, believe me, I know it was true."

Dr. Lovett asked for towels and cold water. Somebody got them—probably Mrs. Bright—and by the time they arrived, Keeton was no longer acting crazy. He was unconscious. Dr. Lovett had Wilder soak the towels in cold water, and upon the physician's instructions, the farmer wrapped the cold towels around his employee's head. They kept the towels wet and waited and hoped that Keeton, whose clothes were almost all torn off at this point, would wake.

He didn't. Not at first. But after fifteen or twenty minutes, Keeton opened his eyes.

Dr. Lovett told reporters that Keeton probably was a few minutes from dying, but the cold water and towels did the trick. It also helped that Keeton had been dragged into the shade.

"I don't remember a thing until I came to with the doctor and Mr. Wilder by me in the shade," Keeton said later.

Keeton, whose head still hurt two days after pulling out his hair, regarded his shredded overalls with some interest. Since you tried to throw nothing away during a decade when nobody had anything, Keeton told the *Des Moines Tribune*, "I guess I can use them for fly chasers for the horses." That would mean he would tie the strips of his overalls to a broom and then with that, wave away flies from the horses. "There wasn't enough left of the hat to save," Keeton added.

Keeton was ordered by Dr. Lovett to stay indoors the rest of the week—and to remain out of the sun for as much as possible the rest of the summer, a tall order for a farmhand. It was good medical advice, but Keeton's family was counting on his salary.

"I'm in a fix," Albert Nickell, Keeton's sixty-one-year-old father-in-law, told a reporter. "I'm about at the end of my rope. My kids haven't got shirts to wear, and I've got all the government loans on my farm that I can get. I don't know what to do. I can't raise much on the place the last few years, and now John can't work. We're in a tough spot."

Still, Nickell hung on to his home and land. The Wilders and Brights remained on their farms. Dr. Lovett continued saving lives and practicing medicine until April 1953, when he retired. He died the following year, of a heart attack, at the age of seventy. John Keeton, meanwhile, lived long enough to see his seventy-fifth birthday, working for a time as a truck driver before returning to working as a farmhand. As alumni of the summer of 1936, it was about as close to a happy ending as you could hope for.

31

JULY 16

Hot Wheels

Today's Death Toll: 800+
Total Death Toll: 5,900+

While drowning victims were often indirect heat victims, the hot weather also increased car accident deaths. It's easy to equate winter with car wrecks—most people would probably rather drive under an unremitting sun than on a sheet of ice. But hot weather creates dangerous driving conditions, too.

For instance, on June 12, near Flagstaff, Arizona, a couple in their sixties stopped at a Native American trading post at the Painted Desert, and the husband mentioned to someone there that the heat made him drowsy while driving. Later in the day, their car and bodies were found in a gully at the edge of the highway.

"A hot muggy weekend that sent hundreds of thousands of southern Californians onto the highways and the beaches left the aftermath of thirteen dead and several others dying today," started off a United Press article on June 22. One of those thirteen deaths was a drowning—and twelve were from car accidents.

Of course, lots of people survived heat-related car accidents over the summer. For instance, on July 11, a motorist in Hamilton, Ontario (103°F), passed out and collided into another driver. They both lived, and the collapsed motorist was charged for reckless driving—but convinced the judge to drop the charges. That same day, in Chicago, fifty-year-old Charles Lob blacked out driving; he wasn't badly hurt, and people found his accident amusing. Lob was a member of the Polar Bears Club; its members purposefully swam in icy Lake Michigan. He could handle the extreme cold but not extreme heat.

Still, chances are, if you lose consciousness while driving, it won't end well. On July 12, in St. Paul, Minnesota (106°F), seven men and one woman passed out while driving; they all died. On July 13, in Washington, Iowa (107°F), a fifty-four-year-old man drove into a ditch and was hurled from the car, which might have still worked out okay if his vehicle hadn't then rolled over on top of him.

In 1936, there was a jump of almost 2,000 traffic fatalities in the United States over the year before, though it's impossible to say how many of the 36,126 automobile deaths were due to the heat or bad driving or if it was simply a case of more traffic on the roads, and so more deaths. Still, it would be foolish to think the heat didn't have an impact. In Toronto, where temperatures were intense, car accidents climbed 2 percent in July over the previous month.

Automotive insurance officials told the *Lansing State Journal* in an article that ran today that the summer heat resulted in a higher toll of insurance claims than the industry typically saw during the winter. You could drive in the freezing cold and would probably be alert and able to react quickly, the insurers said. But in 100-degree plus heat, drivers were sluggish, slow to react, and, in a worst-case scenario, blacking out. Sleep deprivation, due to hot nights, also caused accidents. Another reason for car accidents: automobiles were overheating.

People were overheating, too. If you had a flat that needed changing, an activity that can strain anyone even in cool weather, it might be the last thing you ever did. Today, Bob Green, a forty-two-year-old truck driver, collapsed changing a tire in Seminole, Oklahoma (110°F). He was rushed to the hospital the next day. Green knew his body was shutting down, telling a friend, "I'm dying. I'm not going to last long." Ten minutes later, he was proved correct.

This was a summer in which you also really needed to monitor your tires. An Elgin, Illinois, man who stopped at a local filling station in the middle of the afternoon in mid-July told a reporter that his car developed five pounds of added pressure while driving to the city. A Martinsville, Indiana, man reported his tires acting very odd—as if he was driving on tire rims. He exited his car and found the tires extremely hard, so he let out some air, then drove a few more miles, and had the same problem—the tires were rock hard again. He released more air and kept driving. Finally, he reached home and the temperatures cooled overnight. The next morning, his tires were almost flat.

The heat wave also caused a lot of dangerous tire blowouts. H. W. Jenkins, manager of Minneapolis General Tire company, gave advice to *The Minneapolis Star* readers that was sound then—and now: "Driving fast on a cool day creates an intense heat in tires, and this is multiplied numerous times when a blistering hot sun has baked the pavements. A tire to withstand the intense heat must be sound, otherwise the driver is courting an accident if he persists in driving fast."

For the last several weeks across the country, blowouts routinely ended motorists' lives. A San Francisco married couple was in Nebraska when, at forty miles an hour, their tire blew out, causing the car to roll over three times; the wife died. A sixty-three-year-old was driving in Elkhart, Indiana, when his tires exploded; a tree was the last thing the poor guy saw. In Anadarko, Oklahoma, after a blowout, a twenty-three-year-old Apache school teacher was flung from her car. A fifty-seven-year-old in Chicago also had his tire blow out and he swerved in front of a truck.

On July 12, in Jerseyville, Illinois (105°F), William Evans, fifty, had terrible luck with a tire blow out. His problem started in the afternoon with engine trouble, and a tow truck picked up him and his twelve-year-son. Instead of riding in the tow truck with the driver, Evans and his son rode in their car. This was not a good idea.

While being towed, one of the tires of their car blew out. The tow line snapped and jerked, and Evans's car went rogue, flying free, and slamming into a tree. Evans didn't survive; his son did, barely.

The most prominent example of what a deadly combination heat and tires could be comes courtesy of Louis Murphy, a sixty-one-year-old United States senator. Today, Murphy, a father of five, was behind the wheel of a Packard sedan, driving home to Dubuque, Iowa, after a week's long vacation at Liberty Lodge, a resort near Hayward, Wisconsin. He and his wife, Ellen, were with two friends, Fred Woodward, the publisher of one of Dubuque's newspapers, *Telegraph Herald*, and his wife, Elsie. It was Elsie's car, but Murphy had taken over the driving duties. (Then and now, the publisher of a newspaper vacationing with a US senator would typically be frowned upon, but the two men *were* lifelong friends. Before going into politics, Murphy was a reporter and editor for twenty years in Dubuque and worked at the same paper as Woodward.*)

Near Chippewa Falls (100°F), the Packard's front left tire exploded. Senator Murphy kept the vehicle from veering out of control, and for seconds, it looked like everything was going to be fine, until the right tire also blew out. The vehicle ran into a ditch and rolled over three times, and Murphy was crushed against the steering wheel. A truck driver stopped to help, and he and Woodward pulled Elise and Ellen out of the car.

Senator Murphy was still alive and conscious but that was about all he had going for him. He was in a lot of pain. He was upside down. And the car was on fire.

Woodward and the truck driver extracted the senator, more people came to assist, and the fire was put out. A passerby left to call an ambulance and a doctor. The physician arrived and stayed with Murphy until the ambulance came while his wife and the Woodwards accepted a hospital ride with a Good Samaritan. The Packard was a smoldering heap of scrap metal.

Louis Murphy's lungs were punctured by his ribs, and he was suffering a head injury. Perhaps predictably he arrived at the hospital dead. Ellen was in shock when she learned her husband's fate, and no wonder. A joyous vacation turned into a nightmare due to two blown tires, and the milestone of one of the Murphys' happiest days was now their worst. It was their nineteenth anniversary.

Ontario

Stuck in Windsor and unable to cross the Canadian border, rainmakers Frank Clark and Edward Twardus unsuccessfully tried to meet Duncan Marshall, Ontario Minister of Agriculture. Clark and Twardus told the press that they were offering the province a great deal. They would make

* Since you're wondering, no apparent relation to the legendary reporter Bob Woodward.

it rain within forty-eight hours and end the drought. All for the low price of $1,500 per inch of rainfall for each area of thirty square miles.

Reporters asked why Brantford, where Clark lived, wasn't getting more rain? After all, you'd think Clark would give some free assistance to his hometown and use the city as an example of his rainmaking prowess. Clark explained that he hadn't been using his rainmaking gadgetry lately because somebody in Brantford possessed some electrical equipment that was interfering with it.

Twardus informed the press that along with a rainmaking machine, he also had a sunshine-making machine.

If a storm was approaching, Twardus said his sunshine machine would keep the bad weather at bay within a radius of twenty-five miles. So if you were running a county fair, a horse race, or a baseball game and you needed it to be sunny, for just $1,000 a day, Twardus would keep the skies clear.

Twardus, you will be shocked to hear, had a history of shady behavior. In 1928, right around the time he started talking about his ability to make rain, he lost his New Jersey law license and was jailed for two years because he hired somebody to burn down a building that he was part owner of, so he could profit from the insurance payout.

Twardus remained in the weather business at least until 1950, by then solely focused on professional sun-making. He had cut his price a bit. If you owned a sports team or were organizing a parade and needed to ensure that rain didn't ruin your event, you could hire him to keep your days sunny for a mere $500 a day.

Wisconsin

In Madison, the nude bathers Fred Kleinert and Dolores Westly pled not guilty. They didn't contest being naked in the lake but felt they had good reasons. The judge disagreed, handing them each a $5 fine and $6 in court costs. It was ridiculous compared to what else was happening in the state. In the early hours of Wednesday morning in Chippewa Falls, a fifty-six-year-old farmer died loading hay, and in Mendota, the State Hospital for the Insane revealed that fourteen patients were heat victims, some in their twenties and thirties.

South Dakota

Ernie Pyle, the future Pulitzer Prize–winning war correspondent, wrote the first of several columns showcasing his travels in the Dust Bowl. These were grim times, Pyle observed from Pierre: "Crops are gone. Farmers are broke. The heat is terrific. The whole thing is awful."

Farmers, a group that described most people in South Dakota and across the country, were discouraged. Pyle wrote, "I have found them ready to quit, beaten down by a deadening procession of droughts, low prices, heat, jackrabbits, grasshoppers, beetles, bitter winters, dust, and burning winds." He wrote of South Dakotan heat, "The sun is frightful. It is 106 in the shade. An unspeakably hot wind blows across the prairie. Sticking your hand out the window is like sticking it into an oven."

South Dakota's landscape wasn't much better either, according to Pyle: "From Plankton, westward for 400 miles, there is nothing. Not a blade of live grass, or a green weed, or a tree, except along creek bottoms."

Texas

Papers didn't report his name, but one man in Wichita Falls had an interesting day. He stepped into his shower to cool off. It was 97 degrees, after a couple days of being over 100. The man entered the shower, and seconds later, from his point of view, he was a patient at Wichita General Hospital. In between that time, he strolled down Pearl Avenue completely naked, crooning the tune "Singin' in the Rain."* Police picked him up and took him to the hospital. The man remembered none of this.

* For anyone wondering, "Singin' in the Rain" is best known as the 1952 classic movie musical that starred Gene Kelly, but it was first composed in 1929 and was a popular tune right from the start.

California

Rosalind Russell, twenty-nine years old and future star of movies like *His Girl Friday* and *Gypsy*, collapsed on a sound stage for the movie *Craig's Wife* and was whisked off to Columbia Studio Hospital, where restoratives, probably smelling salts, were given to her. It was 91 outside—but inside the film studio, 103 degrees.

Hollywood was muddling through the heat like every industry. Finally finished with *The Garden of Allah*, Marlene Dietrich was now on an air-conditioned train making its way to New York City, where she and her daughter would sail to London. Jean Harlow, meanwhile, found a place to live in Beverly Hills, a home with a lot of shade and no swimming pool. But a lot of other show business royalty, performers, and crew members were being battered by the heat.

Earlier in the summer, Eleanore Whitney, a nineteen-year-old actress who had a short career in the 1930s in a string of mostly now-forgotten films, suffered heatstroke on a tennis court at the home of film director Mervyn LeRoy. Movie legend Fred Astaire spent at least a day at home nursing a sunburn. Richard Cromwell, who had a good run of films in the 1930s, was also spotted around Hollywood with barbecued skin. Jeanette MacDonald, a popular 1930s actress and singer, called off a trip to New York due to the heat. Burgess Meredith, a character actor who later played the aging trainer in *Rocky*, suffered a California sunburn in July that caused blisters on his lip and delayed shooting of his first starring role in a feature film, *Winterset*.

Actress Carole Lombard wore cold wet cloths tied around her wrists between shooting scenes to stay cool. Adolphe Menjou, a character actor, spent much of the filming of *Wives Never Know* lying in a bed under a lot of covers—and hot studio lights. Actress Joan Bennett bought a "gadget from the east," according to one paper, that "looks something like an old-fashioned stove." Whatever it was, it stored three seventy-five-pound pieces of ice. She used it in her dressing room while filming the comedy romance *Wedding Present* with her costar Cary Grant.

Eleanor Powell, a popular actress and dancer in the 1930s, was gardening at night by electric light.

In the 1936 movie *Pigskin Parade*, featuring future *Wizard of Oz* stars Judy Garland and Jack Haley, a pivotal football scene in a blizzard was filmed in almost 100-degree weather. Extras, surrounded by fake snow (cornflakes), wore fur coats and cheered for the football players. Electric fans performing as wind in a snowstorm may well have kept the actors from passing out.

On July 15, *The Hollywood Reporter* offered an anonymous anecdote about a major movie producer who went on location with the director and actors—and complained bitterly because the director allowed everybody to rest in the late morning and much of the afternoon.

"Can't understand it," said the producer. "Why, you're wasting four hours every day. It's cool enough to carry on. In fact, I feel fine."

A few hours later, the director asked around for the producer—and was told that he was ill due to sunstroke.

Champagne Waltz, starring Fred MacMurray and Jack Oakie, had many scenes with tuxedo-clad actors, and they were all constantly putting on fresh clothes after each take. About a week from today, two dancers, Eleanor Ross and Adele Jerome, collapsed on the set in 104-degree heat.

Entertainment scribe Paul Harrison started off a column, observing of the Southern California heat, "It has been a scorching day, hot enough to thaw the heart of a casting director." Harrison also made the wisecrack that "Donald Duck showed up after lunch at the Disney establishment wearing nothing but his pinfeathers." Harrison continued, "Most of the sound stages, which are about the size of dirigible hangars, are supposed to be air-conditioned, but it's futile when the huge doors have to be opened frequently. Stand-ins for the stars take the worst punishment, because they have to pose for long periods under the glaring lights."

Actors were often wearing tight, hot costumes and trying to keep their film makeup from melting. But it was the extras and crew that got the brunt of the heat. Nine ballet dancers filming the movie *Gold Diggers of 1937* fainted on a sound stage, falling like dominos, according to one report.

After six chorus girls collapsed on the set of *Cain and Mabel* and were carried to the studio hospital, blocks of ice were delivered. The performers sat on it, chewed it, wrapped it in chamois cloths, and put it around their wrists. The electricians were gifted their own hundred-pound block of ice. This was all the doing of Marion Davies, a talented actress who is unfortunately probably best known for being the mistress of newspaper tycoon William Randolph Hearst. She was acutely aware that the set had become unsafe due to the heat outside and the heat from the camera lights.

The sets for the movie, which also starred Clark Gable, were elaborate, and Hearst spent $100,000 to raise the soundstage an additional thirty-five feet. Heat, of course, rises. Technicians brought a thermometer into the rafters of the sound stage one day and found that the temperature was 138 degrees. Electricians on the catwalks during filming were strapped in so if they lost consciousness, at least they wouldn't fall to their deaths. The show must go on, ideally without killing anybody.

Davies recognized that the men above her were suffering to make her look good on film, so she encouraged them to work without their shirts. When Blayney Matthews, head of the Warner Bros. Studio police force, observed the bare-chested electricians, he shouted through the loudspeaker system: "Everyone put your shirts back on, or else get off the set and keep walking." In response, Davies grabbed the microphone and said, "Any electrician who puts his shirt on can leave the set and keep on walking. And furthermore, if you have on shorts, you can take off your pants."

In Los Angeles, Deputy District Attorney Eugene Williams cross-examined Rattlesnake James for four hours. By the end, Williams's collar was soaked with sweat, his hair rumpled, and nerves frayed. James didn't break a sweat, and he never broke from his story of how his wife ended up dead: "I believe she fainted and fell into the water of the fishpond."

In Santa Barbara, Gustaf Meilke, eighty-three, died in a hospital. Yesterday, when it was 87 degrees, the native of Germany was found in his garden, unconscious. Meilke's death was unsettling. It was, Santa Barbara officials believed, the first death by sunstroke in the city's history.

Missouri

Ruby Keeler, the famed actress and dancer—she wowed audiences in the 1933 now-classic movie *42nd Street*—spent part of her summer on a transcontinental automobile trip with her sister and brother. Today, disheveled from 101-degree heat, they entered a posh St. Louis hotel. "The clerk stammered around and said they were pretty hard up for rooms," Keeler told the Associated Press the next day. "We did look pretty bad but finally prevailed upon him to find us a couple of rooms."

In retrospect, that's amusing; little else in Missouri was. Kirksville (102°F) lost two citizens. In Sedalia (106°F), a resident's lawn caught fire. One Sedalia resident was quoted saying, "It's too hot to walk downtown. It's too hot to go any place after you get there. It's too hot to sleep, too hot to stay home and just sit around—in fact, it's just too hot."

Iowa

Sixty babies were at a children's hospital in Iowa City, twice the norm. Most kids were heatstroke patients, and some had pneumonia.

Somebody calculated all the heat deaths in Iowa over the last twelve years—from 1923 to 1935—and concluded that during that time, there were 667 heat-related deaths. In the last two weeks, at least four hundred people died from the heat. Another way to put it: In the last two weeks, there were seven times more heat fatalities in Iowa alone than there were murders in the state in 1935.

Today, it was 100 or more degrees throughout Iowa. There were eight heat deaths in Burlington. Five more in Davenport. Another in Eldridge.

And Iowa City. And Hedrick. And Readlyn. In Bedford, the sun, more than the heat, was the issue.

Emmet Savage, a fifty-year-old farmhand, was riding in the back of a pickup truck, possibly to cool off or because there was no room in the front of the vehicle, with his employer, R. L. Whittington, and another farmhand, Will Underwood, taking those seats. "I did not see the train because of the blinding sun," Whittington said later.

But Savage saw the locomotive coming as the truck headed to the railroad tracks. Savage yelled out a warning and jumped out of the truck, just as Underwood shouted at Whittington. Savage landed on the road and lost his balance while Whittington jerked the throttle wide open. The truck leaped off the tracks, just as the engine rushed by.

Whittington and Underwood gathered their wits and processed their near-death experience, unaware of Savage's decapitated body on the other side of the passing train.

Illinois

The Peoria Journal today reported, "The heat wave is now a 'baker's dozen' having held its unrelenting grip for thirteen days. Every heat record in weather bureau history has been broken. Deaths in and near Peoria near 150. And tomorrow will be hotter." There were heat deaths scattered throughout Illinois today, including East St. Louis, Sugar Loaf Township, and Bennington Township.

Some problems were fixable. The Reidy family in Rock Island awakened at 4 A.M. to discover it hotter in their home than they ever could have imagined, even accounting for the weather. A fire in their oil burning furnace was going full blast. The parents discovered that their three-year-old son turned up the thermostat to 100.

There were similar tales this summer of other children doing similar things. In Reno, Nevada, a police officer was roasting, driving in 96-degree heat, but he was going to the station for ice water an abnormal number of times—until a colleague examined the vehicle and turned off its heater.

New York

After three children drowned in Central Park Lake, New York City police began patrolling twenty acres of water.

Fourteen officers volunteered for lake duty, but before being chosen, had to prove they could swim. They wore bathing suits underneath old uniforms and were allowed to not wear a coat. They still were required to holster a pistol. The officers worked in two shifts, from 8 A.M. to 4 P.M. and 4 P.M. to midnight. At night, the boats were equipped with red lanterns.

The police were hoping to discourage kids from swimming. Central Park Lake had areas as deep as thirty feet and possibly deeper, and in one spot was a sewer outlet with a strong undertow, which is how two children drowned. But it was such a vast body of water, nobody believed that the police's presence would guarantee anybody's safety. As one officer told *The New York Times*, "The kids swim, anyway."

Indeed, kids did, learning the times when the officers rowed past certain areas, but the police department added more officers and boats. The drownings stopped.

Oklahoma

There were six heat victims today. In the evening, in the town of Okmulgee, which saw a high of 106, Jefferson Berryhill, a twenty-seven-year-old Native American, brought his bed outside and eventually fell asleep, his hand dangling off the bed.

Berryhill was jolted to consciousness when he was awakened by an agonizing jolt of pain, and perhaps a terrible odor invading his nostrils and lungs. Then he discovered why he was awake. *His thumb was being chomped on by a skunk.*

Berryhill tried shaking the skunk loose but the animal held on tight. It was a fight to the death, and by the end of it, the skunk lost. What remained of the skunk was not in good enough shape to be tested for rabies, and so Berryhill was immediately treated for the disease. Maybe the treatment worked, or perhaps the heat really had made the skunk insane. Either way, Berryhill didn't get rabies, and he, and his thumb, which eventually recovered, lived a long life.

Pennsylvania

There was another hearing for Marion Shanks, the Philadelphia mom who left two young children tied up in a hot room. She offered her defense: "They looked out the windows and broke things. The children broke everything, even a table. To keep them quiet, that stuff was put up. I was the one to fix the ropes. If the neighbors didn't like it, they should have complained to me instead of to the society."

Shanks delivered her defense in a monotone, listless tone, so maybe even she realized how feeble her excuses sounded.

It came out that while her kids suffered at home, Shanks was at a party. Shanks was sentenced to what the papers called "an indefinite term" in the State Industrial Home for Women at Muncy. Despite Shanks claiming to have tied her kids up, authorities learned that her boyfriend, William Davis, fastened the rope to the floor. He was taken to his new home for the next six months, the House of Correction. Locked up, it's likely that Shanks and Davis spent the rest of the summer yearning for a cool breeze.

The city gave custody of Marion's three boys to the Children's Aid Society and allowed Mrs. Shanks's mother, Catherine Duffey, to care for the eight-year-old girl. If Marion was hoping her mother would come to her defense, she was disappointed. Mrs. Duffey recommended that the court sterilize her daughter.

32

JULY 17

Heat Hilarity

Today's Death Toll: 800+
Total Death Toll: 6,700+

Around the country, wiseacres asked family and friends, "Hot enough for you?" The *Wisconsin State Journal* suggested that if anyone asked you that question and you committed murder, the courts would consider that "justifiable homicide."

As much actual death as there was, people felt that you had to laugh about the absurdity of the weather. This was just a weird time. There were, after all, reports of planted onions *cooking in the ground*, as happened to a La Crosse, Wisconsin, homeowner today.

Around the country, people amused themselves. There were egg frying stunts, and in Burlington, Wisconsin, a housewife put a pan of baked beans on an upstairs porch with a tin floor in 103-degree weather. She said the meal turned out very nicely.

Of course, people were always making cornball jokes about the heat. In mid-July, the wife of Governor Alf Landon, Republican nominee for president, cracked to luncheon guests, "Well, anyway, you can't say Kansas didn't give you a warm welcome." In late August, shortly before the heat wave finally ended, Landon told a crowd in St. Louis, "When I was in Buffalo, I told the folks I should get back to Kansas since I've heard there's been a break in the heat wave. It's only 106 there now." That line got a lot of laughs.

The heat turned up as a joke in comic strips like *Bringing Up Father* and on radio shows with comedians like Bob Hope. One joke circulating around the country—it was so hot, the trees were chasing the dogs.

The knock-knock joke craze was in full swing in the 1930s, and by 1936, if it wasn't at its peak, it was getting there. Newspapers around the country held knock-knock joke contests, paying $1 for a good knock-knock joke. Jokes like: *Knock-knock.* Who's there? *Sarah.* Sarah who? *Sarah doctor in the house?* And: *Knock-knock.* Who's there? *Don.* Don who? *Don by the old mill stream.*

So it's not surprising that there were occasionally some heat-related knock-knock jokes making the rounds during the summer of 1936:

Knock-knock. Who's there? *Hunter.* Hunter who? *A hunter and 12 in the shade.*

(Months earlier, when winter was at its worst, one of the jokes going around was: *Knock-knock.* Who's there? *Vera.* Vera who? *Vera cold weather for this time of year.*)

The Atlanta Constitution published an original knock-knock heat wave joke written by a reader that went as follows:

Knock, knock. Who's there? *Stewart.* Stewart who? *Stewart to do anything but knock knock.*

The paper said the reader was suggesting "Stewart" translates as "too hot" and gave her a one dollar bill as a prize. Well, they couldn't all be winners.

Nebraska

There were six heat deaths today. It's remarkable there weren't more. Hartington and Wausa reached 118 degrees. Dick McFarland, fifteen, was riding his bicycle in Lincoln (111°F) when he blacked out, crashed into a parked car, and was thrown over the handlebars. Ed Schumacher, a forty-six-year-old construction worker in Fremont (111°F), was pushing bricks in a wheelbarrow on scaffolding when he became dizzy and fell twenty-three feet. And a sixteen-year-old boy was missing for most of the day; the sheriff and a search posse found him eight miles from home, wandering around in a heat-stricken daze.

Missouri

Most people probably didn't think they were risking their life working if their career wasn't dangerous or rigorous, which is possibly how Maymie Hinkel saw things. Hinkel was a forty-three-year-old single business owner in Sedalia, which she ran since she bought the place in 1928. She put all her energy into The May-Belle Beauty Shop, friends and associates said, and she tried to offer attractive prices. "Our prices are in reach of everyone," one of Hinkel's 1934 ads promised.

But on July 15, when it hit 112 degrees, Hinkel found working in oppressive heat just as challenging as a construction worker, farmer, or dishwasher might have found it: She passed out. Her beauty shop wouldn't have had much ventilation, and even with the help of four hairstylists, Hinkel was probably on her feet a lot. Hair dryers may have made the room hotter as well. She also had diabetes.

After she lost consciousness, Hinkel's doctor treated her for heat exhaustion, but soon, Hinkel fell into a diabetic coma. She died today.

Hinkel was a pillar of the community, having lived here most of her life, and she taught Sunday school. But life went on. A month after her death, Hinkel's business was purchased by a woman who once ran a competing salon. The May-Belle Beauty Shop changed hands at least one more time and remained open until at least 1970. One year after Maymie Hinkel collapsed in her salon, Ida Hinkel sent out a plaintive message to the universe, hoping at least one soul in Heaven was reading *The Sedalia Democrat*: "Some may think you are forgotten, though on earth, you are no more. But in memory, you are with me, as you always were before. Sadly missed by your mother."

California

The trial of Rattlesnake James continued. Robert James, the "much-married barber," as the papers put it, volunteered to prove that his rattlesnakes, Lethal and Lightning, weren't dangerous, thereby demonstrating that even if he had exposed his wife to the reptiles, which, of course, he didn't, she had been in no danger.

James said that he would gladly put his exposed foot in a box with them. The judge, likely hot and annoyed, with the high temperature outside at 91 degrees, declined the offer. "This courtroom is not a three-ring circus. There's been enough sensationalism already," the judge said. For his part, James insisted that he hadn't killed his wife. "I loved her so much," he said.

Iowa

The day was another of heat and misery. Beulah MacMillan Amie, a missionary, visiting her sister in Des Moines's 104-degree weather, commented to her local paper that she couldn't wait to get back to far cooler weather: the Belgian Congo. "I've never known it to be over 80 degrees on the porch of our mission veranda," she said. In Webster City (105°F), Oliver Dalley, a farmer, brought a gallon glass jar water container with him to stay hydrated. The sun's rays went through the glass and water and ignited his dry oat crop. Five acres burned down.

Ray Schieser, a policeman, was tasked to capture a mad cat in Davenport (103°F), and we'll start this anecdote with the unpleasant ending: Schieser killed the cat. This was, unfortunately, a common scenario. Officers in Davenport were currently shooting about a dog a day. The dogs were said to be enraged, but were probably just in distress from the heat.

This mad cat attacked several small children, so it's understandable that the authorities were called, but when the officer found it around noon it was lying peacefully on a porch. You'd think that Schieser might have tried to pick it up gently or perhaps tried to steer the cat into his car—cat carriers existed, but evidently Schieser didn't have one. Anyway, Schieser picked up the cat by the back of its neck.

Well, go figure—the cat didn't like this. The feline yelped, twisted, and escaped from Schieser's grip—and ripped the leather off his right shoe.

Then the cat sank his claws into the officer's foot. Schieser tried to stop the cat by placing his left shoe on the animal, which was torn apart by the cat's teeth. And Schieser shot the cat.

This was not a good month for Officer Schieser. Five days later, Schieser, probably with sore feet, was on his motorcycle, blissfully unaware that in moments he would be nursing cuts and bruises—after skidding out of control, after his motorcycle tires ran over oil, and after railroad workers accidentally allowed oil to spill into the street.

Minnesota

In Rochester, there were four heat deaths, including three patients at a state hospital. In Minneapolis, four people bit the dust. And in St. Paul, chief of police Clinton Hacker sent out a memo to his police officers that indicated he was now the fashion police. Hacker mandated that officers needed to be attired more professionally, heat or no heat: "Several officers have come to court with sleeves rolled and shirt open at the throat. This makes a bad impression in court."

Illinois

Alton endured nineteen days in July in which the high temperature went over 100, so it's no wonder that Joe Rodriguez, a twenty-seven-year-old steel worker, stopped sleeping where he lived—a boarding house. Rodriguez's go-to "bed" outside was now a sand pile in the town. Every evening, he spread newspapers and slept on the papers and sand. But as people observed later, the sand would have been very soft, but it also would have been hot. Maybe it got too hot. You also wouldn't want to be asleep and get the sand in your mouth.

Nobody knew exactly what happened, but at 5 A.M., a motorman on the streetcar noticed Rodriguez had rolled off the papers and that he was sleeping face down in the sand. Worse, he didn't appear to be asleep.

Ohio

Four thousand swimmers descended upon the Woodland Hills Pool in Cleveland to beat the 82-degree heat. Many swimmers came from the Great Lakes Exposition, a major two-year festival celebrating Cleveland, and of the thousands of people cooling off, there was not one Black swimmer, noted Chester Gillespie, president of the local NAACP chapter in Cleveland. Tomorrow, Gillespie would file civil rights lawsuits against the Great Lakes Exposition.

Black swimmers were legally allowed in the pool. It's just that, as was the case in other states, no Black swimmer felt safe. Black swimmers were sometimes attacked for showing up to swim. Gillespie would charge that the city could be doing more to protect them.

Gillespie, an early leader in the civil rights movement, had done this sort of legal maneuver before. He explained his lawsuits in this way: "I concern myself a great deal with these cases because I feel it my duty to make an example of some of these idiots who persist in deliberately violating your Ohio Civil Rights Law. If we people, who are supposed to know the procedure in such cases, do not take adequate action, we can hardly expect others of our people to make any effort to have their civil rights respected."

Utah

The heat wave may have saved a three-year-old girl's life, another rare case where high temperatures did some good. Nadine Robins wandered away from her parents at a resort in Fishlake National Forest. She was missing for twenty-four hours, while five hundred men and women searched for her in heat hovering around 100 degrees.

It was a precarious place for anyone to become lost, let alone a three-year-old, but on the upside, at night, Nadine was in no danger of freezing or even being cold. As time went on, her parents started wondering if their daughter had been kidnapped, not an unreasonable fear during the 1930s. But Nadine was apparently having the time of her life. It's believed that she ate berries, and when she was located she didn't seem hungry or tired. Rescuers found the three-year-old girl late the next day, happily cooling off in a mountain stream.

Kansas

It was 112 degrees in some towns. An eighty-one-year-old farmer died at his home in Neodesha, as did a two-month-old baby in Hutchinson.

People were trying to sleep, but couldn't. In Emporia, if you could find a cot to buy, it was going for a premium, and chances are you wouldn't find one. People paid for hotel rooms they didn't use. At one hotel, six men were seen bringing out dining room chairs and pairing them up with park benches. They had no blankets or mattresses for padding. They just laid down and made the best of it. Raymond Dean, a public relations man for the Cole Brothers Circus, left his Wichita hotel room and hailed a taxi. Dean had the driver deposit him under a tree, where he slept. That is, until the grasshoppers woke him in the early morning.

Pennsylvania

In the evening, in Wesleyville, a suburb of Erie, Irene Weed, a thirty-three-year-old housewife, knelt in her home with other members of the Church of Nazarene while her husband, Samuel, led them in prayer. Their sons, two and four years old, slept in their bedroom. The pastor was on vacation, and Samuel was its acting minister in his absence.

Neighbors said later that Mr. Weed had acted strangely ever since he had some sort of heatstroke almost a week earlier, on July 12, in 94-degree weather. But on this cool evening, life was pleasant. Hymns were sung, prayers were read, and Samuel Weed ended the gathering at their home with a plea for God's blessing upon everyone present and their families. In retrospect, people would recognize the next day, it was a cry for help.

33

JULY 18

The Scarlet Sin

Today's Death Toll: 800+
Total Death Toll: 7,500+

One of the few upsides of the heat wave was the lack of a crime wave, minus a few tragic instances where the heat accelerated darker urges. But on the whole, nobody had the energy to do anything. Overall crime was down, sometimes way down. By mid-July, Detroit's crime had plunged by 80 percent. A serial killer lurking around Cleveland, Ohio, may have been lying low as well. He was later called the Cleveland Torso Murderer, who may have started killing as early as 1934 and is known to have definitely struck from 1935 to 1938. This summer, a victim was found June 5, and another on July 22, but the body was believed to be months old. The next body was found in September, when temperatures were coming down.

In Springfield, Missouri, a police officer interviewed about the absence of bad guys said, "Crooks are just naturally steering clear of the jail. They know how hot it is over there, and they are taking no chances of being locked up."

In Anderson, Indiana, the local paper interviewed police officers about the weather. William Russell, captain of detectives, said, "There is an apparent decrease in the number of house robberies, hold-ups and other major crimes in Anderson since the heat wave started. It is apparent that the criminal element is just as much affected by the heat as anyone else."

There was still petty theft, said Thomas Estle, a safety officer and juvenile investigator in Anderson: "Boys are stealing more bicycles, ice cream, pop and other articles during this heat wave than ever before." But Madison, Wisconsin, night patrolmen discovered that many shopkeepers were leaving front doors unlocked and the windows wide open. They were too hot and tired to bother locking up, and criminals were too hot and tired to rob them.

The police were equally listless. On July 10, in Des Moines, Iowa, two city detectives approached an employee at a downtown shoe store. The employee ran, and the detectives hurried after him, and one of them fired two shots in the air, but otherwise, they just stood there, watching the guy race through a parking lot and disappear around the county courthouse. When somebody asked why they didn't pursue him, one of the detectives said, "It's too hot for a foot race today."

Unfortunately, the heat wave couldn't stop all crime.

Pennsylvania

Samuel Weed, forty, who up until now had led a quiet, law-abiding, unassuming life as a dutiful husband and father who taught Sunday school, awakened with one item on his to-do list: to hang himself.

Weed lost his nerve, however, and like a couple other madmen earlier in the summer, came up with a different plan: he would kill his family. Around 7 A.M., while his wife and two young sons were sleeping, Weed walked down to his cellar, found a hammer, went back upstairs, and moments later was the embodiment of pure evil. Some papers would blame the hot temperatures for Weed's behavior, calling him a "heat-crazed clerk" who worked for General Electric Company.*

After his grisly work was done, Weed had a change of heart, recognized he was evil, and charged onto the front porch where he spotted his neighbor, Mrs. Edna Reck, who was also a distant relative. "I've killed them," he shouted.

"Killed who?" she screamed.

"The whole family," Weed shouted, racing toward Buffalo Road and flinging his body in front of a passing truck. Glenn Hall, the

* The GE marketing team must have loved the publicity.

twenty-seven-year-old driver, slammed on the brakes as Weed bounced off the windshield and landed on the road. Hall scrambled out of the truck, as did his brother and stepfather, to see if the poor guy was okay, but they quickly understood that no sympathy was required—and that Weed, still very much alive (albeit it with cuts on his face), needed a judge more than a doctor. Weed kept screaming that he had killed his family and wanted to end his life.

Actually, his two-year-old son, Charles, was still breathing. For a few more hours.

Weed tried throwing himself in front of another passing truck, but Hall, his brother, and stepfather prevented him from going anywhere. Someone—probably Mrs. Reck—called the police. Weed told law enforcement that he wanted to purge his family due to "a scarlet sin. I killed them because I had committed a scarlet sin. I didn't want my family to go through life bearing the stigma of that scarlet sin."

Translation, the police assumed: Weed had an affair and, ashamed of his actions, eliminated his family.

The police hauled Weed to a hospital, where he was treated for superficial wounds. Weed was inconsolable, while a police officer, Sam Browne, guarded him. Browne didn't think Weed was much of a threat, though. Browne sat next to his hospital bed and tried to tune Weed out by reading the newspaper.

Bad idea. Browne's gun, sitting in the holster, was in easy reach, and Weed grabbed for it. Browne narrowly dodged the grab and lunged for Weed, who jumped to his feet. The men wrestled for several moments, despite Browne being about sixty-five pounds heavier than the 125-pound Weed. Doctors and nurses rushed into the room. Weed was swiftly fitted into a straitjacket. Later, Weed was questioned by the police and the district attorney, Mortimer Graham.

"What I did this morning was sin against the law of God and man. That's why I tried to kill my wife," Weed said. "My punishment for this will come in the next world."

Not if Graham could help it. He planned on punishing Weed in *this* world. Graham told the press, "The man is a religious fanatic, but he is not insane." Graham said he would try him for three separate murder charges.

"I am led to believe there may be another woman in this case," said Police Chief George Christoff. "What else could this 'scarlet sin' mean? I can see no real reason behind the slaying other than Weed may have felt remorseful about his relations with another woman or girl. With Weed refusing to talk about his 'scarlet sin,' and he will not tell us what the sin is or when it was committed, there is nothing left for us to believe but that somehow, somewhere, another woman enters the picture."

As the day continued, law officials kept asking Weed why he killed his family. "I have committed the unpardonable sin, and I wanted to take them to heaven with me," Weed said. He also said, just as unhelpfully, "I wanted to remove my family, so they wouldn't have to live with me," Weed said. But what was this unpardonable sin? Weed wouldn't say.

For the next several weeks, the police searched the house and neighborhood, hunting for clues and evidence to explain exactly what happened and why. The why wasn't entirely clear, but everyone knew what happened. The murder weapon spoke volumes. Police found the hammer lying near the bodies, covered in blood and matted hair.

Ontario

In northern Ontario, three thousand firefighters battled forest fires while rangers organized a manhunt for an escaped reformatory convict, John Gray, who was said to be crazed by heat and smoke and setting the blazes. Gray escaped with another prisoner, Marshall Johnson, whose body was found three feet deep in a lake. Johnson may have been trying to escape from a fire, but it appeared that Gray may have drowned him. There were also rumors that Gray had managed to secure a rifle. Perhaps not, but he had an axe, authorities said, which is just what you want when you're battling a forest fire—an axe-wielding maniac on the loose.

The Canadian "Mounties" suggested that Gray may have burned up in a fire, but nobody knew for sure. Gray was never seen again.

Illinois

Not a good day for Illinois. There were heat deaths in McLean, Pontiac, and Pana. In Waterman, a psychiatric patient in a hospital due to a nervous breakdown brought on by the heat attacked nurses and doctors and tried to escape. In Edwardsville, another guy thought sleeping on his roof would be a good way to beat the heat. Neighbors found his body in the yard the next morning.

Nebraska

William Sloan, a fifty-six-year-old farmer from Louisville, Nebraska, was hauled into an Omaha court for being drunk and disorderly. His attorney, James Walker, argued that while Sloan "looked, acted, talked and gave forth the odor of a drunken man, he was only the innocent victim of Omaha's heat." Walker said that when Sloan was found the previous day by a policeman at 10th and Howard Streets half-cognizant, it had nothing to do with alcohol.

Sloan, wearing overalls and sporting a Van Dyke beard, testified that he hadn't touched a drop in three years. Judge John Battin was empathetic and accepted the plea. In fact, before the month was out, Battin was sick from the heat and requested a week's vacation.

Iowa

Irma Long, of Woodbury County (103°F), wrote a journal entry on this day, revealing life in the state. "Heat, heat, heat!" she wrote. "It stifles and burns and saturates everything. The beds feel actually hot most of the night. The furniture, too, is not immune. Sometimes we seek stools or chairs without backs in order to get away from the heat on our backs. People all over the countryside are sleeping out of doors, for the houses do not cool off in the evening."

It was, indeed, a miserable day. Edward and Florence Rayhorn, the Des Moines couple who were married for thirty-nine years and freely admitted that the heat was a factor in their wanting to break up, officially divorced.

South Dakota

Ernie Pyle continued traversing the Dust Bowl, profiling Will Keeler, a farmer who lived in Holabird (107°F). If you were going to find the stereotypical citizen who was being ground down by the Great Depression, Keeler fit the bill. The previous autumn, Keeler hadn't been doing too badly: he earned $40 a month from the government by working on roads. But then Keeler caught the flu and was bedridden for two months. Now, Keeler, in poor health, was on government relief, receiving $12 a month.

But it wasn't like Keeler wasn't working. He was, very hard. He simply had nothing to show for it. He planted corn, but the hot winds cooked it. He planted cucumbers, but swarms of heat-thriving grasshoppers ate them. He planted potatoes that were devoured by potato beetles. He owned a milk cow and a couple dozen hens, but with no corn growing, he couldn't feed his anemic livestock, so they couldn't generate milk or eggs. Pyle's column concluded: "So Will Keeler is 65. He's tired and weak. He has one cow and a few chickens and $12 a month. No vegetables. No fruit. No income. No prospects."

"How are you going to get through the winter?" Pyle asked him. "I don't know," Will Keeler said.

Kansas

In Wichita (112.3°F), where you could smell the stench of scorched corn stalks, the city's swimming pool attendance was down. That was blamed on the moms, unenthusiastic to walk with their kids to the swimming pool. Could you blame them? About a dozen people died from the heat just today, including a five-year-old boy. A couple days earlier, a Mrs. Bertha Vann was burning grass cuttings in her backyard, and it was so hot, she didn't notice that her dress was on fire. A neighbor noticed, threw a rug around Vann, and stamped out the flames.

There was little hope of the weather improving any time soon. "The outlook for next week is very discouraging," Snowden Dwight Flora, a prominent federal meteorologist based out of Topeka (110°F), said.

Nobody wanted to hear that. In Garnett (111°F), somebody tallied it up, and seventy-five horses and cattle had died in the last two weeks. In Salina (116°F), the sun shining through a window set a house on fire. In Fredonia, it was hotter than anywhere else in the state and in the country: 121 degrees.

Missouri

The state was an infernal wasteland. Nevada, Missouri, was 117; Joplin was 111. St. Louis (99°F) had twelve citizens die; the 79 percent humidity didn't help. In Willow Springs, customers found an eighty-year-old employee dead in their bank's front doorway. All of which made people wonder if something ominous was happening to the planet. Roscoe Nunn, a St. Louis meteorologist, was asked by a *St. Louis Star and Times* reporter if the climate was changing in today's paper, and his response was emphatic: "No."

Oklahoma

In Alva, the mercury climbed to 120. The following month, an Alva city clerk noted that residents used far more water than they typically did in July, and he speculated that it was because townsfolk were bathing multiple times each week instead of only Saturday night, when people would generally bathe, to be ready for church the next morning.

Nowata also experienced 120 degrees, but because a government thermometer wasn't in the community, the federal government wouldn't accept it. That irked Nowata's citizens. Meanwhile, Alva now had a new record that made them stand out: it had never been 120 anywhere in Oklahoma.

There were a dozen deaths throughout the state, and while crime was easing up throughout the country, that wasn't always the case. Over the weekend, the Oklahoma City police department arrested eighteen men for fighting and drunkenness. "The heat undoubtedly had something to do with it," police chief J. R. Greer said.

34

JULY 19

The Dust Storm

Today's Death Toll: 500+
Total Death Toll: 8,000+

During a heat wave in 2013, sea stars, also known as starfish, began dying by the millions in the Pacific Ocean, particularly on the coast from Alaska to Mexico. They're still dying. From 2014 to 2016, approximately four million common murres, a type of seabird resembling a penguin, died in a north Pacific Ocean heat wave that was nicknamed "the blob." In 2024, at least 234 howler monkeys were heat victims in the tropical forests of the southeastern Mexican state of Tabasco. In 2025, scientists declared that due to melting sea ice, Arctic seals were closer than ever to extinction. In 2026, thousands of flying foxes, also known as fruit bats, were found dead throughout Australia during an extreme heat wave, part of a years-long trend of high temperatures and flying fox annihilation Down Under.

But all of this was foreshadowed during the summer of 1936 when undomesticated animals were suffering as much as domesticated ones. On W. H. Wordeman's farm, near Gettysburg, South Dakota, an Associated Press journalist reported seeing thirst-deranged wild rabbits looking for water, with many lying dead in the yard, thousands of flies feeding upon them. Chickens and turkeys huddled in the shade of a barn, panting. Grasshoppers were out in the fields, eating what they could find.

"Drought has ruined my crops, and now the grasshoppers are getting the ruins," Wordeman said.

Almost anywhere you looked, you could find examples of animals struggling with the heat. On July 10, a Philadelphia Zoo zookeeper saved a four-foot-long king snake from death—and blamed the reptile's odd behavior on the heat. Odd, certainly. The snake was swallowing his own tail. In mid-July, circus elephants in Wichita, Kansas, trumpeted in pain on the hot pavement, so workers put leather pads on their feet. At the Riverview Park Zoo in Omaha, a fox died from the heat, and zoo-keepers constantly hosed off animals to keep them cool. At Milwaukee's Washington Park Zoo, an eleven-year-old chimpanzee named Mary Lou had a heat-caused apoplectic stroke.

Oklahoma farmers noticed that their turkeys drank so much water and ate so many grasshoppers that they were becoming unnaturally fat and flabby, so much so that when they perched in trees, they lost their balance and fell to their deaths. On August 13, on a turkey farm in Lenmore (110°F), 2,200 turkeys perished. A South Dakota teacher in a letter described her cows, which would moo for an hour at a time for water that the family couldn't get because their wells were dry: "Each day, they grow weaker and thinner. The tongues of the oldest have begun to swell. Their eyes are bloodshot."

Early in the 1900s, the farming community learned that sorghum grass, while good for cattle, becomes deadly when it gets really hot; a secondary compound called dhurrin is converted into prussic acid, which will swiftly kill a cow that is grazing on it. This was a summer in which cattle, in states like Wisconsin and Kansas, were dying en masse because the heat poisoned the grass.

Some farm animals found a way to survive, despite the elements. Six hogs belonging to a bank president in Scottsville, Kentucky, were believed to have died—until the executive discovered them in a nearby cave, where they had been staying during the day. At night, they returned to the farm to get water.

Most animals were suffering in some way.

Insects. The abundance of grasshoppers infuriated farmers, but they were delighted that the Mexican bean beetle and European corn borer were dying. One scientist observed that in the farmers' fields, the beetles' pupae and larvae were burning to death.

Across North America, the wax in hives was melting, closing the entrances and making bees homeless, or trapping them inside. If bees weren't dying, they were searching for shade. In Rochester, Indiana, when twenty thousand bees invaded United Brethren Church, Reverend Loren Stine bravely continued delivering his usual Sunday morning sermon, but people could barely hear him over the buzzing. And a Texan was driving a Ford Model T, considered an antique car in 1936, chugging along the highway at eighteen miles an hour, when bees swarmed the car, eager to get some shade. The bees began stinging the driver, who then steered his vehicle over an embankment. No bones broken, he ran for his life, uninjured except for a lot of welts.

Reptiles, scorpions, and fish. In late June, in Trenton, Missouri (107°F), a twenty-two-foot python was found in its display pen, dead. That surprised everyone. Pythons are from the tropics. In mid-July, numerous dead snakes turned up in O'Neill, Nebraska. Thousands of fish, unable to get the oxygen they needed in shallow and hot creeks and ponds, were dying in dozens of states, including Michigan, Kentucky, Ohio, and Oklahoma. In Phoenix, Arizona, miners reported that rattlesnakes, Gila monsters, scorpions, and swarms of tarantulas were all coming into mine shafts to find relief from the heat.

Pets. Today, July 14, Elmer Busse, the director of the Dane County Humane Society in Madison, Wisconsin, said that he had received sixty-three calls in the last week, double the usual, involving reports of dogs being tied up in the sun and locked in apartments without air-conditioning. In mid-July, Buffalo, New York's department of health reported that in the last week, employees collected 245 dogs and cat carcasses in a week, double the norm. (They also found a dead porcupine, guinea hens, pheasants, and rats.)

Not all dogs fared badly. *The Cleveland Plain Dealer* shared stories of how two readers cooled their dogs in the bath enough that they soon understood that if they hopped in the tub and barked, they might receive another shower. Dogs also looked after their owners. Today, near Richmond, Michigan, John Nothaft, manager of a fox farm, collapsed; his two German Shepherds dragged Nothaft into the shade and barked furiously until neighbors came and found him.

Cats were suffering. In mid-July, when it was in the 100s, Mary and George Larrabee of Detroit were driving near Fenton, Michigan, when a cat leaped through one of their car's open windows. The cat went wild, biting and clawing Mary's throat. The two scrambled out of their car, and since the cat wouldn't leave, they rolled up the windows, enough so that it couldn't attack them. Then they started pushing their car down the highway. A state trooper spotted the couple and came to help. He assured them that he could get rid of the cat, opened the door—and was promptly attacked.*

The following month, in Pittsburgh, a police officer watched a white cat chase a squirrel in unforgiveable heat—the cat dropped dead in mid-pursuit.

Birds. Bertrand Cartwright, a British-born Canadian naturalist who wrote a newspaper column called "Wild Winds," suggested that the temperatures inside bird houses were probably making them "death traps." Young purple martins and tree swallows were frequently being found at the foot of bird houses, either dead or barely alive.

Around the country, wildlife experts urged people to fill birdbaths or put out shallow dishes of water for the birds—in the shade, since the water would end up either practically boiling in the sun or evaporating. "This hot, dry summer is bringing them a lot of suffering, more because they can't find water than because of the heat, for birds naturally have a higher temperature than humans and can stand the heat better," said Tom Scott, a wildlife specialist with Iowa State College, in an interview with the Associated Press.

This evening, in St. Louis, at 7:30 P.M., Roy Dickerhoff, the night superintendent at the city morgue, sprayed a paved courtyard outside the back of the building, trying to cool things off, when a pigeon landed and soon collapsed. Dickerhoff brought the pigeon into the autopsy room, which was kept cool due to its proximity to the refrigerating room. For three hours, Dickerhoff periodically sprayed his feathered friend with cold water. He also put out water for it. The pigeon was soon perched on a radiator, trying to preen its saturated feathers. The next morning, he was set outside, where he took to the skies.

Lab animals. At the University of Arkansas, 120 white mice died from the heat in an unair-conditioned building. Researchers, looking for

* It isn't known what happened to the cat. Maybe that's for the best.

something to learn, noted that the stock mice, fed a routine diet, survived while the experimental mice, being fed a controlled diet, did not. (Speaking of mice, the day before, in Pine Bluff, Arkansas [99°F], a woman left a room for a few minutes to get a drink of water and returned to find that a mouse had crawled in front of an electric fan on the floor—and died.)

Wild animals. In South Dakota, in mid-July when temperatures were over 100 and 110, a local government official, S. P. McKenna, the state field man for the division of taxation in Sioux Falls, insisted to the Associated Press, in an article that ran on July 17, that he was not joking when he said that he was driving about twenty miles south of Pierre and saw a coyote chasing a jackrabbit. "Believe it or not, they were both walking," McKenna said. "I stopped the car and watched the chase with several friends who were with me." He believed the jackrabbit got away, adding, "The last we saw of them, the jackrabbit was gaining."

The animal stories get even weirder. Later in the month, Norfolk, Nebraska, had reports of heat-frenzied rabbits taking on dog-like behavior and chasing squirrels and waiting at the bottom of the tree, as if hoping they would come back down and be caught.

And the New York state conservation department announced today that squirrels were attacking homes in Buffalo.

Pennsylvania

Today, for the first time in Pittsburgh's history, with its 101-degree weather, the police force gave their horses the day off. The policemen patrolled on foot.

Utah

At the Hogle Gardens Zoo in Salt Lake City (104°F), two English spotted deer died. Animal lovers were not pleased. In the days to come, the zoo staff would receive holy hell.

New York

The high was 86 degrees in the concrete jungle of Manhattan, when every subway or train commuter's nightmare came true: Chester Johnson, twenty-five, waiting on a platform, passed out and toppled onto the railroad tracks, another unwilling sacrifice to the heat wave. But the train braked hard, stopping just in the nick of time. Johnson made a rapid recovery at the hospital.

Manitoba and British Columbia

The Canadian heat wave was back. Four people went to the hospital in Winnipeg (89°F), and in the last four days, twenty-four people had died from the heat. Nine drowned when seeking relief in creeks and rivers.

In Lytton, British Columbia, the temperature was 100 degrees.

Alberta, Canada; Montana; and South Dakota

A powerful dust storm from Canada—a woman's car in Alberta was overturned—roared into Havre, Montana, a little after 5 P.M. The heat had been miserable (107°F), and then a little after 5 P.M., the dust storm hit, the wind rushing into the town at fifty miles an hour.

After three minutes, the winds slowed to forty miles an hour. Brown dust, so thick that if you were to look across the street you'd only be able to see about halfway, covered the town. Fifteen minutes later, the dust storm was over, heading to Malta, and by 6 P.M., at least it was cooler: 97 degrees.

Next up: South Dakota. In Mitchell, it was 109, until the dust storm came in, and a few minutes later, it was a glorious 77.

Of course, to enjoy the cool weather, you had to be okay with dodging falling trees and being covered in dust. In many South Dakota cities, though, the storm wasn't that bad. The dust clouds were high in the sky and not too many people were choking. There were exceptions, however. In Pierre, the dust was lower to the ground, and the storm stuck around for about a half hour.

Then the dust storm moved on, hugging the ground and invading other states, making its way south, almost as if it was purposefully following the Mississippi River.

Iowa

Before the dust storm hit, the heat came for two men in Cumberland, a man in Keokuk, a woman in Council Bluffs, a woman in Ottumwa, a man in Cedar Falls, and a man in Des Moines. There was a drowning in Muscatine and Washington.

In Sioux City, around 3 P.M., the dust storm invaded. The temperature plunged from 106 degrees to 70 degrees within minutes. Corn was flattened; trees were tossed across highways; electric signs were yanked out of the ground. In nearby Hartley, a church under construction became rubble, and a barn was blown to smithereens, crushing the cattle inside. At about 3:30 P.M., in Ida Grove, the temperature fell from 102 to 82 within thirty minutes; the dust storm lasted forty minutes.

Minnie Dietz, a sixty-five-year-old woman in Manning, stood on her back porch with the back and front doors open. It was a smart cooling tactic, except at this moment. The wind rushed through the house, hurling her down the cement steps. She hit her head, broke one arm, and sprained the other, and one of her legs was badly bruised. She lived but had health issues until her death four years later.

The dust storm hit Des Moines around 7 P.M., and many residents were outside in their beds when seventy-mile gusts came roaring through, toppling power lines and making crackling sounds against the dry and brittle trees. Pajama-clad sleepers ran for their homes or darted inside the nearest building they could find and then shut the doors and windows, if the storm hadn't already shattered them.

Nebraska

There were six heat deaths in Omaha and two drownings in North Platte, and along the banks of the Missouri River, Chester Bozak's clothes and a suicide note were found. This wasn't entirely surprising. Bozak, a twenty-five-year-old brewery worker, had been struggling. He was hospitalized for heatstroke on July 3 and remained at the hospital for several weeks. After his release, he tried jumping off a bridge. He was stopped, but Mrs. Bozak said her husband in recent days had been drinking, and she hadn't seen him for forty-eight hours. It doesn't appear that Bozak was ever seen, dead or alive, again.

Police started a search, but it was short-lived because of the dust storm. Without cell phones or twenty-four-hour cable news, many people weren't aware of it coming and had no reason to suspect ominous weather. The skies were cloudless, there was no breeze, and it was hot. But there were hints of Omaha's oncoming storm. In the evening, at the Missouri River, a thirty-two-year-old man was crossing in water that appeared to be shallow. Just as a bystander said that the current was more dangerous than it might look, the undertow swept the man away.

The dust storm struck at 9 P.M. The eighty-four-mile-per-hour winds ripped down cottonwood trees and buildings and hurled a theater sign into a row of cars, and the temperature dropped from 106 degrees to 68 within fifteen minutes. Roofs of homes and buildings flew off, and more than three hundred power lines snapped. Fans fled from a baseball stadium to find shelter; one witness said that for twenty minutes, there was no visibility.

At Omaha's Carter Lake Club, its members were enjoying the clubhouse and beaches—and staying away from the tennis courts. As the dust storm arrived, the lifeguard ordered the fifty bathers out of the lake, which now resembled a raging ocean. Some people reached the shore in their canoe, and once they scrambled out, the wind flung it a hundred yards back into the water.

Some members couldn't make it off the beach. Three women, holding hands so as not to lose each other and to anchor themselves, knelt on the ground and started praying while dust and sand pelted at them until they began to bleed. Children screamed and cried as their mothers tried to find them in the dust, and once they were reunited, they made their way to whatever shelter they could find.

Inside the club's buildings and bathhouses, everybody stood in shock in their bathing suits, wet and dusty.

Kansas

In Kansas City (105°F), swimmers at the Klamm municipal park swimming pool were complaining that the water was too hot. So park officials ordered eighteen blocks of 100-pound ice and, this morning, dumped them into the pool. In Topeka (100°F), a thirty-seven-year-old meat cutter drowned in the Kansas River. But in the evening, the storm hit, and the temperature fell twenty degrees to 80 in about ninety minutes while the wind did its work, bringing down trees and electrical lines. In Kansas City, a revival tent blew away; four hundred people underneath went racing for cover.

Some states received some welcome rain after the dust storm, but not Kansas.

Missouri

When the dust storm invaded, the temperature in Brookfield fell from 108 degrees to 68, and once the wind whipped into the city, two thousand people watching a softball game scrambled for shelter. As dust pummeled the region, two people were killed: in Independence, a tree limb crashed through the roof of a driver's car, and a seventy-year-old married woman in Cameron returned from church and stepped on a downed power line.

In Pattonsburg, the storm knocked over a revival meeting tent, injuring four women. Around 10 P.M., in Kansas City, as power lines and trees fell, a Trans World Airlines plane was about to take off when the storm hit. The taxiing stopped and passengers were hustled into the airport while twenty employees ran for the aircraft, ten people climbing on each wing, trying not to suffocate on dust and prevent the plane from blowing away.

Oklahoma

Altus set a new heat record, 120 degrees, one that Alva had hit the day before, and many people at the air-conditioned movie theater sat through the same film twice. Residents hung a wet sheet in front of fans and spent time in a bathtub with as cold of water as they could make it. A local doctor suggested taking a piece of surgeon's gauze, dampening it, and placing on your face. Then stick your face near a fan. The gauze acts like a filter, allowing cold and moist water to reach your face, the doctor said. Repeat every five minutes.

The Altus-Times Democrat had a sense of humor about its sweltering day in the sun as the hottest place in the state, saying in an op-ed that for some time, there had been debates about just how hot their city could get, but "our reputation has been saved. We could not exceed Alva's lofty 120 degrees, but we equaled it and once more, our colors floated triumphantly over the entire state. It was just like the good old days before the Hoover depression. No longer would we have to take a back seat to those ambitious cities of the far north like Alva, Ponca City, Bartlesville, Nowata and Guthrie."

In a population of about 8,500, everybody in Altus seems to have survived the 120-degree temperature, which came on a Sunday when a lot of people weren't working. That said, a two-month-old boy died the next morning; the papers never said what from, but it seems a safe assumption that the heat was a factor.

In Tulsa (113°F), thirteen people died, and there were four deaths in nearby Claremore and one in Catoosa. There was one heat victim in Oklahoma City (106°F) and another in Cherokee, a thirty-six-year-old farmhand who might have recovered if somebody found him sooner. He lay in the hot sun for most of the afternoon.

At least some Oklahomans probably welcomed the dust storm that strangled parts of the state deep into the night. Dust rained down and buildings were damaged—the roof of the high school building in Lone Grove was ripped right off—but temperatures did drop. In Tulsa, the temperature fell twenty-two degrees in fourteen minutes.

Texas

In Fort Worth, it was 107 degrees. Wichita Falls was 111. Seymour was 112.5. Most people avoided death, but not everyone. A thirty-six-year-old farm laborer from Thalia took his family to a pond near Vernon (114°F). All was well until he stepped into a seven-foot hole.

The dust storm was sputtering out but still packed a powerful punch late at night in Texas, where it spawned a twister that terrorized the hamlet of Texon. In Pampa, four people were in a car when the dust blew in; the driver couldn't see that part of the road had been washed out in a flood. The nose of the vehicle buried itself in a sandbank, and everybody nursed injuries as severe as a fractured jaw while the dust covered their car.

35

JULY 20

The Grasshoppers

Today's Death Toll: 300+
Total Death Toll: 8,300+

The country continued to struggle with what was appropriate to wear now that nobody wanted to wear anything.

In Cleveland, young ladies fastened safety pins on their swimsuits to get around park bans on two-piece bathing attire that covered a lot of skin but didn't quite join at the waist. The local police were okay with that. An officer told a reporter, "Our orders are that girls' suits must be connected in front, top and bottom, and we don't care how it's done."

In Westport, Connecticut, a politician circulated a petition to require women to wear more than shorts and halter tops in public marketplaces. In Yorktown, New York, the police chief went on record saying that people could wear shorts—but not "shorts that are radically too short."

At the Library of Congress in Washington, DC, men hung their coats on the backs of chairs, and now everyone could see they were wearing polo shirts, a fashion choice that had become popular in the last decade. Somebody objected, and the superintendent, Martin Roberts, agreed. He said the jackets on the chair was "a reasonable concession" to the heat. But polo shirts? That was "going too far." Roberts added, "Not that the library objects to the polo shirts these boys happened to be wearing, but let in one polo shirt and there would be no place to stop. Women readers object to men of years wearing polo shirts, and the Library of Congress considers their point well taken."

In New York City, the men, including the judges, toiled in the courtroom without coats and neckties. In Hackensack, New Jersey, courtrooms, men were also allowed to take off their coats, but they had to still wear a tie.

Iowa

Thomas Graham woke early with the sun and started walking home from the courthouse lawn in Des Moines. It's possible that the eighty-six-year-old retiree got a decent amount of sleep. The night started off badly with the dust storm, but the temperature dropped from around 100 to 78 degrees.

For most of the month, Graham's routine was to sleep at the courthouse. It probably felt like a second home to him. Before retiring, Graham worked for the city government, in the streets department, making sure the roads were well maintained and safe.

Perhaps the streets were not as safe with Graham off the job. He crossed at a corner of two streets but went diagonally across the road, which probably wasn't the wisest decision, because a car came out of nowhere—at least from Graham's perspective.

The vehicle ran over Graham and dragged him for sixty-five feet, and after his body somehow freed itself from the automobile, the car kept going. Two army lieutenants witnessed the whole episode. The twenty-nine-year-old driver was tracked down later in the day; the police, engaging in some nifty detective work, matched the broken glass on the street and found that it fit with the broken headlight on the suspect's car. But if the heat wave had been a villain, it probably would have felt like it did its job well. The punishment didn't fit the crime. Graham was dead forever, and his killer went to jail for five months.

About the time Thomas Graham was meeting his end, Lowell Otte was going through his own personal hell.

Otte, thirty-two years old and a resident of Sidney, had problems long before the heat wave, but the weather worsened them, friends said. A physician backed them up, telling reporters, "He has had a background of mental disturbance. The intense heat during the last two weeks, and the severe windstorm last night, aggravated the condition."

For anyone already depressed and distressed by the heat, a dust storm *would* aggravate that. The evening before, a sunset church service at Waubonsie Park was interrupted. Buildings lost roofs. Trees fell, some on powerlines. All of Sidney was plunged into darkness, while the wind howled and dust smothered the land.

Otte led a charmed life once, but things seemed to be falling apart now. He had been a college football star at the University of Iowa and a top-flight academic who wrote poetry. Then he worked as an assistant athletic coach at Tarkio College in Missouri. But that position ended in 1935 after he got into a fight—with the coach. He hung on to employment at the college, working as a resident adviser at one of the dorms. He lost his job in February, however, after reports that he got a little rough with two unruly students. A month later, he was working at some stockyards. That couldn't have helped his confidence.

His wife, Mary, retained her secretarial position at Tarkio College, and they may have been living apart. Newspaper accounts hint that she was now living in Tarkio, Missouri, thirty-five miles away. Lowell was living with his mother, Armada—everyone called her Mada—and his stepfather, Albert Jorgenson. He and Mada married in 1919, when Lowell was fourteen.

Lowell's ill health the last several years led to bouts with manic depression and being hospitalized several times due to nervous breakdowns. But Lowell's mindset also may have been influenced by four other relatives who ended their lives, including a cousin, Harold Otte, six months earlier. Mada found Harold hanging from the rafters of their barn.

All of that considered, if this morning Lowell Otte was standing on the edge of an abyss of despair, as the coroner said, the dust storm and heat may have pushed him over it. It had been over 100 degrees every day for days. Yesterday, it was 106 degrees. This morning, it was probably in the 80s, heading toward a high of 90.

Around 8 A.M., Otte stepped into a shed. Mada Jorgenson had just returned home from a night shift at the hospital in nearby Hamburg. She was with her husband, who had picked her up, and they heard a 12-gauge shotgun blast. Mada and Albert darted out of their house and followed the noise, running toward the worst moment of their lives.

Oklahoma

Charles Gilbreth and his wife moved from Wewoka to their son's home in Cushing. This may have been a good life decision, but physically doing it at 3 P.M., when it was 107 degrees, was not. Almost as soon as their belongings were inside, the fifty-nine-year-old husband, father, and newly retired meat cutter realized he didn't feel well. By evening Gilbreth, who evidently suffered a heart attack, was calling family members so he could bid farewell. He was no hypochondriac. A physician got to the house, and Gilbreth had said his final goodbyes.

In Muskogee county, Gin Ki, a sixty-five-year-old chef and Chinese immigrant, was taken to the hospital with an internal temperature of 107. He lived another ten years, however, undoubtedly thanks to his ice bath. The three major hospitals in Tulsa were using three tons of ice a day to treat patients. It took an average of a hundred pounds of chipped ice to begin with, and then the medical staff covered the patients continually with ice packs until people's temperatures reached normal.

Unless they didn't. Across the state, where it was well over 100 degrees and in many communities over 110, there were approximately thirty heat victims, including a salesman, a baker, a cardiologist, a retired banker, a retired farmer, and a laborer. Many residents collapsed and died in the hospital several days later.

One of those was August Frederick Kaufman, who was walking in downtown Tulsa when he fainted. Kaufman was a sixty-three-year-old Switzerland-born artist who for years commanded serious attention and money, though when he moved to the United States in 1918 to New York City and then to Tulsa, he never quite recaptured the earlier acclaim of his career. As *The Oklahoma Courier* put it, "He was internationally famous as a portrait painter. He operated here as an interior decorator for several years, but the pinch of the depression and the ebbing of his great talent with advancing years brought him to virtual obscurity." His last few years, as the economy fractured, the portrait painter was painting houses.

Unlike the path taken by some artists, his death didn't help with the obscurity problem.

California

It was only 84 degrees in San Diego, but that was the highest temperature in fifty-nine years, and the humidity was 68 percent. For the sixth day in a row, it was over 90 degrees in Los Angeles, and there were four heat victims. In parts of Southern California, temperatures were well over 100, and a dishwasher in a restaurant in Brawley was found dead at home after he didn't show up for work. A twenty-five-year-old Bakersfield man died. So did three people in El Centro. A forty-four-year-old tried to cool off in the Kern River and was swept into the rapids. In Lost Hills, a thirst-quenched family drank water, but it was impure. Everyone became sick, and the family's four-month-old son died.

Kansas

Six heat deaths today. The heat was so bad in Wichita (106°F) that Sterling Davis, a farmer, reported his cow was producing sour milk.

Nebraska

There were four heat deaths in Omaha (90°F). And to make things even more miserable for people, municipal pools were closed; the water had to be emptied and the dust cleaned out.

Washington

For the second day in a row, it was over 100 degrees virtually everywhere, and the heat took out a seventy-seven-year-old Mason City woman and a mail carrier in Yakima. A thirteen-year-old Cedarville boy drowned. The heat *almost* killed Harry Ikeda. In Chewelah, the fifty-eight-year-old collapsed while operating a gasoline speeder—a small vehicle made for train tracks, similar to a handcar, only it's fueled by gas. Ikeda's gasoline speeder rammed into a parked train. He woke in the hospital with a concussion and possibly a fractured skull. He had no memory of the crash, which was probably just as well.

Myrtle Gaylord, a columnist for *The Spokane Press*, probably spoke for everyone when she wrote, "When it's officially 100 in the shade, and unofficially anywhere from 114 to 120 almost anywhere, there's no use trying to think or talk about anything but the weather." Later in her column, which was probably written today in 103-degree heat but ran the next day, when the high was 101, Gaylord wrote, "There are folks who suggest that nudism would be fine in this temperature. Maybe so." But she observed that the people who suggested going naked usually had a physique that made her inclined "to believe that clothes for most of us, even at 100 in the shade, are a blessing in disguise."

Oregon and Idaho

La Grande, Oregon's newspaper, described life in 103-degree heat: "Society is practically at a standstill, with only a few organizations attempting to meet—and most of these take the meeting out to the park or some similar place and turn it into a picnic."

The hottest spot in Idaho was in Lewiston (110°F). Beachgoers crowded the Snake and Clearwater Rivers. Predictably, several people lost their lives.

South Dakota

From Rapid City, where the high was 89 degrees, journalist Ernie Pyle wrote about the heat-driven grasshopper plague. Pyle wrote, "All of a sudden, they are streaking around in all directions, like bullets in the war posters. They jump so fast that each one makes a sort of black streak. They smack and hang all over the car. I was continually dodging and blinking. When you see one coming straight at you, you instinctively duck. And just as you do, he hits the windshield with a pop that sounds as if you'd thrown a rock."

After driving for three miles through clouds of grasshoppers, Pyle stopped at the first town he found and purchased a grasshopper screen to go over his radiator.

"Nearly every car out here has one. It costs 85 cents, and is made of window screening, cut to fit your radiator," Pyle wrote. "If you don't have one, the grasshoppers stick in the radiator, and the first thing you know the surface is solid with them, and no air can get through, and your engine gets hot."

A mechanic swept the dead grasshoppers out of Pyle's radiator with a broom before installing the screen. "I was silly enough to count them. There were 284 stuck in the radiator," wrote Pyle, who estimated that a third of his driving time was spent traveling through grasshoppers.

Nine days earlier, Martin Kane, a United Press staff correspondent, drove through Jamestown, North Dakota, and described the grasshoppers hitting his car in 118-degree weather, splattering "against the windshield like machine gun fire."

"There are never less than half a dozen in the car with me," Pyle wrote. "About three times a day, one gets up my pants leg, and I have to stop and fish him out. You're liable to find them in your hotel room, or in your shirt in the morning, or hopping around the tables in the best restaurants. They don't hurt you, of course, but they get in the way."

Actually, grasshoppers *could* hurt you. In mid-July, in Montana, a mother heard her one-year-old scream. She swooped him up; a grasshopper had nibbled on the infant's ear until it bled. In late July, in Lewistown, Montana,

William Kirkendall was driving when a grasshopper landed in his eye; he lost control and his gravel truck overturned three times. Kirkendall lived, but around the same time, a Nebraska woman tried to brush a grasshopper off her ankle and lost control of her car, crashing into a ditch, and her passenger, a six-year-old cousin, was killed.

The grasshoppers were everywhere and devoured almost anything. In July, in Kansas City, a councilman and coal company executive came into his downtown office and found a potted plant picked clean by the grasshoppers that came in through the window. He was on the fifth floor.

Pyle wrote about the poison that the government used to kill the grasshoppers called "paris green," a poisonous green copper and arsenic compound. The poison killed the grasshoppers but didn't seem to make much of a difference. Pyle wrote, "As one farmer says, 'For every one that dies, a thousand come to his funeral.' It's like trying to bore a hole in water." The poison also may have done more harm than good, according to Pyle: "The farmers say that when it rains after poison is spread, the poison washes off and runs down to the water holes and poisons the cattle and birds. They say that quite a few cattle have been killed, and that you hardly ever see birds any more."

Utah

In Salt Lake City, all eyes were on the Hogle Gardens Zoo, where two beloved English spotted deer died yesterday. J. C. Flint, the local veterinarian, examined the deer corpses and came away with a damning conclusion. "It is my opinion that the condition of the deer was brought on by the intense heat and the lack of shelter at the Hogle Gardens Zoo," he said.

The remaining two deer wouldn't live much longer if something wasn't done, Flint said, informing *The Salt Lake Tribune* that the dead deer hadn't touched a drop of water for three days. It was easy to understand why. Their only water was in a rusty barrel, black and stagnated.

The water, Dr. Flint said, was "unfit for anything, human or animal, to drink." There was no vegetation for the deer, nor shelter. Grace Hyslop, the zoo's society president, promised, "If no action is taken, I'll get 100 volunteer workers and do the necessary work myself, if city commissioners insist on letting animals die tortured deaths from neglect."

New York

Police rescued Rose Crimmins today. The eighty-year-old widow in Rockland Lake had been held captive by a sixty-five-year-old woman, Mary Moss, who physicians described as "deranged" by the heat. Temperatures had fallen into the 80s, but the humidity was 80 percent. Crimmins had befriended Moss, who was incredibly lonely. Crimmins may have been lonely, too, but she really went the extra mile. Crimmins invited Moss to leave the nursing home and become her roommate.

The expression "no good deed goes unpunished" was invented for times like these. Moss moved in, locked Crimmins in a bedroom, and threatened to burn the house down. For twenty-four hours, Crimmins begged Moss not to light matches. At some point, a neighbor visited, heard the conversation, and called the police.

Pennsylvania

In Erie, Pennsylvania, the media continued to discuss the Samuel Weed case. Weed was strapped into his hospital bed and Leroy Search, a county detective, told the press that there was no evidence of Weed having an affair.

"We can't find a thing of questionable or irregular nature. Weed spent nights at home, often making toys for his children and was an earnest religious worker. We cannot find anything that would indicate there had ever been another woman in his life," Search said.

The neighbors were insistent that Weed wasn't dating another woman. The police were starting to believe that maybe Weed was a model husband who, due to the intense heat, actually lost his mind and did the unthinkable.

Ohio

People's morale was flagging, nerves were on edge and the heat was becoming a way of life. Today, the *Cincinnati Enquirer* reported that on a recent "comfortable night," a young woman in the city was seen waving a fan back and forth, even though the evening temperatures were mild. "I got so used to fanning in the last week that I can't stop," said the woman, continuing to fan.

36

JULY 21
The Icebox

Today's Death Toll: 300+
Total Death Toll: 8,600+

Air-conditioning wasn't the only appliance and industry thriving during the summer of 1936. Shower baths and shower cabinets (a shower without the bathtub) were in great demand. Many American homes still had outhouses and people bathed in outdoor tubs, but more and more people liked the idea of bathing indoors.

Refrigerators also were having a banner year. Sales were up before the heat wave, during it, and afterward. There was ample room for growth in the industry, with prices still out of reach for Depression-era families. Thirty years later, Patrick Ryan Jr., load promotion supervisor of Illinois Power Co., told his local paper, *The Decatur Daily Review*, that refrigerators made up less than 10 percent of all home food cooling equipment in 1936. Most Decatur residents, he said, kept food in iceboxes.

Iceboxes did a reasonably good job of keeping food cool. The wooden icebox was well-insulated, often with tin or zinc, and it stored a large block of ice near the top of the box, and underneath were several shelves where you put your food. But if you have trouble keeping your refrigerator tidy today, you'd love maintaining an icebox, which could almost feel like a full-time job.

You'd regularly pay your iceman, who continually put a block of ice in your icebox. Then, because the icebox didn't have many shelves, you had to go to the store more often. A good icebox had a drain or pan to catch the ice as it leaks. But you had to empty the pan, and if you forgot or didn't have a pan, you'd be cleaning up melting ice a lot.

Your iceman probably brought a block of ice almost daily, maybe even twice a day, especially in the summer, coming inside your home to put the ice in the icebox. But if you were between deliveries, and your ice had mostly melted, eating your food could become chancy. There were numerous food poisoning incidents that made local headlines around the country, all believed to have been due to food being exposed to temperatures in the 90s and 100s. You really wanted to make sure your icebox was functioning well during a heat wave.

In Jefferson City, Missouri, Eva Bremerman, a community nurse, told her local paper that she knew of at least a dozen families "already fighting off illness caused by food which was tainted by the hot weather." She added, "Babies are in distress, and families all over the city have been forced to eat food which they knew was not good. If ice is not provided, we can expect many families to become ill."

If an icebox wasn't available, experts advised putting baby bottles with milk in a large pan filled with cool water, but change the pan frequently. Or you could put milk in a fruit jar, provided the jar had been boiled, sealed with a tightly screwed—and then keep the jar suspended in a pail in the upper part of your water well. It was also recommended that you store the jar of milk in a cellar or springhouse, where the milk would hopefully keep better.

North Dakota

Ernie Pyle continued his tour of the Dust Bowl, and he wrote of driving with a North Dakotan and stopping in front of a farmhouse a few miles west of Rhame. "Can we get a drink out of your well?" Pyle asked. The farmer agreed. "You have to drink often when it's 110 degrees," wrote Pyle.

Idaho

It was 103 degrees in Boise, and at the statehouse, government officials muddled through the day. The *Idaho Statesman* painted a portrait of what it was like: “Executives sat in front of huge whirring fans, languidly stirring papers about and doing their best to simulate activity—without any tangible results so far as newsmen were concerned. Clerks listlessly lifted heavy ledgers around, mentally groaning at every step; stenographers pecked half-heartedly at typewriter keys.”

Lewiston reached 110 degrees, and the state’s ice industry started having problems filling orders. Typically, ice executives said, ice could be frozen and ready for transport in eighteen to twenty hours, but during hot weather like they were having, it took forty-eight hours.

Indiana

A forty-seven-year-old in Indianapolis who spent the previous night drinking slept on the courthouse lawn and awakened this morning to discover his pants had been stolen, along with $50 and his slippers. On his way home, without pants and shoes, identification, or money, and with alcohol on his breath, he encountered a police officer—who promptly arrested him.

Pennsylvania

Samuel Weed, in Erie, still in a hospital bed, still wearing a straitjacket, told the press, “I can’t understand why they are keeping me here. I want to plead guilty and get this thing over with—the sooner, the better.”

Weed would see a judge soon. The district attorney and police captain planned to have their hospitalized prisoner arraigned after his family’s funeral later in the day.

Iowa

From his apartment window, Dr. George Mogridge of the Iowa Institution for Feeble-Minded Children watched the children he used to oversee, who were watching a band concert. It was a pleasant moment at a time when Mogridge was not feeling well. In his diary, he wrote, "Cool again. Clear." The high was 92 degrees, but compared to the last couple weeks, it probably felt cool. And then on another line, "Slight blood in spittoon."*

Around 8:30 P.M., Mogridge died. Somebody later wrote in the diary that Dr. Mogridge's body was found in the bathroom. He was said to have had a heart attack or stroke. Nobody blamed the heat for Mogridge's death, possibly because it was so "cool" outside.

California

It was 119 degrees in El Centro and 122 in Brawley. At least six people around here died, including a baby and a man in his fifties, who newspapers described as a one-armed, heavily tattooed, unidentified transient.

One California resident was taking chances with the sun—and knew better. Jean Harlow was seen on Catalina Island, sunbathing with her mother. It's easy to see why Harlow would want to relax on what was then, and still is, an island paradise, albeit a tourist magnet. But sunbathing was a worse health risk for Harlow than most people, and she couldn't seem to resist the allure of those rays.

* A metal container made, specifically, for people to spit into.

37

JULY 22

The Misery Index

Today's Death Toll: 200+
Total Death Toll: 8,800+

There's a reason hell is depicted as fire and unending heat. When you're freezing, you can pile on layers of clothing and blankets and possibly achieve a sense of comfort. But when you're hot and miserable, after removing your layers, there isn't much left to do—except think about how hot and miserable you are.

It seems impossible to overstate how clammy and uncomfortable people felt this summer. The heat was always with you, unless you were fortunate enough to work somewhere cool, like a movie theater or perhaps a department store.

Some people were more uncomfortable than others. Jacqueline Jean Benson was born in Chicago on January 14 during the terrible winter, weighing twelve ounces. She was, up to this point, the smallest baby to have been born and survived, and was now a minor celebrity. In mid-July, she had trouble eating, which everybody blamed on the heat. But Benson rallied and ultimately grew up to be an elementary school teacher. Then there was poor Robert Wadlow, who lived in Alton, Illinois, which bore the brunt of a lot of heat this summer. Wadlow was eighteen and something of a national celebrity. He was the world's tallest person, and he still holds the record. He was 8 feet 5 inches tall, and he weighed 425 pounds. His shoe size was thirty-nine. When you have that much body mass, you tend to be hotter than the average-sized person, and Wadlow felt every degree of heat the summer was dishing out.

He spent some of the summer at state fairs, trying to earn a living but with ambitions of studying law. "I'm not a sideshow freak, and I don't intend to be one," he told a reporter. But it was a lousy summer for Wadlow, who spent as much time as he could in front of electric fans and in swimming pools. He died way too young, in 1940, at the age of twenty-two.

The misery index also depended on where you lived. In *The Arizona Republic*, an August 2 op-ed observed that their state was just as hot as it was in the Midwest and East, but citizens were doing just fine, partially because everyone was accustomed to the heat: "Men and women in Arizona do not suddenly fall on the street or highway as they do in eastern and northern communities. Their heat strikes in darkness as well as midday, while in our higher altitudes and clearer atmosphere, night almost invariably brings relief."

The Arizona Republican was onto something. Similar to what was happening in Nevada, Arizona's low humidity and dry air protected it. Many other states' humidity essentially created a quilt of water vapor that blocked the night's heat from escaping. For instance, on July 14, when the summer was doing its worst to the United States, in Winslow, Arizona, residents were sleeping in 60-degree weather; in Springfield, Illinois, everyone was tossing and turning in 84 degrees. For most of the country, daily life was almost unbearable. Helen Lavasseur, when she was ninety-five years old in 2011, told the Madison, Wisconsin, newspaper all about the summer of 1936: "It was too hot to do anything. It hurt to walk on the sidewalk. I thought our furniture was going to burn up." Lavasseur slept outside with a friend in a big yard behind a boarding house.

Lavasseur, then a college student, did accounting work for a dentist. "I had a little fan on the floor, but it was too hot to do any work," she said, remembering a day when the temperature reached 106. "We had to wear stockings then, and I asked my boss if I could take them off. He said yes. Finally, I asked if I could go home, and he said, 'Yes, go.'"

In 1976, forty years after the 1936 heat wave, Marguerite Lienlokken, a resident of La Crosse, Wisconsin, recalled to her local paper that when she was twenty-five years old and very pregnant, "we'd lie down in front of the door on a blanket, make newspapers into fans and fan ourselves to sleep." Her seventy-eight-year-old grandfather had a fatal heart attack in 108-degree weather, on July 14, 1936.

In 1987, Richard Middleton, a resident of Bloomington, Illinois, told his paper that in 1936, he had a new job with the National Bank of

Bloomington: "It was so darned hot that I'd wear a clean white shirt. And I'd bring two dry white shirts with me."

One reader writing to a newspaper in Orchard, Nebraska, in August 1936, described life this way: "The scorching heat and wind torment us for the day. At last, at night, we go to bed only to roll and dream of destruction and starving livestock."

Pearl Levy, ninety-five years old in 1993 when she was interviewed about the '36 heat wave by *The New York Times*, remembered, "People had to get out of the streets, but the subway was smothering, withering. I remember distinctly that when I was out on the street, it was like the street was full of hot steam. The heat came up from the sidewalk, and it would envelop your whole body and face."

In 1982, Helen Clark, of Columbus, Ohio, recalled the candles in her home melting, without lighting a match. "I spent most of my time at night on the floor under the window," she said. Her husband, Vic, remembered a picnic that the Clarks attempted and the dessert they brought with them. On the way there, they tried to keep cool in the car by hanging a wet towel in the window. It didn't work. "But it was so hot, the cake melted down," he said.

Alpha Knipp, who lived in Hugo, Oklahoma, discussed the heat wave in a 1980 interview with the Texas paper *Paris News*. She said it was 118 degrees inside her house. "The beds were hot, so you didn't want to lay down. The chairs were hot, so you didn't want to sit down," she said. A ceiling fan that her husband bought didn't help much either, she added: "All it did was stir around the hot air."

An anonymous female Oklahoma newspaper columnist with the *Monkogee Daily Phoenix and Times-Democrat* offered her take on the summer in a column that ran on July 19: "On a day like this, I'm supposed to sit at a typewriter in a newspaper office and write a column. My typewriter is so hot that it burns my fingers."

James Melton, a popular radio singer, snapped to one reporter, "Keep cool? Are you trying to be funny? I change shirts every hour." His laundry bill, he added, had gone way up. "That in itself burns me," he said.

And some people must have felt like they just couldn't win. On July 14, an Elkhart, Indiana, man was overcome by the heat in a factory and rushed to the hospital; the next day, he went swimming and almost drowned.

The heat affected virtually every element of life. For instance, in Creston, Iowa, business owners and employees drank the well water near Black's Laundry for years without an issue. But in early July, everybody noticed the water didn't taste so great, and there was an odor. The fire department investigated and stuck a hose into the well, adding fresh water. Eventually, the old water came flushing out along with a pile of dead, wet crickets. The firefighters said the heat drove the insects to the darkness and dampness of the well, and the townspeople were super grossed out to realize that for some time now, they had been essentially drinking cricket juice.

Indiana

Dr. Herman Morgan, the secretary at the Board of Public Health for Indianapolis, announced the number of burial permits that were issued the week of July 15 when the heat wave was at its worst: 243. Typically, that number would have been around 135. "There is no way of determining just how many deaths were caused by the heat," Morgan said. "It undoubtedly acted as a contributory cause in a number of cases where persons were suffering from chronic ailments or age infirmities."

Physicians often referred to heat as a contributory cause or contributing factor in a patient's death. On July 13, John McMahon, a sixty-eight-year-old buyer of horses and mules in Cannelton, Indiana, may have been doomed the moment a mule kicked him, but his doctor said the 107.5-degree temperature robbed him of any chance of rebounding. On July 15, in Cincinnati, a twenty-four-year-old pregnant woman died. She had the measles and didn't have much of a chance, since the highly contagious virus-caused disease was often a death sentence, with no vaccine for it yet. Still, the doctors concluded the heat signed her death warrant.

And this evening, in an extreme example of the heat being a contributing factor to somebody's demise, on a train near Valparaiso, a sixty-five-year-old

Minnesotan, believed to be mad from the heat, jumped through the window of a moving train, flinging his body to the earth.

California

Age was catching up with Tom Dunfield. He was a restaurant owner in Princeton and seventy-seven years old, which was considered getting up there in 1936. Losing his patience with everybody, today, Dunfield fired buckshot at a dairyman who stepped onto his property.

He was swiftly arrested, although he got out two days later after posting a $1,000 bond. But then he was taken into custody again for threatening a neighbor.

"If you don't keep those chickens out of my yard, I'll kill them. Yes, I'll kill the chickens and you, too," Dunfield snapped. When a judge heard the case in early August, the neighbor said, "Dunfield lately has become so abusive and threatening that I haven't slept in my own home for a week."

Dunfield suggested that the heat had gotten to him. "I never meant to kill anybody. I'd swear that on a stack of Bibles as high as my head," Dunfield said.

The heat defense worked, and Dunfield didn't serve jail time. It didn't hurt that Dunfield promised to move in with family members in another town. He spent the next decade as a resident of Colusa.

Mexico

The heat wave didn't stop at the southern border of the United States. In Mexicali, the capital state of the Mexican state of Baja, California, five people died from the heat.

Pennsylvania

Philadelphia could claim the nation's worst mom, but Erie had a runner-up or, depending on your point of view, the best mother-in-law: Alice Chapin, fifty-three years old and the mother of the late Irene Weed. Obviously, Alice was speaking during an emotionally turbulent time and perhaps later regretted her words. Or maybe she didn't have regrets. Perhaps Alice was leaning on her faith, and she may have truly felt the heat affected her son-in-law. But you have to wonder what Irene would have made of her mother's generous defense of her husband, Sam Weed. Remember, Weed *killed* Alice's daughter. With a hammer.

"I forgive Sam," Alice Chapin told reporters. "I will go to the hospital to see Sam. He will need someone to help him. There is no other woman in his life. I know his past life. If my daughter were alive and able to talk, she would forgive Sam for what he has done."

"The law may call it murder, but I don't . . . It wasn't Sam who actually killed them," Chapin insisted to reporters, presumably suggesting he was out of his mind or possessed by the devil. "They were on a constant honeymoon despite the fact they had been married for eight years. The law will eventually take its course. But I still believe in him. He was an adorable husband and a marvelous son-in-law."

Utah

Even without the heat, Ralph McCollin was on the hot seat. In the wake of the death of two deer at the Hogle Gardens Zoo, McCollin, the director, was sacked. McCollin mounted an aggressive defense in the media: "I don't know why my resignation has been asked for," he said. "I have worked at the zoo for four years. I came here at the request of the zoological society after drastic promises, never fulfilled, were made. I found the zoo in a deplorable condition and tried to remedy the situation."

According to McCollin, before his arrival, "The cages had never been cleaned, and it took us eight days to clean eight of them. The monkey island was filthy. The society decided to make a garden out of the property and took money which should have been used for the animals. I set about to get animals so the property would not be a barnyard but a zoo. I did everything I could to cut expenses. I've never got a dime for the use of my car, nor a gallon of gasoline. I spent my own postage getting feed. All last winter the water line was on top of the ground. I recently counted sixty-two leaks in it. I have had to haul water in milk cans for the animals. There has never been a day that I have not gone over the zoo grounds fifteen times in the interest of the animals. I have been working 18 to 20 hours a day. I think I've done my part."

McCollin may have had a case. *The Salt Lake Tribune* found that the previous spring, McCollin petitioned the Salt Lake City commission for funds to provide shelter and shade for the deer. In his written appeal, he predicted an expensive tragedy would befall the deer without a sun shield and stated that the water conditions at the zoo were inadequate.

Sixty-two years after the first American zoo opened in Philadelphia, there was still a learning curve at zoos, and McCollin likely made mistakes with the deer and all the animals—his four-year-old son used to play with Rex, the lion, when he was a cub. But now the city was paying attention. McCollin was handed his walking papers, and the zoo society president put out a five-step plan, which stated "that immediate relief in the form of shelters from the summer's intense heat be given the remaining deer in the zoo. This should be done today, before more animals die from the conditions existing there."

"They had to make a goat out of someone, and I guess I'm it," McCollin said to a reporter.

McCollin's day got worse. That evening, while he was at a lodge meeting, his wife, Geraldine, started a fire in their gas stove with a gasoline can. It exploded, and though she wasn't injured or blown up, the kitchen was immediately in flames.

Geraldine's parents were in town for a long visit, and her dad grabbed the blazing gas can. He carried it from the house and became badly burned on his arms, hands, and right leg—while his daughter, wife, and grandkids raced out of the house. Still, while the McCollin family lost their main source of income during the Great Depression, and some members were almost killed or burned and saw half their uninsured home go up in flames, they were all alive. Compared to a lot of families this summer, it was still a pretty good day.

38

JULY 24

In the Heat of the Night

Today's Death Toll: 200+
Total Death Toll: 9,000+

Millions of Americans were discovering that there was a reason their ancestors started sleeping indoors. Even if you weren't hit by a car or bitten by a skunk, there were a lot of downsides to sleeping under the stars.

Bill Tucker, a reporter, and later advertising manager, for the *Holdenville Daily News*, described sleeping outside in Oklahoma City. "Nightly marches are joined in by whole families," Tucker wrote, describing what he saw in his neighborhood and maybe drawing upon his small household—he and his wife had a seven-year-old daughter. "First, one member will sojourn to the yard, maybe carrying his or her sleeping paraphernalia, if not already prepared for the retreat from the hot house. Next, some other member will join the procession—and another, and another. The more outside would-be sleepers, the merrier—for the mosquitoes."

Tucker lamented that a family member would comment about the mosquitoes, and then another family member would say something, and before you know it, the complaints about the mosquitoes would drown the noise of the mosquitoes. "Victims get up, walk into the house, try sleeping there, but are driven back into the yard because of the heat," wrote Tucker, before suggesting that some larger families should consider appointing a parade marshal.

Hazel Fowler, a thirty-one-year-old reporter in Norman, Oklahoma, wrote of a similar experience: "We reasoned that after 10 or 11 o'clock, things would quiet down, and we could settle down for some of that cool, refreshing slumber we'd heard so much about." It was not to be. Fowler wrote, "People walked incessantly up and down that sidewalk, stray dogs and cats paid frequent visits to our bedside, radios blared out with baseball reports, cars kept flashing their lights in our eyes. Sleep was impossible."

Indeed: birds chirping at dawn; swarms of mosquitoes, flies and gnats; milkmen tiptoeing around sleeping bodies on the porch and unsuccessfully trying to be quiet. In some states, people snoring were at risk of grasshoppers jumping into their mouth. In Elk City, Oklahoma, residents sleeping on lawns discovered that red ants adjusted their schedules to the heat, resting in the day and coming out at night.

If you lived in an area with snakes, you might find yourself sharing your bed with one, as happened to a terrified man in Ontario. In Marysville, Kansas, two men slept on cots on a lawn when they were awakened by a hissing snake and a frantic alley cat. They tried capturing the snake, but it got away. The next morning, they found the cat, dead from a snake bite. A lot of Marysville residents also reported being chewed on by beetles and finding blisters on their skin in the morning.

You weren't necessarily safe from snakes inside. The morning of July 10, an older married couple in Mitchell, Indiana, discovered a big brown and black spotted snake resting in their bird cage, minus two birds. Their daughter and her husband had spent the night, and they all queasily concluded the snake came through the open window and slithered right over the sleeping couple.

Stray dogs were a nuisance. One guy in Sedalia, Missouri, slept outside with his family, and when a dog bothered him, the guy tried slugging the animal, missed, and gave his wife a black eye.

The mayor of Durant, Oklahoma, was concerned about dogs roaming the streets and carrying rabies, which had been an issue. With more people sleeping outside, he issued an unsettling edict: stray dogs caught would be killed.

Pet dogs were also challenging. Your dog might be indoors, barking wildly throughout the night because of the people sleeping in their yards. But if you kept your dog with you outside, they'd still bark—or find another way to wake everyone up. The Tulsa police chief awakened one morning after a next-door neighbor's dog licked him on his face. In the same city, the city auditor awoke to find somebody's puppy scampering on his chest.

Frank Greenwald of Whiting, Indiana, fell asleep in the middle of the day on his porch on July 13, and his own dog stole his upper false teeth—from his mouth. Greenwald wasn't sure how that happened without him waking up, but if he was like a lot of Americans, he was sleep-deprived, and once asleep, probably out cold.

Something similar happened to Charley Drake, in Broken Bow, Nebraska. He and his family were in a tent, and Drake removed his false teeth before going to bed. The next morning, the teeth were missing. But Mrs. Drake noticed a neighbor's small dog that quickly became the main suspect. They found the false teeth, eventually. The dog had buried them.

The great outdoors as a bedroom also wasn't a place for people who were jumpy. Harry Bowers, who owned a piano service company in Tucson, Arizona, was in his backyard when he was awakened by a fierce wild animal hidden in foliage near his fence. He dispatched his bulldog to attack, but his pet was too smart to go after it. Bowers pulled out a revolver, but it didn't work. So he contacted the police.

The police fanned out across his yard, searching for a ferocious, perhaps rabid, animal. They did not find it. They did, however, discover an adorable porcupine trying to get through a fence. They put it in a box and took it back to the station, where one of the officers seemed partial to keeping it.

There was no shortage of ways you could be roused from your slumber if you were outside. In Jacksonville, Illinois, people dozing in a park were disturbed by fishermen walking around with flashlights, looking for night-crawlers. In downtown Cincinnati, a twenty-four-year-old man bedded down in the grass at Central Parkway and Vine Street, and a passerby dropped a bottle on the sidewalk. It shattered, and glass struck him in the face.

Even going from the indoors to sleep outdoors wasn't necessarily a straightforward process. On July 28, a married woman in Lebanon, Tennessee, decided to sleep on her porch. In the dark, she fell down the stairs and fractured both arms.

Hospital patients wanted to go outside but usually were stuck sweating inside. Dr. Courtney Townsend, of Paris, Texas, told his hometown paper in 1980, "Patients would have to have their bed clothes changed two or three times a night."

But arguably, the people who had it the worst were those who worked the night shift—and slept during the day when temperatures were the highest. In Russell, Kentucky, during mid-July, a railroad man told his newspaper that he had about a week, where he averaged two hours of shuteye a day, because he couldn't sleep when he was sweating.

North Dakota

From the city of Bismarck, Ernie Pyle concluded his tour of the Dust Bowl and observed, "The whole United States seems to be tortured and wounded in varying degrees with drought and heat, but in the bowl, there is complete destruction." He also wrote, "Living is far from pleasant in the bowl this summer. The hot wind blows all day, and the fields are bare, and there is no shade anywhere. The heat is constantly terrific. A hundred and ten is nothing at all. It seems to stay nearly as hot at night as in the daytime. The last few days have been slightly cooler. But for more than a week, I slept not more than three hours a night."

Nebraska

It was 113 degrees in Omaha, and Tom Ryan, a sixty-year-old laborer with no permanent address, was found on a street, unconscious and dying. The next day a former classmate shared some recollections with the local paper. One can only wonder what Ryan would have made of the memories, if he had been around to read them.

When Ryan was younger, according to the classmate, he was "handsome and a good dresser" and his nickname was "Pretty Tom." But Ryan was no financial wizard, according to the classmate: "He inherited a tidy sum of money, but didn't hang on to it."

Wyoming

Heat expanded railroad tracks near Rock Springs (91°F), causing twenty-four cars from a passenger train heading from Denver to Salt Lake City to depart from the tracks. There were two deaths—and a lot of injuries.

California

The heat wave's talents extended beyond murder. It may have killed a career.

Trini Varela was born in Mexico but soon after moved to Tucson, Arizona, with her family and became an American citizen. She saw her singing career take off at age sixteen after being discovered by a local tenor. She moved to Los Angeles, staying with relatives and taking vocal lessons with Florencio Constantino. The acclaimed Spanish operatic tenor, who was late in his career, was charmed by the young woman's talent and reportedly said, "Instead of paying me for testing your voice, it is I who should pay you for the pleasure of listening to you sing."

By the 1920s, Miss Varela was making a pretty good name for herself performing on the stage. In the 1930s, she appeared in vaudeville, recording music, and making appearances in movie shorts such as *La Cucaracha* in 1934. *The Plainsman*, a now-classic Western, was to be the thirty-six-year-old's first appearance in a feature film, one starring Gary Cooper and Jean Arthur and directed by Cecil B. DeMille.

The first day of filming was done in Calabasas, where it was in the low 90s, and events became a little chaotic. Arthur was riding on a stagecoach, holding the reins of six horses that suddenly bolted. Three extras were slightly injured trying to stop the horses. Cooper, sitting next to Arthur, managed to stop the horses, but the actress was thrown about, ending the ride with a bruised hand. And somewhere in this mess, Trini Varela passed out from the heat.

So the first day of filming for *The Plainsman* was memorable. But Varela didn't experience the second. She recovered from her prostration but didn't appear in *The Plainsman*. Going forward, she married in 1937 and appeared in a smattering of films, in mostly uncredited or minor roles, such as playing

"Mexican woman" in the 1948 film *Angel in Exile.* Her greatest brush with fame was singing the only musical number in the 1943 classic *For Whom the Bell Tolls*, starring Ingrid Bergman and, as it worked out, Gary Cooper. She died in 1977, hopefully having had a happy and fulfilling life, but one in which she never achieved the stardom she appeared to be on the verge of until one hot day in 1936.

39

JULY 25

The Politics of Heat

Today's Death Toll: 100+
Total Death Toll: 9,100+

It was inevitable that the heat wave would become embroiled in politics. Why not? It affected everything else. Low turnout for primary elections was blamed on high temperatures. Some voters, meanwhile, blamed politicians for the weather. "When Republicans were leading this country, we would have a day or two of heat but not prolonged like recent droughts," a reader wrote to Bloomington, Illinois's newspaper, *The Pantagraph*. "Therefore, if you like this heat and prolonged drought, re-elect Roosevelt. If you want weather and rain like we should have, elect Landon."

Deila Tefertiller, from Greenfield, Missouri, wrote *The Parsons Sun* and confidently stated that if Alf Landon was elected, he would make it rain. The editors responded that "if Alf can make it rain, we would like for him to demonstrate a little here at home."

Democrats also weren't above blaming Republicans for the weather. One political joke making the rounds: "It's a Republican heat wave on account of there's no relief."

Even local politicians took heat for the heat. Today, Councilman Earl Stephens of Parkersburg, West Virginia (87°F), after weeks in the 90s and 100s, complained to a reporter that voters blamed him for not fixing the weather. "It's a dog's life," Stephens said.

In Canada, a politician leveraged the heat wave as a reason to vote for him. Jim Litterick ran for the Communist Party to become a member of the Manitoba Legislative Assembly. Litterick wrote an opinion piece for *The*

Winnipeg Tribune that ran on July 11. Whatever you make of his politics, Litterick's op-ed provides an interesting snapshot of what the heat was like for the downtrodden.

"We have experienced intensive heat," Litterick wrote. "Severe suffering has been experienced, but who has borne the brunt of the suffering? Just imagine, if you can, four thousand single men, crowded into a huge dining hall not equipped with fans or other devices for cooling the hall, sitting down to hot soup, mulligan stew and mushed up boiled potatoes, etc. These single unemployed men must eat this hot greasy mess, no matter how nauseating it is, or else go hungry."

Litterick painted a grim portrait of the poor in a sweltering climate: "Many hundreds of old houses in Winnipeg, which should have been razed years ago as unfit for habitation, are crowded with working class families who are unable to sleep in them for the heat, and on top of that many of them are vermin ridden. Most of these houses have no proper screening to protect the inhabitants from flies and mosquitoes. They are like furnaces in hot weather and like ice boxes in winter."

But if you were rich, Litterick stated, you didn't do so badly. He described "the capitalist class" as feasting on "iced tea, cooled salads, frozen fruit desserts, highballs in cracked ice, screened porches in the shade, cool shower baths, excursions to the country house by the lake and fast motors to carry them."

Litterick's column may have resonated with voters, since he won a seat in the assembly. But that was his high point; things got rough for him early during World War II. In 1940, Canada outlawed communism, and he was kicked off the assembly. He went into hiding and gave himself up to the Royal Canadian Mounted Police in 1942. A year later, he worked in a clothing factory, and he appears to have dropped off the map after that.

It was an uncomfortable time to be any politician trying to go about their normal business. Campaigning was curtailed. Nathan Bachman, a Democratic senator from Chattanooga, toured his state in July but didn't make any speeches. "It's too hot to speak," he said. On July 8, in Chicago, Charlton McVeigh, assistant to the chair of the Republican National Committee, collapsed. He fell from his chair during a conference at the committee headquarters. He writhed in agony on the floor while anxious employees called for a doctor and pressed ice packs on him.

In August, when Secretary of the Interior Harold Ickes had a disagreement with President Roosevelt, he was asked if he might quit. Ickes quipped, "I am not going to resign during this hot weather as long as I have an air-cooled office."

Michigan and Nebraska

The heat was breaking in Michigan (it was 87 degrees today in Detroit), but victims were still turning up. James Parks, a sixty-five-year-old from Detroit, was found by a highway worker today. He had been dead, it was believed, for about two weeks. Omaha, Nebraska, lost two people today. It was 114 degrees and 116 in neighboring towns.

Missouri

In Joplin (98°F), children skipped through a free street shower set up by the firemen with their hoses or a fire hydrant. For the last three days, stoic, rugged firemen watched the children enviously. But not today. They put on their bathing suits and ran through the shower with them.

Please hang on to that imagery for a moment, because the rest of the day was Satan's playground.

In St. Louis (102°F), the Sears, Roebuck & Co building's air-conditioning system was in overdrive, which is how Joseph Johnston, a sixteen-year-old working for his uncle, a carpenter, found himself at 6 A.M. on the roof of a three-story building. He stood on a derrick, a platform with a crane attached, cranking a handle and lowering on a wire a 250-pound container of filtering fluid used in the store's cooling plant. But the 250-pound drum was too heavy for the platform. When the drum reached the second floor, it suddenly plummeted the rest of the way, yanking the wire and platform off the roof, with the doomed teenager standing on it.

Preston Armstrong, a fifty-seven-year-old roofer in Grant City (111°F), was on the sloped roof of a business when he became dizzy and lost his balance, tumbling off.

And the high was 96 degrees in Poplar Bluff, where four young children playfully ducked their heads in a tub of water in a barn at a dairy farm. It was a heartwarming portrait of old-fashioned goodness and Americana until a fourteen-month-old girl drowned in front of the other kids.

40

JULY 26

The Business of Heat

Today's Death Toll: 100+
Total Death Toll: 9,200+

The heat wave was good and bad for business. In mid-July, a Muncie, Indiana, company reported selling one hundred tons of ice a day, compared to their usual seventy-five to eighty. About the same time, a report found that in Decatur, Illinois, ice cream consumption shot up 250 percent. Agriculture, as an industry, was not so hot, because it was so hot. In Pennsylvania, with thousands of chickens dying, July's egg production dropped 20 percent.

Swimsuits, suntan lotion, beach merchandise, and even lawn and garden ornament sales were up, since people were going outside to escape the heat inside. In Wichita, druggists reported selling lots of soap: to cool and clean off, people were taking more baths. Drugstore soda fountains were also doing very well.

Sales of milk did a brisk business as usual, but in Lorain, Ohio, the secretary of the milk board pleaded for housewives to return their empty milk bottles. During extreme weather, the secretary said, households often forgot to leave their empties on the porch for the milkmen to pick up. There was a shortage, with missing bottles increasing by an average of ten thousand a day.

Dry cleaners were booming because of the sweat factor. A Pittsburgh laundry service reported that in their first week of July, they had as many clientele as they did through June.

Vacationers and business travelers flocked to air-conditioned cars, boosting the passenger train industry. In fact, because passenger trains were so prevalent, people were making short trips to a few cities away in air-conditioned comfort instead of their cars. In Michigan, in mid-July, old-timers said that the empty roads were about as barren as they were during the pre-automobile days.

Even with people driving less, mechanics saw an uptick in business due to tire blowouts and overheated motors. And as you would expect, stores couldn't keep electric fans in stock. A shop in Pittsfield, Massachusetts, reported that electric fan sales had tripled. In Saginaw, Michigan, a tobacco and novelty shop was doing poor business in July—until they sold electric fans. They sold out immediately.

Actually, any fan was going to sell. As *Billboard* magazine put it, "Outstanding is the demand for fans at this season, and it matters not whether it's an electric fan or the hand paper fan."

The funeral industry flourished. Florists made a mint, too, selling funeral flowers, but running out of them was a problem—and keeping them from wilting in the heat. Even eye doctors reported robust business. The glare from the sun causes eyestrain, observed one Hutchinson, Kansas, optometrist. Taxi services were also thriving; it was too hot to walk.

In Antigo, Wisconsin, merchants reported selling a lot of cowbells. With the grass dried and dead in fields, farmers let their cattle feed in the woods; the cowbells made it easier to find them. And beer sales were way up in some cities. In mid-July, in Milwaukee, breweries were operating twenty-four hours a day; beer sales jumped 75 percent.

But many businesses were battered. Around the country, mills, plants, factories, and foundries closed early or didn't open. While the term "essential workers" wouldn't be bandied about in the way it was during the pandemic that hit in 2020, people in 1936 had similar discussions. An op-ed in *The Decatur Daily Review* remarked on July 15 that in recent days, "in many cities, factories closed for at least part of the day. There are services, however, that cannot let down. We expect the ice factories to keep going full blast, we want the men to keep the fires up under the boilers in the water works; trains must run on time and men must fire the engines; electricity must keep flowing to refrigerators, fans and lights and somewhere along the line there are men in boiler rooms keeping the generators running. We may complain of the heat but if any of the services that we are used to having in this modern world should fail we would complain bitterly about it."

Still, some businesses simply couldn't run normally. On July 15, inside the Hobart foundry in Troy, Ohio, temperatures were 140 degrees. Even the most hard-headed business owner recognized that employees couldn't last long in those conditions.

So especially in mid-July, construction crews halted work, business meetings were scrubbed and livestock trading sessions closed early. For some companies, this was unheard of. On July 15, an employee at the American Car and Foundry Company in St. Charles, Missouri (109°F), was taken to the hospital for a heatstroke, and at 2:30 P.M., the powers-that-be gave the rest of the men the day off. One employee told his local paper that it was the first time something like this had happened in thirty-five years of working there.

Naturally, they were told to report to work the next morning.

Restaurants and retailers struggled. A bank president in Aberdeen, South Dakota, said, "It is definitely noticeable that there are not so many people coming to town and that the number of business transactions have decreased. While the deposit levels of banks are generally up, activity is down."

At the Quality Shop in Beckley, West Virginia, James Pickus said, "Warm weather—especially very hot weather—is bad for us. Customers come in, but they aren't willing to try on clothing. They are too warm—perspiring—and they don't want clothes sticking to them."

Retailers from jewelry stores to furniture and grocery started offering free giveaways to entice customers to drop by—and buy. Electric fans were popular gifts. Some stores brought in a special guest to attract crowds, like the robot known as Monsieur X, a "mechanical man." Monsieur X toured the country ever since he (well, it) came on the scene in 1933 at the Chicago World's Fair. Appearances generally worked like this: the robot was brought to a store, and townspeople would admire the modern marvel, which could run, walk, pick up objects, and point to people in the audience. Then, hopefully, after being entertained, the townsfolk would buy stuff.

But it didn't quite work out the way a Mexico, Missouri, drugstore owner hoped, since it was 115 degrees outside. Monsieur X overheated, and "he" must have looked to be in bad shape because an employee, eighteen-year-old Pearl Bramblett, screamed and fainted. Fortunately, Bramblett was revived. So was Monsieur X.

Other businesses tried to attract more customers by making their premises cool and comfortable. Movie theaters that offered air-conditioning had no trouble selling tickets. Movie theaters that lacked it had trouble filling seats.

Theaters featuring live performers rarely had air-conditioning, probably due to budgetary reasons—live performers cost far more than films you could show repeatedly. But the heat was turning off customers. One *New York Times* reader griped in a July 12 letter, "As one of at least six million people who spend the summer in New York, I view with dismay the legitimate theatres' backwardness in installing cooling systems." According to *Variety*, one July evening at a theater in Yonkers showing *The Bat*, a stage play that is said to have influenced the superhero comic book character Batman, there was a crowd of ten, and two were shills. Most patrons were simply not in the mood to be hot and entertained, with a few exceptions. Jazz legend Louis Armstrong drew crowds wherever he went, no matter how sweaty it got.

The famed Belasco Theatre, started by theater producer and playwright David Belasco, which is still showing Broadway shows in New York City, attracted crowds after a member of the Belasco management sighed and said he wished the theater had a cooling system. The prop man overheard the guy and said, "Why there is one, that Belasco himself devised." A man was sent to the roof with a blow torch to burn the cobwebs out of the air ducts, and they were soon—with the help of cakes of ice—able to get cool air blown into the theater.

Having opened his theater in 1907, Belasco's air-conditioning system was primitive, but it worked.

California

In Southern California, it was in the 80s, 90s and 100s, depending how far inland you went. Naturally, everyone went to the water, and twenty-nine-year-old film actress Janet Gaynor was among them. She also almost became another drowning statistic at a Los Angeles beach. Gaynor and a male companion were wading in the water, fifty yards from shore, when she stepped into a hole, lost her balance, and was swept away by a riptide. But she kept calm and swam with the current, shouting for help. A lifeguard heard her crying out and saved her.

Oregon

On July 21, Lee Fook, a seventy-seven-year-old Chinese American, was discovered lying on railroad tracks in Portland, semiconscious. It was 84 degrees. Papers reported that Fook was a heat victim; the coroner suggested it was hardening of the arteries and possibly senility. Whatever took his life today, Fook was coming to a sad ending to what was probably a hard life. Born in China, Fook emigrated to the United States in 1875 and found employment at a laundry service, infamous for its sweatbox-like conditions. Languishing in a hospital bed for five days may well have been the only rest Fook ever had.

Kansas

Leona Butterfield woke on her front porch in Wichita around 3 A.M., due to a breeze on her neck and something blowing in her face. Sleeping near the thirty-six-year-old was her husband and five of her seven children. Leona put her hands around her neck and head and woke her spouse.

She asked, "Claude, where is my hair?"

Leona still had hair, but her long locks were gone.

Perplexed, Claude discovered her missing hair at the head of Leona's makeshift bed. In fact, it was her own cut hair that woke her up, but in her sleep fog and the darkness, she hadn't realized it. They then understood that somehow, somebody snuck up in the middle of the night and, without waking anyone, cut off Leona's long locks of hair so that it was now a short bob.

"It was a strange feeling, to feel the night air on my neck and find what was my long hair blowing into my face," Leona said to a reporter the next day.

The police chief assured the public, many of whom slept outside, that they would investigate, but they came up empty. The chief speculated that the creepy act could have been a simple case of vandalism, revenge from somebody who didn't like Mrs. Butterfield, or possibly even the act of a sex pervert.

Oklahoma

Donald Knepper didn't seem the murderous type. The twenty-four-year-old was a Oklahoma City college graduate who graduated with honors. But he spent time in a mental institution from 1930 to 1931, so he had some issues. Still, he never displayed violent behavior.

But for the last two days, his son had acted strangely, his father, Frank, told authorities. The heat affected Donald's mind, Frank suggested.

Frank may have had a point. For over two weeks, the high was 100 and often over 110. Yesterday afternoon, when Donald hoed a garden, it was 103 degrees. Then, today, shortly after midnight, for reasons nobody understood, Donald left his bedding on the front porch and went to the house next door where his seventy-five-year-old grandmother lay in bed. She was housesitting, and her husband was spending the night at another daughter's home.

Like his father, Donald was also at a loss to explain why he strangled his grandmother then slashed her throat with his pocketknife. All he could say was that he gave into a "strange impulse."

"Saturday night, I was just too weak to resist, I guess. I can't remember wanting to kill my grandmother. I don't think I even wanted to hurt her," Donald told a reporter the next day from his jail cell. Donald remembered his grandmother as a wonderful woman. "She would do anything for me . . . my grandmother was swell to me," Donald said. In fact, she once said that Donald was her favorite grandson, but it was a designation she probably took back in the moments when he choked the life out of her.

About a month later, Donald was returned to a state mental institution.

Iowa

On a day when it would be 110 in Lidderdale, at 9 A.M., the heat selected a twelve-month-old baby with a heart condition. A little later, George Gigl, seventy-three, decided he could no longer fight the heat. Gigl, a divorced grandfather and farmer who lived near Waterloo, was a portrait of sadness. The last several months were not good for him. Gigl had a farm but lived with a son, Ray. Before that, he was a resident at a hospital for the insane, in Independence, Iowa, committed there for drinking too much.

He drank, he said, because he had financial worries. Now, on top of it all, it was so damn hot. A hired hand on Ray's farm made the observation that Gigl seemed really bothered by the heat.

The heat, his drinking, his financial struggles: it was too much. In the early afternoon, when the temperature was approaching 109 degrees, George Gigl removed his right shoe and right sock. He placed the muzzle of a 12-guage shotgun in his mouth. With his big toe, he pulled the trigger.

41

JULY 28

The Blame Game

Today's Death Toll: 100+
Total Death Toll: 9,300+

Rightly or wrongly, the heat was blamed for virtually everything. It was a convenient scapegoat, but often an accurate one.

In July, a St. Louis advertising company filed a motion for a new trial. The Dutton Advertising Company won its lawsuit against an insurance company, but their attorneys argued the jury became prejudicial against their client for prolonging proceedings under uncomfortable circumstances—it was 90 degrees outside every day of the trial—and awarded the firm less than they asked for. The judge said he would take it under advisement, but the appeal failed.

In a similar vein, in late August, Willis Reed, a Nebraska lawyer and former attorney general, appealed a decision, asking the court if he could present overlooked details that he didn't bring up in oral arguments. Reed blamed his screw-up on working "during the extreme heat and drought." He also said the court "considered the case during the extreme hot weather of June and July 1936" and that "extreme weather was not conducive to cool and deliberate discussion of the facts and law."

The judges couldn't have liked hearing that. The decision was not reversed.

On July 14, after Minneapolis golfer Patty Berg, an eighteen-year-old four years away from turning pro, was pulled over for speeding (thirty-five miles over the thirty-mile limit), she told the judge, "I was just taking a crowd of girlfriends to the lake to cool off." (She also blamed her driving habits on visiting Europe, where she said there were no speed limits.) The judge was unmoved. Berg was fined $10 and court costs.

In late August, Nathan Choderker, twenty-five, a collar salesman—he sold men's shirts—robbed a store in Rockland, Pennsylvania. It was a dramatic robbery. He grabbed a female employee's purse with $200 in it and ran down three flights of an "up" escalator to escape. He was tackled by an employee, fought with him, and kept running, crashing through a glass door. After he was dragged into court, he blamed the hot weather, telling the judge, "I didn't know what I was doing—the heat got me." Denied bail, Choderker was led back to a cell.

In August, Charles P. Taft, chief adviser to Republican nominee for president, Governor Alf Landon, announced he was taking a leave of absence. The Topeka heat was blamed for harming Taft's health, but it was an open secret that one of Landon's biggest donors didn't like Taft. Indeed, after Taft "recovered," his campaign role was reduced.

Companies blamed the heat when sales were down, and pastors warned parishioners not to blame the heat for not attending church. One reverend said that if you went anywhere despite the heat, you could also come into church. A pastor in Atwood, Kansas, urged his parishioners to not let "the hot weather keep us away from God's house. The devil doesn't quit because of the heat, so why should we?"

Sports teams blamed the heat when they lost (but never seemed to give credit to opponents for winning despite the weather). The heat was blamed for an uptick in divorces; in Wichita, Kansas, there were 132 divorces in July, instead of the average 80. (But maybe the heat strengthened some couples, too, suggested a Parsons, Kansas, writer, who wrote in his local paper, "A fellow and his girl who can love each other through this sweaty, sticky weather, will never be found in the divorce courts later in life.")

In Kansas City, Missouri, Rose Chaus, the social head of the welfare department, blamed the heat for lousy family values, observing, "There has been a great increase in the number of wife-deserters since this hot weather began."

Two businessmen in Indiana blamed losing a collective $909 on the heat. When they pulled out their handkerchiefs to mop their sweaty brows, they said, they must have pulled out their wallets and checks, which fell onto the ground.

On a day when there were heat deaths in states that included South Carolina, Oklahoma, Nebraska, Wisconsin, and Ohio, you could blame the heat on just about anything, because it affected almost everything.

Nebraska

Eldridge Stratton, a thirty-four-year-old shoe salesman, died in 89-degree heat, declared the coroner. Stratton's mother, however, blamed two men who attacked and beat up her son earlier in the month, taking his clothes, shoes, and briefcase and leaving him naked in an alley. The doctor who performed the autopsy saw no evidence that the beating ended his life, just the heat. It was one hot month for Omaha, however. The day Stratton was beat to a pulp, it was 101 degrees.

Three miles east, in the town of Arnold (100°F), four teenagers went out to dinner and were going to see a movie, but instead, around 8:30 P.M., they went for a swim in a gravel-pit pond on a farm. The farmer generously allowed everyone to swim here. Too bad he wasn't a jerk.

Merton Condron, weeks away from his nineteenth birthday, was his high school valedictorian two years earlier in nearby Anselmo—and was now a clerk at an Arnold general merchandise store. Norma Jean Condron, his wife (also weeks from turning nineteen), had lived in Arnold her entire life. They brought to the gravel-pit pond Norma's fourteen-year-old friend Lois Shields and Rudy Morgan, sixteen, a cousin of Merton's from Denver. He had been staying with the couple for the last few days.

It was dark. The girls couldn't swim but waded in the water while Merton and Rudy took turns jumping off a diving board. Then, suddenly, the ground beneath Norma Jean and Lois disappeared. Lois emerged above water just long enough to shout for help.

Merton and Rudy dove after them. Rudy grabbed Lois's hair, pulling her to the pond's shore while Merton swam after his wife. Rudy and Lois both could make out Merton reaching Norma Jean, who in her panic, pulled him under the water.

Rudy broke off a thick tree branch and waded back in so the couple could grab it when they resurfaced. They didn't.

Rudy bolted for the Condrons' car to get help but it wouldn't start, so he ran and ran until he reached the farmhouse. Soon a small crowd of volunteers descended upon the gravel pit, searching for the Condrons.

The double funeral was packed, crowded with townspeople, friends, and family, including Norma Jean's parents, four sisters, and three brothers, and Merton's parents and nine siblings. Eight days earlier, they were all celebrating Merton and Norma Jean's wedding. The newlyweds were buried together in one casket.

Ohio

Dr. Clarence A. Mills, a professor at the University of Cincinnati, told the Associated Press that the world was generally getting warmer. It had been rising for some time, according to Mills, who asserted that temperatures around the globe had been climbing since 1850 and that eventually, there may be ramifications. "As we move into a cycle of higher temperatures, we conceivably may record a gradual decrease in world population. Fertility of animals goes down as temperatures increase," he said. Mills added, "We have been going away from the Ice Age for 20,000 years, and we are still going away."

Iowa

In Davenport, a forty-one-year-old man was found dead in a shed. A sixty-four-year-old woman in Spencer, Iowa, was discovered hanging from a noose in her chicken house—a heat suicide, the coroner ruled. Across the state, the summer and the Great Depression conspired to create fields of nightmares, with rows of yellow-gray wilted corn and ruined dreams.

But people still had groceries to buy, jobs to perform, and friends and family to visit. Emma Hubbs was a thirteen-year-old who lived in Carlisle, but today she was visiting relatives in Des Moines with her mom and fifteen-month-old baby brother while the rest of the family stayed at home. It was 97 degrees, after several days in the 100s. Behind the cousins' house was a swimming hole. It was also once a gravel pit.

Emma and her two cousins, Mary Daniels, twelve, and Dorothy Daniels, ten, were given permission to swim there while the parents and baby stayed in or near the house. Dorothy was on a floating board but didn't know how to swim, which is where the trouble started. That is, Dorothy fell off and started the process of drowning.

Emma was an experienced swimmer. She went to help Dorothy, who grabbed Emma around the neck. Now Emma was underwater while Dorothy tried to stay above it.

Mary—perhaps not the best swimmer—pushed the floating board toward Dorothy, who grabbed it and kicked her way back to shore.

Emma was still underwater.

Nobody knew what to do. Then, from out of nowhere, Merval Byerly appeared. The fourteen-year-old boy was swimming on the other side of the gravel pit when he heard screaming. It isn't clear if he ran around the pit or swam across it, but suddenly, he was there, and he pulled Emma to the shore.

Emma was unconscious, on her way to dying. Fortunately, two adults were nearby working on a WPA project and they began trying to resuscitate the young teenager. By now, word was getting out, and two police officers joined the let's-save-this-girl's-life undertaking. Before long, Emma was breathing again, and she was taken to the hospital.

A lot of factors saved Emma. It was lucky that the police officers were in close proximity. It was fortunate that two down-on-their-luck adults, working on a WPA project, were also at the right place at the right time, and because the WPA existed, indirectly, Franklin Roosevelt's administration helped to save Emma's life. But the main hero of the day—besides Emma and Mary, who both played a part in saving Dorothy's life—was, of course, Merval Byerly. He wasn't supposed to be there. Merval should have been at nearby Sunset Beach which had lifeguards and bathrooms.

In fact, Merval's parents forbade him to swim at the gravel pit. If he had been a little more obedient, or less hot, it's almost certain that Emma Hubbs would have died.

Emma told the local press that evening, "It was awful. I knew what was happening, and I just couldn't do anything about it. I've never been afraid of the water before. I sure was then."

She also said that the "first and last thing" she thought of when she was still conscious "was that I would never see my baby brother again."

Merval went onto marry, have kids, and became a department manager and general foreman at the Firestone Tire & Rubber Co. before dying too young, at the age of fifty-nine. Shortly after rescuing Emma, Merval said in an interview, "I thought I would catch it when the folks found out I had gone in swimming there. But for some reason, I didn't. They told me in no uncertain terms, though, that I wasn't ever to go back there again—ever!"

But there's more to the story. Emma lived not only because Merval was in the right place at the right time and had pluck and bravado. Somewhere along the way to Sunset Beach, Merval discovered he didn't have the money to pay for a ticket to enter the grounds. That's when he decided to visit the gravel pit. Emma Hubbs got to grow up and marry a man named Virgil and live to be seventy-four years old and have five children, fifteen grandchildren, and numerous great-grandchildren—all because of a lost dime.

42

JULY 29

Don't Think About the Heat

Today's Death Toll: 100+
Total Death Toll: 9,400+

Newspapers throughout the country offered advice for cooling off, often providing lame tips such as don't think about the heat. There were also helpful if obvious suggestions, such as don't overdo it and consume plenty of water. Some doctors recommended that people drink as many as sixteen glasses of water a day.

Physicians also pushed people to add half a tablespoon of salt a day to a glass of water, and companies gave their employees salt tablets. In fact, the Ford automobile factories had slim glass containers loaded with salt pills at every drinking fountain. Employees were encouraged to press the button, and a pill came out of a slot, like a gumball machine; everyone was urged to take four a day. Ford started this in 1935 in response to the 1934 heat wave, when the company averaged four hundred employees collapsing per day.

It wasn't bad advice; when people sweat, electrolytes that include sodium are released. And bodies need salt. But before anyone rushes out to buy salt during the next heat wave, consult your doctor first. The sodium suggestions aren't as on target now because people already have a salt-heavy diet, thanks to processed foods.

Mercifully, people's insanity about wearing lots of clothing no matter how hot it was didn't extend to young children. As one newspaper column advised: "Keep the baby in the coolest part of the house, see that his bed is well screened and if it's extra hot, let him sleep naked as a jaybird."

Some doctors felt adults should also skimp on their wardrobe. Dr. Herman Bundesen, president of the Chicago Board of Health, recommended wearing only enough clothes to satisfy the police.

Several days from now, newspapers ran an article by Dr. Warren Draper, assistant surgeon-general of the US public health service, first published during the summer of 1935, in which he urged everyone to pay attention to how they dressed: "Regarding the matter of clothing in hot weather, it seems rather ridiculous that convention should require that men perspire with a collar and necktie around their necks, their bodies enclosed in two or three thicknesses of clothing and only their faces and hands exposed to the cooling, soothing, and stimulating action of the circulating air upon the skin. The women with low necks and bare arms and shoulders are much more comfortably and healthfully dressed and certainly arouse our envy."

Margaret Chandler Porter, a columnist for the *St. Louis Globe-Democrat*, offered marital advice for these hot and irritable times. Much of Porter's advice was typical for 1936, writing, "A frown between the eyes, tight little lines around the mouth and a tendency to take exception to the simplest statement are all red flags announcing, 'Danger ahead!'" She advised, "Be tolerant of the change—it is only temporary, and a tactful wife, a cool shower and a frosty drink will do much to restore him to his usual charming self."

But Porter defended housewives, too, writing, "Of course, this doesn't mean that only the breadwinners should be handled gently during the good old summertime. The little woman who has coped with household problems during the long hot day, has struggled vainly to amuse the children, and has spent weary hours working for others (without pay) is very apt to find herself mighty snappy about 5:30 in the afternoon."

The heat was wearing down men, women, and children. Predictably, there were heat deaths scattered across America today, in states like Kansas, Missouri, Massachusetts, Oklahoma, Pennsylvania, and Nebraska.

Florida

Residents were used to high temperatures and humidity. But in Tallahassee, the 97-degree weather was too much for Paul Freeman, two weeks into a three-year burglary sentence. Freeman was working with prisoners on a road when he had a fatal heatstroke. He was buried in a nearby cemetery. Near Apalachicola, the mid-90s heat warped train tracks, enough that a bridge collapsed as an engine and nine cars began to cross it. Fourteen people were injured.

Pennsylvania

Every July 29, since 1875, the good people of Waynesburg had come to expect rain. It all started when a farmer, whose birthday was July 29, mentioned to Bill Allison, a pharmacist in the city, "It's darn funny, but it will rain today—always does on July 29." Allison started keeping track of the rainfall, and it turned out the farmer was right. Slowly but surely, people began placing bets on whether it would rain on July 29. It didn't in 1880, nor in 1930. But otherwise . . .

People were so confident it would rain today that they walked out into the sun with raincoats and umbrellas.

And rain it did, at 9:16 A.M., a true downpour for several minutes, ensuring the temperature went no higher than 84 degrees. Townspeople poured out into the streets, cheering and singing. Some people gathered inside the drugstore where it all started, only now it was owned by a guy named Byron Daily, to look at the tattered rain logbook that was usually kept in a safe.

Even now, every July 29, Waynesburg holds an annual Rain Day festival. Everyone is terribly disappointed if it doesn't rain.

California

Barbara Pepper, a twenty-one-year-old actress, looked outside her Hollywood home and spotted Fred Radke, a tourist from Tacoma,

Washington, looking unwell. Pepper told a reporter that Radke was "acting strangely. He seemed a little uncertain in his movements. He would take a few steps, then stop. Finally, I saw him lean against a tree."

Then he was lying, and dying, in the grass. Pepper went to check on him and ran back into her house, told her maid to call a doctor, and brought the man a glass of cold water. "I don't know how I knew, but I was sure he was having a heart attack," Pepper said.

A doctor credited Pepper for saving the man's life. Whether it was the heat that did him in or something else—temperatures were in the 80s—Pepper was featured in numerous newspapers around the country, with her photo and a small headline reading "Saves Heat Victim."

Barbara Pepper later went onto greater fame as a character actress, playing Doris Ziffel on the 1960s sitcoms *Petticoat Junction* and *Green Acres*.

Iowa

Edward and Florence Rayhorn, the couple in their sixties who divorced because of the heat, remarried today. Florence said that an argument exacerbated by the weather led to the divorce. According to friends, Edward, a salesman, used his persuasion techniques to convince Florence to stick around.

"We won't be so hasty next time," Florence told a Des Moines reporter. Mr. Rayhorn agreed, promising that this new marriage would endure. "This isn't going to be one a heat wave can break up," he said. And then the couple departed in an automobile, going for an evening "honeymoon" ride, and they lived (happily?) ever after.

Oklahoma

Harry Wahlgren, a forty-six-year-old federal meteorologist who lived in Oklahoma City, was beloved. He was a local legend, an icon, a state treasure.

In 1933, oilman Charles Urschel was kidnapped by George "Machine Gun" Kelly. Urschel kept a mental record of the weather, and when he was freed nine days later, Wahlgren got wind of the details and concluded the oilman had been kept near Paradise, Texas. Wahlgren informed the FBI, who quickly captured five of the kidnappers. Wahlgren received a letter of commendation from FBI director J. Edgar Hoover.

Wahlgren also spent the 1930s reporting on the dust storms from the Dust Bowl. That, too, endeared him to Oklahomans. In fact, in 1936, Wahlgren was so well liked that some good-natured if anemic knock-knock jokes based on him were circulating around the state.

—*Knock-knock.* —Who's there? —*Wahlgren.* —Wahlgren who? —*Wahlgren when it rains.*

—*Knock-knock.* —Who's there? —*Wahlgren.* —Wahlgren who? —*Wahlgren and bear the heat.*

(Translation for those who don't quite get it: replace "Wahlgren" with "We'll grin.")

Today, Wahlgren was driving around Vian (110°F) to inspect some weather observation stations when he passed out. Wahlgren's wife, Maude, grabbed the wheel and managed to stop the vehicle. Then she drove them to a drugstore. Somebody carried Wahlgren into the back room, where his head was doused in a bucket of ice water. A doctor was called.

After Wahlgren was revived, he was heard to say, "Thank heaven I'm not in Oklahoma City. The newspapers would never let me hear the end of this." Of course, word got out, and *The Oklahoman* ran a big story the next day and was a little cheeky, saying Wahlgren didn't merely pass out but that he "folded up like a camp stool."

43

JULY 30

The Air Age

Today's Death Toll: 50+
Total Death Toll: 9,450+

Harry Wahlgren recovered from his heat scare with ice packs on his head. Still, he had a sense of humor about it, telling an *Oklahoman* reporter, "I've had enough. I've taken one of my own bitter pills. It will be cooler today. I can't let this go on."

Wahlgren also shared a few details about how his doctor saved him: "He brought me around to consciousness before he discovered I was a weatherman. Had he known me when he arrived, I probably would be pushing up daisies today. Why is it people don't like weathermen?"

Maude Wahlgren possessed a similar wit. "Anyone who would give the city the weather he's given it deserves a taste of heat prostration," she said.

But it was Harry who kept making wisecracks throughout his bedridden interview:

"Next time we need an inspection trip, I'll send my assistant, Mr. Whitney. I'm afraid the sun has been laying for me and finally caught me out in the open."

"Sure, I thought I was a big husky guy who could take it. I noticed the farmers up there in the eastern part of the state were sitting under shade trees all day. That looked kind of sissy to me."

"The best way to avoid heat prostration is to go to Alaska for the summer. The next best way is to stay in somebody's basement all day. If you can't do either of these, become a weatherman and predict misery for someone else."

Wahlgren said his doctor recommended ice packs and electric fans, adding, "The doctor wasn't very clear, but a heat prostration does something to your brain. In a way, I'm glad I had this prostration. It is definite proof I have a brain."

Ohio

Good news!—the nation would see fewer heat fatalities in the years to come, promised Roy Miller, director of sales promotion for Air-temp Corp., when speaking to the Rotary Club at a luncheon at the Dayton Biltmore Hotel. "We are standing at the threshold of what we will go down in history as the 'air age,'" Miller said. "Rapid aerial transportation is considered a matter of course; music, speeches and all manner of things come to us over the air by radio; before long, television will be definitely accomplished. The last decade has taught us that we can control the atmospheric conditions in which we live, work and play. The comfort and well-being of the civilized world has been affected tremendously."

Near Dayton, in Springfield, it was 58 degrees in the morning, leading local meteorologists to declare the heat wave over. Several hours later, W. N. Alexander, a weatherman in Columbus, declared: "It being practically the end of July, there is every reason to believe that from now on, we'll have normal temperatures. Our extreme weather usually comes in June and July. Of course, we'll have some hot days in August, but there is nothing in the field of observation to indicate any more extreme weather this summer."

Meteorologist W. C. Devereaux in Cincinnati was even more confident: "The backbone of the heat wave of the summer is broken."

They weren't entirely wrong, just mostly. The weather across the country was, for the moment, calming down. In St. Louis, the last two days of July were in the 80s. Even parts of Kansas, after a long run of 100-plus days, were getting a short string of 90-degree days.

You couldn't blame meteorologists or regular folks for thinking that the heat wave might be over. But they were wrong; and before August was over, some would be dead wrong.

AUGUST

THE DEATH DAYS OF AUGUST

44
AUGUST 3
The Reprieve

Today's Death Toll: 30+
Total Death Toll: 9,600+

For a handful of days, sweat-drenched Americans were given something of a reprieve. The last day of July and the first several days of August, parts of the country enjoyed slightly lower temperatures (80s and 90s instead of 100s and 110s) and rain and fewer fatalities.

But on August 3, temperatures started climbing again. The heat took out today an eleven-year-old with a heart condition in Port Chester, New York, where it was in the 80s, a forty-eight-year-old foundry worker in Baltimore (95°F), and a thirty-eight-year-old housewife in Philadelphia (95°F). There were also drownings throughout the country.

The cracks in the ground between rows of cotton were so wide that farmers said it could be dangerous just walking around and inspecting the crops. Prairie fires were occurring with regularity. On delivery trucks, glass soda bottles exploded in the heat. And people continued to die.

Massachusetts

In Woburn (95°F), the caddies at the Woburn Country Club were on their second day of a strike, and golfers were obliged to carry their own bags. Around 2 P.M., Boston residents began noticing a tiny black insect in abundance: marsh flies. They were an annual visitor, but nobody remembered seeing millions of these insects. The heat brought them out, according to Boston's health commissioner.

And the marsh flies stuck around. Four days later, it put an ice cream stand temporarily out of business in Scituate due to customers steering clear. Nobody was too excited about eating an ice cream cone covered in marsh flies.

Missouri

In Kansas City (97°F), a heat victim was found dead in a boarding house. Nobody knew who he was, but eventually the police discovered he was Fred Bailey, a forty-three-year-old from Macon, Georgia, who was migrating west looking for work. He was positively identified because relatives in Macon told authorities that their missing kin had the big toe on his right foot amputated. And this guy, sure enough . . .

California

Between shooting scenes for *Libeled Lady*, Jean Harlow struggled to look fresh for the cameras. The cast included William Powell, Myrna Loy, and Spencer Tracy, and they were filming in Culver Studios, a suburb of Los Angeles, and the town of Sonora, where today it was 101 degrees.

Entertainment writer Paul Harrison's column would run in a couple days—it was probably today when he was observing the filming—and he outlined some of the concessions the cast and crew made for the heat. Powell's tailor created a shirt that had a special "heat wave collar" for him, a half-size larger than his ordinary collars, cut high and narrow in the back, low and long in the front. His porous linen shirt had short sleeves and buttoned halfway down the front, with no back, making the sport jacket he wore over the shirt more comfortable.

As for Harlow, Harrison wrote, "she sat at the makeup table in her dressing room while her maid ran a comb through her hair every few seconds to keep it from looking damp and wilted. The actress would pat continually at face and neck with a big puff and brown powder. Another maid was busy writing out big squares of chamois in a bucket of ice water and applying them, cold but dry, to the Harlow forehead and nape of the neck. The procedure reminded you of a fighter being worked over between rounds."

As Harrison wrote, "Pretty soon director Conway called, 'All right, Jean,' and she returned to the set for some more broiling under the lights."

It didn't look glamorous, but, hey, it was Hollywood, and Harlow, albeit sweaty, was still living the life of luxury. But the heat wave was about to catch up with her.

45

AUGUST 8
Sleeping Outdoors? Bring a Flashlight.

Today's Death Toll: 30+
Total Death Toll: 9,630+

Today was a relatively quiet Saturday in the nation. There were drownings in Wisconsin, Iowa, and Texas, and it was still plenty hot. In Wellington, Kansas, it was 111 degrees. But mostly, it was a quiet day. Mostly.

California

In the San Bernardino Valley, it was 106 degrees. The intense heat was pushing people to the beaches, and it's understandable that anyone with the means to frequently escape the heat and go somewhere like Catalina Island would. With her mother, Jean Harlow did just that. But once again, the actress just couldn't help herself. She went sunbathing, and during her risky dalliance with the sun, fell asleep.

Texas

Police led a man off a Houston hotel roof for sunbathing in the nude. The hotel guest complained that the authorities were being unreasonable and that it was "hot as blue blazes." Also, he was alone on the roof. So who called the cops? Office managers in higher buildings. They couldn't get their employees to stop watching the naked man sunbathing.

Oklahoma

Alexander Rhoten, a ninety-year-old farmer, was the talk of the town in Bluejacket. His body was found alongside the road yesterday, six hours after his death. The sheriff and coroner initially believed his cuts and bruises were from a hit-and-run until they concluded he passed out in 96-degree heat. It also surfaced that people in a cattle truck saw the dazed farmer staggering around in his field. The truck didn't stop. They thought Rhoten was drunk.

Missouri

Gladys Gregg and her husband, Arthur, a truck driver, came up with a plan. They lived in Hammond, Louisiana. He had to go to Chicago. She had friends in Kansas City. They decided to drive together to Kansas City. Gladys, twenty-five, would stay with a friend, while Arthur drove to Chicago.

Gladys's friends owned a boarding house, and she asked for a room facing the garage roof—and her wish was granted. Gladys apparently figured she would sleep on the roof of this abandoned building while other boarders were bedded down.

In the darkness of night, probably still in the 80s—it was 88 degrees at 9 P.M. —Mrs. Gregg exited her window and went onto the garage roof, probably clutching a pillow and blanket. It's unclear if she was crawling on the roof or walking, but she probably had a 98 percent chance of everything being fine. She was unaware, however, of a skylight on the roof. Or if she knew, she didn't know that it was no longer boarded up; the boards were blown off in the recent dust storm. The skylight glass, if it was there, couldn't withstand the weight of a person standing on it.

Outdoor sleepers and tenants heard bloodcurdling screams as Gladys plunged twenty feet toward a concrete floor, headfirst.

A few hours later, Clarke Armstrong, thirty-four, also a resident of Kansas City, took some bedding onto the roof of his house's back porch.

He slipped or tripped and dropped twenty-five feet, his body slamming into his car, hitting the radiator. He was badly hurt with compression fractures, a cut and bruises. Still, unlike Gladys, who survived for a few hours at St. Margaret's Hospital, Armstrong lived.

46

AUGUST 10

"It Is a Disaster . . ."

Today's Death Toll: 50+
Total Death Toll: 9,680+

Three weeks away from September, and the summer ground on. The day before, the heat snuffed out an elevator operator in Volga, South Dakota (97°F). The poor kid was just seventeen years old—probably working in a small room with little to no ventilation, in the middle of a very hot building, wearing a heavy, dark, long-sleeved uniform. There were also heat deaths today in Missouri, Pennsylvania, and Texas, where a sixty-nine-year-old tried to help his wife, who was overcome on their front porch in the heat. He did help her, and she lived—but he died of a heart attack.

If anything, the summer was getting worse, not better. Howard Hunter, assistant federal administrator of drought relief, declared in Chicago that it was "no longer just a drought—it is a disaster."

Texas

Wallace Lamar, a prominent sixty-one-year-old stockman-farmer, found himself stranded on the highway, his auto trailer stuck in a ditch, north of Graford. It was 100 degrees. Maybe he would have also been doomed if he stayed with his vehicle, but looking for help was not a wise decision. He was discovered unconscious by the road and would die two hours later.

Pennsylvania

In Pittsburgh, thirty-two-year-old John Shaw was hauled into court for stealing a case of beer from a distribution company truck. Temptation got the better of him, a regretful Shaw told the judge, adding that the extreme heat "just naturally made me thirsty."

Maybe the judge wasn't one to imbibe. Shaw was sentenced to three months.

Utah

Claude Beatty, throughout the 1930s until his death in 1965, was world-famous for his animal training act, especially with lions. Earlier in the summer, the thirty-three-year-old performed in Kansas City, Missouri, doing his lion and tiger act, and some of the animals tried unsuccessfully to maul him, "giving the crowd its only chilling moments since the heat wave started," wrote an Associated Press reporter. Afterward, in a circus dressing wagon interview, Beatty blamed the 116-degree temperature for the incident.

"Lions' and tigers' tempers flare in the extreme heat the same as a man's. The animals are sluggish in the heat. It's hard to make them snap out of it—and when they do, the chances are, they'll snap at you," Beatty said, adding that three of his lions were taking a break for the summer because he couldn't trust them.

Today, Beatty toured the Hogle Gardens Zoo, site of the dead deer controversy. He was not impressed. Beatty said of the elephant house: "It's poorly ventilated. In fact, it isn't ventilated at all." He didn't like the monkeys living with the elephants. "The monkeys cause the worst stench. They should be quartered in a separate enclosure. Monkeys are the hardest animals to keep clean." He also thought the monkeys' water supply was "pretty dirty."

Beatty thought the lion cages were spacious enough but needed shade. The buffalo and elk corrals were "well situated" and "ample," Beatty said.

But he unleashed his harshest commentary for how the zoo took care of the bears.

"Those bears are in the most cruel location the human imagination could devise," Beatty said, describing their lair as a concrete well sunk into the top of sunbaked hillside. "It's a soup kettle of heat, and in the winter . . . Lord, how do they keep from being frozen to death? Heat will kill bears, and so will cold. There isn't a chance of a breeze reaching to the bottom of that thing, and in the winter, it must be a bed of ice and snow."

Mr. Beatty said the bear pit and other animal quarters should have been built into a hillside, not sunk on top of one, so they could get the benefit of shade and shelter. He added: "Those bears are in terrible shape in their present location. I saw nine of 14 polar bears freeze to death in Peru, Indiana, because they were kept in a place like that."

Beatty remarked of the deer corrals: "No wonder two of them died in the heat. No shade . . . no shelter . . . nothing . . . and this zoo is full of shade in most places . . . Whoever laid out this zoo certainly didn't know anything about zoos."

Beatty suggested the Hogle Gardens Zoo pattern itself after the Cincinnati Zoo, adding, "but it would cost plenty of money. Unless the city has the money, it might as well abandon Hogle Gardens."

The Hogle Gardens Zoo now has an excellent reputation, but back then, for the zoo staff and everyone who wanted it to succeed, the reports were as damning as the heat.

Kansas

In Elsmore, Alec McCullough played a baseball game in punishing heat. But that's probably not how he met his end.

The thirty-eight-year-old worked at a train station depot and would have been better off spending some low-energy quality time with his wife and kids at their farm near Neosho Falls. Instead, McCullough squatted near home plate with his catcher's mitt. He swung for home runs and attempted to steal bases.

After a few innings, he became sick. Still, before the end of the game, McCullough recovered and suggested he resume his position as catcher. But good judgment prevailed, and McCullough didn't. He soon went to a house, possibly a teammate's, in the city of Moran, where he had a meal.

We don't know what culinary choices McCullough had. Maybe nobody trusted what was in the icebox, if the ice was melting. Perhaps nobody felt like cooking. All we know is that McCullough had some food from a can.

Shortly after the meal, McCullough again became ill, enough that a doctor was summoned. That was yesterday. This morning, McCullough died at the hospital. Doctors weren't sure if heat sickness killed McCullough or if he became ill from food poisoning. While canned food tends to not go bad, the contents can spoil, especially when temperatures hit 75 degrees or more. When McCullough sat down for his meal, it was 113 degrees.

Illinois

Two eleven-year-old boys, Harold Griffin and David Johnson, were practicing target shooting with their rifles in Jerseyville (95°F). Their parents told them to be careful, and maybe they were. David was lying on the ground, watching Harold fire the rifle, and that probably seemed like a safe place. But in David's sweaty hands, his rifle slipped, and a round went right into his friend's foot.

Many of us, after being shot in the foot, would probably be screaming, crying, cursing, and maybe hopping on the good foot and shouting for a medic. Harold, however, regarded his foot and then took the shoe off and started to cut the bullet out with his pocketknife. Sure, why not?

David suggested his friend not do that, since it could become infected, and they made their way through town until they found a doctor.

Oklahoma

In Norman, home of the University of Oklahoma, female students attending summer school were receiving compliments for their dresses; they were decorated with tiny thermometers. Joy Saxon, the college student who started the fad, said at least a hundred people a day asked her what the temperature was.

But most of the state wasn't having as much fun. Oklahoma saw temperatures as high as 116 today. There was a death in Miami, Farwell, and Seminole.

There were two heat victims in Oklahoma City. One of those, Dave Campbell, a sixty-five-year-old unemployed carpenter, died in his trailer. Mobile trailers have never been known as being particularly safe, given that they're the first things to go in a tornado. But the first trailer homes, which came on the scene during the 1930s, were generally built of metal. Metal roofs, metal walls. By sleeping indoors, even with the windows open, Campbell was essentially a human meat pie baking inside an oven.

47

AUGUST 11

Air-Conditioning All of North America

Today's Death Toll: 100+
Total Death Toll: 9,780+

Every day was a clarion call that air-conditioning's time had come, but it needed to be cheaper for it to truly go mainstream. On July 13, a Wisconsin opinion piece in *Oshkosh Northwestern* practically demanded the air-conditioning industry get its act together, declaring, "We hope to push air-conditioning to the point where these cooling devices will be in every home, office, theater, hospital, church and other buildings. And we also want air-conditioned automobiles."

Charles Driscoll, a columnist for *The Atlanta Journal*, correctly predicted on August 13 that it would take two generations before air-conditioning was everywhere. But it would happen, Driscoll asserted: "The next generation of indoor workers (if revolution does not destroy the world we know) will live and work in cool, clean air all the time. There will be no permanent buildings that are not air-conditioned."

Driscoll felt that everyone's health would benefit: "I believe that air-conditioning in homes is likely to increase the efficiency of all brain workers and probably of muscle-workers as well. A man who works hard with his body all day generally will sleep, no matter how hot the weather, if he is well."

Still, while air-conditioning wasn't quite taking over the country, it was making progress. In mid-July, Minneapolis's mayor announced that some of the city's biggest hospitals would be air-conditioned before the year was up. In late July, in Columbus, Ohio, a rarity opened: an air-conditioned veterinary hospital. In Washington, DC, the Capitol building was in the process of installing air-conditioning, although it wouldn't be finished this summer. The hope was that air-conditioning would end what Congressmen referred to as "hot weather legislation," in which a lot of bad or rushed decisions and laws were made because politicians were in a hurry to get out of the building and somewhere cooler.

An Illinois paper, *The Decatur Daily Review*, reported in mid-July that retailers had more inquiries about air-conditioning systems from prospective buyers in the last twelve days than in all previous time. Air-conditioning sales had increased by 75 percent, the paper said, and 200 percent in the region.

A *Decatur Herald* op-ed that ran on July 8 suggested that air-conditioning could eventually stop heat waves in their tracks: "A modern world has come to the conclusion that science can accomplish most anything it attempts," the paper stated optimistically, and suggested a wild idea—perhaps scientists could erect a dozen steel towers at strategic points and air-condition the entire continent. The op-ed concluded: "An idle fancy? Consider the radio."

California

Jean Harlow was in agony. Her body was feeling the full effects of having fallen asleep while sunbathing two days earlier. Harlow had second-degree burns covering her body.

According to the book *Jean Harlow: Tarnished Angel* by David Bret, an hour after returning to her Beverly Hills home, the actress collapsed with a temperature of 103. Her mother, who wasn't a fan of doctors, didn't want Harlow to receive medical care for a condition caused by God and one that could be remedied by prayer, but William Powell, Harlow's costar and beau, overruled the mother. He called a doctor. Maybe in this case, however, the mom had a point. The doctor lanced, drained, and sprayed Harlow's blisters on her back and limbs with boric acid. It was a then-typical way to treat skin, but the chemical is now primarily used as a pesticide.

The boric acid treatment didn't work. Harlow was admitted to the hospital.

Oklahoma

In Guthrie (114°F), if you were one of the ten diners or waitstaff in Mrs. Effie Pike's lunch stand, you watched a loaf of bread, wrapped in wax paper, burst into flames. Mrs. Pike later made a fairly obvious statement to the press: "It could have been that the sunlight reflecting through a window pane intensified the heat."

In Tulsa, Martha Lay, known as "Grandma" to everyone, remarked to a reporter, "Never in all my life did I feel the heat as badly as I did yesterday." That was saying something. Grandma Martha Lay had just celebrated her 109th birthday.*

US Rep. Samuel Chapman Massingale of Oklahoma sent an appeal to President Roosevelt for help. It was a long telegram, but the main point of the message was "All red tape should be cut to avert human suffering."

Indeed, there were at least a dozen deaths in the state today. A few stand out for horrifying details or poignancy. In Maud (114°F), William Meeks, a forty-year-old, collapsed. Maybe in different circumstances, he could have been revived, but he fainted on top of a massive oil derrick. He fell eighty-four feet, landing on another part of the derrick.

In Durant (114°F), forty-six-year-old Joe Price lived with his aging parents. He chipped ice, put it in a bathtub outside, and filled it up with water. He didn't even bother getting undressed. He sunk into the water and moments later, his dad heard him groan and splash in the tub. Something about the sound disturbed his father, who went to check on him. His son was in the middle of getting out of the tub when he fell over, dead.

Maybe, in some ways, Price was living on borrowed time. Decades earlier, Price served fourteen months overseas in the World War, often on the front lines. In 1935, he survived a serious scrape with a guy named Snuffy Jackman Mead, who stabbed him three times with a knife in the stomach, knife, and wrist. Price was surrounded by death even on the job; he worked

* Grandma Martha Lay survived the heat wave, passing on, on August 24, 1940, a few weeks after she turned 113.

in the marble tombstone business. Price undoubtedly wasn't expecting to be his own customer this soon.

Price died far too young but experienced over double as much life as Joe Steele. The seventeen-year-old high school valedictorian spent the summer working for a resort at the Lake of the Ozarks, Missouri, and was set to attend college in the fall. He was called back to his home in Kellyville, however, because his fifteen-year-old brother John collapsed in the heat and fell from an upper level of the barn. Yesterday, Joe visited John in the hospital in Bristow (114°F) and took over his chores. But Joe, too, became overheated. He took a bath in cold well water and went to an air-conditioned theater, but it didn't help. He became ill that night, and this morning, he died.

His mom collapsed in shock and grief. She and John were still in the hospital recovering when Joe was buried. His classmates served as pallbearers.

Texas

Five Texans succumbed to the heat. In Gainesville, a sun-kink occurred and a freight train derailed. The railroad crew detached the still-standing cars and kept chugging along—until another sun-kink occurred just past a bridge. Five train cars toppled into a field, and the gasoline saturating the grass caused a fire. When a fire crew came to put it out, one fireman was killed.

Some Fort Worth firemen, however, had an easier project. They received a frantic call that nine-year-old Billy Burke was stuck on the roof of his family's house.

Billy was bouncing a rubber ball that flew onto the roof and lodged behind the chimney. Billy decided to get it—which meant he had to cross a hot gravel driveway, and then, once on the roof, he walked across hot tar shingles. By then, his feet were so burned that he refused to come down. He just made himself as comfortable as he could until his parents sent for firemen to rescue him.

48

AUGUST 12

We Repeat, He Wasn't Wearing Shorts

Today's Death Toll: 100+
Total Death Toll: 9,880

It wasn't enough to beat up America. The heat wave was back to pummeling Canada. The last few days had seen 100-plus degree weather in three of Canada's provinces. Crops were suffering, grasshoppers were flourishing, and in the town of Milk River, Alberta, sheep were dying.

It was bad everywhere. In Washington state, where temperatures were in the 80s, there were four drownings. In Wells, Minnesota, the 91-degree heat took the life of a middle-aged engineer at the light plant, or as it would be called now, the electric company. In Indiana, 101-degree heat stamped out a forty-four-year-old factory worker already ill from heatstroke in July. In Monroe, Louisiana, 100-degree-plus heat flicked away a sixty-four-year-old butcher.

But a few states were *really* struggling.

Kansas

In Wichita, it was 114 degrees—and the thirty-seventh 100-degree-plus day this summer. Citizens were irritated with each other. One woman reported that her neighbor had been working on his car at night, making sleep impossible. Another griped about neighbors playing their radios "loud and late." One housewife said that she hung up clothes to dry, and neighborhood kids threw rocks and dirt on them, meaning another hot day redoing laundry. Wichita police also reported an unusually large number of prowlers walking into homes while residents slept outside.

Oklahoma

At midnight, in Miami, it was 95 degrees. The low, at 8 A.M., was 93 degrees. Many people didn't even bother to attempt sleeping. It was, as the local paper said, "practically impossible."

In Oulstee (107°F), citizens reported that Turkey Creek was dry; that was the town's water supply. Oklahoma City had at least ten heat victims today. For the second day in a row, a prisoner died at McAlester Prison, in McAlester (107°F): a twenty-nine-year-old who was in jail for kidnapping a little girl. Probably not too many people showed up to his funeral.

Altus, again, saw its temperature reach 120 degrees. Weather observers said that it might have gone higher, but 120 was as high as the city's thermometer went.

Life nonetheless unfolded somewhat normally in Altus. The paper reported the library was full of people reading newspapers and magazines. "The only complaint," said the librarian, "is that most of them reach the second-floor puffing and panting and wishing the building had an elevator." The library's phone kept ringing, too, with people asking how hot it was.

Somebody on kitchen duty in an Altus café put a pot of beans on a shelf to soak overnight only to discover thirty minutes later that the beans were cooked. An anonymous housewife said her housekeeping was kept to a minimum, adding, "It's too hot for any of us to sleep inside. We eat on the back porch and spend evenings on the lawn."

Jasper Pendleton caused a stir because he appeared to be *wearing shorts* while riding a bicycle. Pendleton defused the controversy by explaining that, no, in trying to cool off, he merely rolled up his trousers to his knees.

49

AUGUST 13

The Heat's Unforgiving Grip

Today's Death Toll: 220+
Total Death Toll: 10,100+

Highways exploding and expanding railroad tracks and steel drawbridges weren't the only way the heat affected the country's infrastructure. Virtually nothing was safe from the heat's unforgiving grip.

Tar left a lot to be desired as a building material; for instance, a spark from a chimney could land on a tar roof and ignite. But this summer, tar melted off roofs. In Kansas, a roof's tin grating caused tar to melt over wiring in the building, setting it aflame. In Hastings, Nebraska, the fire station's tar roof melted until firefighters continually sprayed it with cold water. A hotel in Canada had its tar roof melt into a drainpipe. Nobody had any idea until it rained. The pipe burst and it leaked through a linen closet on each floor, the water eventually reached the basement.

Houses, even those without tar roofs, were constantly catching fire. So were barns and fields. In Ashland, Wisconsin, the fire chief believed three grass fires started due to litter: empty glass pop bottles acted like a magnifying glass, concentrating the sun's rays and setting fire to the earth.

In Lawton, Oklahoma, the townspeople briefly lost power on a day when it was 105 degrees because a cable buried underground caught fire.

A Pennsylvania trolley car derailed rounding a curve because normally, grease was applied to the curved track to help the trolley navigate it; the heat dried the grease.

The heat was blamed for a clock on a courthouse in Petersburg, Virginia, going haywire on July 16, striking 130 times before it wore itself out. Four days later, in Springfield, Ohio, the county courthouse clock began striking at the right hour for the first time in years.

The heat didn't just harm big clocks; wristwatches were affected. Joe Bryan, a Chickasha, Oklahoma, watch dealer told his local paper: "We've been having more trouble keeping watches regulated this summer than I've ever experienced." The problem was that the fine parts in watches needed to be lubricated. The drops of oil inside the watch were evaporating in the heat. People were also looking down at their watches, only to realize they were rusting.

In New York City, an absent-minded man left his false teeth on a windowsill, and within an hour, they melted. In Clarissa, Minnesota, in July, it got up to 104, and a married woman smelled smoke. In her backyard, she found a pile of sawdust smoldering. In Oklahoma, iron bedstands were burning holes in blankets. A Toronto, Kansas, housewife put a cherry pie on the windowsill to cool off, and she might as well have put it back in the oven: the sun burned the crust.

In late July, in Dickens, Iowa, a fire broke out two days in a row at Norvil Crews's farm. The farmhands extinguished it the first day but couldn't figure out why the fire started. After the second day of fires, they scrutinized the farm more carefully. Someone noticed a car parked in the yard at another farm, facing toward the Crews's field. They concluded that the sun's rays, falling on the windshield, made a strong, sharp reflection at the exact point where the fire first broke out a quarter of a mile away. The car was moved, and the fires stopped.

Today, in Belleville, Kansas (114°F), a Ford Model T burst into flames. The sun hit the windshield at just the right angle, enough to set the front seat cushion ablaze.

The most obscure things were affected by the heat. Professional wallpaper hangers discovered that when you put the wallpaper with the glue on the wall, it immediately dried, so you couldn't adjust it even a few seconds later. Across the country, the heat warped safes so they couldn't close. In mid-July, in Sturgis, Michigan, the 100-plus degree heat warped the metal on the vault at Citizens State Bank, making it impossible to open. The bank had to request emergency supplies of cash from nearby banks.

In St. Nazianz, Wisconsin, the varnish on a woman's picture frames melted off; she caught enough in a bowl that she used it to varnish part of her kitchen floor. In mid-July, a woman from Urbana, Ohio, drove to Columbus and when she opened her purse, she discovered the rubber lining melted all over her money, which she had to wash before she could use any of it. Golfers swung their clubs, only to have their golf balls explode into white dust.

On July 10, at Trachtenberg's Drug Store in Montclair, New Jersey, the caps on perfume bottles all popped off, and perfume drenched the window. But on the plus side, in front of the same store, workmen painting traffic lines in the road reported that the paint dried in three minutes, less than half the usual time.

Even grocery shopping, at least in one Springfield, Missouri, store, was indirectly affected by the heat. Housewives complained that butchers were shortchanging them on meat. Weight inspectors discovered that the electric fans blowing air was hitting the scales and adding two to three ounces of weight, giving the housewives less meat for their money. The fans were moved.

Trash collection was affected, too. Cities reminded residents to keep a tight lid on their metal garbage cans. Otherwise, flies would breed, and you'd smell the stench of rotting rubbish. But there were problems with keeping lids on too tight. In Reading, Pennsylvania, gas formed inside the cans, and the hotter it got, the more pressurized the can became. Nobody was injured, but the lids occasionally popped off, followed by a noise that sounded like cannon fire. It was even more dangerous in Lancaster, Ohio, when the combination of heat and sewer gas that had been collecting sent manhole covers popping off, flying as high as four feet in the air.

Oklahoma

When the staff entered the courthouse in the morning in Muskogee (106°F), a bronze chandelier was on the floor, having fallen forty feet and crushed a chair where the assistant US district attorney usually sat. Everyone figured that the previous day's heat (108°F) caused the bronze to expand, loosening the fixture from its bronze chains. The fallen chandelier was six hundred pounds. The assistant US district attorney said he would be carefully eyeing the other two bronze chandeliers in the courthouse.

Today, twenty-eight people across Oklahoma died from the heat. In Blackwell (112°F), the weather bureau's office received three hundred calls an hour.

Securing accurate temperature readings could be difficult for members of the public, far harder than it is now (just look at your phone). Your newspaper wasn't much help (it could tell you yesterday's temperature but could only make a guess for today's). You had to listen for a weather report on the radio, look at an outdoor thermometer, call somewhere that might know the temperature, like the weather bureau, or seek out friends or family who might know.

The latter was risky; weather could inspire town gossip. In July, rumors circulated in Emporia, Kansas, that the newspaper, chamber of commerce, and the local weather observer were telling the public that it was cooler than it was because they thought the hot temperatures were bad for business. The rumor spread because Emporia's city thermometer showed 114 degrees when some neighboring towns registered as high as 120. People knew they were hot, they just weren't always certain *how* hot.

In northeast Oklahoma, fishermen and volunteers rescued fish from shallow pools of water. The county and city of Pawhuska provided trucks and tanks to transfer the fish to deeper water, and the Pawhuska Ice Company donated ice to put in the tanks. It was a two-day project, but unfortunately, some volunteers scooped up other critters like turtles and snakes, removing them, not recognizing their value to a creek.

In Altus, the temperature reached 116 degrees. This morning, a resident, Charles Simpson, awakened on his lawn to find his pants stolen, along with the pockets' contents: five dollars, a gold watch, a pocketknife, and a pencil. In response, Altus's police chief suggested that lawn sleepers leave their valuables inside their house. Given how some thieves were going inside the homes when people slept outside, this was shaky advice.

Really, nothing was safe from thieves, as an Oklahoma City family discovered a few weeks earlier. Thieves crept into a family's backyard in the daytime and made off with two of their mattresses and quilts.

Texas

There were sixteen heat deaths and drownings. A fifty-three-year-old peddler from Fort Worth spent his last minutes fixing a flat tire along a highway, likely blown out from the 105-degree heat, when a car clipped him.

California

In San Jose (93°F), a thirty-two-year-old mechanic died while fixing a truck. In Stockton (101°F), two parents created a horrific cautionary tale by putting their baby boy in a bathtub to cool him off. They left the water running with the drain open while they tended to other things. They were unaware of their eight-month-old bumping into the drain, closing it.

Pennsylvania

Normally, it would be news when a twenty-six-year-old factory worker dies of a heat-induced heart attack in a city like York (94°F). This summer, it was just another Thursday.

Missouri

Um, make that three? In St. Joseph (110°F), at *The St. Joseph Gazette*, Arnold Bailey, a thirty-two-year-old a telegraph editor, had written the headline, "Two Overcome by Heat," with his pencil, when he got woozy and passed out. Bailey was taken to the hospital, where his wife was a nurse. He recovered. Elsie Mae Cremeens, forty-five, manager of a Brookfield clothing store, however, did not. She passed out at work. Brookfield (108°F) was not doing well. Farmers were saying that their corn crops were 100 percent ruined.

New York

Thurman Jackson, thirty-one years old, was performing on a stage when he collapsed in the heat.

Jackson was performing with the Negro Theater division of the Federal Theater at the Lafayette, which was in Harlem. Jackson was a White actor playing the part of Captain Sap Rogers in the three-act folk play *Turpentine*. He had been performing since 1925, when he departed his hometown of East Point, Georgia, to try to make it big.

For several years, Jackson traveled in states such as Louisiana, North Carolina, and Pennsylvania, and became known—at least in theater circles—for his comic roles. He went to New York City in the late 1920s to make it in the motion-picture business, but that went nowhere. By 1930, Jackson was in St. Louis, managing a theater and engaged. She was an attractive young woman from a well-to do family, and he was impoverished during the Great Depression. It was a short marriage.

Jackson returned to acting and New York City. As his limp body was carried off stage, it looked like his career was coming to an end. It was 90 degrees outside and probably much worse inside. Plus, Jackson was wearing a heavy costume. He was whisked off to Harlem Hospital, as several newspapers dutifully reported.

An understudy stepped into his role—and happily, Jackson recovered. While he never achieved his dreams of stardom during his sixty-three years on the planet, he made a living doing something he loved. Not a bad way to spend a life. But the actor certainly had some bad luck. In 1937, when Jackson was in his dressing room rehearsing for a one-act play written by famed playwright Eugene O'Neill, the actor recalled fainting in the heat, and griped to a public relations man about his lack of publicity.

"The only time I get my name in the papers is when I go to the hospital," Jackson complained.

Frustrated, Jackson walked toward steps that led to the stage, but then he stumbled and tumbled down the stairs.

"He's in Harlem Hospital," New York's *Daily News* reported.

50

AUGUST 14

The Hangman

Today's Death Toll: 200+
Total Death Toll: 10,300+

The summer of 1936 was the story of the summer, but it wasn't the only story. Rattlesnake James was finally off the front pages; a jury spent seven hours deliberating in late July but found him guilty. He would be hanged, though it took time for the appeals process to play out, and he didn't go to the gallows until 1942. Today, the big news story centered around Rainey Bethea.

In Owensboro, Kentucky, Bethea was brought out to hang at dawn, his punishment for murdering a seventy-year-old White woman in her apartment in June. After he was caught, Bethea pled guilty. Whether he was a murderer or not, in retrospect, you don't have to be a lawyer to realize that this legal case looks like a sorry mess. It took a jury four and a half minutes to decide that he would hang. His appeals process took about two months.

But what really interested the media and public was that a White *female* sheriff, Florence Thompson, was going to pull the lever that would release the trap door and hang the Black twenty-six-year-old.

Today, an ugly scene played out, one that seems to fit in perfectly with the dystopian, catastrophic summer the nation was suffering through.

It was already warm—about 76 degrees when Bethea was brought to the hanging platform at 5:20 A.M. in front of an audience of 20,000 spectators. This ended up being the last public hanging in America. It's easy to see why. By now, every other state in the country had outlawed public hangings (hangings behind prison walls still occurred until 1996), and many of Kentucky's residents were uncomfortable with the bloodthirsty reaction of the crowd. One man interviewed said he came from Jacksonville, Florida, to watch the execution with several of his friends. At 5:28 A.M., with a professional hangman stepping in at the last moment to do the grim task for Thompson, Bethea's body dropped, and the crowd cheered.

By the afternoon, the crowd was long gone, and the mercury was climbing to 99 degrees.

Kansas and Illinois

In Hutchinson (113°F, yesterday and today), parents awoke to find their son, a toddler, wasn't in bed. They called the police, who rushed over to the house and found him outside, where it was cooler, sleeping comfortably on the running board of the family car.

Gerald McNaught, a seven-year-old boy from Kenawee, Illinois, was having trouble sleeping, and it was decided that he could accompany his father, Albert, to his job on the night shift at the water company. While Albert worked, Gerald would sleep in the car.

The plan partially worked: Gerald slept, but two thieves stole the car. Gerald half awakened and was aware that two men were in the vehicle, but he thought it was his father and a friend. Gerald went back to sleep, and the accidental kidnappers later apparently discovered the boy and left him, unhurt, and the car in the town of Galva. The men were never caught.

Pennsylvania

Louis Jaffe was riding in a junk wagon pulled by a horse that the Philadelphia media dubbed Donald. At 12:30 P.M., Donald lay down in the middle of the street, at 11th Street and Ridge Avenue.

Concerned, Jaffe got off the wagon and loosened the horse's harness, and Donald opened an eye and looked at him; Jaffe removed the rest of the harness, figuring Donald needed it off to recover. But immediately, the horse jumped up—and bolted, racing down 11th Street.

Cars swerved to miss Donald and almost slammed into each other. Donald was already slowing to a trot, then laid down in the middle of the street in front of the police station on 11th and Winter. An officer, John Anderson, approached, and Donald jumped up, sending the officer tumbling to the ground.

Galloping for just a bit, the horse lay down again at 9th and Winter. But a police car soon appeared with two officers in the car and Anderson standing on the running board and swinging a lariat. Donald jumped up again, flicked his tail, and ran down 9th Street to Race, toward traffic at the Delaware River Bridge entrance. Buses slammed on brakes; cars bumped into each other; pedestrians scampered; police whistles blew.

At 7th Street, Anderson tossed the lariat, looking triumphant—until the lasso missed. The horse dashed up a sidewalk, with pedestrians scattering. Another police officer tossed a lasso—and also missed.

But at Cherry Street, Donald slowed down to a trot. The heat was too much, and the horse allowed Anderson, on the running board and sweating profusely, to put a halter over his head. Anderson tied the rope to a post and called the Society for the Prevention of Cruelty to Animals. The SPCA brought a bucket of water, and Donald greedily drank it up.

Missouri

2 A.M. Samuel Stanborn, a Kansas City resident, unable to sleep, decided to take a middle-of-the-night stroll. He encountered two muggers and was robbed of $10.

5:45 A.M. Two Columbia police officers locked up a prisoner, James Bach. They had traveled with him the previous day and all night from Denver. They planned to spend the night in Salina, Kansas, but the high was 118, hot enough to kill two residents; figuring they'd never get any sleep, the officers kept driving. It was a productive drive: Bach confessed to the murder—several times.

Late afternoon. In Kansas City, J. T. Ethington, a broom salesman, rested in a doorway at Twelfth and Central Streets. Or he may have collapsed. He wasn't sure. Either way, Ethington woke up and discovered a thief had stolen what he was selling: eighteen brooms, eighteen whiskbrooms, and four brushes.

Crime was clearly an issue for Kansas, but residents were more interested in the weather. The mayor's office in Kansas City (113°F) was besieged with desperate phone calls from residents asking for the temperature.

Oklahoma

In Seminole (106°F), a gas station went up in a blaze of glory. There were numerous theories why, but certainly the heat didn't help matters.

Three people were killed; one man's body in the explosion flew twenty-five feet. Two filling stations burned down as well as six small houses. Three trucks burned to the ground. Seconds before the explosion, a man went to relieve himself in an outhouse behind the filling station. People shouted, "Oh, he's dead!" But moments later, the man slowly walked out of the outhouse, carefully buttoning his pants and looking around to see what the commotion was.

Iowa

Maybe Pearl Strawhacker's anger had nothing to do with the temperature, though it's easy to make the connection between the forty-five-year-old farmer's short fuse and the 104-degree heat. Strawhacker kept calling the telephone operator (perhaps to ask how hot it was?), over and over, but nobody answered.

Hopefully the thirty days in jail he received from the judge was worth it. Because eventually, Strawhacker decided he had enough with the endless ringing. Strawhacker grabbed his axe and stormed over to the telephone pole in front of his house, swinging it and cursing loudly with each chop.

Nebraska

In Valentine, a weekly newspaper, *The Republican*, featured a headline on August 7 that said, "Hot Weather Vanishes."

But the next day, the high was 104. It remained around 100 for the next week.

Today, *The Republican* printed a lengthy article explaining how they usually don't indulge in apologies for articles due to "a long experience having proved that rehashing a story only makes it worse, unless a serious injustice has been done someone." But last week's article required a mea culpa. Ever since the article ran, "the publisher has been subjected to jeering remarks concerning the trustworthiness of his news—hence this retraction. The heat wave has not vanished."

51

AUGUST 15

The Climatologists

Today's Death Toll: 100+
Total Death Toll: 10,400+

Snip, snip. That was the sound of red tape being cut. The Department of Agriculture placed seven more counties on an official emergency drought list; there were now 977 counties on the list, covering twenty-two states. Half of the country looked like the Dust Bowl.

In a column running in newspapers across the country today, Clarence Mills, professor of experimental medicine, University of Cincinnati, wrote, "we are now in a period of irregularly rising world temperatures, which, according to studies on tree rings and alluvial deposits, may continue many decades yet."

He added, "The rise has been proceeding with irregular relapses into colder periods, since about 1850. And as earth temperatures rise, summer heat and aridity grow more severe in portions of continents far inland from the source of moisture, such as the great plains area."

Mills was one of many scientists studying the climate. Ellsworth Huntington, a Yale geography professor, was still well-known for a book he wrote twenty-one years earlier called *Civilization and Climate*, which examined climate's role in shaping societies, including the ups and downs of the Roman Empire.* Earlier this year, archaeologist Earl Bell announced he had discovered a 4,000-year-old Indian village in Boyd County, Nebraska,

* The Roman Empire started when the weather was warm, wet, and predictable; its end coincided when the world was going through some serious upheaval, with volcanic activity and cold temperatures.

that had been wiped out during a drought. It was a discovery that hit a little too close to home, given the current conditions.

Frank Thone, a well-known science writer of the time, didn't see a climate change crisis, and his view reflected that of many scientists of the day. He stated in a column which was heavily syndicated over the summer, "Climates do change, but not in a human lifetime, or even in a whole row of generations. Permanent climactic changes are jobs for the millennia."

But climate change, as a concept, was a topic of national conversation. In early July, Secretary of Agriculture Henry A. Wallace made news when talking to students at Northwestern University. He was asked about "weather change," as in whether the weather was changing for good, and he said that it was "conceivable" that it was transforming into something new, permanently.

On a day when there were heat deaths around the country, including Oklahoma, Missouri, Texas, and New York City, Wallace said, "If the weather of the United States really is changing, it is essential that we study it as a great national problem," though he made it clear that it was "premature" to make any conclusions.

New Jersey

Estelle Hartz, a twenty-one-year-old saleswoman, fainted in 90-degree heat while walking on Broad Street in Elizabeth. Police officer William Kroeschel was soon on the scene. The forty-one-year-old officer called for an ambulance at St. Elizabeth Hospital. A bystander, however, called Elizabeth General. The first ambulance arrived, collected Hartz, and sped back toward St. Elizabeth Hospital with Kroeschel standing on the vehicle's running board.

It wasn't the safest way to travel, but this was done all the time. In most cases, Kroeschel probably would have been fine. But the ambulances that were called were ignoring traffic lights, and the ambulance *with* Hartz crashed into the ambulance coming *for* Hartz.

Everyone survived—except Kroeschel. There was a lot of anger that this happened, and the two drivers were both initially in legal hot water, though nothing came of it, since both men were doing what they had been trained to do. But for a moment, it seemed as if heads would roll. "We are going to treat this like any other fatal automobile accident," the city prosecutor promised.

Minnesota

In Minneapolis, Frank Carlson, a sixty-six-year-old driver from Aitkin, was believed to have passed out in 90-degree heat. If the heat didn't kill him, the impact of the crash did. Witnesses saw him slump over at the wheel as he rounded a curve, right before his vehicle smashed into the Johnson Brick and Tile Company, the radiator and front end of the car leaving a gaping hole in the ten-inch-thick brick wall.

Missouri

Orpha Martin, her husband Robert, and three of their sons slept on their front porch in Albany on a night when the low was in the 80s. Around 11:45 P.M., a gun was fired, a .38, and a bullet pierced Mrs. Martin's left arm and lodged itself deep into her back. At about 3:30 A.M., a doctor had removed the bullet, and for the rest of the night, and the next day, she was carefully monitored by the physician. Orpha survived.

But who shot the gun, and why, became a local mystery. A $100 reward was put up by the city, and the prevailing theory was that a drunken motorist passing by fired it. Others thought somebody might have been shooting at a dog. Robert was a railroad employee, and Orpha was a housewife; the kids were kids; they had no known enemies.

The dog theory was correct. George Sowards, twenty-seven years old, shot at a pack of barking dogs that were keeping his family awake. Sowards kept quiet because he was afraid. Mr. Martin was boiling mad, and Sowards worried that volunteering what he did might be his own death sentence. He said nothing until a couple weeks later, when the prosecutor and sheriff, who had done lot of investigative work, appeared on his doorstep. Once he was questioned, Sowards confessed.

Sowards didn't go to jail. The prosecutor believed it was an accident, and Robert Martin didn't press charges. Orpha Martin probably never slept outside again.

New York

The heat wave was back in New York City (90°F). Meyer Goodman, a thirty-two-year-old, bought a newspaper with his seven-year-old son, possibly hoping to look for a job in the classifieds, since he was unemployed. But instead of going to their apartment, Goodman told his son he wanted to read on the roof of a neighboring building, where it was cooler, and sent the boy up to his mother. On the roof, Goodman became dizzy from the heat and fell off, plunging five stories. Incredibly, he lived, but he fractured both legs, and when his wife heard about the fall, she became hysterical and also needed medical attention.

It was a day in which an estimated million-plus people sought relief at Coney Island and the Rockaways, a southern peninsula on Long Island that was a popular beach destination.

One of those beachgoers stopped that Saturday afternoon to confess her sins at St. Joseph's Catholic Church in Babylon, a neighborhood on Long Island. After confessing to Father Christopher Donoghue, the assistant pastor, the red-haired twenty-one-year-old went to a pew to say penance in the sparsely populated church.

Father James Smith was watching. He did not like what he was seeing. The young woman was kneeling with several other young women her age, and the forty-two-year-old priest felt that she was sinning in the moment, wearing clothing that might have been passable for the beach but not for church. He told her, "Go home and dress like other women in the house of God." The young woman objected. "You can't put me out of the church," she said.

Smith didn't like that. As he recalled later, "I grabbed her by the wrist and dragged her from the pew."

Halfway down the aisle, the young lady agreed to leave quietly, saying, "Never mind dragging me out."

She left but later returned with a high-necked jacket, covering her previously bare arms. Smith, however, saw her coming and refused to let her back in until she wore a skirt. She left. And that was that, Smith believed. But as he would discover over the next few days, that was not that.

52
AUGUST 16
The Sermon

Today's Death Toll: 50+
Total Death Toll: 10,450+

The solar assassin was slowing down, selecting fewer targets. There were heat deaths in Arkansas, Nebraska, Oklahoma, Missouri, and Illinois, but people were finding ways coping with the high temperatures. For the most part.

Ohio

Father Charles Coughlin, a controversial man with a popular radio show, became a brief victim of the heat wave when he made a speech in Cleveland (86°F). He was in front of a crowd and being broadcast on the radio, perspiring heavily, in the middle of what the *Jewish Advocate* referred to as one of his "anti-Semitic utterances," when suddenly Coughlin said, "I am too ill to continue."

Then, as the priest later put it, "Everything went black." Coughlin fainted, falling into the arms of a nearby police officer. Two police detectives took him to a car, and as he sat in the front passenger seat, covering his eyes with his heat and slumping down in his seat, an eager fan came up to shake Coughlin's hand. Coughlin weakly shook it, then the car sped to his hotel. He was ordered by doctors to stay in bed for the next week.

California

Walter Soucie, a thirty-six-year-old who lived in Del Paso Heights, and Samuel Bell, a twelve-year-old Black boy, were driving near Clarksville, where the temperature was in the 90s, and maybe higher. In the middle of the desert, their car overheated on the Sacramento-Placerville-Reno highway.

Little is known about Bell, but Soucie had a colorful past, engaging in odd jobs throughout the 1930s, including riding bulls. Most recently, he traveled with the Al G. Barnes Circus.* When the circus reached Fargo, North Dakota, Soucie decided he had enough and hitchhiked home in early August. He was now employed as a laborer at a plant nursery.

With the radiator boiling, Soucie pulled over to the side of the road, and the two set off to look for water. They didn't notice a pool of water close to the highway. Instead, they walked toward what looked like a creek bed about a hundred or so yards from the freeway.

"I saw the green grass down by the creek and figured I'd find water there," Soucie later said. "And then I saw the most horrible sight I've ever seen."

Soucie and Bell stared at the remains of a nude woman, lying in the dry ravine, face down; several of her toes were missing. Animals had fed on her over the last two or three months. Soucie and Bell hurried on foot until they found a telephone.

When the police got a look at her, she looked to be twenty-five years old, was five foot three inches tall, and had jet-black hair. On her left hip was a tattoo featuring a heart with a dagger in it and the initials "IE H" in the middle. Red polish was still on her fingernails. Her face was badly bruised and two teeth were missing, possibly removed from whoever murdered her, the police thought.

Sheriff George Smith told reporters the woman "must have been the victim of sex-crazed kidnappers." He added, "No one would wander there in the nude. She must have been brought here from some outside city, possibly Sacramento."

Law enforcement suspected she might be a taxi dancer, a profession in which women accepted money to be a dance partner. There was a trend of taxi dancers getting tattoos with either their partners' names on them, or their own. Complicating matters, several women had recently gone

* The same circus where Wally the elephant "worked" before being sold to the Fleishhacker Zoo in San Francisco.

missing and seemed like possible candidates to be the woman found in the dry creek bed.

"A great many young women seem to have gone in for tattoo designs on their legs," said Clarence Morrill, chief of the State Crime Bureau.

The police kept finding and ruling out possible victims. The authorities interviewed around 150 tattoo artists and found one who recognized his own work, but couldn't discern who the client was. The woman's identity is still a mystery.

Soucie was about to have a few bad weeks. First, he never got his car working again. Second, he briefly became a murder suspect. The police were suspicious that Soucie and the kid hadn't gone to the water closer to the road to fill the car radiator, but they dropped their theory after confirming Soucie's traveling circus alibi. It was a dumb theory. Why would Soucie risk "discovering" this dead body and calling the police, months after getting away with murder?

And a few weeks later, after grocery shopping, Soucie did some hitchhiking. He secured a ride from two men. Shortly thereafter, the car stopped on a city street and the men pulled out a gun, ordered Soucie out of the vehicle, and robbed him of his groceries and cash—after first punching him in the face.

New York

Father James Smith, the Catholic priest on Long Island who tossed out a young woman from his church the day before, based today's sermon on that incident. As a general rule, in the hot summers, Smith didn't deliver a Sunday sermon. He made an exception today as the mercury headed to a high of 91 degrees.

According to papers who reported on it, Smith's sermon, or at least some of it, went as follows:

> Some months ago, I asked the women of the parish not to come into the church without hats, as it was not very respectful to the

> Blessed Sacrament. I never thought that it would be necessary for me to ask them to come in fully dressed. Last night, however, I was compelled to eject—and when I say eject, I mean to forcibly eject—a young woman who brazenly insisted upon coming into this house of God showing her bare back, and she even had the audacity to argue with me.
>
> Christ drove the money changers from the temple, and I'll drive any such morons from the house of God back to the gutter where they belong and whence they probably sprung. Everybody knows that I am as anxious as anybody else that the women, God bless them, should be comfortably clothed in this warm weather, but I have a strong objection to, and I will not tolerate, any women coming into the house of God improperly clothed. She is doing nothing but distracting others who are attempting to pray, and she knows it. I'll chase from this house of God any woman who attempts to come in here dressed as was that woman last night.

Smith delivered his service throughout the morning for the 8, 9, 10, and 11 o'clock masses. According to the news media, at one point, Smith said of the woman he ejected, "I had to drag her from the pew." He also said, "I was forced to eject a young hussy who came into church barebacked and whose appearance in the house of God was a desecration and a sacrilege." And, "The ladies must be cool, but I don't propose to allow half-naked, unladylike morons to enter my church."

Just to be clear, the woman in question was wearing a halter top and slacks. She also had a red bandanna in her hair.

Smith probably persuaded some or all of his congregation that church was not the place to wear comfortable, cooler clothing. He certainly vented. He probably felt better for it. And he thought that was the end of the conversation. He was wrong.

53

AUGUST 17

Father Smith vs. the Hussy

Today's Death Toll: 100+
Total Death Toll: 10,500+

The woman tossed out of the church was not happy about it. Her name was Rena Breen. She was deeply religious and now very embarrassed. She outed herself today in the media, and Breen revealed that she had consulted assistant district attorney Lindsay Henry to see if she might carry out a lawsuit against Father Smith.

Henry wouldn't take the case. The priest was on solid legal ground when kicking her out, Henry said. In fact, he suggested Breen apologize publicly to the priest, pointing out that she wouldn't have been publicly humiliated had she not gone public. That sounds like a fair point, but Breen's friends attended Sunday services and they all knew who Reverend Smith was talking about. Breen felt her identity was already public, at least in her own neighborhood.

Breen told the press that she was still looking for an attorney who would represent her and sue Smith for slander unless he apologized in a reasonable amount of time. For his part, Smith wasn't in the apologizing mood.

Smith explained his position to reporters and the public this way: "If a woman was to be received by the King of England, she would never get past the gates of Buckingham Palace if she was dressed as was that woman in church. The guards would not permit her to enter. If a woman was to be received by the President of the United States, Secret Service operatives would put her out of the White House if she was to come there, in halter and slacks. If such attire is not good enough for the King of England or the President of the United States, surely it is not good enough for Christ, who is the king of kings."

Breen didn't see it that way. "God, if not Father Smith, would not criticize me for my attire," she said, though she did concede she would "never again enter a church in slacks."

What hurt Breen was the brusque manner in which Smith had treated her and how he referred to her in the sermon. "Father Smith came down the aisle and told me that I was half naked and to go out and put my clothes on," said Breen, who saw things differently. In any case, Breen obliged, going to the boarding house where she lived, putting on either a high-necked jacket or sweater—Breen called it a jacket; Smith referred to it as a sweater—but she was still wearing her slacks. The way Breen saw it, it wasn't a big deal.

"There were about 15 other persons in the church, and nobody was paying any attention to me. I was not conspicuous in the least," Breen said. "I maintained and still believe that I was properly dressed for church. If he says that I am a moron and he should have dragged me to the gutter whence I sprang, then a convent of the Catholic Church must be the gutter, for that was where I was reared."

Indeed, Breen spent about six years in a Catholic convent in Ireland. Her mother died when she was six, and Breen's father, a policeman, didn't feel equipped to raise a little girl, so off she went to the convent, where she remained until she was fourteen. She returned to New York to go to high school. Of the priest's behavior, Breen said, he was "absolutely wrong."

For his part, Father Smith felt Breen's behavior was "sacrilegious." But Smith wasn't only irked with Breen's wardrobe choices—he also criticized the general public's tastes. He told reporters that both shorts and slacks were improper for street wear, and he agreed with the ruling in Yonkers when a city judge fined a man and woman $10 each for wearing shorts in public. Smith wasn't a fan of anything that smelled of impropriety, which is a quality that many people want in a priest.

Smith was also something of a crusader when it came to making his viewpoints clear. Two years earlier, Smith picketed a Long Island movie theater for showing Mae West's *Belle of the Nineties*, saying that it wasn't fit for his congregation to see. Smith kept attendance low at that theater, although Mae West's career seems to have not suffered too much.

More recently, there had been his fiery sermon admonishing lady parishioners for not wearing hats in church. Even if you liked the custom of women wearing hats and gloves to church, there's no question that it was a dangerous ritual in the summer. If it was hot in the church, the more you covered up, the hotter you were going to be, and by the way, the men had it better than the women (per custom, the men were required to *remove* their hats in church). Indeed, on August 9, a sixty-seven-year-old woman died of a heart episode at a Pittsburgh Presbyterian church service in the morning when it was in the 70s and heading toward a high of 89; one would assume she was wearing a hat and gloves.

The bickering between Smith and Breen would soon die out, but not for a few more days. Meanwhile, today, there were heat deaths across the country, including in Missouri, Indiana, and Louisiana.

Massachusetts

In Boston, it was 89 degrees, and yet another person—a seventy-seven-year-old woman—learned the dangers of leaning out a window, two stories high, to catch a breeze when you might fall or lose consciousness.

Guy Roberts, a forty-nine-year-old World War I veteran from Lynn, collapsed after arriving at work. Roberts, a WPA supervisor overseeing a project, was sent home. He died, and his body was returned to where he was working—Pine Grove Cemetery.

Oklahoma

It was well over 100 degrees throughout the state—in Shawnee, it was 117—and Oklahomans were dropping dead. In Muskogee. In Okmulgee. Vinita. Shidler. Peters Prairie. Baxter Springs. In Tulsa, William Morris, a fifty-six-year-old divorced café owner, in the morning drove to get a load of fresh tomatoes in the town of Claremore. On his way back, he took a shortcut on a lesser-traveled road and hit a pile of chat, a type of gravel, in the middle of the road, and became stuck.

Police said that from the looks of things, Morris took his shirt off, attempted to free his vehicle, gave up, and started walking down the road in 108-degree heat, leaving his vehicle and tomatoes behind. But about a hundred yards from his car, and five hours before the authorities discovered his body, Morris was hit with a heart attack. He toppled into a ditch.

Tennessee

A month after a prisoner died due to the heat, Chattanooga was still sending Black prisoners to the rock quarry. But now they were supposedly allowed a few hours of rest every day.

If that policy was instituted, along with his youth, perhaps that saved Eddie White's life. White was eighteen years old when he was sent to the prison's quarry after being arrested for trespassing in a railyard and unable to pay the $50 fine (a little over $1,000 in today's dollars). In the afternoon, White collapsed. The hospital fixed him up though, good as new, so he could be returned to toil in the quarry.

54

AUGUST 18

The "Scarlet Sin" Slayer Gets His Due

Today's Death Toll: 100+
Total Death Toll: 10,600+

The heat was changing what people could count on. In about a week, a writer in Kingfisher, Oklahoma, would mention in the local paper that what people historically could look to as a sign for better or worse weather was no longer available. Usually, the writer said, you could listen for the call of the yellow-billed cuckoo, which cawed before and during a storm, so much that many people called them "rain crows." When there was a wet moon (when the crescent moon is in the shape of a bowl), that was said to mean rain is coming. Winds from the east, the birds gathering in flocks, and rheumatic corn and bunion pains—it all meant a rainstorm was coming.

But not this summer.

There were heat deaths today in scattered states across the nation, including Kentucky, Oklahoma, Massachusetts, Nebraska, and Kansas. The only thing anyone could count on right now was that wherever you went, it was hot.

New York

Six men who had a beer keg party in Brooklyn's Brower Park at 3 A.M. were hauled into court for public intoxication. The judge asked for their plea, and they all said they were guilty—and added that it was too hot to sleep. The judge agreed and suspended their sentence.

Meanwhile, other people were weighing in on the war of words between Father James Smith and Rena Breen. Mostly, the only people who would admit their feelings about the matter in public were those who sided with Father Smith.

As one op-ed in the Somerset, Pennsylvania, paper *The Daily American* observed, "One might pray in halter and slacks in one's own closet, but when a woman goes in halter and slacks to church, it is difficult to imagine that her purpose is pious."

The Reverend Patrick Coyne, in Toronto, took up for Father Smith and said, "I would throw any girls who appeared in my church in slacks out of the door." Another Toronto priest, Father S. McGrath, said while it was difficult to decide what one would do until an incident occurred, he would certainly take some action. A fellow priest in Brooklyn said that he wouldn't have ejected Breen from the church, but he would have called the police to let them do it.

But some religious leaders appeared to align themselves with Breen. Reverend Peter Joshua, of the Central Presbyterian Church in Huntington, Long Island, said the rule against improper apparel should also be applied to men who came into church wearing golf clothes. One reverend said that he would have allowed Breen to stay once her back was covered, that the slacks were all right. A pastor's son and theology student said Breen was in the wrong, but acknowledged, "If a girl in halter and slacks felt the need of prayer greatly, I think she should be permitted."

Father Smith continued doing interviews. "I'm not trying to be the czar of fashion, but the exposure of a woman's back in church when the sacrament is in the tabernacle is disrespectful," Smith said. "I don't mind summer dresses, low cut and sleeveless, but the general tendency toward nudism is abhorrent. I don't think shorts are decent apparel for women in or out of church. I don't like shirtless swimming suits for men or halters on women on beaches, but they appear popular."

Breen decided not to sue, but she wasn't eager to meet Father Smith to apologize or have a discussion. "I'm not going to do anything. I won't listen to anything. I just want to forget it all," Breen said.

Smith felt the same way, saying, "I don't want to talk any more about it. The whole incident was unfortunate, especially in the publicity given it. I guess we both went a little too strong. And let me tell you, this is not the first time I've ordered a girl from church for improper apparel. But the others left without protest or comment when I directed it. This girl didn't, and that's what upset me."

Oklahoma

"It's too hot," Judge C. Guy Cutlip said, postponing a murder trial in Seminole, where it was 105 degrees, explaining, "Jurors can't think properly." If it rains within the week, Cutlip said that they would hold the trial the following Tuesday. "If it doesn't, we'll just hold up the trial until it does," the judge said. "It is simply too hot to attempt to hold a trial such as this in such uncomfortable, unhealthy weather."

The trial would not be held until October.

Kansas

In Topeka, it was over 100 degrees. For the forty-fifth day in a row. Federal forecaster A. D. Robb said there was no relief in sight. Tomorrow, he correctly predicted, it would be 100 degrees—for the forty-sixth day in a row.

Missouri

In St. Louis, there were four heat deaths today, and in 106-degree weather, Bill Lurie showed up at the National Public Parks Tennis Tournament, the favorite to win the men's singles championship. But the twenty-three-year-old Lurie must have suspected he was doomed the moment he reached the court. Where the heat was reflecting off the court, a thermometer reading said that it was 136 degrees, and Lurie was coming off a sleepless night.

Lurie's opponent must have slept better than he did. Lurie lost all four sets.

Pennsylvania

A sentence was handed down today to Samuel Weed, the accused "scarlet sin" slayer, as the press now called him. The district attorney Mortimer Graham announced Weed had been found a victim of "criminal mania," a legal term describing somebody who was insane. Despite promising that Weed would be charged for three separate murders, Graham decided no trial was needed. The man needed help.

Weed was sent to the Fairview State Hospital for the Criminal Insane in Carbondale, Pennsylvania. Still, for anyone who thought Weed got off easy, this was no vacation. The patients were in cells, there were guards, and many of Weed's fellow inmates also murdered their families.

There Weed remained until March 30, 1943, when he was pronounced cured and returned to Erie County prison. Not long afterward, he was released to the custody of his sister and brother-in-law, who lived near Westfield, New York. He was, according to accounts, kept under constant surveillance—after all, who could trust him? Family members said Weed was despondent over his actions. In the moments before he murdered his family, he initially intended to kill himself. On January 26, 1950, Weed reverted to the original plan, and was found hanging from a high bedpost in his upstairs bedroom.

55

AUGUST 19

Extreme Weather

Today's Death Toll: 150+
Total Death Toll: 10,750+

There was a drought, but it wasn't as if states never saw rain. Heat-fueled thunderstorms affected many citizens, especially on the East Coast. And people in 1936 understood the correlation between the heat wave and other forms of extreme weather.

After a severe thunderstorm ripped through New England on July 9, newspaper articles referred to Delia Glides, a sixty-two-year-old in Lawrence, Massachusetts, as a "heat victim," even though her end came not from the sun but the clouds. When Glides opened a window to observe the incoming storm, lightning struck her nightgown, catching it on fire; she died in the hospital from her burns. Another storm followed on July 10: in Hazleton, Pennsylvania, two girls took shelter in a garage, and a blast of wind lifted the structure into the air and carelessly tossed it aside. The girls survived—the garage had no floor.

The paper of record for Bloomsburg, Pennsylvania, described a July 14 storm that attacked Berwick, in which a young adult was struck by lightning and small buildings were leveled, as "the latest of the freak storms that have been sweeping this section since the heat wave began."

On July 16, at a Columbus, Indiana, farm, stone-sized hail slaughtered sixty young chickens, some of them old enough, it was said, to be in frying pans. On July 19, in Valley City, North Dakota, a storm dropped enough hail that farmers used snow shovels to remove it from their flattened crops. On July 20, a county agent in Holdenville, Oklahoma, described the hail that killed chickens and damaged crops as "big as goose eggs."

On August 4, in Boston, the Associated Press said of a storm, "Mother Nature electrocuted or blew Mr. Heat Wave into temporary oblivion, at least today, but caused widespread damage and at least one death." That death involved a car crash with a driver thrown into oblivion.

With the ongoing drought, the rain was welcome, but the lightning wasn't. Wooden barns, bone dry and surrounded by brittle grass, were fire traps. Today, a Pennsylvania farmer, Roy Beck, was in his barn when lightning hit. He was knocked out cold; the only reason he escaped dying in a fire is that his frightened horse, trying to escape, kicked him in the stomach. Beck was jolted awake and fled his burning barn. Across most of the country, there was no rain, no lighting. Just relentless heat that took out victims in Oklahoma, Illinois, Kentucky, and Texas, among other states.

New York

Rena Breen was having second thoughts about not suing Father Smith. After meeting with her father for two hours, Miss Breen announced she *would* take legal action against the priest unless he apologized within a reasonable time. Breen said of her dad, "He agreed with me that I had been viciously and unjustly slandered. Today, my father is going to consult an attorney. Unless a public apology is received within a reasonable time, I am going to sue."

Father Smith didn't sound like a man planning to apologize. He said he received hundreds of letters, cards, and telegrams from the East and some further west than Chicago, most commending him. A few anonymous letters, he said, were critical.

Tennessee

It was not a good day to be Harry Smith in Memphis (97°F). At 9:45 A.M., Harry Smith, fifty-nine, a former cook at St. Joseph's Hospital, was discovered unconscious on a tennis court on the hospital grounds. He was taken into the hospital, where he soon died. Later in the day, the body of Harry Smith, a fifty-six-year-old farmer, was found in one of his fields. There were approximately another dozen Harry Smiths who lived in Memphis, but they all made it through the day okay.

Indiana

After a day of scattered people dying and collapsing across the state, in the evening, at his house in Vincennes (107°F), Murl Winters, a twenty-four-year-old shoe factory employee, lowered himself into a bathtub of cold water. Then he reached over to turn on an electric fan, which turned out to be a big mistake. It fell into the water. Winters was instantly electrocuted.

That would have been the end of poor Murl Winters, but one of his parents heard the fan spinning in the water. It was dreadful chaos: the fan was unplugged, the fire department was called, and a pulmotor was brought to the house. Winters was revived and lived to marry, become a machinist, and enjoy being alive for another sixty-nine years.

Nebraska

A woman drowned in a Scottsbluff sand-pit swimming hole. A seventy-three-year-old news vendor made news by becoming a heat victim in Omaha (94°F). And Peter Jensen, a sixty-five-year-old in charge of the city parks in Omaha, devastated his family by taking his life—and probably forever haunted the coal dealer who wanted to ask about a fuel order and discovered his body hanging from double binding twine in the basement of the main greenhouse's boiler room.

Jensen's family, which included three sons and thirteen grandchildren, blamed the heat for his suicide. His wife told the authorities that her husband had said, "My flowers are fading and dying, and I feel that like them, I, too, am wilting away in this heat." He also said, "The heat is destroying the flowers and me."

It seems unlikely that any gardener could have kept Omaha's gardens thriving, and unfortunately, Jensen apparently saw his inability to keep the foliage and flora from dying as a moral failing. Jensen took his profession so seriously that decades earlier, when he was new on the job, he traveled to his home country of Denmark to study horticulture and floriculture, and ever since, maintained the plants in the greenhouses, keeping the parks beautiful and the flowers and trees healthy. By all accounts, he did a splendid job—until this summer.

Missouri

At 1 A.M., it was 89 degrees in St. Louis, and by 5 A.M., it hit a low of 86. Then the temperature hustled to a high of 105. Thomas Braddock, a sixty-year-old divorced retired interior decorator who didn't have a phone, had written to one of his daughters in the city saying he wasn't doing well, and today, at 4 P.M., Tessie Benson, thirty-six, came for a visit. Worried, she decided to drive him back to her house. They were crossing the MacArthur Bridge over the Mississippi River when he lost consciousness. She sped home and called a doctor, who confirmed her worst fears. Braddock was one of at least six heat deaths today.

In Kansas City (107°F), the paper ran a story about an unidentified body that had been found at Nineteenth and Walnut streets. He was believed to have worked in construction. When he was found, he was still alive, unconscious but mumbling, saying things like "Unload that load of sand," and "Get the men working."

"The heat victim appeared to be about 55 years old," stated *The Kansas City Times*. "He had blue eyes and light hair; was 5 feet 8 inches tall and weighed about 185 pounds. He had large scars on his right shoulder and right hip. He was dressed in working clothes. The body is at the Mast mortuary, 3146 Main street."

The next day, Charles Ronicke, a carpenter, was identified by family or friends. As life's final insult, the paper guessed him to be ten years older than his actual age.

56

AUGUST 20

Amnesia

Today's Death Toll: 100+
Total Death Toll: 10,850+

In 1987, there was a famous anti-drug commercial in which an actor demonstrates the dangers of drug abuse by holding up an egg and saying, "This is your brain." He motions to a frying pan and says, "This is drugs." He cracks open the egg and plops it on a hot skillet and says, "This is your brain on drugs." That's a fitting analogy for what heat does to one's brain. Studies have repeatedly shown that people don't function well in the heat. Our brains become fried—or if you prefer, scrambled.

That may explain all the amnesia cases this summer. On August 18, a middle-aged man collapsed in Oklahoma City. He was taken to the hospital and revived—but he had no idea who he was. "I can't remember a thing that happened before yesterday," he told a reporter the next day as he munched a dinner of fried chicken at Oklahoma General Hospital and police pondered who he might be.

"I have a pain in the top of my head which runs almost clear around—like something was pressing down on me," said the man, about forty-five and balding. "I know what is going on now, but I can't remember anything before that. I can't even remember my own name or anything about my family. Isn't that funny?"

Today, the man remembered. He was Everett Bass, a salesman from Wichita, Kansas. Bass told doctors that he was worried about business and marital difficulties when he decided to hitchhike to Oklahoma City and, somewhere along the way, lost his memory. Given that amnesia is rare and something you might more commonly see in a movie or a sitcom, a cynic might conclude that Bass was milking his "amnesia" so he could relax in the hospital (albeit one without air-conditioning). But let's give the man the benefit of the doubt. Bass was one of about half a dozen known amnesia cases that summer.

In fact, Bass was the third amnesia victim to come to Oklahoma City in a matter of months. The first time was in April, when the temperature had been in the low 90s; a young man was brought to the police station, only knowing that Franklin Roosevelt was the president. It was weeks before his identity was known. On July 18, when it was 110 degrees, a twenty-one-year-old man told two passersby in Oklahoma City that he was lost and, by the way, he couldn't remember his name. He was taken to the city police station.

Having been through this recently, Captain L. J. Hilbert cleared everybody out of his office and grilled the twenty-one-year-old for ninety minutes, hoping something would click. Eventually, when Hilbert mentioned the state capital, the young man remembered that he had been riding a bus. Hilbert pulled out a map, pointing to various towns. The man recalled playing football in one of the towns, and they kept going until he remembered his phone number. The captain called, reached his sister, and learned the man's name was Carl Godsey. It was a name that meant nothing to the captain or likely anyone reading this, but Carl Godsey was thrilled.

When discussing Everett Bass, Hilbert told the local press that amnesia cases occur all over the country during torrid heat spells. He wasn't incorrect.

Manuel Jordan, forty-two, of Lowell, Massachusetts, wandered around Detroit's Union Station for two days until, on July 13, employees called the police, who learned the guy didn't know who he was. Doctors examining him said the heat caused his amnesia. In mid-July, in Los Angeles, where the temperatures had been in the 90s, sunstroke led to a man having amnesia, according to the *Los Angeles Times*. On July 29, when it was 90 degrees and following a string of 100-plus degree days, Ruth Price, twenty-six years old, walked into a St. Louis police station, having no idea who she was. Two days later, at a hospital, she remembered: she was a divorcée and had a six-year-old son, and she lost her memory riding a streetcar. Her family was alerted.

Thomas Gaines, eighty, was a nursing home resident wandering around St. Louis on August 10, with no memory of who he was. He may have had an age-related disease such as dementia, but it was 96 degrees that day, so who's to say? But the case of James Carson Staat, another St. Louis resident, had all the hallmarks of heat-induced amnesia. On August 6, the thirty-nine-year-old left for work and failed to come home that night. His family learned that he didn't report to his job at Anheuser Busch. Four days later, he was found sitting on a street corner, dazed and with no memory of what happened.

His wife, Lulu, however, remembered that ten days before his disappearance, he and four other coworkers suffered heatstroke. At least one employee died. Ever since, Staat had complained of a heavy, depressing feeling in his head. Staat eventually regained his memory and stuck around another twenty-four years, but the incident seems to have steamrolled his life. He was soon no longer working for Anheuser Busch, instead working for his parents' business, and he was divorced about a year later.

Arkansas, Kentucky, Mississippi

The heat continued to kill: A forty-three-year-old woman in Harrison, Arkansas (107°F); an eighty-five-year-old printing shop owner in Newport, Kentucky (97°F); and Jake Smith, a Black plantation worker, age unknown, in Clarksdale, Mississippi (101°F).

Missouri

In downtown St. Louis (102°F), James Dorney sat on the windowsill of the second-story floor of Father Dempsey's Hotel. Started by a priest who died months ago, the hotel offered cheap lodging but not much in the way of ventilation. Maybe Dorney, a forty-five-year-old chauffeur, wasn't scared of heights or felt supremely confident that nothing would go wrong if he sat in the windowsill and cooled off.

He fell asleep.

When the police found Dorney on the ground, he was alive and able to converse. But Dorney had a severe head injury, or a "broken skull," as one paper called it. He lasted another five days.

Five additional St. Louis residents died, and the heat took out two men in Kansas City: a sixty-year-old male resident of a homeless shelter and a thirty-five-year-old car salesman. In Lansing, a fifty-two-year-old man convicted of assault died in a state prison.

Both St. Charles and Thayer were undergoing serious ice shortages. That was a problem for many cities. The heat wave wouldn't end, demand was high, and companies couldn't produce ice fast enough. Nothing was happening fast enough: In Farmington, it was announced that the new municipal swimming pool wouldn't be ready for use until deep into the fall, when nobody would need it.

When the heat wasn't deadly, it was inconvenient. In Webster Groves (105°F), a police officer told a young woman holding an ice cream cone that she was parked in a restricted zone. She regarded her ice cream and said, "Hold the cone, please, until I move my car." The officer agreed, and the woman moved her vehicle. By the time she returned, ice cream had dripped over the cone, down the officer's white shirt sleeves, and onto the sidewalk while amused spectators gathered to watch the scene.

Tennessee

Anyone in the reading audience a movie producer? If you make a prequel to the movie *Home Alone*, you could focus on the ancestors of the bad guys—and take some inspiration from Otis Stanfield, twenty-five, and Robert Powers, twenty-two, who were both serving time at a Nashville prison. Stanfield robbed a bank and was discovered at his house, hiding in a closet, and was now doing twenty years. Powers robbed a businessman with a friend; they bonked him on the head and stole about fifty bucks, and now he was doing five-to-ten. Stanfield and Powers were both thrown into prison in 1934.

Several months later, four of Powers's friends were arrested for smuggling two saws into the prison. Now, Powers was going to try escaping again with his new pal. Stanfield and Powers asked a fellow inmate to nail them up in a package case full of stockings that would be shipped from the prison hosiery mill. They had a small crowbar inside the crate with them, and the plan was that once they were outside the prison walls, they would pry the lid off.

Solid plan, except they neglected to consider the 100-degree heat, and that as hot as it was in a prison cell, it might be worse inside a wooden crate. About thirty minutes after they wedged themselves into the crate, a surprised guard noticed the lid of the wooden box slowly rise. He went to investigate and discovered the men near collapse. The prison physicians said that if they hadn't used the crowbar to open the crate, they wouldn't have survived in the box much longer.

The escape attempt probably didn't help reduce their sentences.

57

AUGUST 21

The Parking Brake

Today's Death Toll: 150+
Total Death Toll: 11,000+

Who was dying in the heat wave? As you would expect, mostly society's most vulnerable citizens—the youngest children, the oldest adults, the working class, and the poorest members of a community. On July 20, the *St. Louis Star and Times* ran a story in which Dr. Lee Cady, president of the St. Louis Medical Society, examined the death records of the 295 heat victims. Cady felt that at least three-fourths of the deaths were preventable.

Cody was probably right that the deaths were preventable, but if you had a demanding occupation, were sandwiched into a tenement apartment with no cooling system with thirty other roommates, or in any number of other situations, taking precautions might have been next to impossible. Today, Domety Gillituck, a thirty-year-old Russian immigrant and cook at a Springfield, Illinois hotel, worked when it was 104 degrees outside, and inside was probably far worse. But Gillituck was probably grateful to be employed and may have felt as though he didn't have any choice but to work himself to death, which he did.

The rich were vulnerable to the heat too, just *less* vulnerable. "It is easy to be comfortable in America—if you have the price. And the price is not high. It is merely that, little as it is, scarcely anybody has it," wrote Chester Harvey Rowell, a newspaper editor with a column in *The Napa Valley Register*. He discussed the cost of air-conditioning in a July 15 column and commented that if you were rich, you could pay for air-conditioning and basically "buy the weather."

Meanwhile, lower class families were relying on the generosity of the rich and middle class to donate money to ice funds so they could get ice and milk to stay cool and nourished. Edna Mae Wray, of the United Charities of Chicago, on July 19 outlined some typical situations she encountered: "The Visiting Nurse Association gave one family an ice box, but they couldn't buy ice to put in it. A neighbor gave another $1 a week ago, but when the ice from that dollar was gone, they had nothing, and the baby was very sickly. We rushed ice tickets out to all of them, and I am certain it saved their lives. I have been swamped with calls today. New babies and heart cases. A hospital called, asking us to give ice to a cardiac patient who must have ice packs. A special worker called, asking ice for a mother with nine children. Her husband died before the last baby, now 15 months old, was born."

Today was another hot one. Heat killed people in numerous states, including Tennessee, Nebraska, Oklahoma, Kentucky, Ohio, Indiana, Iowa, Kansas, and Texas.

Indiana

The squirrels in Bedford (108°F) usually found sustenance from walnut, hickory, and beechnut trees. But the trees were dead. So the squirrels foraged for what they could find in the cornfields. Infuriated Bedford farmers who typically didn't allow hunting on their property invited hunters to come on out and make a day of it.

But squirrel hunters, who normally would have jumped at the chance, weren't obliging. It was too hot to hunt, and hunters figured they'd have to hustle to get to an icebox, since the meat would quickly spoil.

New York

The drama between Rena Breen and Father Smith was still resonating with some members of the public. One reader of the *Buffalo Courier Express* wrote a letter to the editor and signed their name "Puzzled." The reader took

Father Smith to task saying, in part, that "he basely defamed her character and humiliated her to such an extent that her faith in her religion has been shaken and may soon be lost."

California

Jean Harlow was recovering at home and reportedly sifting through fan mail, many of which included suggestions for treating an extreme sunburn. Ultimately, Harlow's Catalina Island beach tanning incident cost the studio more than $30,000 to delay filming on *Libeled Lady*. But Harlow accommodated *Libeled Lady* director Jack Conway as much as she could. Her bedroom was now a soundstage.

Conway brought the sound equipment to her home. While the actress was in the hospital, he shot every scene he could that didn't involve Harlow, but today, lying in bed, she read dialogue into the microphone. "If I felt a little better, I'd say this was an ideal way to go to work," she told a reporter.

New Mexico

After leaving their hotel in Taos, Clifford Burr, an auto mechanic, was possibly behind the wheel at first, until his wife, Grace, took over. The Burrs were en route, with their five-year-old daughter, Norma June, to Albuquerque. The plan was to visit relatives and escape the heat. Not that there was any getting away from it. Albuquerque's high for the day was 91.

But it was cooler weather than what the Burrs experienced in Benton, Kansas, which was in a streak of 100-plus degree days.

Clifford's asthma was aggravated by the heat, and between Santa Fe and Albuquerque, his health deteriorated. Grace sped toward Albuquerque, believing her husband was in mortal danger.

She was right. Around noon, Clifford was gone. In what must have been the worst road trip ever, Grace drove herself, her daughter, and her dead husband the rest of the way to Mr. Burr's cousins.

Missouri

If you weren't sleeping at night, you were going to try to fill those hours somehow. Four friends in St. Louis found themselves in that situation today. Theodore Morse, thirty-six, Wally Martin, twenty-six, Frances Martin, twenty-two, and Anna Arney, twenty-three, were looking to keep themselves busy between midnight and dawn.

Yesterday evening, on August 20, Wally was at a café with his sister Frances and Anna when they ran into Ted, as everyone called Theodore. Ted was accompanied by a woman. The five wiled away the hours then moved their party to Ted's hotel, where he was living after separating from his wife, Mavis, about a year earlier.

Eventually, they called it a night. Around 2 A.M., Ted dropped Wally, Frances, and Anna off at their boarding home—and he took his date home. About an hour later, Ted returned to his three friends and said, "It's too hot to sleep. Let's go swimming."

Ted was a veterinarian who worked as a federal meat inspector. Assuming he had to work Thursday morning, he evidently wasn't concerned about being on the job within several hours, functioning on zero sleep. Nor, apparently, was Wally, a clerk at a Kroger grocery store. That said, many people weren't sleeping, no matter what they did. The evening before, at 8 P.M., it was 96 degrees. By 9 P.M., it had cooled off to 93. Around the time Morse suggested a swim, the unofficial temperature taken by amateur forecasters was 80 degrees.

They ended up about ten miles away from the city, at Meramec River, at 4 A.M. Swimming in a river in complete blackness. What could go wrong?

The four friends soon found out. About halfway across the river, Ted shouted for help. Wally swam after him. Ted said that he was too exhausted to swim any further. He couldn't touch the bottom; the river was ten feet deep. Wally tried to help Ted swim to shore, but his energy was now fading quickly, too.

"Go get a boat," Ted said. "I think I can stay on top until you get back."

Wally didn't waste time. He swam about sixty feet until he could stand. Then he ran another forty feet to the shoreline. Where Frances and Anna were isn't clear, but Wally desperately looked for a boat. Two boats were locked up at the pier. A third was unlocked—but with no oars. Wally took it into the water, paddling with his hands.

Wally later guessed that only a few minutes passed from the time he left Ted to when he returned. Wally shouted and shouted, but there was no sound or sign of Ted. Wally made his way back to the shore and found his sister and Anna. Without a car on this side of the river, it took some time to find a police station. By 7 A.M., they finally reported the drowning. A stepbrother was called, as was Ted's wife in Little Rock, Arkansas.

At least eleven other people throughout Missouri died today because of the 100-plus degree heat. Ted Morse was fished out of the river at half past noon.

Illinois

In Alton (103°F), families, as per the new usual, bedded down outside for the evening. Frank Belcher, sixty-nine years old, could see it all happening on his street from his front porch. He was a watchman, known now as a security guard, for a shoe factory. But for now, he was observing the neighborhood and taking it easy. When suddenly he noticed his car.

The parking brake wasn't on. The car was moving.

If someone didn't stop it, the car was going to roll down the driveway and across the street into a neighbor's front yard. Where three young children were on blankets, fast asleep.

Belcher jumped to his feet. He ran for his car and got onto the running board and opened the driver's door—and fell off. The car kept going. Two of the three children on the lawn were directly in the vehicle's path.

Down at the Ford residence, sitting on the front porch, were two of the children's parents, Edward and Margart, and a set of grandparents (Margart's parents). Edward's sister lived here, but she wasn't around, probably waitressing tables, which she had to do ever since her deadbeat husband split. The adults noticed that across the street, a car was backing out of a driveway and initially thought nothing of it. But then they saw Belcher running for his car.

Edward, a store clerk, vaulted over the banister of the front porch and sprinted for the children in the car's path: his five-year-old nephew and his nine-month-old son, Edward Jr.

It was a race between a father and a driverless car. Ford was fast, but the car was faster. There was no time for Ford to do anything but hurl himself into the open door and grab for the steering wheel, except he missed the door, so he tried to stop the car by sticking his arm underneath the car, and got himself tangled up in the tires and wheel's spokes—right as the car ran over the children.

Soon, the parents would discover that both children were fine, other than some bruises on the five-year-old's hips.

But it was melee at first, with the adults—including neighbors who heard the screams, and poor Mr. Belcher who felt terrible about the whole thing—pulling the children from under the car, then everyone racing to the hospital to get the kids looked over. Also being examined was Edward Ford, whose arm was banged up, but it would heal.

That the kids didn't die was something of a miracle. The adults weren't entirely certain, but from what they could discern from the tire tracks, one of the car's wheels had run right over Edward Ford Jr.

58

AUGUST 22

At Least There Was Popcorn

Today's Death Toll: 200+
Total Death Toll: 11,200+

It had been the worst summer for agriculture that anyone could remember. In Warsaw, Indiana, on July 10, a grocery store owner discovered that his grapes—on display in the store—had turned into raisins. Across North America, in places like Ontario, Michigan, and Wisconsin, there were reports of baked apples on trees.

A farmer in Riverwood, Indiana, walked through his field and said the beans in the pods were so dry that you could hear them rattle.

When you stepped on heat-burned grass, it crunched. W. B. Danning, the secretary of the Nebraska Department of Agriculture, on July 11, toured the city of Lincoln and didn't mean it as a good thing when he said, "Nebraska corn fields are the cleanest I ever saw them—practically weedless." He added, "Weeds need rain to grow, too."

Gardens were ruined. At the Huntington Inn in the town of Louisiana, Missouri, a petunia bed and its blossoms were not only decimated—two ornamental tin birds in the flowerbed melted.

A Linton, Indiana, farm wife went to the hen house to collect eggs, found that they were completely cooked, and served them at a luncheon. In Barry, Illinois, in early August, Cloyd Winner, a farmer, proudly showed neighbors an ear of his corn. Half of the kernels had turned into popcorn. Something similar happened later in the month to a farmer in Alton, Illinois, and Bristow, Oklahoma, and in September to farmers in Brownstown, Indiana, and near Eastland, Texas.

When the heat wasn't throttling agriculture, it was throttling the humans. People died in numerous states today, including Missouri, Illinois, Kansas, Kentucky, Maryland, and Ohio.

Ohio

Clarence Mills, University of Cincinnati climatologist, had another column syndicated by the Associated Press. Once again, Mills essentially shouted from the rooftops, in an understated and verbose way, that the climate was changing. It wasn't changing rapidly, he acknowledged, but it was changing too fast for comfort. And he wanted society to do something about it.

"We, as individuals with daily living problems to face, have only an abstract interest in climactic fluctuations of past centuries, even though these fluctuations may have changed the destiny of nations," Mills wrote. "We have a most intense and vital concern, however, with the fluctuations that may be taking place today to effect radical alterations in living conditions and the problems of individual existence. That such changes are in progress can scarcely be doubted by anyone who cares to look closely in the subject."

Oklahoma

Mabel Bassett, state commissioner of charities and corrections based out of Oklahoma City, shut down the city jail in Chandler (104°F); it was too hot to safely imprison anyone. She was planning to visit Madill in a couple days to investigate the death of a prisoner who seemed to be a heat victim. The constant 100-degree heat was wearing down the sixty-year-old politician, wife, and mother of three, who was known in the state for fighting for the downtrodden. Today, Oklahoma's largest women's prison is named after Mabel Bassett.

Bassett told an Associated Press reporter that she couldn't wait for cooler weather, remarking, "I not only get calls about child beatings, spats and hot jails all day, but at home before breakfast and after bedtime."

Indiana

At a gravel-pit swimming hole near the Mid-West Cement Company in North Manchester (98°F), a fourteen-year-old boy, Edward Bergk, and his twelve-year-old cousin, Walter Ehnen, came for some relief and fun. Their parents warned them about coming here, but Edward was confident they could avoid a deep hole the adults were worried about.

Edward didn't avoid it. Walter was just learning to swim and ill-equipped to help his cousin. Walter shouted to four boys off in the distance that Edward was drowning. Maybe nothing could have been done, but nothing *was* done. The boys thought Walter was kidding.

In Valparaiso (97°F), ninety miles away, more than two hundred mostly middle-aged nudists hung out at the Lake of the Woods Club. There, they played ping-pong and volleyball, and engaged in archery. Men, women, and children cooled off in the lake, but they all worried about sunburns in places they normally wouldn't worry about. Russell Abbott, president of the international nudist's conference, told reporters that he was developing a two-thousand-acre nudist colony at Mays Landing in New Jersey. Membership and interest in nudist colonies were up. Abbott admitted, "perhaps the weather had something to do with it."

The naked members weren't *entirely* naked. Some wore shoes. They also all wore chains with name tags that said, "Hi, neighbor. I'm___"

At the opening meeting, one of the naked officials told the naked members to remember to pay the $1 membership registration fee. The official said, "I know none of you have the money with you now, but later you can get a bill and see us at the clubhouse." Late into the night, there were professional dancers (also nude), but when it came time to dance the foxtrot, the young adults who did so were all clothed. Even nudists in 1936 had their limits.

Nebraska

At the Harr Ice factory in Ainsworth, Wallie Allen hauled blocks into a storage cooling unit, which made him a sweaty mess, despite it being so cold.

The twenty-one-year-old went outside for some fresh air. He sat on a chair or bench, or possibly on one of the sacks of grain lying around; somebody was grinding corn very close by. Exhausted, Allen leaned his head against the ice plant's wall. He was talking to a couple coworkers, perhaps discussing the hard work of the job or the miserable weather they were having. It was in the low 90s and would soon drift back into the 100s for a few more days.

While Allen was talking, his coworkers were alarmed to see him slump over against a sack of grain. He was dead. They soon understood what happened. The corn grinder motor had shorted out; 220 volts traveled from it, going to the damp ground where Allen had planted his feet, onward through his sweaty body, and then to his head, which had been leaning against a metal wall.

Tennessee

In Chattanooga, Hubert "Swifty" Wright, eighteen, was working the night shift at a company that made broilers and sought out a cool place to take a nap. At 2 A.M., he found it: he climbed inside a three-foot long broiler steel drum being constructed for an oil company.

Wright fell into a deep sleep, so deep that he didn't notice when a crane picked up the steel drum—and lowered it into an annealing furnace.

59

AUGUST 23

One More Reason to Not Sleep Outdoors

Today's Death Toll: 200+
Total Death Toll: 11,400+

At an Ohio county fair, where the temperature was 95 degrees, 125 people were treated for heat ailments. There were drownings throughout North America, from Michigan and Ohio to Pennsylvania, Texas, Virginia, Ontario, and Quebec. There were heat deaths in Illinois, Kansas, Maryland, and Pennsylvania. The heat wave was slowing down, but it was still dangerous out there.

New York

Reporters were quick to spot Rena Breen going to church Sunday morning, one week after Father James Smith eviscerated her in his sermon. Miss Breen steered clear of Smith's church and went to the 8 A.M. service at St. Patrick's Church in Bayshore, Long Island. Breen didn't say much to the media, but she did make at least one comment to a reporter, saying, "I've had about 60 or 70 letters, and most of the writers think Father Smith was entirely too harsh in his action."

At his service, Father Smith made no mention of the controversy. The mini scandal faded away, and three years later, Miss Breen went onto marry a baker and had at least three children. She appears to have never spoken to the media again about the clothing incident and died in 1997. Smith also stopped discussing the matter and led two more churches before dying of a heart condition in 1959.

For Miss Breen's part, today, she wore to church a yellow dress, brown jacket, a white hat, and gloves.

California

The high in Pasadena was 95. An estimated half a million people crowded Southern California's beaches. One of those bathers on a Santa Monica beach was Jane Withers, a famous child actress. Tomorrow, the studio physician would send the severely sunburned ten-year-old home, ordering bedrest for a few days—and Jean Harlow, recovered from her sunburn, returned to MGM's studio to continue filming *Libeled Lady*.

Kentucky

Foster Bennett, a forty-eight-year-old carpenter in Hartford, which was suffering 100-plus temperatures in the day and the 70s at night, set up his bed in a two-person swing in the front yard. That ensured he would get fresh, cool air, since he would constantly be in motion. His wife figured she'd tough it out in the house.

Unfortunately for Mr. Bennett, he didn't account for a guy driving his truck, coming from Owensboro and heading home to Centertown. The driver was speeding and upon realizing he was going to miss his street, turned too fast. His truck leaped over a ditch and crashed into Bennett and his swing before smashing into the Bennett's bedroom.

Mrs. Bennett was uninjured. Mr. Bennett was badly bruised, and his right leg was broken into two pieces. Still, Bennett was alive, and on this sweltering day, five of his fellow Kentuckians couldn't say the same.

Indiana

Another hot, cruel day, with temperatures reaching the low 100s. There were four people taken out by the heat, including a fifty-eight-year-old water carrier from Crawfordsville who passed out on a construction site—then an eight-ton truck ran over him.

In the morning, George Kelly, a sixty-year-old Indianapolis farmer, told his wife that he was going for a walk in the woods. By noon, he hadn't returned, and she became alarmed. Mrs. Kelly, her son, and neighbors went searching for him in the 100-degree heat. On the edge of a gravel-pit swimming hole, they found his clothes and a suicide note.

Another Indianapolis resident attempted to drown himself today: Bernard Waller, seventy-four. He put stones and iron in his pants pockets and walked into a canal, but somebody spotted him, and when he was neck-deep in water, the police pulled Waller out. On the bank of the canal, the police found a suicide note in his coat that began "Dear Wife" in which he asked to be forgiven for what he was about to do.

In his note, Waller requested that his wife, Louise, give his brother his razor blades and to his sons, all his clothes, "except the ones you bury me in," and suggested to his wife that she "look under the linoleum."

Police took Waller home, but Louise wasn't there. They arrested him on a charge of vagrancy so they could keep him in a cell, safe. When Mrs. Waller met with the officers, she told them her husband suffered sunstroke the previous Wednesday and that he had said he "could not stand it much longer." Louise promised that she would get her husband help at a hospital. Later, she looked under the linoleum, where she found $75.

New Jersey

Maybe George Mallalieu, seventy-four, had a sneaking suspicion his time on earth was short or perhaps he simply possessed uncanny timing. Hours before his death, Mallalieu, a retired businessman, consulted his attorney about changes in his will, which isn't even the weird part of this story. After his meeting, Mallalieu, a lifelong golf enthusiast, played a game at the North Jersey Country Club Golf Course in Preakness (87°F).

Deep into the game, Grace Crew, a club member and Mallalieu's competitor, bent over to take a swing at the sixteenth hole. When she looked up, she screamed—Mallalieu was lying on the ground.

Several caddies ran to get medical help while golfers administered first aid. Eventually, the golf club manager and a physician drove up in a golf cart. Mallalieu was pronounced dead. But what really rattled everybody was the exchange that Mallalieu had earlier with another golfer. At the eleventh hole, Alice McBride, a fellow member about twenty years younger, warned Mallalieu that he shouldn't be on the links. She said it was too hot. Unconcerned, Mallalieu cheerfully replied, "I don't know any better place to die than here."

60

AUGUST 24

Frozen Feet

Today's Death Toll: 200+
Total Death Toll: 11,600+

Across the country, the heat was still hunting for victims:

- Missouri. A Bactrian camel—two humps—in a Missouri circus train collapsed near Kansas City (109°F) and was put out of his misery. A forty-five-year-old man lost his life in the heat, and a Kansas City citizen was arrested for opening the water to a fire hydrant. "I'm a taxpayer," Joseph Centimano, twenty-four, protested. The police were sympathetic but said he'd have to settle things with the water department.
- Indiana. Many of the 50,000 people who showed up to an Indiana American Legion parade in Indianapolis (108°F) required first aid, and five people were rushed to the hospital. In Edinburgh (108°F), a retired office worker was mowing his lawn and became so weak that he couldn't walk. He crawled to his kitchen door, where his wife later found him. He lived.
- Illinois. In Chicago, at 5 P.M., the high was 96 degrees, a record that hadn't been matched in sixty-three years, back in 1873.* At least one death was blamed on the heat.

* Chicago started keeping daily weather records in 1860, though in 1871, they were all lost in the Great Chicago Fire. Weather observations began again in 1872.

- Nebraska. In Fremont (107°F), a seventy-three-year-old building caretaker was found dead on the second floor.
- Ohio. A fifty-seven-year-old farmer working in the fields died in Columbus (91°F). There were three drownings. And a sixty-seven-year-old farmer, Cyrus Sherman Yarnell, died of "frozen feet." When the news came out the next day, the media loved that—man dies of frozen feet in 100-degree weather! But his death was hardly amusing. His feet froze in twenty below zero weather, and because they were never amputated, gangrene eventually set in.
- New Jersey. In Paulsboro (92°F), a thirty-five-year-old collapsed on a street and died soon after.
- Kansas. In Topeka (110°F), two men died. In Wichita, it was 104 degrees, the eighteenth day in a row the city experienced temperatures over 100.
- Oklahoma. In Lahoma (109°F), the heat took out a seventy-four-year-old retired farmer.
- California. In San Francisco (72°F), a black tomcat got stuck in a maze of pipes. City officials believed the cat went into the pipes to drink water and escape the heat, or rather, the humidity, which was high, over 80 and 90 percent the last couple mornings. William Polk, an employee with the Society for the Prevention of Cruelty to Animals, crawled through a thirty-inch wide pipe and found and rescued the cat—after crawling underground for forty city blocks.

61

AUGUST 25
Frozen Pipes

Today's Death Toll: 200+
Total Death Toll: 11,800+

Across the country, people must have been looking longingly at their calendar. Autumn wasn't too far away.

But for now, there were numerous heat deaths in Oklahoma, Maryland, Ohio, Indiana, Illinois, Kansas, Iowa, and Washington, DC, with temperatures in the 90s and 100s. A seventy-four-year-old truck driver decided he couldn't take the heat any longer and ended his life with a gun. In Washington, DC, where the high was 96 degrees with unusually high humidity, a mother found her seven-month-old baby dead in his crib.

Pennsylvania

Harvey Snyder was a sixty-year-old farmer in York County (95°F), pushing a heavy wheelbarrow of green corn for his cattle. Worried family members later went looking for him, and his eighteen-year-old daughter found him lying dead in a field. Snyder was well over two hundred pounds, and his home was a quarter mile away. Family members and neighbors unceremoniously put him into the wheelbarrow and took him back to the house.

At about 7:25 P.M., in the same county, George Stout, a barker for a motordrome, a course where auto, truck, and motorcycle races were held, became a heat victim. He was looking over cars and trucks, preparing for the next day's show, when he collapsed. The coroner, Lloyd Zech, who examined both Stout and Snyder, remarked that he had been on the job for almost a dozen years. More people died from the heat this summer than in the previous eleven years combined, Zech said.

Kentucky

In Bromley, Walter Sheid, a fire captain, revived Mary Huddleston, thirty-one, and her fourteen-month-old daughter, Marie, who both passed out. But he couldn't understand Huddleston at first and thought she was still suffering. Actually, she was deaf and mute. In an age before sign language interpreters were common, it took a while for Sheid to get information for his report.

Missouri

Urban Gates, a tavern owner, called his friend Edward McEvilly, a plumber, and asked him if he could "come over and thaw out the pipes in my basement." McEvilly mopped his brow, turned up the electric fan to high speed, and asked if he had heard correctly.

Gates assured him that he had, and so McEvilly showed up at his friend's door. Gates greeted him wearing a heavy bathrobe. A dog, all curled up, shivered and whined in a corner. An amazed McEvilly followed Gates to the basement. Down there, McEvilly discovered that the furnace was tightly packed with cracked ice. A blower fan whirred beneath the grating. According to the local papers, the conversation went like this:

"There, my water pipes are frozen up," Gates said.

How, wondered McEvilly, did this happen?

"It was like this. I got tired of the heat last night, so about 2 A.M., I went down and brought 400 pounds of ice," Gates said. (It must have been a sweaty journey, bringing ice from the tavern to his basement. Gates had one leg and presumably a prosthetic due to a hunting accident in 1931; the following year, he opened his tavern.) After putting ice in his furnace, Gates said, "I cranked it up, opened the drafts and closed the windows."

The blower in the furnace then went to work, Gates explained, saying, "Soon, I had to have a blanket, and I covered up the dog. Then I needed more cover, and I went to get a drink, but there wasn't any water. It looks like the pipes run through the place where I put the ice."

McEvilly examined the hot water pipes. They were, indeed, frozen. Two basement windows had cracked from the change in temperature. "I can't thaw the pipes out unless we get rid of the ice," McEvilly said. Gates sent his pal away, deciding he would rather be cold with frozen pipes than endure the heat.

62

AUGUST 26

Ice Shortages

Today's Death Toll: 100+
Total Death Toll: 11,900+

President Franklin Roosevelt announced that he would visit areas of the country where the drought had hit the hardest. He left today, riding in a special presidential air-conditioned train. The heat wave was almost over, but for some parts of the country, and some people, it was still an apocalyptic furnace. There were several deaths in Iowa, Kentucky, and Missouri, including a forty-year-old telegraph lineman in Cole Junction. He was found by his coworkers, strapped to a telephone pole, yet another case of sweat and electricity being a deadly combination.

Oklahoma

John Westbrook, divorced for a year, was remarried to a woman twelve years his junior. Yesterday, in Atoka, Westbrook drove a lumber truck for his employer with two young sons, Richard, four, and Johnnie, eight, sitting with him in the front seat.

That is, they were until a rough patch in the road, then Johnnie was no longer in the truck. Instead, he was under the wheels of the vehicle.

The father slammed on the brakes and quickly got Johnnie to the hospital, but today, the boy died of internal injuries. One can only imagine what went through the mind of John's ex-wife, Eva Westbrook, when more details came out, and if she ever again allowed him anywhere near their other son.

Johnnie was thrown from the truck because of a bumpy ride, and in an age before seat belts were common. But what sealed Johnnie's fate and what makes one question his father's judgment in having kids ride with him is that several days earlier, to keep the vehicle as cool as possible, Westbrook removed the truck's doors.

Kentucky

Today, with temperatures in the 90s and low 100s, five citizens' lives came to an unplanned end. And because of the heat, Cannelton was experiencing an ice crisis. The town had been securing its ice from a manufacturer in Owensboro, Kentucky, but Owensboro now had an ice shortage.

This was becoming the norm. East Texas was facing an ice shortage. Cities in Louisiana were getting ice from Chicago ever since St. Louis, their normal supplier, had a shortage, which meant cities throughout Missouri were now struggling to give their residents ice. Cities like Camdenton, Missouri, announced a shortage, and that they would soon get ice from Tennessee. Jerseyville, Illinois, was also in the midst of an ice shortage: ice was restricted to homes needing it for food preservation only, and businesses with air-cooling systems, like movie theaters, would be cut off from ice until a shipment from Chicago could make it in.

These shortages created a cascading effect. Vevey, Indiana's ice plant generated twelve tons of ice every twenty-four hours, but being overtaxed with orders for the last two weeks, the factory secured ice from Madison, Indiana. Then Madison ran out of ice and bought ice from Indianapolis, which this week declared itself unable to fulfill orders, so they started ordering ice from a storage plant in Covington, Kentucky.

63

AUGUST 27

Thank God Feathers Weren't Involved

Today's Death Toll: 50+
Total Death Toll: 11,950+

For a heat wave that everyone hoped and believed was in its last throes, given what the calendar indicated, it was still packing a powerful punch. People were still dying, although by the end of the day, the feel-good stories were at last starting to outnumber the tragic tales.

Illinois, Indiana, Ohio, and West Virginia

Between the four states, there were at least eight deaths and drownings. They were all people just trying to live their lives despite the temperatures. For instance, when she collapsed, Ida Epple, a thirty-two-year-old housewife and mother in New Boston, Indiana (102.4°F), was making jelly in her kitchen.

Missouri

In Kansas City, it was over 100 degrees for the sixteenth day in a row—and the forty-ninth day of over 100 for the entire summer. In the town of Nevada (108°F), a mule working the fields was taken to some water but fell over, dead. Seven more people died in St. Louis (100°F), including Eugene Young, a fifty-nine-year-old restaurant dishwasher who collapsed on the job. The restaurant, on Gravois Avenue, was in a working class community, which means the kitchen was probably cramped, and Young was bombarded by the heat from the coal-operated stoves. Young, like so many working stiffs in the Great Depression, knew he had two terrible choices—quit and forgo a steady paycheck, or tough it out and hope not to die. His hands and arms were likely soaked in scalding water. The ventilation in the kitchen was probably subpar at best. He would have been on his feet for hours at a time in conditions that were akin to a constant steam bath. Many family members take solace when somebody dies doing what they love. Young's family almost certainly didn't get to say that.

Iowa

August Meyer, on a road crew in Waukon, was filling a barrel with tar to be used on Black Hawk Bridge. Tar can do odd things when it gets hot. The day's high was 85 degrees, not so hot comparatively speaking, but a few days earlier it was 100 degrees, and we don't know how the tar was stored. The liquid expanded in the barrel, shooting into Meyer's face, covering his eyes. Fortunately, Meyer was able to remove it. Something similar happened earlier in the summer to a workman in Salamanca, New York, who was near a barrel of tar when it exploded all over him. It took hours to get cleaned off.

Tennessee

In Nashville (101°F), a nineteen-year-old horse named Minnie, who everyone adored, was pulling a vegetable cart and collapsed. "She just got overheated and fell out," a townsperson told the *Nashville Banner*. Twelve men secured wooden boards, lifted Minnie onto them, and carried her to the owner's home. Everyone hoped for the best, but the owner reluctantly called two policemen to put Minnie out of her misery.

Ready, aim . . . wait a minute. The officers really liked horses, and one of them said that he thought he detected a glint of life in Minnie's eyes.

The pistols were reholstered and a veterinarian was summoned to see if something could be done. The next day, Minnie was wearing a straw hat and taking it easy in the shade.

Kansas

In Topeka, it was 104 degrees. It had been over 100 for nineteen days in a row, and it was the fifty-ninth day this summer that the mercury was over 100. But in Wichita, after twenty consecutive days of ranging from 100 to 114 degrees, the residents were celebrating. The high was only 98.

The next day, *The Wichita Eagle* stated, "To Wichitans, it felt like a spring day, and the evening was distinctly cooler and more comfortable."

64

AUGUST 28
Public Service Announcement: Gas Is Flammable

Today's Death Toll: 20+
Total Death Toll: 11,970+

The heat wave wasn't quite over. For instance, in Louisville, Kentucky (100°F), a forty-two-year-old sheet metal worker passed out but was later revived. And there were still a few other states that were stuck in a heat loop.

Pennsylvania

In Uniontown, a boy working for Raymond and Nehls, confectioners at East Main Street and Stewart Avenue, soaked a mop with gasoline to clean spots on the floor.

That may sound odd, but gasoline is effective at cleaning grease. But people of this era seemed to have not yet received the memo that you shouldn't combine gas with searing temperatures. For instance, earlier this month, Elda Harding, a twenty-year-old housewife in Burley, Idaho, hoping to kill the odor of some stink bugs, put a pan of turpentine on the stove. In the least surprising outcome ever, the turpentine caught on fire and burned Harding's hands and legs. She raced out of the house, stamped the flames out, and returned to the front door, only to encounter her husband who was in the midst of throwing the fire—still in the pan—outside.

Harding caught on fire *again*. She did survive, had kids, and hopefully led a happy life, passing in 1994.

We could go on all day with ill-fated gasoline and turpentine cleaning attempts, but let's get back to this boy working for Raymond and Nehls. Today, the heat wasn't terrible—in the low 80s—but it was hot enough. The boy scrubbed the floor of the confectionary shop and then put the mop out the back door, resting it on heat-scorched bricks.

At that moment, next door, Agnes Callahan came outside to get some fresh air. Her husband owned a pool hall. One newspaper described her as a "well known Negress of Tariff Alley." Another paper called her a "human torch," which was unfortunately appropriate on this day.

As the mop's cloth hit the bricks, it went into a blaze; flames encircled Callahan and caught her stockings and dress afire. The horrified boy watched Mrs. Callahan save her own life by rolling on the ground and snuffing out the fire with her hands. She suffered burns on the lower part of her limbs and bruises on her knees and arms but was otherwise okay. She was given medical attention at home by a doctor, and hopefully the boy never again mopped floors with gasoline.

Missouri

Near Jasper (97°F), an eighty-four-year-old woman died at 3:15 P.M. from illness and heat exhaustion. While St. Louis weather forecasters predicted relief soon, four more city dwellers died from the 98-degree heat.

Kansas

In Manhattan, the high was 96, but by nightfall, it was 43 degrees.

Dr. Will McClung was feeling better, *The Wichita Beacon* reported today. This was welcome news. Last winter, the pastor of First Baptist Church had a heart attack. He pulled through, but his health hadn't been the same, and on July 13, when it was 101 in Wichita, McClung asked the church if he could take the rest of the year off to recuperate.

To his parishioners, McClung seemed like a sitting duck, so everyone pooled their money for an air-conditioning system to be installed in their pastor's bedroom. Everyone attributed his recovery to the miracle of air-conditioning. McClung lived another fifteen months, but without his fellow townspeople, he probably wouldn't have made it through the summer.

Indiana

In Evansville (104°F), a sixty-nine-year-old died. Elsewhere in the city, a news reporter jumped out of his car, rushing over to a body lying on the sidewalk—and practically jumped out of his skin when the guy sat up. "Of course, I'm all right," the man explained to the terrified reporter. "The sidewalk here beneath this tree is the coolest spot I've found in days. Just the place for a bit of shut eye."

65

AUGUST 29

Sweet Relief

Today's Death Toll: 10+
Total Death Toll: 11,990+

In cities across the country, the heat wave finally lifted, dropping forty degrees in some places. The high was 87 in Louisville, fifteen degrees cooler than the day before. Some drought-stricken communities even received rain. In Clinton, Oklahoma, they had a downpour of 1.25 inches. The heat wave, many weathermen promised, was finally over, and this time, they were mostly right.

Today, D. L. Sutherland, president of the Sutherland Air-Conditioning corporation, announced that a model home was being built in Minneapolis, and it would boast a year-round air-conditioning system. "It is now possible for the owner of the small or average size house to live in air-conditioned comfort, the cost of the air-conditioning installation being well within the range of the average budget."

Sutherland was overly optimistic. But the entire summer of 1936 was an advertisement for air-conditioning's importance.

There were some drownings, but the only heat victim today seems to have been M. C. Larson, who was sixty-nine years old. Larson lived in a county nursing home in Falls City, Nebraska. The high was 86, but Larson sputtered out due to a heatstroke he suffered about two weeks earlier, when it was 110 degrees.

An editor's note at the top of *The Wichita Eagle* that morning pretty much said it all: "Yesterday's temperatures in Kansas dropped 25 degrees. Perhaps there will be some frost on the pumpkins after all, if there were any pumpkins."

Epilogue

September: The Slow Cool Down

September's Death Toll: 50+
Death Toll: 12,000+

On September 1, the heat wave was over. Sort of.

As is typical with September weather, there were still hot days. Schools around the country delayed the start of their year by a few weeks, or instead had students come in for half days—and one can imagine the chorus of groans if any teacher announced to the class, "I'd like you to write a 'how I spent my summer' essay." But temperatures were coming down, and the country started processing what they had endured.

In a September 3 newspaper opinion piece, a writer in Columbia, Missouri, put it this way: "The heat was so terrible that it was just an effort to live. Days of heat and nights of heat, made living almost unendurable . . . One began to wonder, before the break in the heat wave came, just how much longer one could carry on. One grew philosophical about it and didn't particularly care just what happened."

In his fireside chat of September 6, 1936, President Roosevelt said this about the nine states he toured during America's worst summer: "I talked with families who had lost their wheat crop, lost their corn crop, lost their livestock, lost the water in their well, lost their garden and come through to the end of the summer without one dollar of cash resources, facing a winter without feed or food—facing a planting season without seed to put in the ground. I shall never forget the fields of wheat so blasted by heat that they cannot be harvested. I shall never forget field after field of corn stunted, earless and stripped of leaves, for what the sun left the grasshoppers took. I saw brown pastures which would not keep a cow on fifty acres."

Near the end of the year, Andrew Hamrick, a federal meteorologist in Kansas City, Missouri, said in an interview: "It was a record-breaking year in that it went from one extreme to another. It was a year of excesses—excesses in heat, cold and dryness. We have had in other years the extreme in one, but never before a combination of all three."

People were still passing out, and there were still heat fatalities. September 6 was a particularly terrible day, with people in Oklahoma, Missouri, Michigan, and Pennsylvania succumbing to either the heat or a heat-related illness brought on weeks earlier. In the case of Pennsylvania, David Benson, a thirty-five-year-old unmarried barber from West Chester, died from a sunburn. In the waning days of August, Benson had been on a vacation in the Carolinas, according to press reports, possibly going to a beach in Charleston, South Carolina, or perhaps somewhere around Evergreen, North Carolina, where his parents lived.

By the time he returned home, Benson was cooked to a crisp. On August 25, his doctor sent him to the hospital. On September 3, physicians gave Benson a transfusion of blood, donated by a friend. It didn't help. On September 6, at 1:10 P.M., Benson died, and the following day, his body was sent to his parents.

By now, Jean Harlow, fully recovered from her sunburn, had finished filming *Libeled Lady* and already moved onto shooting *Personal Property*. But her bouts with the sun, especially the last one, had weakened her immune system and overall health. In January of 1937, Harlow developed influenza, and a few months later, after getting her wisdom teeth removed, came down with sepsis and was hospitalized. She retained her active life as a movie star for a little longer, but on May 20, when filming *Saratoga*, Harlow's health started going downhill again. By June 6, 1937, she was comatose in a hospital, and she died the following day with costar and real-life lover William Powell at her bedside, as well as her mother, stepfather, and cousin.

There were, and still are, numerous theories about what killed Harlow, with suggestions from heavy drinking to the toxic fumes in her hair dye.

Still, as *The New York Times* observed in her obituary, Harlow had been in dismal health for about a year, and among other things, they noted her "acute case of sunburn" from the summer of 1936. As *Variety* observed around the time of her death, "The case of the late Jean Harlow's sunburn, which left so much scar tissue, it led to fatal complications, is one of the many Hollywood accidents traceable to ol' Sol's shafts."

The coroner listed kidney failure as the cause of Harlow's death, but it's been established that heat-related illnesses and dehydration can lead to a decline in kidney function. It may be that, in a sense, Jean Harlow was the last victim of America's worst heat wave.

Throughout September, the heat wave was still fighting to stay relevant, and occasionally coming back to life, like a Hollywood movie villain that just won't die. Over the next few weeks, there were heat victims throughout the country, in states like Oklahoma, Illinois, Missouri, and Ohio. Decomposed bodies were turning up, too. On September 8, the body of William Zumalt, a seventy-three-year-old nursing home resident, was discovered in Columbia, Missouri, and the coroner listed him as a probable heat victim. It sure looks that way. On July 23, when the high was 103, Zumalt packed up his things and told his fellow residents that he was going to talk to the governor to get his pension. He had departed before to visit relatives, so nobody was too concerned, but eventually, the sheriff was notified about Zumalt's absence. It doesn't appear that Zumalt met with the governor or that anyone looked too hard for him. His cheap-looking suitcase and badly decomposed body, dressed in blue overalls, a shirt, and heavy work boots, was discovered by a farmhand plowing a field about two hundred yards from the nursing home.

Still, overall, the bodies, the deaths, and heat-related injury toll dropped significantly in September, and most of the country moved on. Scientists, however, were interested in what the country had experienced. The medical world was discussing a study, released in late August, from the Harvard School of Public Health, which suggested that if premature babies were birthed in an air-conditioned room, their survival would shoot up 26 percent. It wasn't really the heat that was the problem for premature infants, said C. P. Yaglou, a professor of industrial hygiene, but the humidity. Yaglou also told an Associated Press reporter that the benefits of air-conditioning in hospitals were a net plus for people with hay fever and asthma—though he acknowledged that air-conditioning occasionally made hay fever sufferers worse.

In November, the University of Buffalo revealed that they started a year-long study back in July following four medical students who would eat and sleep at the school, in air-conditioned rooms, with their diets controlled so they consumed the same number of calories. The goal was to decide whether climate had any effect on the individual expenditure of energy.

Clarence Mills, the University of Cincinnati climatologist, meanwhile, urged the nation to embrace air-conditioning. In a column for the Associated Press that ran in early September, Mills observed that more people died from the heat when they were working indoors than those who worked outdoors, but he asserted that air-conditioning could fix that. He also mentioned his concerns about climate change. He didn't use that phrase, but he wrote (with italics added to help the words jump out): "In this picture of *generally rising world temperatures*, more complete control of interior environments comes to assume a place of great importance, just how great we can as yet little more than guess."

Of course, nobody needed convincing that air-conditioning was necessary and important. It probably would have become mainstream sooner than it did, but World War II throttled the residential air-conditioning industry; instead of installing them in homes, air conditioners cooled warships, cargo ships, factories, and munitions plants. But once the war was over, throughout the late 1940s, the 1950s, and the 1960s, air-conditioning became far more prevalent in society.

Clarence Mills continued discussing climate change, as did other scientists. Two years later, in 1938, Arthur Coleman, a geologist in Toronto, gave a talk to the Geological Society of America and predicted the future with "New York's deserted skyscrapers rising as steep walled rocks from a shallow sea." Coleman added, "But the possibility of this taking place is so far in the future that real estate owners need not begin to worry in our generation."

Indeed, their generation didn't worry. Nor did the next. Or the next.

Mills died in 1974, but until then, spent the rest of his life studying climate change and air pollution. Humanity, Dr. Mills said in a 1949 interview, "is in reality a pawn of the environmental forces encompassing him, being pushed forward to a vantage point at one time, or held in lethargic bondage at another. Here is a challenge of the first magnitude—can human intelligence find an effective answer?" As a *St. Louis Post Dispatch* article that Mills was interviewed in observed, "Most experts agree that it is getting warmer and that the upward swing has been going on for about 100 years. Records of 400 meteorological stations all over the world show a decided shift toward higher temperatures." That article ran on April 8, 1953.

In a 1955 article that Mills appeared in, in a Pasadena, California newspaper, the author started off with "The world's climate is undergoing a slow but profound change; summers are getting longer and hotter, winters are growing milder and shorter; and as icecaps are retreating, oceans are steadily rising."

The 1936 heat wave eventually sputtered out. Winter came, and there was no heat wave of 1937 that gripped the country. Meanwhile, the Dust Bowl era was coming to a close. There's some debate whether the end of the Dust Bowl concluded in 1936 or if it was closer to 1940. But that, too, ended, with significant and copious amounts of rain extinguishing the long drought.

But the nation didn't really ruminate much on the summer of 1936. People were thrilled to reach the part of the calendar with cooler weather and didn't want to think about what had just happened, just as there probably aren't all that many people nostalgic to revisit the good old days of the COVID-19 pandemic. Besides, there was still the rest of the Great Depression to endure, and then World War II. The summer of 1936 quickly became relegated to a historical footnote—but those who lived through it didn't exactly forget. As a 1954 United Press article that ran in Indiana papers stated of the 1936 heat wave, "Most adults past 25 or 30 years of age remember that summer well. They still talk about it and probably will be reminiscing about it in rocking chairs half a century from now."

Today, those rocking chairs are empty, and the 1936 heat wave may be all but forgotten, but its victims shouldn't be. It's easy to imagine their ghostly forms roaming lonely country roads where they once fell, farm fields where they collapsed, and beautiful but deadly swimming holes where they drowned—and being disappointed at how little has still been done to combat climate change and the deadly heat that will come with it.

The heat victims of yesteryear should be a warning to a warming planet of what can happen when humans ignore their reality and don't practice a little restraint. The modern mass availability of air-conditioning and emergency cooling centers in cities has made us forget the mortal dangers of heat. If temperatures keep rising, eventually, there will be no escape. That is, of course, exactly what the heat wave wants: to return and create a sequel that makes everyone wistful for the summer of 1936. In the meantime, the heat watches and waits, biding its time, preparing to strike and come for us and all we hold dear. You may think you can spend most of your life in air-conditioned comfort, but the heat wave is cunning. The heat wave is patient. It knows you'll have to step outside eventually.

That may sound absurdly alarmist, and it is—but the alarm was sounded in 1936, and it has been ringing ever since.

Notes and Research and Acknowledgments

I often wrote this book in the comfort of air-conditioning, so the first person in the long list of those I should probably thank for helping me write this book is Willis Carrier. Without his invention, I'm sure fewer of us would be around, including myself. I don't think I would have fared well during the summer of 1936, especially if I took my twenty-first century middle-aged body back there and had to leave my high blood pressure medication behind.

This is the part of the book where I'm supposed to show my work and offer pages of citations for each anecdote and item mentioned in the book—and as with my previous book *Washed Away*, that's not quite what is about to happen. I'm always impressed with the authors who provide fifty or so pages of documentation showing where they found each fact. I almost don't know how they do it—if they belong to a secret bibliography club or use special software that I'm not privy to, or if they're wealthy enough to hire research assistants to compile every document they touch. But for me, citing every source I come across becomes untenable. For starters, when I uncover any historical anecdote or fact, I rarely rely on one source; I cross-reference as many other sources as I can find, so one sentence may be connected to five sources. It's also expensive for the reader. According to my publisher, the longer the book, the pricier it is, and a fifty-page bibliography just makes the book more expensive (or I'd have to cut fifty pages from the narrative).

(Economics is also why I wasn't permitted to write a longer book. I wanted to write a chapter for every day of May through September, but I was given some malarkey about how most readers might not be excited about reading over 120 chapters and spending $90 on a book. You would have done that, right? Who's with me?)

But, look, if any researcher wants to dig into the anecdotes referenced in *The Summer of Death*, it wouldn't be hard to retrace my steps. Virtually anything mentioned in the book is tied to a day and community; go into the newspaper archives and you should find what you're looking for. The entire book is practically a bibliography.

Still, for those who are curious how this all came together, a sampling of the newspapers I consulted include: *The Dallas Morning News*, *The Denver Post*, *The Cincinnati Enquirer*, *The Washington Post*, *The New York Times*, *The South Bend Tribune*, *The Indianapolis Star*, *The Muscatine Journal* (Iowa), *The Ithaca Journal* (New York), *The Capital Times* (Madison, Wisconsin), *The Daily Chronicle* (DeKalb County, Illinois), *The Ann Arbor News*, *Springfield News-Sun* (Ohio), *The Berwyn News* (Illinois), *Detroit Free Press*, *Green Bay Press-Gazette* . . . and on and on. For any community mentioned in the book, you can assume I probably read all or most of its hometown newspapers. While writing this book, I essentially lived at the websites of Newspapers.com, NewspaperArchive.com, and GenealogyBank.com.

Ancestry.com was also a big help in researching the lives of almost everyone mentioned in the book. I also pored through many magazines of the era (the August 1, 1936, issue of *Broadcast Magazine* was where I read about a radio orchestra performing in their underwear), including 1936 issues of *Variety*, *The Hollywood Reporter*, *Time*, and *Newsweek*, and 1936 journals such as *Climatological Data*, produced by the U.S. Department of Agriculture, and Weather Bureau and *Public Health Reports* by the United States Public Health Service.

Another vital resource that I used over and over was ExtremeWeatherWatch.com. What a wonderful website. You can go back to almost every day of every year (provided weather records were taken) in North America and other countries around the world and find out what the high and low temperatures were. Between ExtremeWeatherWatch.com and the newspapers, I generally could determine the high and low temperature of every day (often to the hour, thanks to the newspapers). If I didn't know a community's temperature, I went with the temperature of the nearest community. My quest for temperature accuracy may not have been a perfect system, but I do feel like it worked pretty well.

I also contacted a number of historical societies, generally to confirm information or fill in gaps in my knowledge. I really appreciate the help given to me by Phil Sutton, a volunteer at the Oklahoma Historical Society; Holly Stephenson at the St. Joseph Co. Historical Society in Michigan; Bonnie Mitchell, a curator at the Jackson County Historical Society in Iowa; and Dick Kunau, a lifelong resident of Preston, Iowa (Bonnie and Dick confirmed that after the enormous thermometer on the roof of the Maybohm garage in Preston caught on fire thanks to the heat, the entire building didn't burn down to the ground . . . it's a little detail, but the newspaper coverage of the fire was scant, and I didn't want to suggest the building burned down if it didn't). Also thanks to Candi Barnhart, the curator at Holmes County Historical Society in Ohio; and Rochelle Gridley, assistant archivist, and Bill Kemp, librarian, at the McLean County Museum of History in Bloomington, Illinois. And a grateful shout out to Crystal Laudeman and Jacob Huss, archivists at the Midland County Historical Society in Michigan.

Kaitlyn J. Dodds, a researcher who came recommended by the librarians at the University of Iowa, helped me get my hands on George Mogridge's diary. Chamisa Redmond, a senior information and reference specialist at the Library of Congress, helped me track down James Hardy, the archivist at Bob Hope Legacy, LLC, who gave me approval to look through some of the famous comedian's radio shows. Unfortunately, while Hope joked about the heat wave quite extensively, the jokes were parts of skits that didn't translate well to a book and I wound up cutting everything, but I still appreciate Hardy's help. I also want to thank Sharon Purtee, director of the Donald C. Harrison Health Sciences Library and Henry R. Winkler Center & Cataloging Librarian at the University of Cincinnati. She was able to get me the personal files of Clarence Mills, who was a climatologist before the term was invented.

And even though it was a brief email exchange, I really appreciated "meeting" Anne Serling, daughter of Rod Serling. I was hoping she would regale me with stories of how her dad talked incessantly about the 1936 heat wave and how it influenced *The Twilight Zone* episode "The Midnight Sun." Alas, he didn't, and she couldn't confirm that childhood memories from the summer stuck with him until adulthood. I obviously suspect it did.

I'd also like to recognize Travis O'Brien, a professor at the Indiana University Bloomington (my alma mater!) Department of Earth and Atmospheric Sciences. He had some very helpful meteorological insight into the weather of 1936. I also want to acknowledge Zachary Schlader, an associate professor in the School of Public Health at Indiana University Bloomington, who gave me some insight into how the heat affects the body. Many thanks to Kelly Enright, the curator of campus collections and associate professor at Flagler College in St. Augustine, Florida. She doesn't appear in the book (except here) but she was helpful in taking the time to discuss how employees reacted (or didn't react) to unsafe and hot conditions in the workplace. And a thank you to Dr. John Hinshaw, chair of social sciences and professor of history at Lebanon Valley College in Annville, Pennsylvania.

I tried to reach out to a few descendants of heat victims to learn more about some of the people in the book. I often wasn't too successful—people marry and change their names and so on—and I often got sidetracked anyway by dozens of other anecdotes I was researching. But I did track down Katherine Hope Cull, who introduced me to her mother, Mary Cull, the daughter of Marjorie Anne Stekl. Marjorie saved her cousin Herman (Tuppy) from drowning, and it was fun to make that connection with Mary and pick up a few extra details on what happened that day that the newspapers didn't mention—and to learn more about Marjorie's life after the summer of 1936.

Of course, it goes without saying that if there are any errors in the book, they are mine and mine alone.

I had help in writing this book that went beyond the research and writing. Laurie Abkemeier has been my agent for a little over twenty years. This is the fourth book of mine that she has guided through the publishing process, and while a couple of my books' sales probably paid for her kids' shoelaces and maybe a box of cereal, and despite her being busy representing a lot of best-selling authors, she has nonetheless stuck with me. I'm very lucky to have her in my corner. Somehow convincing her to represent me was one of the smartest things I've done.

I also want to offer my sincere gratitude to Jessica Case and her husband Claiborne Hancock, the publishers of Pegasus Books. This book exists because of them. Without Jessica and Claiborne, I'd have been reduced to standing on a city street corner chasing after people saying, "Excuse me, sir and ma'am, let me regale you with the entire story of the summer of 1936—hey, no need to call the cops, I didn't mean to follow you into your SUV. Wait, is that mace? [anguished scream]"

Sorry, I watch too many sitcoms. Anyway, Jessica is also my editor, a skilled wordsmith who always has smart advice on how to make a book better, and she's a dream to work with. Every writer should be so fortunate to have a Jessica Case in their life. And I've now been fortunate enough to have her edit two of my books. I also need to thank Victoria Rose, a skilled copyeditor who polished my prose. I'd also like to thank Maria Fernandez, a senior designer. She does a lot of unglamorous work that, among other things, makes the font and overall book look better. I'm really appreciative, and a big shoutout, to Lori Paximadis, a very skilled proofreader. I am sure throughout the editing process, I kept her busy.

I kept a lot of people busy. I'm very grateful to Ally Purcell, an editorial assistant at Pegasus Books, who read the book at the last minute and found five grammatical fender benders. And a hat tip to those who read my book before publication to offer blurbs for the book jacket: I'm extremely grateful to Kenn Kaufman, Eric Klinenberg, and Jen Carfagno, but I have to give a special shoutout to Jen, who made some helpful geographical and weather-related suggestions that improved the book.

I'd like to mention several close friends of mine—to thank them profusely in print for their friendship and encouragement—but now that I think about it, I'll feel bad for any other good friends of mine who I didn't put in the book. Boy, this is just too much pressure. Well, I'm sure I'll come back to this later and add them in. [Editor's note: He didn't.]

Finally, I need to thank some of my family members: Susan Kailholz, my ex-wife and the mother of our kids, and her mother, Eileen (salt of the earth), have been stalwart and supportive cheerleaders of my writing career. And, of course, my parents, Jim and Rita. You know those TV insurance commercials that are always joking about how we need to avoid turning into our parents? Well, I should be so lucky. They're my role models. My younger brother, Kevin Williams, is my rock and sounding board, and I'm sure he is sick of hearing about the summer of 1936. I also want to thank my daughters, Isabelle and Lorelei, now twenty-four and twenty-two, who have infused my life with more meaning than I can express, and I'd like to say more sappy things about them, but I can already imagine their eyes rolling. Still, I couldn't be more proud of them. Isabelle teaches pre-K at Head Start, and Lorelei's beginning a career in social work. (Like their writer father, they apparently both decided to take a vow of poverty.)

And, finally, I'd like to thank you—the reader. For starters, simply by reading this book, you're keeping the pastime of reading alive (plus, hey, my career). So, seriously, thanks for reading *The Summer of Death* and coming on this adventure with me. It can be difficult to find time to leisurely read anything in what many people have rightfully called "the attention economy," and we all have a lot of distractions competing for our time. But by paying attention to another time, you're also helping to keep history alive.

And maybe you're helping to keep all of us alive. As the saying goes, those who cannot remember the past are condemned to repeat it. But, you know, I don't want to end this on a downer. There are a lot of smart people out there, and the youngest generations, if not everyone in the older ones, seem to fully get that there's a looming climate-change crisis on the horizon. We may not be able to do much to avoid some of the future calamitous heat waves that may have us in their sights, but I have a feeling that someday, before too long, the world is going to buckle down and put "fixing climate change" higher on its to-do list. Until then, however, remember to use sunscreen, stay cool, don't overexert yourself too much in the heat, and keep hydrated.

Index

D

E

T

Y

Z